THE EMERGENCE OF ISRAEL IN THE TWELFTH AND ELEVENTH CENTURIES B.C.E.

Society of Biblical Literature

Biblical Encyclopedia
Leo G. Perdue, Series Editor

An English Translation of Biblische Enzyklopädie
Walter Dietrich and Wolfgang Stegemann, Editors

Volume 2

The Emergence of Israel in the Twelfth and Eleventh Centuries B.C.E.

THE EMERGENCE OF ISRAEL IN THE TWELFTH AND ELEVENTH CENTURIES B.C.E.

by

Volkmar Fritz

Translated by James W. Barker

Society of Biblical Literature
Atlanta

THE EMERGENCE OF ISRAEL IN THE TWELFTH AND ELEVENTH CENTURIES B.C.E.

Copyright © 2011 by the Society of Biblical Literature

A translation of Die Entstehung Israels im 12. und 11. Jahrhundert v. Chr. (1996), published under license from © W. Kohlhammer GmbH Stuttgart.

All rights reserved. No part of this work may be reproduced or transmitted in any form or by any means, electronic or mechanical, including photocopying and recording, or by means of any information storage or retrieval system, except as may be expressly permitted by the 1976 Copyright Act or in writing from the publisher. Requests for permission should be addressed in writing to the Rights and Permissions Office, Society of Biblical Literature, 825 Houston Mill Road, Atlanta, GA 30329 USA.

Library of Congress Cataloging-in-Publication Data

Fritz, Volkmar.
 [Entstehung Israels im 12. und 11. Jahrhundert v. Chr. English]
 The emergence of Israel in the 12th and 11th centuries BCE / by Volkmar ; translated by James W. Barker.
  p. cm. — (Society of Biblical Literature biblical encyclopedia series ; no. 2)
 Includes bibliographical references and indexes.
 ISBN: 978-1-58983-262-6 (paper binding : alk. paper) — ISBN 978-1-58983-633-4 (electronic format)
 1. Jews—History—To 1200 B.C. 2. Bible. O.T.—History of Biblical events. 3. Judaism—History. I. Title.
 DS121.F7513 2012
 222'.2095—dc23   2011042797

19 18 17 16 15 14 13 12 11   5 4 3 2 1
Printed in the United States of America on acid-free, recycled paper conforming to ANSI/NISO Z39.48-1992 (R1997) and ISO 9706:1994 standards for paper permanence.

Dedicated to the memory of
Aharon Kempinski,
colleague and friend

Contents

Abbreviations xi
Timetables xv
Map: Palestine in the Iron Age xvii
Acknowledgments for Figures xviii

I.   The Biblical Portrait of the Era 1

I.1.   Representation 1
      I.1.1.   Sojourn in the Eastern Transjordan (Num 21–36) 2
      I.1.2.   Moses' Farewell Speech (Deut 1–34) 3
      I.1.3.   Taking the Western Transjordan (Josh 1–24) 4
      I.1.4.   The Period of the Judges (Judg 1–21) 6

I.2.   Questions 8
      I.2.1.   Sojourn in the Eastern Transjordan (Num 21–36) 12
      I.2.1.1. The Supplements (Num 25–31 and 33–36) 13
      I.2.1.2. The Balaam Oracles (Num 22–24) 16
      I.2.1.3. Taking the Eastern Transjordan (Num 21 and 32) 18
      I.2.1.4. Repetition of the Trip from Horeb to the Jordan (Deut 1–3) .. 23
      I.2.2.   Taking the Western Transjordan (Josh 1–24) 25
      I.2.2.1. Conquest of the Land (Josh 1–24) 26
      I.2.2.2. Allocation of the Land (Josh 13–19) 31
      I.2.2.3. Joshua's Farewell Speech (Josh 24) 33
      I.2.3.   Judges and Deliverers (Judg 1–21) 35
      I.2.3.1. History of the Deliverers (Judg 3–16) 37
      I.2.3.2. The Appendices (Judg 17–21) 51
      I.2.3.3. The Prologue (Judg 1:2) 54
      I.2.4.   The Tribal Sayings 59
      I.2.5.   Syntheses 61

II.   Historical Reconstruction of the Epoch 67

II.1. Chronological Framework 67

CONTENTS

- II.2. Canaan at the End of the Late Bronze Age 70
  - II.2.1. The Collapse of the Canaanite City-States 72
  - II.2.2. The Canaanites 76
  - II.2.3. Israel and the Merneptah Stele 80
- II.3. The Resettlement of the Land in the Early Iron Age (1200–1000) 82
  - II.3.1. Settlement Regions 83
  - II.3.2. Settlement Form 85
  - II.3.3. Economic System and Social Structure 103
  - II.3.4. Material Culture 109
  - II.3.5. Alphabetic Script 115
- II.4. The Land Acquisition 117
  - II.4.1. Land Acquisition Theories 120
  - II.4.2. The Ḫapiru 126
  - II.4.3. Nomads in the Second Half of the Second Millennium 130
  - II.4.4. The New Settlement Form and the Origin of Its Inhabitants 135
- II.5. The Life of the Tribes in the Cultivated Land 139
  - II.5.1. The System of the Tribes 139
  - II.5.2. Yahweh War 145
  - II.5.3. The Tribes' Habitations 147
- II.6. The Religion of Yahweh 157
  - II.6.1. The Name of Yahweh 159
  - II.6.2. Local Deities 166
  - II.6.3. The God of the Ancestors 170
  - II.6.4. Cultic Artifacts 173
  - II.6.4.1. The Ark 173
  - II.6.4.2. The Teraphim 175
  - II.6.4.3. The Oracle by Casting Lots 177
  - II.6.5. Cultic Sites 179
- II.7. The Philistines 182
  - II.7.1. Name and Origin 183
  - II.7.2. Settlement History 186
  - II.7.3. Material Culture 188
  - II.7.3.1. Architecture 188
  - II.7.3.2. Cult 189
  - II.7.3.3. Burial 191
  - II.7.3.4. Pottery 192

| | II.7.3.5. | Metallurgy .... 195 |
| | II.7.4. | History and Significance .... 196 |

II.8. Neighboring Peoples 197
    II.8.1. Phoenicians 198
    II.8.2. Arameans 199
    II.8.3. Ammonites 200
    II.8.4. Moabites 202
    II.8.5. Edomites 203
    II.8.6. Midianites 205
    II.8.7. Amalekites 207

III. The Literature of the Era 209

III.1. Hymns of praise 210

III.2. Riddles 216

III.3. Fables 220

III.4. The Role of Oral Tradition 224

III.5. On the Concept of the Legend 235

IV. The Theological Significance of the Epoch 241

Index of Place Names 247
Index of Modern Authors 249
Index of Biblical References 255

Abbreviations

AA	*Archäologischer Anzeiger*
ÄA	*Ägyptologische Abhandlungen*
AASF	Annales Academiae Scientiarum Fennicae
AASOR	Annual of the American Schools of Oriental Research
ÄAT	*Ägypten und Altes Testament*
AB	Anchor Bible
ABLAK	*Aufsätze zur Biblischen Landes- und Altertumskunde*
ADAJ	*Annual of the Department of Antiquities of Jordan*
ADPV	Abhandlungen des Deutschen Palästinavereins
AJA	*American Journal of Archaeology*
AJBI	*Annual of the Japanese Biblical Institute*
AnBib	Analecta Biblica
ANET	*Ancient Near Eastern Texts Relating to the Old Testament.* Edited by James B. Pritchard. 3rd ed. Princeton, N.J.: Princeton Universitiy Press, 1969.
AOAT	Alter Orient und Altes Testament
AOS	American Oriental Series
ASOR	American Schools of Oriental Research
ASTI	*Annual of the Swedish Theological Institute*
ATANT	Abhandlungen zur Theologie des Alten und Neuen Testaments
ATD	Das Alte Testament Deutsch
BA	*Biblical Archaeologist*
BASOR	*Bulletin of the American Schools of Oriental Research*
BBB	Bonner Biblische Beiträge
BETL	Bibliotheca ephemeridum theologicarum lovaniensium
Bib	*Biblica*
BK	Biblischer Kommentar
BN	*Biblische Notizen*
BTAVO	Beihefte zum Tübinger Atlas des Vorderen Orients
BWANT	Beiträge zur Wissenschaft vom Alten und Neuen Testament
BWAT	Beiträge zur Wissenschaft vom Alten Testament
BZ	*Biblische Zeitschrift*

BZAW	Beihefte zur Zeitschrift für die alttestamentliche Wissenschaft
CahRB	Cahiers de la Revue biblique
CBOT	Coniectanea Biblica, Old Testament Series
CBQ	Catholic Biblical Quarterly
EvT	Evangelische Theologie
FB	Forschung zur Bibel
FRLANT	Forschungen zur Religion und Literatur des Alten und Neuen Testaments
HAL	Ludwig Koehler, Walter Baumgartner, and J. J. Stamm. Hebräisches und Aramäisches Lexikon zum Alten Testament. New ed. Leiden: Brill, 1967–1995.
HAT	Handbuch zum Alten Testament
HSM	Harvard Semitic Monographs
HTR	Harvard Theological Review
HUCA	Hebrew Union College Annual
IEJ	Israel Exploration Journal
IWW	Internationale Wochenschrift für Wissenschaft, Kunst und Technik
JBL	Journal of BiblicaL Literature
JdI	Jahrbuch des Deutschen Archäologischen Instituts
JNES	Journal of Near Eastern Studies
JPOS	Journal of the Palestine Oriental Society
JSOT	Journal for the Study of the Old Testament
JSOTSup	Journal for the Study of the Old Testament Supplement Series
JSS	Journal of Semitic Studies
JTS	Journal of Theological Studies
KS	Kleine Schriften zur Geschichte des Volkes Israel
LÄ	Lexikon der Ägyptologie. Edited by Wolfgang Helck, Eberhard Otto, and Wolfhart Westendorf. Wiesbaden: Harrassowitz, 1972.
MAOG	Mitteilungen der Altorientalischen Gesellschaft
MDOG	Mitteilungen der Deutschen Orient-Gesellschaft
MThSt	Marburger Theologische Studien
MUSJ	Mélanges de l'Université Saint-Joseph
NEAEHL	The New Encyclopedia of Archaeological Excavations in the Holy Land. Edited by Ephraim Stern. 4 vols. Jerusalem: Israel Exploration Society and Carta, 1993.
OA	Oriens Antiquus
OBO	Orbis Biblicus et Orientalis
OLA	Orientalia lovaniensia analecta
OTL	Old Testament Library

OTS	Oudtestamentische Studien
PEFA	*Palestine Exploration Fund Annual*
PEFQS	Palestine Exploration Fund Quarterly Statement
PEQ	*Palestine Exploration Quarterly*
PJ	*Palästina-Jahrbuch*
QDAP	*Quarterly of the Department of Antiquities of Palestine*
RB	*Revue biblique*
RlA	*Reallexikon der Assyriologie und vorderasiatischen Archäologie.* Edited by Erich Ebeling et al. Berlin: de Gruyter, 1928–.
SAVK	Schweizerisches Archiv für Volkskunde
SBLDS	Society of Biblical Literarture Dissertation Series
SBLMS	Society of Biblical Literature Monograph Series
SBS	Stuttgarter Bibelstudien
SBT	Studies in Biblical Theology
SEÅ	*Svensk exegetisk årsbok*
SHAJ	Studies in the History and Archaeology of Jordan
SJOT	*Scandanavian Journal of the Old Testament*
SMA	Studies in Mediterranean Archaeology
SS	Studii Semitici, Rome
SSN	Studia semitica neerlandica
ST	*Studia Theologica*
STANT	Studien zum Alten und Neuen Testament
TB	Theologische Bücherei: Neudrucke und Berichte aus dem 20. Jahrhundert
TDOT	*Theological Dictionary of the Old Testament.* Edited by G. Johannes Botterweck, Helmer Ringgren, and Heinz-Josef Fabry. Translated by John T. Willis, Geoffrey W. Bromiley, and D. E. Green. 15 vols. Grand Rapids: Eerdmans, 1974–.
ThSt	Theologische Studien
ThWAT	*Theologisches Wörterbuch zum Alten Testament.* Edited by G. Johannes Botterweck and Helmer Ringgren. Stuttgart: Kohlhammer, 1970–.
TLZ	*Theologische Literaturzeitung*
TRE	*Theologische Realenzyklopädie.* Edited by Gerhard Krause and Gerhard Müller. Berlin: de Gruyter, 1977–.
TRu	*Theologische Rundschau*
TTZ	*Trierer theologische Zeitschrift*
TUAT	*Texte aus der Umwelt des Alten Testaments.* Edited by Otto Kaiser. 3 vols. Gütersloh: Mohn, 1982–1997.
TynBul	*Tyndale Bulletin*
TZ	*Theologische Zeitschrift*

UF	*Ugarit-Forschungen*
VT	*Vetus Testamentum*
VTSup	Supplements to Vetus Testamentum
WMANT	Wissenschaftliche Monographien zum Alten und Neuen Testament
WO	*Die Welt des Orients*
WVDOG	Wissenschaftliche Veröffentlichungen der Deutschen Orientgesellschaft
ZAW	*Zeitschrift für die alttestamentliche Wissenschaft*
ZDMG	*Zeitschrift der deutschen morgenländischen Gesellschaft*
ZDPV	*Zeitschrift des deutschen Palästinas-Vereins*

Timetables

Nearly all the sketches of ancient Near Eastern chronology differ from one another, even the ones in the individual volumes of the Biblical Encyclopedia series. The dates in this volume take the following timetables as a basis.

Eras of Biblical Archaeology

Neolithic	8000–4000
Chalcolithic	4000–3150
Early Bronze I	3150–2950
Early Bronze II	2950–2650
Early Bronze III	2650–2350
Early Bronze IV	2350–2150
Middle Bronze I	2150–1950
Middle Bronze II A	1950–1750
Middle Bronze II B	1750–1550
Late Bonze I	1550–1400
Late Bonze II	1400–1200
Iron I	1200–1000
Iron II A	1000–900
Iron II B	900–700
Iron II C	700–587
Iron III	587–332

Chronology of Egyptian History

Predynastic Kings	ca. 3000–2950

Early Dynastic Period
  1st Dynasty   ca. 2970–2950
  2nd Dynasty   ca. 2770–2640
Archaic Period   ca. 2640–2155
  3rd Dynasty   ca. 2640–2570
  4th Dynasty   ca. 2575–2465
  5th Dynasty   ca. 2465–2325
  6th Dynasty   ca. 2325–2155
  7th Dynasty   ca. 2155
  8th Dynasty   ca. 2155–2134
First Intermediate Period   2134–1991
  9th–11th Dynasties
Middle Kingdom   1991–ca. 1650
  12th Dynasty   1991–1785
  13th Dynasty   ca. 1785–1650
  14th Dynasty   ca. 1715–1650
Second Intermediate Period (Hyksos)   ca. 1650–1551
  15th–17th Dynasties
New Kingdom   1552–1070   (1540–1070)
  18th Dynasty   1551–1306   (1540–1295)
  19th Dynasty   1306–1186   (1295–1188)
  20th Dynasty   1186–1070
Late Period
  21st Dynasty   1070–945
  22nd Dynasty   945–722
  23rd Dynasty   808–715
  24th Dynasty   725–712
  25th Dynasty   712–664
  26th Dynasty   664–525
Persian Rule   525–404

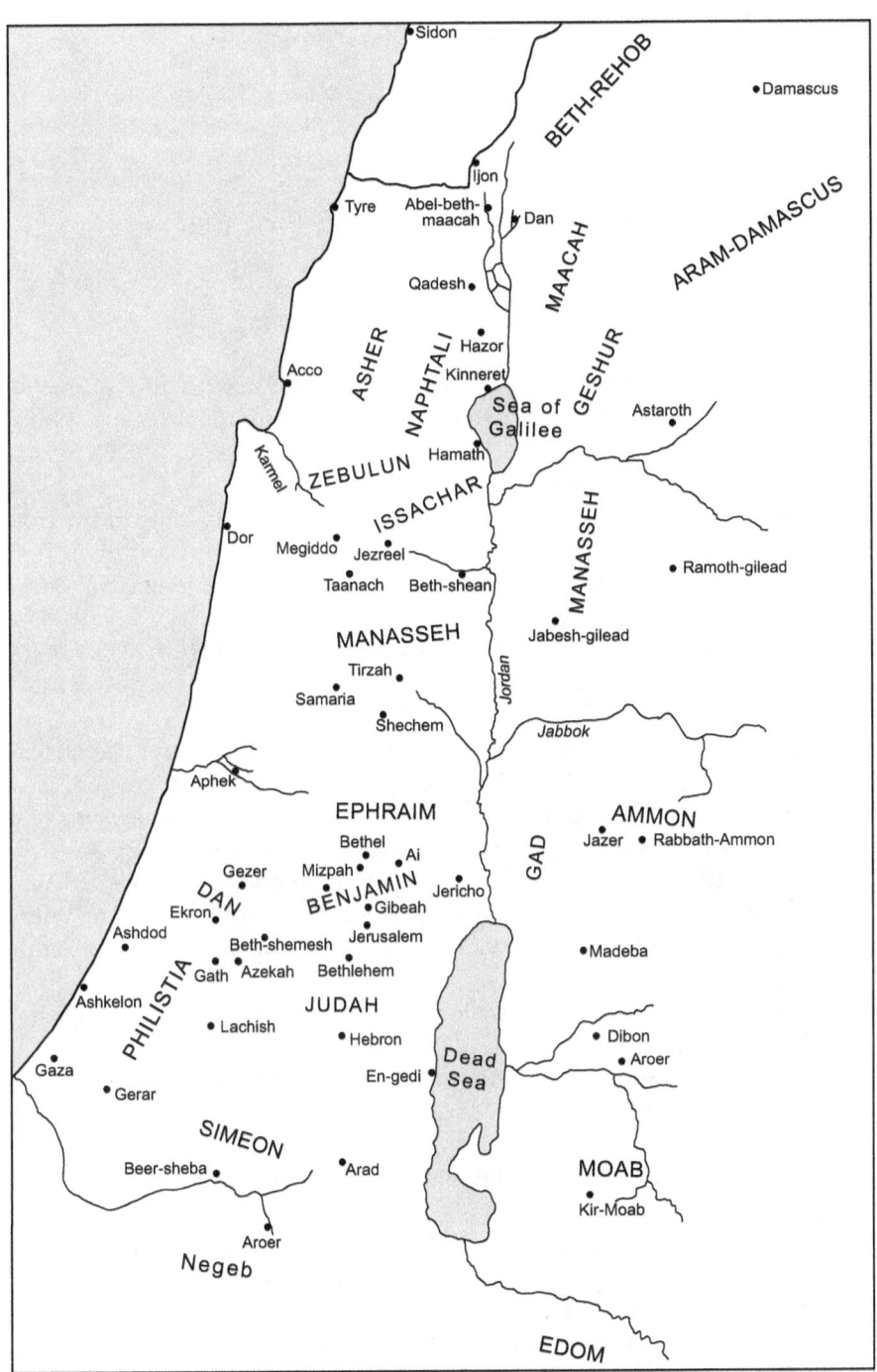

Palestine in the Iron Age

Acknowledgments for Figures

Figs. 1–4, 7, 10–11. After Israel Finkelstein, *The Archaeology of the Israelite Settlement* (trans. D. Saltz; Jerusalem: Israel Exploration Society, 1988), (1) 95 fig. 28, (2) 115 fig. 35, (3) 189 fig. 55, (4) 223 fig. 70, (7) 254 fig. 86, (10) 239 fig. 76, (11) 78 fig. 21.

Fig. 5. After Zeev Herzog, "Settlement and Fortification Planning in the Iron Age," in *The Architecture of Ancient Israel: From the Prehistoric to the Persian Periods* (ed. Aharon Kempinski and Ronny Reich; Jerusalem: Israel Exploration Society, 1992), 235 fig. 4.

Fig. 6. After Joseph A. Callaway, "Raddana, Khirbet," *NEAEHL* 4:1253.

Fig. 8. After Amihai Mazar, "Giloh: An Early Israelite Settlement near Jerusalem ," *IEJ* 31 (1981): 6 fig. 2.

Fig. 9. After Adam Zertal, "An Early Iron Age Cultic Site on Mount Ebal: Excavation Seasons 1982–1987," *Tel Aviv* 13–14 (1986–1987): 107 fig. 2.

Fig. 12. After Zeev Herzog, *Beer-sheba II: The Early Iron Age Settlements* (Tel Aviv: Tel Aviv University, Institute of Archaeology, 1984), 79 fig. 34.

Figs. 13–14. After Volkmar Fritz and Aharon Kempinski, *Ergebnisse der Ausgrabungen auf der Ḥirbet el-Mšāš (Tēl Māśōś)* (3 vols.; ADPV 6; Wiesbaden: Harrassowitz, 1972–1975, 1983), (13) 12 fig. 2, by Thomas Stahlheber, and (14) 32 fig. 5.

Fig. 15. After M. Kochavi, "An Ostracon of the Period of the Judges from 'Izbet Ṣarṭah," *Tel Aviv* 4 (1977): 5 fig. 3.

Fig. 16. After Gordon Loud, *The Megiddo Ivories* (University of Chicago Oriental Institute Publications 52; Chicago: University of Chicago Press, 1939), pl. 4:2b.

Fig. 17. After Amihai Mazar, "Additional Philistine Temples at Tell Qasile," *BA* 40 (1977): 83.

Fig. 18. After Moshe Dothan, *Ashdod II–III: The Second and Third Seasons of Excavations, 1963,1965* ('Atiqot 9–10; Jerusalem: Department of Antiquities and Museums, 1971), 193 fig. 91:1.

Fig. 19. After Trude Dothan, *The Philistines and Their Material Culture* (New Haven: Yale University Press, 1982), 107 fig. 8.

I. The Biblical Portrait of the Era

I.1. Representation

The biblical historical record knows of two events concerning the history of the people prior to the formation of the state and the monarchy: the exodus from Egypt under the leadership of Moses (Exod 1–14) and the entry into the promised land under the leadership of Joshua (Josh 1–12). The exodus of the people from Egypt had the goal of acquiring the land of Canaan, and the exodus achieves fulfillment when the Israelites occupy the land. That connection is stated explicitly in God's speech to Moses: "I have come down to deliver them out of the hand of the Egyptians, and to bring them up out of that land to a good and broad land" (Exod 3:8). The geographic data that correspond to the wandering in the wilderness (Exod 15:22–18:27 and Num 10:11–20:29) initially follows the exodus, which is broken up by the sojourn at Sinai (Exod 19:1–Num 10:10).

The land acquisition should actually follow the wandering in the wilderness. On account of the bad report concerning the promised land on the part of the spies, the people are punished with an additional sojourn in the wilderness (Num 14:10–35). An unauthorized attempt to push forward into the scouted land from the south proves unsuccessful (Num 14:39–45). Israel's additional sojourn in the wilderness ends with the departure from Kadesh in Num 20:22. The narrative about taking the land in Josh 1–12 presupposes that the people crossed the Jordan and went up to Jericho from the east. Thus, before they can begin to take the land, the people have to acquire the land east of the Jordan. For that to be the case, the people have to move out of the wilderness at the eastern edge of Sinai into the region east of the Jordan. Thus, the sojourn in the eastern Transjordan stands between the wandering in the wilderness (Exod 15–18; Num 10–20) and the land acquisition (Josh 1–12).

I.1.1. Sojourn in the Eastern Transjordan (Num 21–36)

The last venture in connection with the wilderness journey leads to a siege by the Canaanites at the place called Hormah (Num 21:1–3). What was probably originally an independent local tradition unrelated to the land acquisition ends up in its current context describing an event on the way into the eastern Transjordan. The ensuing narrative of the brazen serpent (Num 21:4–9) is not localized and serves again to exemplify both the people's disobedience and Moses' mediation of God's salvific acts. The wider journey moves out of the region of the Negeb, where Hormah is to be found, through the region east of Arabah to the mountain of Pisgah at the heights of Jericho (Num 21:10–20). The battle against Kings Sihon of Heshbon (Ḥesbān) and Og of Bashan ends with the capture of these regions. The capture of the eastern Transjordan comes to a close with the victory over these two kings (Num 21:21–35). At the same time, the story serves as the point of departure for the subsequent land acquisition described in Josh 1–12. The procession in the eastern Transjordan turns out to be indispensable for the conquest of the land, which now takes place coming out of the east. The entire episode of Num 21–36 serves as a link to connect to the events reported in the book of Joshua.

The narrative of the seer Balaam in Num 22–24 forms a self-contained complex. During the sojourn in the plains of Moab at the northern edge of the Dead Sea, Balak, the king of the Moabites, calls Balaam son of Beor at Pethor, which is on the Euphrates, with the intention of cursing Israel. On the way to Moab, the messenger of Yahweh stands in the path, at first seen only by the ass Balaam is riding. Balaam comes away from the encounter with the instruction, "Go with the men; but speak only what I tell you to speak" (Num 22:35). After the requested curse is changed three times to a blessing in Balaam's mouth, Balak chases him away but not before hearing a fourth blessing over Israel. In the end, Balaam returns to his homeland.

Additional individual episodes follow that describe the sojourn in the eastern Transjordan. At Shittim the people fall away and worship Baal of Peor, and so the chiefs are put to death (Num 25:1–5). When an Israelite by the name of Zimri marries a Midianite woman, the priest Phinehas grabs a spear and pierces the two of them (Num 25:6–18). Next comes the census of the tribes and clans in Num 26 (corresponding to the order of the camps in Num 1–10), but the Levites are listed separately from the twelve tribes because of their special appointment. In additional regulations, the daughter's right of inheritance (Num 27:1–11), the appointment of Joshua as Moses' successor (Num 27:12–23), and various offerings, festivals, and oaths (Num 28–30) are regulated. The war to conquer the Midianites (Num 31) ends with precise instructions concerning handling the booty, according to which people and livestock are exterminated—although only a representative number are killed—and items of precious metals merely undergo a process of purification.

Numbers 32 returns to the theme of taking the land. Since the Reubenites and Gadites own so much livestock, they ask Moses for a place to settle in the land already conquered east of the Jordan. Moses grants their request on the condition that both tribes participate in the ensuing conquest of the land west of the Jordan. The northern portion of the eastern Transjordan is allotted to the tribes of Reuben and Gad and to the half-tribe of Manasseh. This arrangement establishes the settlement of the eastern Transjordan and secures the conquest of the western Transjordan by all Israel. With Moses' allocation, the conquered eastern Transjordan becomes a legitimate settlement area for Israel. The long record in Num 33:1–49 brings the acquisition of the eastern Transjordan to a conclusion insofar as the itinerary presents a summary of the preceding journeys from the exodus up to the present location in "Abel-shittim in the plains of Moab." Precise instructions follow regarding the expulsion of the Canaanites as well as the conquest and distribution of the western Transjordan (Num 33:50–34:29). This is followed up with further instructions from Moses regarding cities for the Levites and cities of refuge. The acquisition of the eastern Transjordan ends with a view of the impending conquest of the western Transjordan as the promised land.

I.1.2. Moses' Farewell Speech (Deut 1–34)

The substantial legal collection of Deuteronomy, which is stylized as Moses' farewell speech, stands between the narratives of the sojourn in the eastern Transjordan (Num 21–36) and the seizure of the land (Josh 1–12). The Sinai tradition is made up predominantly of Exod 19–40, Lev 1–27, and Num 1–9. Harking back to the Sinai tradition, Deuteronomy will lay out a recapitulation of the law prior to the acquisition of the promised land and, by way of introduction, will give a recapitulation of the narrative of the journey from Horeb to the Jordan in Deut 1–3 (cf. §I.2.1.4). Other ancillary pieces conclude the book: a collection of tribal sayings in Deut 33 and the narrative of Moses' death in Deut 34. At this point, Moses' work was fulfilled, and, not being exempt from punishment, he was to die before reaching the beloved land. The end of Deuteronomy reaches a decisive point both functionally and literarily. Functionally the giving of the law concludes definitively with the death of the mediator. Literarily no further legal texts follow; instead, a long historical narrative runs from Joshua through 1–2 Kings. Nevertheless, the book of Deuteronomy stands at the head of the complex of the books of Joshua, Judges, 1–2 Samuel, and 1–2 Kings. Given the unity of its representation, the entire narrative procession from the beginning of Deuteronomy to the end of 2 Kings is summarily designated as "Deuteronomistic History" (cf. §I.2). The Jews and Samaritans would join the book of Deuteronomy to the four preceding books of Genesis, Exodus, Leviticus, and Numbers to form a unit named *Torah*, since most of the texts contain instruction. This presupposes that after the combination of the historical narrative of the books Genesis to Numbers with the Deuteronomistic History, Deuteronomy was separated out from the Deuteronomistic History based on its content and combined with the four books, Genesis, Exodus, Leviticus, and Numbers to form a whole (see Otto Kaiser, *Grundriß der Einleitung in die kanonischen und deuterokanonischen Schriften des Alten Testaments*, Band 1, *Die erzählenden Werke* [Gütersloh: Gütersloher Verlagshaus Gerd Mohn, 1992], 47–131).

Except for the narrative parts at the beginning and end, Deuteronomy represents a law collection that on linguistic and historical grounds is to be dated no earlier than the end of the monarchy. Based on its content, Deuteronomy consequently does not actually belong to the genre of historical narrative. Rather, Deuteronomy is *sui generis*, and all of its historical presentation is preceded by a historical preface in chapters 1–3. The so-called farewell speech of Moses therefore is not taken into account for the subsequent representation of Israel's history because of the data it contains and its late time of composition; thus, Deuteronomy is not a source for Israel's sojourn in the land east of the Jordan.

I.1.3. Taking the Western Transjordan (Josh 1–24)

The conquest narrative begins in the book of Joshua with Yahweh commissioning Joshua as the new leader of the people after the death of Moses (cf. Deut 34:1–9). Joshua initially sends two scouts to Jericho, whom Rahab hides and rescues; therefore they promise to spare her when the city is taken (Josh 2). This is followed up with the people crossing the Jordan on dry ground, since the water miraculously stops flowing when the ark reaches the shore. To commemorate this miracle, twelve stones from the riverbed are set up in Gilgal (Josh 3:4). As the first act in the promised land, Joshua has all the men undergo circumcision, the practice having been abandoned during the wandering in the wilderness (Josh 5:1–9). The people's provision of manna from heaven comes to an end with the Feast of Passover, since now they can find sustenance from the produce of the land. Joshua's encounter with the messenger of Yahweh confirms his commission (Josh 5:13–15). The destruction of Jericho occurs miraculously after several days of parading and raising the war cry, which results in the walls collapsing in on themselves; Rahab and her family are spared during the capture of the city (Josh 6). The conquest of Ai fails because Achan sins against God by taking some of the devoted things; thus God's anger burns against Israel. However, stoning Achan would restore the disrupted relationship between God and the people (Josh 7). The renewed attack on Ai is carried out using ambush tactics and ends with the annihilation of the enemy army; the king is hung, and the city burned with fire.

At Mount Ebal Joshua builds an altar, offering sacrifice there and inscribing a copy of the law of Moses on the stone; afterwards, the law is read before all the people (Josh 8:30–35). The inhabitants of Gibeon and three other cities in the area cunningly get Joshua to agree to a treaty; in this way they avoid annihilation but become servants involved in maintaining the temple (Josh 9). In a large battle at Gibeon, Joshua battles the five allied kings of Jerusalem, Hebron, Jarmuth, Lachish, and Eglon (10:1–14), who are hung after being found hidden in a cave at Makkedah (10:15–27). In independent actions, numerous cities in the Judean mountains are conquered and the inhabitants killed until the entirety of southern Canaan is subdued (10:28–43). Similarly, the kings in the north are attacked in the battle at the waters of Merom; Hazor is smitten and burned to the ground, and the other cities are defeated and annihilated (11:1–23). The ensuing conclusion to the conquest of the western Transjordan consists of a long list of the places of the conquered kings (12:1–24).

The allotment of the land presupposes its conquest, and the seizure requires a firm delineation of the settlement regions. Thus, the individual places are either listed or their borders are delineated. Moses had already explicitly divided the land east of the Jordan among the tribes of Reuben, Gad, and the half-tribe of Manasseh (Josh 13). The allotment of Hebron to Caleb (Josh 14) takes place with reference to his special role in the reconnaissance of the land (cf. Num 13–14). Especially lengthy is the description of the borders and list of places for Judah (Josh 15), whereas for Ephraim and Manasseh only a summary of the border is discussed (Josh 16–17). The remaining tribes of Benjamin, Simeon, Zebulun, Issachar, Asher, Dan, and Naphtali are allotted their settlement regions by seven lots (Josh 18–19). Cities of refuge are determined for cases of manslaughter (Josh 10), and the landless Levites receive some cities within every tribe as settlement regions (Josh 21). A special altar will be set up for the tribes east of the Jordan for offering sacrifices (Josh 22). Joshua's two farewell speeches deal with faithfulness to the law and to the covenant with Yahweh as the only God (Josh 23:1–24:28). Finally, there are notices about Joshua's death and the burial places of Joshua, Joseph, and Eleazer the priest (Josh 24:29–33).

The book of Joshua shows a clear development that remains consistent up through the conclusion (see §I.2.2). The occupation of the land under Joshua's leadership is accomplished by warlike seizure (Josh 1–12) and by peaceful donation (Josh 13–24). The two parts of conquering and distributing the land belong together as mutually dependent. A definite organization is discernible in the two parts, namely, the orientation and ordering of the procession from south to north. The first part concludes with a summary in the form of a list of conquered cities (12:1–24); the second part ends with a final notice (19:49a) and is followed by Joshua's last words (24:1–28). The speech is the high point of the book, because it reads through a depiction of the past and introduces a view of the people's subsequent history in the land. The entire narrative of taking the land, with its two different halves of warfare and distribution, comes to an appropriate conclusion with the covenant scene. Both parts are held together by a literary frame made up of biographical comments about the figure of Joshua. Joshua's commission (1:1–6) and death (24:29–31) stand at the beginning and end of the process of taking the land. The book of Joshua thus proves itself to be a consciously fashioned literary work.

The bookends of Joshua's commission and death are enough to hold the book together, because Joshua is the bearer of the action in the book named for him. Joshua is the only leading figure throughout, and other characters appear only in marginal roles as is necessary to move the action along. Joshua takes over the leading role of Moses with respect to taking the land. Just as Moses determined the conditions for Israel's livelihood by giving the law, Joshua laid the groundwork for the people's life thereafter by conquering and dividing the land. The Joshua tradition views him as the sole and unique leading figure after Moses. On the analogy of the call of Moses in Exod 3, the tradition of Josh 5:13–15 is built up further so that Joshua gradually appears as a second Moses. Consequently, Joshua's significance would be mentioned in different ways in the preceding historical representation in order to prepare his role (cf. Exod 17:8–16; 24:12–14; 32:17; 33:11; Num 11:28; 13:16; 14:6–38; 26:65).

I.1.4. The Period of the Judges (Judg 1–21)

The subsequent history of the first generations after the taking of the land is narrated as the work of judges. The tradition explicitly differentiates between two groups of judges. The "major" judges display heroic acts and, for a specified time, serve as new leaders of the people of Israel so as to save them from their enemies. The "minor" judges always serve a leading role for more years. The two groups are also different in terms of their commissioning, such that Jephthah is listed as both a "major" and a "minor" judge.

Proceeding from the concepts of the taking and distributing the land in the book of Joshua, the representation of the time of the judges begins with episodes concerning battles in the land as well as a list of the unconquered cities arranged according to the individual tribes (Judg 1). This somewhat negative record of the land's possession is followed by the appearance of the messenger of Yahweh before the people (2:1–5), the recapitulation of the report of Joshua's death (2:6–10), and a theological-historical assessment of the time of the judges (2:11–23). After setting up the situation of the era (3:1–6), Othniel, Ehud, and Shamgar, the first three judges, are introduced as tribal heroes (3:7–31). Only the assassination of the Moabite king Eglon by the left-handed Ehud is described in any detail as a courageous act. Othniel is accompanied by forty years of peace and Ehud by eighty years of peace. The battle at Kishon near Megiddo, where tribes fight a coalition of Canaanite kings, is told in the double-tradition of the prose report in Judg 4 and the song of praise in Judg 5. Alongside the general depiction of the battle, the ignominious death of the enemy commander Sisera as a result of the brave action of Jael is especially highlighted. The result is a forty-year period of rest.

As is also true of the "major" judges Jephthah and Samson, Gideon's story is told in a cycle of narratives (Judg 6–8). Apart from the actual battle against the Midianites, the cycle contains several episodes: Gideon's call as a commander, the destruction of the altar of Baal, an expedition in the land east of the Jordan, and Gideon's refusal of the offer for him to rule. During his lifetime, the land had forty years of rest from its enemies. The form of the judges' history is abandoned at the cessation of the rule of Abimelech of Shechem, and his death at the siege of Thebez is narrated without identifying him as a judge. The succeeding narratives are interrupted with a record of the "minor" judges Tola and Jair (Judg 10:1–5), whose activities spanned twenty-three and twenty-two years respectively. A general summary follows from there, describing the historical situation according to the theological motif of sin and punishment (10:6–16). The Jephthah traditions include the narrative of his victory over the Ammonites, his selection as head of the Gileadites, his negotiation with the Ammonites, and the short report of an intertribal battle with the Ephraimites (10:17–12:7). Next comes a report of the "minor" judges Ibzan, Elon, and Abdon, who held office for seven, ten, and eight years respectively (12:8–15). Samson's battle against the Philistines comprises individual acts of bravery such as the destruction of crops and clobbering the enemy army with the jawbone of an ass. When Delilah betrays Samson to his enemies, his story concludes with a final superhuman feat that leads to his death (Judg 14–16). The complete narrative cycle is preceded by his special birth and his appointment as a Nazirite (Judg 13). After the Amorites, Moabites, Canaanites, Midianites, and Ammonites, the Philistines appear in the Samson narrative as the enemies of Israel. The motif of Israel's salvation from their enemies thus comes to a close.

Two appendices follow: one narrates Micah's installation of the Levite as a priest, the wandering of the Danites in their new settlement region at the upper reaches of the Jordan, and the conquering of the city Laish (Judg 17–18). The other appendix recounts the bloody feud between all the other tribes and the tribe of Benjamin from the beginning of the conflict up to the abduction of the women at Shiloh (Judg 19–21). Both cases deal with inner-Israelite disputes that carry local significance. The situations also carry the pressure to resolve matters peacefully in order to avoid certain further conflicts involving quests for land or blood vengeance. Several times it is pointed out that at that time there was no king ruling in Israel (17:6; 18:1; 19:1; 21:25). This statement prefigures the beginning of the history of the monarchy as told in 1–2 Samuel, where Samuel represents the last judge in Israel and Saul becomes the first king.

The book of Judges evinces a completely different structure than the book of Joshua. The plot is basically carried out by the characters of the judges, who fight and conquer Israel's enemies in the course of history before the monarchy. Fully formed complexes of tradition accompany three of the major judges: Gideon (Judg 6–8), Jephthah (Judg 10:17–12:7), and Samson (Judg 13–16). The biggest difference in the collection of these three narratives goes back to the fact that they were formed during different eras of the monarchic period. They have in common the commission to act as judge by divine inspiration. Overall, Judges contains extraordinarily disparate material (see §I.2.3), from which only the Song of Deborah (Judg 5) in its raw material reaches back to the premonarchic era (see §III.1). Every other piece describes the history prior to the monarchy in light of the monarchy. As in the book of Joshua, the leading idea is thus the concept that God truly determines the course of history, but humans as active agents also take decisive action in their situation. The ideal kind of action is the people's salvation from their enemies. Since one individual will no longer characterize an entire era, the succession of acting characters will be placed in a chronological list and classified historically (see §II.1). The form of historical writing in Judges differs substantially from Joshua. There is no longer a progressive narrative held together by one character who determines the course of history. Instead, there is a succession of different periods of threat and well-being (rest) according to which the people's well-being depends on their good conduct.

I.2. Questions

Auld, A. Graeme. *Joshua, Moses and the Land: Tetrateuch–Pentateuch–Hexateuch in a Generation since 1938* (Edinburgh: T&T Clark,1980). **Cross**, Frank Moore. "The

Themes of the Book of Kings and the Structure of the Deuteronomistic History," in idem, *Canaanite Myth and Hebrew Epic: Essays in the History of the Religion of Israel* (Cambridge, Mass.: Harvard University Press, 1973), 274–89. **Dietrich**, Walter. *Prophetie und Geschichte: Eine redaktionsgeschichtliche Untersuchung zum deuteronomistischen Geschichtswerk* (FRLANT 108; Göttingen: Vandenhoeck & Ruprecht, 1972). **Friedman**, Richard Elliott. *The Exile and Biblical Narrative: The Formation of the Deuteronomistic and Priestly Works* (HSM 22; Chico, Calif.: Scholars Press, 1981). **Nelson**, Richard D. *The Double Redaction of the Deuteronomistic History* (JSOTSup 18; Sheffield: JSOT Press, 1981). **Noth**, Martin. *Überlieferungsgeschichtliche Studien* (2nd ed.; Tübingen: M. Niemeyer, 1957). **Peckham**, Brian. *The Composition of the Deuteronomistic History* (HSM 35; Atlanta: Scholars Press, 1985). **Polzin**, Robert. *Moses and the Deuteronomist: Deuteronomy, Joshua, Judges* (A Literary Study of the Deuteronomic History 1; New York: Seabury, 1980). **Smend**, Rudolf. "Das Gesetz und die Völker: Die Mitte des Alten Testaments," in *Gesammelte Studien I* (BEvT 99; Munich: Kaiser, 1986), 124–37. **Weippert**, Helga. "Das deuteronomistische Geschichtswerk: Sein Ziel und Ende in der neueren Forschung," *TRu* 50 (1985): 213–49. **Veijola**, Timo. *Das Königtum in der Beurteilung der deuteronomistischen Historiographie: Eine redaktionsgeschichtliche Untersuchung* (AASF, Ser. B, 198; Helsinki: Suomalainen Tiedeakatemia, 1977).**Wolff**, Hans Walter. "Das Kerygma des deuteronomistischen Geschichtswerkes," in *Gesammelte Studien zum Alten Testament* (TB 22; Munich: Kaiser, 1964), 308–24. See now also: **Römer**, Thomas. *The So-Called Deuteronomistic History: A Sociological, Historical, and Literary Introduction* (New York: T&T Clark, 2007).

The narrative complexes of Num 21–36, Josh 1–24, and Judg 1–21 do not give a comprehensive picture of the era. Instead, the historiography strings together individual narratives of different lengths that are broken up by formulaic pieces and lists. Up to the beginning of the book of Judges, the narrative is not held together by a chronological framework and is only occasionally bound together by back references (see Josh 9:1–4; 10:1, 2; 11:1–3). In addition, the locations in the book of Joshua have only a loose framework and no workable geographic structure. Each narrative stands on its own, and only the succession of narratives can form a course of evenly matched events; however, this by no means presents the entire history history of the era from the taking of the land to the beginning of the monarchy. The conquest of the land is limited to the acquisition of a few cities. The only actual land-acquisition narratives are for Jericho and Ai (Josh 6 and 8); the annihilation of additional cities in the south and north is conveyed merely by short reports or formulaic phrases (Josh 10 and 11). In fact, not even all of the thirty-one Canaanite cities enumerated in Josh 12 are named in the preceding text. This enumeration gives the appearance of accurateness without having to claim correspondence to the mediation of historical reality.

Similarly unsatisfactory are the matters concerning the traditions of the book of Judges. Here, by way of summary statements, there is the impression of a succession of different judges, but neither the individual deeds of the judge characters nor the sparse statements concerning the individual agents of the judicial office can actually fill the historical space of almost two hundred years. The mediated portrait of occasional victories over the enemies and the peaceful functioning of a total of five "minor" judges is by no means able to represent the life of the Israelite tribes over several generations.

Biblical historiography thus attempts to visualize historical events vividly by the example of a few narratives and to then break up the in-between space with notes or lists. A section such as the victory over Jericho in Josh 6 stands for the whole; an individual event covers a wide field of historical events that light up for a moment but are not represented in their entire spatial and temporal expanse. The intention of biblical historiographers is thus clear: in individual events, history will be expressed as an event and as a consequence of God's action. The biblical conception of history thus differs fundamentally from the principles of modern historiography. According to the methods of historical scholarship, only that which is verifiable according to time and place can count as historical. Each event is questioned with respect to its assumptions, its sequence, and its consequences. Only that which can be verified in place and time as human action can count as historical reality. The prerequisite for this critical inquiry concerning the actual events is a literary-critical examination of the sources. Literary criticism inquires not only about the literary integrity of a text and about the growth of the text complex but also about the time of composition and the author. Not until after the necessary classification of a text regarding the features of its formation can the question be posed concerning the inclusion of older tradition and concerning its usefulness as a historical source. The literary-critical analysis tries to clarify the conditions for all additional work on the text by determining for each literary unity the composition and origin in addition to the original *Sitz im Leben*. *Sitz im Leben* thus concerns not only the original place of the formation of a text in the life of the community but also the question concerning the socioeconomic milieu of the one bearing the tradition.

All further work presupposes the analysis of the sources by means of literary criticism. Historical statements can thus be made only after the critical examination of the formation, age, and intention of the respective literary sources. The literary-critical investigation is thus the irrevocable prerequisite for all further research into the biblical texts.

The books of Joshua and Judges are part of the so-called Deuteronomistic History. This extensive historical representation reaches from Deut 1–3 up to the end of 2 Kings and thus comprises the entire span of Israel prior to and up through the formation of the state, from the sojourn in the eastern Transjordan to the collapse of the monarchy. The intention of the work is the interpretation of the history of Israel as a break from the exclusive worship of Yahweh in the only place chosen by Yahweh himself, the Jerusalem temple, as demanded in Deuteronomy; such an interpretation attempts to explain the collapse of the monarchy, the destruction of the temple, and the fate of the exile. The blame for the consequences of falling away lies most notably on the kings, since they seduced the people to the cults of foreign gods by not enforcing the demand of the Deuteronomic command. In addition to this show of self-blamed fate, the Deuteronomistic History nevertheless also serves to anchor divine salvific appointments in history. In the book of Joshua there is appropriation of the land, and in the book of Judges there is salvation from the enemies; which, as irrevocable salvific deeds of Yahweh, also continues to belong to the people who come from that history. Thus, this representation puts the entire history of Israel under the will of Yahweh, but it also clarifies how strongly Israel is bound to its God throughout its history.

The formation of the Deuteronomistic History is explained by two different hypotheses that are mutually exclusive:

1. The strata model posits a foundational element that was worked over several times. According to this theory, the composition of the original work took place by the reception of older traditions on the part of an unknown Deuteronomistic Historian (DtrH) during the exilic period. This historical-theological design became supplemented literarily by a later "Deuteronomist," who most notably emphasized the law mediated by Moses as the irrevocable guiding principle for human action; on account of this Torah-oriented *Tendenz*, the author is designated as the Nomist (DtrN). An additional layer can be ascertained by the expansion of prophetic narratives (DtrP) in the books of Kings (R. Smend, T. Veijola).

2. The incremental model maintains the composition of a foundational element during the late monarchic period. This historical work of the monarchic period initially reached only to the time of Josiah, but after the collapse of the state of Judah the work was updated by an expansion up to the end of the monarchy. With this addition, the older part was also redacted. The Deuteronomistic History thus belongs in the late monarchic period, and only in light of historical experience was it built up to its current capacity by its corresponding expansion (F. M. Cross, R. D. Nelson).

According to both hypotheses, an older foundational document is distinguished from redactional revision and expansion. However, whereas by the strata model the Deuteronomistic History first stemmed from the exilic period and the additional literary layers were attached still later in the postexilic period, the incremental model counts on an older design from the late monarchic period that was then completed in the exilic and postexilic periods respectively. According to both hypotheses, a foundational document must be distinguished from the literary revisions.

The following analysis and representation will rely on the strata model, holding that the oldest version of the complete work goes back to the Deuteronomistic Historian (DtrH); however, the additional revisions are not classified precisely and thus no redactional layer will be assigned. In any case, the view of the older research, that the books of Joshua and Judges are the continuation of the sources represented in the Pentateuch, is to be given up. The question pertains most importantly to the older traditions included in the framework of the Deuteronomistic Historian's work of history. The significance and purpose of the original design were the reasonable explanation of the historical development of the monarchic period. The sole criterion for judgment about the history was the people's behavior in view of the demand to worship Yahweh as the one and only God as programmatically established in Deuteronomy. The collapse of the monarchy was explained by the people's misbehavior. The demise of the state with the destruction of the temple is blamed on the people themselves insofar as they turned toward other gods and thus fell away from Yahweh.

I.2.1. Sojourn in the Eastern Transjordan (Num 21–36)

Fritz, Volkmar. *Israel in der Wüste: Traditionsgeschichtliche Untersuchung der Wüstenüberlieferung des Jahwisten* (MThSt 7; Marburg: N.G. Elwert, 1970). **Noth**, Martin. *Numbers: A Commentary* (trans. James D. Martin; OTL; Philadelphia: Westminster, 1968). **Rudolph**, Wilhelm. *Der "Elohist" von Exodus bis Josua* (BZAW 68; Berlin: Töpelmann, 1938). **Stuart**, Aaron. *Mose und Israel im Konflikt: Eine redaktionsgeschichtliche Studie zu den Wüstenerzählungen* (OBO 98; Freiburg, Switzerland: Universitätsverlag, 1990).

The course of the action is broken up again and again by pieces that do not belong to the narrative and turn out to be insertions. By various supplements, the Sinai narrative already grew to a considerable complex of legal and cultic regulations. Likewise, the narrative of the additional course of the wandering in the wilderness and the path through the eastern Transjordan in Num 10 and 11 was filled in with numerous expansions that have nothing to do with the actual course of events. Within the narrative complex following the departure from Kadesh in Num 21–36, there are numerous supplements of various types:

1. Narratives that take place in the eastern Transjordan (Num 22–24; 25; 31)
2. Lists and registers (Num 26; 33)
3. Legal or cultic regulations (27:1–11; 28:1–30:1; 30:2–17; 36)
4. Looking forward to taking the western Transjordan under the leadership of Joshua (27:12–23; 33:50–34:29; 35)

With the exception of the Balaam narrative in Num 22–24, in terms of language and outlook, all these pieces are developments of the postexilic period. By their insertion behind Num 21, it is thus certain that the norms and practices of this era of formative Judaism were to be legitimated by corresponding examples and decisions from the time of Moses. After singling out all the supplements, only Num 21 and 32 are considered as land-acquisition narratives for the eastern Transjordan.

I.2.1.1. The Supplements (Num 25–31 and 33–36)

The core of the episode in Num 25 is the falling away to the idolatry of the Moabites in Baal of Peor (25:1–5); all the remaining pieces are literarily dependent on this section (see Noth, *Numbers*, 195–99). Yet even in the starting point there is no old tradition, since the connection between foreign women and seduction to idolatry represents a typical postexilic topos (cf. Ezra 9). The naming of the place by no means indicates an old place tradition, since the name Peor is probably identical to Beth-Peor. The original name was only subsequently changed by the theophoric element Baal in order to achieve a point of departure for the narrative concerning the apostasy from Yahweh (cf. Hos 9:10). The place Beth-Peor was again named as a deposit of Israel in Moab (Deut 3:29; 4:46; 34:6) in addition to belonging to the region of Reuben in Josh 13:20; concerning the unknown location, on the basis of the statement by Eusebius (*Onomasticon* 48.3–5) it is to be found in the region east of Heshbon. A cultic site for Baal is by no means necessarily presupposed, since the very place name is sufficient as a starting point for the narrative.

The population census in Num 26 is a complement to Num 1:20–47, and the sequence of tribes agrees in both tables (on the tribal system, see §II.5.1). A clan list underlies the census, as it is a secondary interpolation also in Gen 46:8–25. "The secondary character of the figures that are given vis-à-vis the clan list is clear from the fact that the actual content of the clan list has no bearing on them, since they do not refer to the individual clans but only to each tribe as a whole. The clan list has therefore been utilized simply as a tribal register" (Noth, *Numbers*, 203). The genesis and age of the clan list are just as unknown as the origin of the figures. Even the deviation to the summary statements conveyed in Num 1:20–47 cannot be explained. Since neither the clan list nor the figures correspond to real relationships in Israel's history, they can be understood only as a fictive stocktaking, which the Priestly Document's system of tribes already presupposes. Therefore, the clan list must be later than the Priestly Document. Thus, the list originally had nothing to do with the land-acquisition narrative.

The piece in Num 27:1–11 brings about by divine decision a ruling to a legal case using the example of the named Zelophehad from Num 26:33. In case of the death without male heirs, the inheritance is determined exactly. In the supplement of Num 36, this regulation is updated further. With regard to content, both sections fall from the framework and were not original components of the land-acquisition narrative.

The announcement of the death of Moses and the installation of Joshua as his successor (Num 27:12–23) presupposes the punishment of Moses and Aaron (Num 20:1–3) and must therefore be later than the Priestly Document. The announcement of the death of Moses is repeated once again in Deut 32:48–52 in the framework of the Deuteronomistic History, and then the death is reported in Deut 34:1a, 7–9. The appointment of Joshua as his successor is also stereotypically connected with the reference to Moses' death in Deut 3:23–29; 31:1–8; Josh 1:1, 2. Here is thus a pronounced connecting piece that already knows the outstanding role of Joshua in the land acquisition and emphasizes the God-willed continuation of his leadership. The section was intended as a literary bridge and was hardly constitutive of the land-acquisition narrative.

The systematic compilation of all the offerings into the calendrical arrangement for the different days and the individual feasts of the year in Num 28:1–30:1 presupposes the offering instruction of Lev 1–7, the feast calendar in Lev 23, and the supplements in Num 15:1–16 (see Noth, *Numbers*, 219–23). As a late literary construction, it is a supplement that reflects the practice of the postexilic period of an indeterminate time.

With the commitment to the vow made by women, Num 30:2–17 deals with a particular problem of cultic practice in the postexilic period. The remarks are practically unique and are a literary insertion.

The narrative about the war against the Midianites in Num 31 is a late piece in terms of form and content,[1] which was prepared for by Num 25:16–

---

1. Ernst Axel Knauf, *Midian: Untersuchungen zur Geschichte Palästinas und Nordarabiens am Ende des 2. Jahrtausends v. Chr.* (ADPV 10; Wiesbaden: Harrassowitz, 1988), 160–69; contra Otto Eissfeldt, "Protektorat der Midianiter über ihre Nachbarn im letzten Viertel des 2. Jahrtausends v.Chr.," in *Kleine Schriften V* (Tübingen: Mohr Siebeck, 1973), 94–105; William J. Dumbrell, "Midian—A Land or a League?" *VT* 25 (1975): 323–37.

18. The actual war report is "remarkably colourless and schematized and lacking in concrete details, so that it is difficult to see in it an independent element of tradition" (Noth, *Numbers*, 228). The additional explanations are directed toward the legitimate dealings with booty and the adherence to cultic purity. The entire entity has the character of a constructed example narrative, and the choice of the Midianites as the enemies of Israel probably refers to the Gideon tradition (Judg 6–8). The chapter is a supplement to the sojourn of Israel in the eastern Transjordan that is later than Num 25:1–15 and stems from a priestly circle at the earliest.

Numbers 33:1–49 brings about a recapitulation of the wilderness trip in the form of an index of stations; this reaches from Ramses as the place of departure for the exodus in Exod 12:37 to the location reached in the eastern Transjordan that is marked by the name Abel-shittim. A list underlies the index of stations as the nucleus, which describes a journey through the eastern Transjordan to Ezion-geber and from there possibly to northwest Arabia.[2] The original meaning of this list can no longer be discerned, since the location of a majority of the places has not been determined. The greatest probability is that a description of the route was included, without that having to mean the "pilgrimage journey to Sinai" (Noth, "Der Wallfahrtsweg zum Sinai [Nu 33]"). Presumably this has to do with a description of a journey from the time of the Assyrian and Babylonian dominance during the eighth to sixth centuries, when the numerous campaigns demanded the fixing of firmer routes. The starting point remains unclear, whereas the end point was in the eastern Transjordan, which facilitated the inclusion of the list in this context. The original index was filled in with the locations from the wilderness tradition (Exod 15–Num 20). The piece thus presupposes the existing narrative connection and goes back to the scholarly work of a redactor in the postexilic period.

The instructions for taking the land in the eastern Transjordan in Num 33:5–34:29 are a conglomeration of later pieces. Numbers 33:50–56 refers back to the narrative of the book of Joshua and includes the key Deuteronomistic

---

2. George W. Coats, "The Wilderness Itinerary," *CBQ* 34 (1972): 135–52; G. I. Davies, "The Wilderness Itineraries: A Comparative Study," *TynBul* 25 (1974): 46–81; idem, "The Wilderness Itineraries and the Composition of the Pentateuch," *VT* 33 (1983): 1–13; Zechariah Kallai, "The Wandering-Traditions from Kadesh-Barnea to Canaan: A Study in Biblical Historiography," *JSS* 33 (1982): 175–184; J. Maxwell Miller, "The Israelite Journey Through (Around) Moab and Moabite Toponymy," *JBL* 108 (1989): 577–95; Martin Noth, "Der Wallfahrtsweg zum Sinai (Nu 33)," *ABLAK* 1 (1971): 55–74; Jerome T. Walsh, "From Egypt to Moab: A Source-Critical Analysis of the Wilderness Itinerary," *CBQ* 39 (1977): 20–33; Wolfgang Zwickel, "Der Durchzug der Israeliten durch das Ostjordanland," *UF* 22 (1990): 475–95.

concepts ירש ("to take possession") and נחל ("to receive as an inherited possession"). The description of the borders in Num 34:1–12 even leaves out the land east of the Jordan and thus stands in contradiction to Num 32, where the eastern Transjordan is distributed to the tribes Reuben and Gad. This border description has as a presupposition the idea of the cultic impurity of the land east of the Jordan (cf. Josh 22) and probably goes back initially to the priestly circle. The same border demarcation is found also in Ezek 47:15–20 in the framework of the idealized land distribution of the postexilic period, in which the land west of the Jordan is distributed schematically among the twelve tribes without consideration of the historical data. With Num 34:13–15, the land distribution of Josh 13–19 is established as an instruction by Moses. The names of the list in Num 34:17–18 correspond to those of Num 1:5–15 and 13:4–56, although they are not always identical. The entire section proves to be a redactional combination, which already presupposes the process of the historical narrative in the Deuteronomistic History.

The instructions for cities of refuge and cities for the Levites in Num 35 point ahead to Josh 20–21 and are literarily dependent on the explanation there.[3]

I.2.1.2. The Balaam Oracles (Num 22–24)

Donner, Herbert. "Balaam Pseudopropheta," in *Beiträge zur alttestamentlichen Theologie: Festschrift für Walther Zimmerli zum 70. Geburtstag* (ed. Herbert Donner, Robert Hanhart, and Rudolf Smend; Göttingen: Vandenhoeck & Ruprecht, 1977), 112–23. **Gross**, Walter. *Bileam: Literar- und formkritische Untersuchung des Prosa in Num 22–24* (STANT 38; Munich: Kösel, 1973). **Moore**, Michael S. *The Balaam Traditions: Their Character and Development* (SBLDS 113; Atlanta: Scholars Press, 1990). **Mowinckel**, Sigmund. "Der Ursprung der Bil'amsage," *ZAW* 48 (1930): 233–71. **Safren**, Jonathan D. "Balaam and Abraham," *VT* 38 (1988): 105–13. **Schmidt**, Ludwig. "Die alttestamentliche Bileamüberlieferung," *BZ* NS 23 (1979): 234–61. **Zobel**, Hans-Jürgen. "Bileam-Lieder und Bileam-Erzählung," in *Die Hebräische Bibel und ihre zweifache Nachgeschichte: Festschrift für Rolf Rendtorff zum 65. Geburtstag* (ed. Erhard Blum, Christian Macholz, and Ekkehard W. Stegemann; Neukirchen-Vluyn: Neukirchener, 1990), 141–54. See now also: **Van Seters**, John. "From Faithful Prophet to Villain: Observations on the Tradition History of the Balaam Story," in *A Biblical Itinerary: In Search of Method, Form, and Content; Essays in Honor of George W. Coats* (ed. Eugene E. Carpenter; JSOTSup 240; Sheffield: Sheffield Academic Press, 1997), 126–32. **Moberly**, R. W. L. "On Learning to Be a True Prophet: The Story of

---

3. See Martin Noth, *Das Buch Josua* (2nd ed.; HAT 1/7; Tübingen: Mohr Siebeck, 1953), 127.

Balaam and His Ass," in *New Heaven and New Earth: Prophecy and the Millennium; Essays in Honour of Anthony Gelston* (ed. P. J. Harland and C. T. R. Hayward; VTSup 77; Leiden: Brill, 1999), 1–17. **Sals**, Ulrike. "The Hybrid Story of Balaam (Numbers 22–24): Theology for the Diaspora in the Torah," *BibInt* 16 (2008): 315–35. **Kooten**, George H. van, and Jacques van **Ruiten**, eds. *The Prestige of the Pagan Prophet Balaam in Judaism, Early Christianity and Islam* (Themes in Biblical Narrative 11; Leiden: Brill, 2008).

Numbers 22:1–24:25 represents a self-contained narrative that was fit into the context by the redactor of 22:2–4a. The connecting element for the addition to Num 21 is Moab as the place of the plot. The narrative about Balaam, who was called by the Moabite king Balak to announce destruction but instead pronounced salvation over Israel, shows a successive growth. Numbers 23:26–24:44 was probably first added to the third and fourth sayings in the postexilic period (W. Gross). Yet there is also a supplemental addition with the ass episode (22:22–35) to clarify that the foreign figure did not act and speak without divine providence, although the transfer of the title "prophet" to Balaam is particularly avoided. The two episodes in 22:7–20 were originally independent narratives pertaining to the character Balaam and were presumably added into the context only later. The original narrative thus contained only the foundational element of 22:4b–6, 21, 36–41 and 23:1–25. Possibly the closing comment in 24:25 already concluded the oldest version. In this context, the question can remain open as to whether the foundational layer already belonged to the pre-Priestly historical writings or was added afterward as a self-contained construction independent of the older Tetrateuch narrative. Within the narrative, any kind of reference to the land acquisition is still lacking. The Balaam narrative thus developed independently of the idea of a sojourn by Israel in the eastern Transjordan; rather, the foundational layer already figures on a settled Israel. Since the first and second sayings reflect the special position of Israel among the peoples, they were composed over the course of the monarchic period at the earliest. The addition of the material in the tradition complex located in the eastern Transjordan probably did not take place until after the addition of Num 24:1–24 in the postexilic period.

The inscriptions on the plastered wall of Tell Deir 'Allā from the eighth century (*TUAT* 2:138–48) names a Balaam, son of Beor, in connection with soothsaying (*Weissagungen*).[4] Even if the Aramaic text shows no immedi-

---

4. Jo Ann Hackett, *The Balaam Text from Deir 'Allā* (HSM 31; Chico, Calif: Scholars Press, 1984); J. Hoftijzer and G. van der Kooij, *Aramaic Texts from Deir 'Allā* (Documenta et monumenta Orientis antiqui 19; Leiden: Brill, 1976); Hans-Peter Müller, "Die aramäische Inschrift von Deir 'Allā und die älteren Bileamsprüche," *ZAW* 94 (1982): 214–44; P. Kyle

ate connection to the biblical tradition, Balaam is nevertheless attested in an extrabiblical source. On account of the fragmentary state of preservation and numerous uncertainties in terms of reading and the interpretation of this text, the details of the extrabiblical oracle remain largely unclear. Nevertheless, it is clear that the Balaam tradition of Israel was adopted and built up out of foreign material. Within the biblical tradition, the character Balaam was further developed. In Deut 23:5–6; Josh 24:9–10; and Neh 13:2, Balaam is mentioned according to his role in Num 22–24. However, in Num 31:16 he is brought into connection with the event of Num 25:1–15; consequently, in Num 31:8 he is killed along with the five kings of the Midianites. In Josh 13:22 he is finally disqualified as one who practiced divination (קוסם). In subsequent interpretation, Balaam was reevaluated as a false prophet (cf. H. Donner) who is detestable in spite of his blessings, given that only God turned the disastrous intention into the opposite redeeming promise.

I.2.1.3. Taking the Eastern Transjordan (Num 21 and 32)

Bartlett, John R. "The Conquest of Sihon's Kingdom: A Literary Re-examination," *JBL* 97 (1978): 347–51. **Kallai**, Zecharia. "Conquest and Settlement of the Trans-Jordan," *ZDPV* 99 (1983): 110–18. **Noth**, Martin. "Nu 21 als Glied der 'Hexateuch'-Erzählung," *ABLAK* 1 (1971): 75–101. **Noth**. "Israelitische Stämme zwischen Ammon und Moab," *ABLAK* 1 (1971): 391–433. **Schmitt**, H.-Ch. "Das Hesbonlied Num 21,27aβb–30 und die Geschichte der Stadt Hesbon," *ZDPV* 104 (1988): 26–43. **Van Seters**, John. "The Conquest of Sihon's Kingdom: A Literary Examination, *JBL* 91 (1972): 182–97. **Van Seters**. "Once Again—The Conquest of Sihon's Kingdom," *JBL* 99 (1980): 117–19. **Weippert**, Manfred. "The Israelite 'Conquest' and the Evidence of Transjordan," in *Symposia Celebrating the Seventy-fifth Anniversary of the Founding of the American Schools of Oriental Research (1900–1975)* (ed. Frank Moore Cross; Cambridge, Mass.: ASOR, 1979), 15–34. **Wüst**, Manfried. *Untersuchungen zu den siedlungsgeographischen Texten des Alten Testaments I* (BTAVO, Reihe B, 9; Wiesbaden: Reichert, 1975).

Numbers 21 is made up of different literary units, which are independent of one another and are to be analyzed individually:

McCarter, "The Balaam Texts from Deir 'Alla: The First Combination," *BASOR* 239 (1980): 49–60; Victor Sasson, "The Book of Oracular Visions of Balaam from Deir Alla," *UF* 17 (1986): 283–309; Helga and Manfred Weippert, "Die 'Bileam'-Inschrift von *Tell Dēr Allā*," *ZDPV* 98 (1982): 77–103. See now also Hendricus Jacobus Franken, "Balaam at Deir 'Alla and the Cult of Baal," in *Archaeology, History and Culture in Palestine and the Near East: Essays in Memory of Albert E. Glock* (ed. Tomis Kapitan; ASOR Books 3; Atlanta: Scholars Press, 1999), 183–202.

— Defeating the Canaanites in Negeb (21:1-3)
— The Brazen Serpent (21:4-9)
— The Journey to Moab (21:10-20)
— The Victory over Sihon (21:21-31)
— The Conquest of Jazer (21:32)
— The Victory over Og (21:33-35)

Of these pieces, 21:1-3 takes place in the Negeb, but the short narrative frames the prelude to the theme of land acquisition. A literary connection to the preceding narratives in Num 20 is not given. The death of Moses and Aaron prior to reaching the land is established by the last wilderness tradition in Num 20:1-13.[5] The piece following from there, Num 20:14-21, is a late construction that is only secondary to this position. The death of Aaron in 20:22-29 is narrated directly in connection with the departure from Kadesh. The scene of this event, the mountain Hor, cannot be located but is probably to be found in the vicinity of Kadesh, the headwaters ʿÊn el-Qudērāt. In any case, this mountain was west of the Arabah, and only in the postexilic period would it be confused with the Ğebel Hārūn by Petra to the east side of the Arabah (cf. Josephus, *Antiquities* 4.4.7 §§82-84). With this narrative of the death of Aaron, the Priestly Document breaks off; it has no interest in the wider course of the land-acquisition narrative and is represented no further in the book of Joshua. The report about the death of Moses in Deut 34:1a, 7-9 is constitutive of the Deuteronomistic History and is not embedded by the Priestly Document.[6]

As an independent narrative, Num 21:1-3 does not provide an itinerary note but is clearly in the region of the Negeb, given the name of Hormah. Hormah has still not been located, but other citations suggest that it is definitely to be found in the Negeb (cf. Num 14:45; Deut 1:44; Josh 12:14; 15:30; Judg 1:17; 1 Sam 30:30); the attachment to the Tell el-Ḥýuwelīfe by Nadav Naʾaman ("The Inheritance of the Sons of Simeon," *ZDPV* 96 [1980]: 142-43) is possible but not conclusive. In a style noticeably colorless and austere, Num 21:1-3 is largely composed of stiff expressions. Since the piece can be spun entirely out of the wordplay of the name Hormah with the verb חרם ("to consecrate to destruction"), there is hardly evidence of an old tradition about a place here. (The naming of the king of Arad is a gloss anyway.) Therefore, the narrative appears to be a late construction that was not yet constitutive

---

5. F. Kohata, "Die priesterschriftliche Überlieferungsgeschichte von Num XX 1-13," *AJBI* 3 (1977): 3-34; William H. C. Propp, "The Rock of Aaron and the Sin of Moses," *JBL* 107 (1988): 19-26.

6. Lothar Perlitt, "Priesterschrift im Deuteronomium?" *ZAW* 100 (1988): 65-88.

of the pre-Priestly historical writings. Apparently it was created for this place in order to fill in the gap between the departure from the wilderness and the land acquisition in the eastern Transjordan. The shaping and insertion of the piece are not explained by the naming of the place Hormah at the end of the Yahwistic story of the spies in Num 14:45. In Num 21:1–3 the setback narrated there concerning the land acquisition is balanced out, so that the wider process takes place against a background of success.

The story of the brazen serpent (Num 21:4–9) is fit into the context by the itinerary note in 21:4a. The instructions concerning the route are redactional, adopted from Exod 15:22 and Num 20:22, thus presupposing the wilderness tradition in the combined form of the older historical work and the Priestly Document. The narrative establishes the making of the object described as the "brazen serpent" (נחש הנחשת) by Moses. This cannot be dissociated from the cultic idol named the נחשתן ("brazen serpent") that was removed from the temple of Jerusalem by Hezekiah (2 Kgs 18:4). Since that representation of a serpent goes back explicitly to Moses, the story of the serpent plague in the wilderness and its management by Moses can with great probability be seen as an etiology for this cult idol in the temple of Jerusalem. This connection between cult object and narrative dates the formation of the piece to the monarchic period. All that is presupposed is thus the idea of a wandering in the wilderness, as it was given by the pre-Priestly historical writings. It is also certainly conceivable that the narrative was first created in the postexilic period on the basis of 2 Kgs 18:4. In any case, Num 21:4b–9 does not belong to the pre-Priestly historical narrative, but rather was only subsequently interpolated to this position as an appendix to the wilderness tradition. The redactional transition in Num 21:4a, by the avoidance of Edom, presupposes the late literary compilation of Num 20:14–21; the insertion of the piece thus belongs in the late redactional work after the exile. It cannot be decided whether the narrative of the brazen serpent emerged already in the monarchic period or represents a postexilic construction based on 2 Kgs 18:4. In any case, a narrative inserted in the last possible place, which can assert no claim to a long tradition and great age, merely took up the idea of Israel's wilderness migration.

The route from the wilderness west to the Arabah in the eastern Transjordan is broken up by the itinerary in Num 21:10–20. Included in this is the so-called Well Song (Num 21:17b–18a), which is passed off explicitly as a citation from the "Book of the Wars of Yahweh," but possibly stems from oral tradition. Concerning the places of the itinerary, the first two—Oboth and Iye-abarim—are also named in Num 33:44 and could be adopted from there. The Wadi Zered is likewise in Deut 2:13; the place Bamoth occurs again in Num 22:41; the top of Pisgah is named also in Num 23:14–15, and

Yeshimon [Heb. יְשִׁי(מֹ)ן(ה)‎; Eng. "(the) wilderness"] appears in Num 23:28 as well as in Deut 32:10. Apart from Arnon and Zered, the remaining names are entirely unknown. Although the connection of the itinerary cannot be explained by this attestation, this proves nonetheless to be a redactional connecting piece, "with which a later hand has endeavoured, as best he could, to compensate for the lack of connection of which he was aware and which really exists, between the stories already related as still taking place on the edge of the desert and the following accounts of the conquest" (Noth, *Numbers*, 159).

In the narrative about the victory over Sihon, the king of the Ammonites (Num 21:21–31), the so-called Heshbon Song (Num 21:27–30) represents an independent unit that is integrated with the Sihon story such that Heshbon is made into a city of Sihon (21:25b–26). Hans-Christoph Schmitt ("Das Hesbonlied Num 21,27aβb–30," *ZDPV* 104 [1988]: 26–43) demonstrated that the Heshbon Song was composed during the time of Assyrian dominance over the cities in the eastern Transjordan in the seventh century. However, even the narrative in Num 21:21–25a, 31 about the victory of Israel at Jahaz (Ḫirbet Medēniyeh) does not go back to an old tradition and was not a component of the pre-Priestly Tetrateuch narrative. The piece is a literary construction, having the motif of the refusal to march through and the common parlance of military actions. The place list introduced by Num 21:25a possibly was broken off by the insertion of the Heshbon Song. Presumably this core piece of east Jordanian land-acquisition narrative was created subsequently in order to bridge the gap between the wilderness traditions (Exod 15–Num 20) and the land-acquisition narrative in the book of Joshua.

The note concerning the conquest of Jazer in Num 21:32 has no point of departure at all in the context but have arisen because of the naming of the land Jazer in Num 32:1. According to the additional citations, the place appears to have had a certain significance (cf. Num 32:3, 35; Josh 13:25; 21:39; 2 Sam 24:5; Isa 16:8; 1 Chr 6:66; 26:31). Its location is unknown, but according to the statement by Eusebius (*Onomasticon* 104.13–19) it is to be found approximately ten Roman miles west of ʿAmmān in the upper reaches of Wadi Saʿab. The isolated place and the stereotypic common parlance show the redactional character of this note. Its insertion goes back to the redactional work in the postexilic period.

A redactional insertion is likewise found in the passage of the victory over Og of Bashan in Num 21:33–35. On account of the broad verbal agreement with Deut 3:1–3, this piece is considered to have been adopted from the introduction to the Deuteronomistic History in Deut 1–3.

Numbers 22:1 is the redactional transition to the incorporation of the Balaam narrative. The general place statement, "the plains region of Moab"

(עַרְבוֹת מוֹאָב), is also used elsewhere by the redactors (cf. Num 26:3, 63; 31:12; 33:48, 49, 50; 35:1; 36:13; Deut 34:1, 8; Josh 13:32) in order to mark the end of the procession in the eastern Transjordan.

In Num 32, verses 39–42 represent an addition to the preceding narrative in order to establish the instruction of individual clans to certain settlement regions. Those notes are thus redactional supplements, which either—as in the case of Gilead—correspond to the general conception or were simply constructed out of the names. These comments were added in order to supplement the narrative about Moses' awarding land to Reuben and Gad with the naming of the Manassite clans and thus to complete the taking of the eastern Transjordan corresponding subsequently to the ideas of the monarchic period.

The narrative concerning the allocation of the land east of the Jordan to the tribes Reuben and Gad (Num 32:1–38) is indeed self-contained, but the foundational element was expanded by numerous additions (cf. Wüst, *Siedlungsgeographischen Texten*, 95–99). The plot amounts to the construction of the cities cited by name in 32:34–38 and originally contained only the introduction (32:1), the request by the concerned tribes (32:16) including the associated assurance (32:17), and the granting of this request by Moses (32:24). Prior to verse 24, 32:20aα could still have stood as an introduction to the verbal discourse. The original narrative thus comprised only 32:1, 16, 17, 20aα, 24, 34–38; all additional parts are secondary insertions. The sequence of the individual materials of the redaction need not be discussed here. The foundational element at one time had the allocation of the tribal regions to Reuben and Gad as its content, but at the same time it secured the participation of these tribes in the conquest of the western Transjordan in view of Josh 1–12.

In the narrative of Num 32:1, 16, 17, 20aα, 24, 34–38, the taking of the eastern Transjordan is represented as a peaceable procedure, which certainly does not preclude a preceding partial conquest. The tribes rich in livestock, Reuben and Gad, approach Moses with the request concerning the construction of cities (32:1, 16) and declare that they are prepared to take up arms and participate in the conquest of the western Transjordan (32:17). Consequently, Moses gives permission to build the cities (32:20aα, 24), which are then listed by name. Given that the history has in view the acquisition of the western Transjordan, as it is narrated in Josh 1–12, its belonging to the pre-Priestly historical writings is ruled out, since that document knew only of a land acquisition from the south. It is rather a connecting piece that was conceived by adopting a list of east Jordanian cities in view of the land acquisition narrative in the Deuteronomistic History. The main point of the story lies solely in the fact that the east Jordanian tribes participate in the seizure of the western Transjordan, even though through Moses they had already obtained their residence across the Jordan.

The two pieces Num 21:21–31 and 32:1, 16, 17, 20aα, 24, 34–38, thus present a land-taking narrative for the eastern Transjordan analogous to that of the western Transjordan in Josh 1–24. Reported are both the conquest by all Israel and the bestowal of the region to the tribes there. The foundational element of Num 21–36 thus involves both defeat of enemies and allocation of land for the constitutive elements for the land seizure. As necessary literary transitions, Num 21:21–31 and 32:1, 16, 17, 20aα, 24, 34–38 were created by a Deuteronomistic author in order to close the existing gap between the wandering in the wilderness (Exod 15–Num 20) and the acquisition of the land west of the Jordan (Josh 1–24). By further replenishments and additions, this east Jordanian land-acquisition narrative became largely overgrown.

Nevertheless, the intention of the foundational element is clearly discernible. The land seizure in the eastern Transjordan was carried out in the same way as in the western Transjordan: from the conquest follows the allocation of the land. The composition of this literary bridge took place either in connection with the creation of the Deuteronomistic History or a bit later in the fifth century. Older traditions do not underlie the two pieces; therefore, these sections are ruled out as historical sources for the history of the eastern Transjordan in the premonarchic era. The narratives do not reflect historical circumstances but instead attest postexilic notions of these occurrences and developments. The east Jordanian land-acquisition narrative, then, by the inclusion of numerous supplements, grew into a considerable complex with its own literary weight. The accumulation of different materials is determined by the character of Moses, by whose authority different individual questions could be decided as having the force of law. Since Deuteronomy was fixed as an enclosed unit, no further additions were allowed; in addition, the Sinai pericope had likewise already grown to a fixed size. In the postexilic period, additional materials could be accommodated only at the end point of the wandering through the land east of the Jordan, which at the same time represented the end of Moses' journey through life.

I.2.1.4. Repetition of the Trip from Horeb to the Jordan (Deut 1–3)

Lohfink, Norbert. "Darstellungskunst und Theologie in Dtn 1,6–3,29," in idem, *Studien zum Deuteronomium und zur deuteronomistischen Literatur I* (Stuttgarter biblische Aufsatzbände; Stuttgart: Katholisches Bibelwerk, 1990), 15–44. **McKenzie**, John L. "The Historical Prologue of Deuteronomy," in *Papers: Fourth World Congress of Jewish Studies* (2 vols.; Jerusalem: World Union of Jewish Studies, 1967,

1968), 1:95–101. **Mittmann**, Siegfried. *Deuteronomium 1,1–6,3 literarkritisch und traditionsgeschtlich untersucht* (BZAW 139; Berlin: de Gruyter, 1975). **Perlitt**, Lothar. "Deuteronomium 1–3 im Streit der exegetischen Methoden," in *Das Deuteronomium: Entstehung, Gestalt und Botschaft* (ed. Norbert Lohfink; BETL 68; Leuven: University Press, 1985), 149–63. **Perlitt**. *Deuteronomium* (BK Altes Testament 5; Neukirchen-Vluyn: Neukirchener, 1990–). **Veijola**, Timo. "Principal Observations on the Basic Story in Deuteronomy 1–3," in *Wünschet Jerusalem Frieden: Collected Communications to the XIIth Congress of the International Organization for the Study of the Old Testament, Jerusalem 1986* (ed. Matthias Augustin and Klaus-Dietrich Schunck; Beiträge zur Erforschung des Alten Testaments und des antiken Judentums 13; New York: Lang, 1988), 249–59.

In Deut 1–3, the journey from Horeb by way of Kadesh in the eastern Transjordan is narrated once again. Regardless of possible revisions and expansions, this repetition has a connection to the events depicted in Num 10–32. This renewed narrative uses the first person so that the entire report is stylized as a speech by Moses. As such, this retelling refers less to the ensuing preaching of Deuteronomic law than to the narrative of the conquest of the western Transjordan in Josh 1–12, beginning with the installation of Joshua in Josh 1. Since the summary of Deut 1–3 is clearly intended as a continuation, it can only be interpreted as an introduction to the entire work of the Deuteronomistic Historian. The Deuteronomistic History begins with Deut 1–3 and represents the history of the people Israel from the land seizure to the end of the monarchy in Judah.

In the repetition of Deut 1–3, the available material from Num 10–32 was strongly condensed and reduced to the most important events. From the *Vorlage* there is merely a selection that is limited in essence to the story of the spies in Num 13–14, the confrontations in the eastern Transjordan in Num 21, and the allocation of the settlement regions to the east Jordanian tribes in Num 32. The structure of Deut 1–3 corresponds in a noticeable way to the structure of the book of Joshua, although the acquisition of the western Transjordan was represented in far more detail. By this reduction down to the crucial occurrences, the Deuteronomistic Historian created a new historical narrative with a new *Tendenz*. The given material was "literarily compressed, geographically oriented, adapted to the form of a speech, and articulated as standardized theology" ("literarisch kompirmiert, geographisch orientiert, in der Redeform aneinander adaptiert und theologisch einheitlich akzentuiert" [Perlitt, *Deuteronomium*, 30]) In this way, the sojourn in the wilderness is expanded to forty years in order to enforce consistently the punishment of the generation of the exodus, since these were prohibited from acquiring the promised land on account of disobedience. This expansion of the time in the wilderness required in turn the choice of Kadesh-barnea as a stopover for the people in the wilderness prior to taking the land. The building up out of given material thus shows a consistent historiographic concept.

I.2.2. Taking the Western Transjordan (Josh 1–24)

Auld, A. Graeme. *Joshua, Moses and the Land: Tetrateuch–Pentateuch–Hexateuch in a Generation since 1938* (Edinburgh: T&T Clark, 1980). **Fritz**, Volkmar. *Das Buch Josua* (HAT I/7; Tübingen: Mohr Siebeck, 1994). **Smend**, Rudolf. "Das Gesetz und die Völker," in *Die Mitte des Alten Testaments: Gesammelte Studien II* (BEvT 99; Munich: Kaiser, 1986), 124–37. **Van Seters**, John. *In Search of History: Historiography in the Ancient World and the Origins of Biblical History* (New Haven: Yale University Press, 1983). See now also: **Nelson**, Richard D. *Joshua: A Commentary* (OTL; Louisville: Westminster John Knox, 1997).

Literarily the book of Joshua is a self-contained unit, the contents of which subdivide into two parts. The book is framed by two announcements to the character Joshua, the leading figure after Moses: in 1:1–6 Joshua is instructed by God concerning the land seizure, and in 24:29–31 his death is reported after the completion of his life's work. Apparently here lies a certain shaping of the book, in which conquest and allocation of the land are represented as the work of one man. Within the book a clear break lies between Josh 12 and 13. Joshua 13:1abα, 7 is marked as a reinsertion, and the list in 12:1–24 should summarize the conclusion of the previous conquests. For both parts, separate concluding formulas are found in 11:16–20 and 19:49a. The book of Joshua proves to be a consciously shaped composition with a bipartite construction, but the whole is held together by the overall leading figure of Joshua.

The comment about the conclusion to the land distribution in 19:49a—far before the end of the book—already shows evidence of the book's subsequent expansion. In the last chapter, the lists of cities of refuge and cities for the Levites (Josh 20–21) are supplements to the instruction of tribal territories. No independent document underlies the two. Joshua 20 goes back to Deut 19, and Josh 21 is a redactional compilation from the place names occurring in Josh 13–19 (cf. Fritz, *Josua*, 212). The narrative of Josh 22 is stylized according to the Priestly Document and is close to the conception of the border description in Num 34:1–12, in which the eastern Transjordan was definitely ruled out as a residence for the Israelite tribes. In view of the question of cultic purity, chapter 22 will thus add the necessary correction to the concept that the eastern Transjordan belongs to Israel as landed property. Joshua 23 is a duplicate of the farewell speech of Joshua in Josh 24; with the first speech, the Deuteronomistic redactor added what he missed in Josh 24: the covenant to the Torah of Moses and the forbidding of marriage to foreign women (cf. R. Smend). The last large unit of the book is Joshua's speech in 24:1–28; from there only the note about the death and burial of Joshua is yet to follow in 24:29–31 as the actual conclusion of the book.

I.2.2.1. Conquest of the Land (Josh 1–24)

The commission of Joshua, which originally comprised only 1:1–6, was supplemented several times: by 1:7–9 as well as by 1:10, 11, and 12–18. The piece constructs the literary frame of the book, which presupposes the location of the eastern Transjordan, though it is not named. The reference to the death of Moses narrated in Deut 34:1a, 7–9 represents a close literary connection with Deuteronomy as the final speech of Moses.

The reconnaissance narrative in Josh 2 was, apart from short supplements, largely expanded particularly in the central part (2:8–14). This expansion contains the unusual statement about the land grant by Yahweh in the mouth of Rahab (2:9a) as well as the promise of the spies to spare Rahab (2:12–14a). Actually the exploration of the land is a superfluous act; originally the foundational element of the narrative (2:1–3, 4b, 5–7, 15–17a, 18, 19, 21–23) was probably a history of the conquest, which contained the fall of the city by means of treason. The motif of the red thread in the window of the city wall through which the spies entered (2:18, 21) refers to that former conclusion. In its current context, this characteristic serves to make the house that is to be spared completely conspicuous. Since the thread is nevertheless attached to the outside of the city wall, this identification can originally have been meant only to mark the way into the city for the invaders. The original conclusion was then omitted in favor of Josh 6. The foundational layer of Josh 2 thus goes back to a pre-Deuteronomistic land-acquisition narrative about the conquest of Jericho.

The narrative about crossing over the Jordan (Josh 3; 4) is difficult to unravel literarily, since the foundational element was worked over several times.[7] The miraculous crossing through the Jordan, in the original version,

---

7. See Jan Dus, "Die Analyse zweier Ladeerzählungen des Josuabuches (Jos 3.4 und 6)," *ZAW* 72 (1960): 107–34; F. Langlamet, *Gilgal et les récits de la traversée du Jourdain, Jos. III–IV* (CahRB 11; Paris: Gabalda, 1969); Johann Maier, *Das altisraelitische Ladeheiligtum* (BZAW 93; Berlin: Töpelmann, 1965); Eckart Otto, *Das Mazzotfest in Gilgal* (BWANT 107; Stuttgart: Kollhammer, 1975); Brian Peckham, "The Composition of Joshua 3–4," *CBQ* 46 (1984): 413–31; J. R. Porter, "The Background of Joshua 3–5," *SEÅ* 36 (1971): 5–23; Paul P. Saydon, "The Crossing of the Jordan, Jos. chaps. 3 and 4," *CBQ* 12 (1950): 194–207; J. Alberto Soggin, "Gilgal, Passah und Landnahme: Eine neue Untersuchung des kultischen

comprised at most 3:1, 14a, 15a, 16; 4:11a, 18. The adoption of an older tradition is not recognizable. Instead, there is a literary construction analogous to the march through the sea in Exod 14, whereby the ark effects the standstill of the waters at the Jordan. The growth of the first narrative thus necessitates, on the one hand, that the role of the ark was at one point further accentuated and emphasized, and, on the other hand, that the report of the erection of a stone pillar in Gilgal (4:1–9, 20–24) was inserted. (The division of the text into two parallel narrative threads fails, given that the miracle in 3:16 and the corresponding restoration of the water to its former fluid state in 4:18b are only narrated once each time.) In the process of growth, the miraculous nature of the event was enhanced further and further. Nevertheless, Gilgal was not established as a cultic celebration or legitimated as a cultic place in any of the versions.

In Josh 5, verse 1 is a summary of the Deuteronomistic redaction. The short center section concerning circumcision in 5:2, 3, 8 was supplemented by redaction (5:4–7, 9) in order to establish the necessity of the practice in more detail. The note about the end of the manna in 5:10–12* is a supplement by a redactor. The accompanying reference back to the narrative about the manna miracle in Exod 16 presumes an interim Tetrateuch narrative prior to the Deuteronomistic History. The celebration of the first Passover Feast in the land (Josh 5:10b, 11*, 12b) was then brought in secondarily to the note about the end of the manna. In 5:13–15 a narrative about the promise of Yahweh's help in the conquest of Jericho and the land (Josh 5:13, 14a) is reshaped into a special commission of Joshua by the army commander Yahweh. Thereby Joshua is placed in parallel to Moses: Joshua obediently performs commensurate gestures and realizes that he will lead Israel into the land, not out of his own impetus or for his own fame but rather by divine commission.

The representation of the conquest of Jericho in Josh 6 was worked over several times in order to emphasize particularly the role of the ark and the ram horns in the event. As such, the fall of the city was narrated from the beginning as a miracle; indeed the wall collapsed simply from the war cry. Given the obligatory consecration to destruction, only Rahab and her family were spared—hence the explicit reference back to the events of Josh 2 (Josh 6:22–23). The foundational layer merely comprised 6:1, 2a, 3*, 4aβ, 5, 7a, 14,

---

Zusammenhangs der Kap. iii–vi des Josuabuches," in *Volume du Congrès: Genève, 1965* (VTSup 15; Leiden: Brill, 1965); Ernst Vogt, "Die Erzählung vom Jordanübergang Josue 3–4," *Bib* 46 (1965): 125–48. See now also Jan A. Wagenaar, "Crossing the Sea of Reeds (Exod 13–14) and the Jordan (Josh 3–4): A Priestly Framework for the Wilderness Wandering," in *Studies in the Book of Exodus: Redaction, Reception, Interpretation* (ed. Marc Vervenne; BETL 126; Leuven: Peeters, 1996), 461–70.

15a, 20b, 21–24a.[8] The older version of the capture of the city by treason was replaced with this later literary construction.

Joshua 7 is a type of didactic narrative that is enclosed and artfully constructed. The narrative consistently displays the carrying out of the death penalty for transgression in carrying out the consecration to destruction. An older *Vorlage* is not recognizable, and the possibility of an oral tradition that was at one time confined to the Valley of Achor is ruled out. Exemplifying the consequences of transgression in the consecration of certain goods, the narrative has been constructed using literary *topoi* clearly in view of the ensuing story of the conquest of the city Ai.

In Josh 8 a literary kernel was worked over several times and expanded. The original version contained only the following parts: advance and preparation (8:10–12), the attack by the inhabitants (8:14–15), conquest of the city (8:19), annihilation of the inhabitants (8:21), and the demise of the king of Ai (8:23, 29). The conquest of Ai is narrated schematically and by use of the universally recognized motifs of ambush and pretending to run away. Confining the event to the wreckage site of Ai may imply a local tradition, but such a local tradition could have originated only during the monarchic period; that is, the idea of a military land seizure by all the Israelite tribes first originated in the time of the state and was by no means available in the premonarchic era.[9] Only after the unification of the Israelite tribes under the leadership of a king could the concept of a land acquisition by all Israel be constructed; moreover, the explanation of a stone heap in Ai as a burial mound of a former king of the city in the time before the land seizure could be developed. For the oldest version, the structure, style, and vocabulary suggest a land-taking narrative that is older than the composition of the book of Joshua. Such a narrative about the conquest of Ai could be formed only in the course of the monarchic period. In any case, there is not an older tradition from before the monarchic period. The piece in Josh 8:30–35 is a supplement that is inconsistent and is

---

8. Cf. Ludger Schwienhorst-Schönberger, *Die Eroberung Jerichos: Exegetische Untersuchung zu Josua 6* (SBS 122; Stuttgart: Katholisches Bibelwerk, 1986), 122. On Josh 6, see now also Daniel E. Fleming, "The Seven-Day Siege of Jericho in Holy War," in *Ki Baruch Hu: Ancient Near Eastern, Biblical, and Judaic Studies in Honor of Baruch A. Levine* (ed. Robert Chazan, William W. Hallo, and Lawrence H. Schiffman; Winona Lake, Ind.: Eisenbrauns, 1999): 211–28; Frédéric Gangloff, "Joshua 6: Holy War or Extermination by Divine Command (*herem*)?" *Theological Review* 25 (2004): 3–23.

9. Arnulf Kuschke, "Hiwwiter in Ha'ai?" in *Wort und Geschichte: Festschrift für Karl Elliger zum 70. Geburtstag* (ed. Hartmut Gese and Hans Peter Rüger; AOAT 18; Kevelaer: Butzon & Bercker, 1973); Martin Noth, "Bethel und Ai," *ABLAK* 1 (1971): 210–28; Ziony Zevit, "Archaeological and Literary Stratigraphy in Joshua 7–8," *BASOR* 251 (1983): 23–35.

dependent in its different elements on the regulations in Deut 27:5-7. The supplement aims to show that Joshua performed the first offering in the land.

In Josh 9, verses 3-15a represent a self-contained narrative that requires no continuation.[10] Its purpose is to explain the juxtaposition of Canaanite and Israelite population, given the otherwise common practice of annihilation in the land seizure. This juxtaposition of the two population groups was still not a questioned fact at the beginning of the monarchic period; thus 2 Sam 21:1-14 expressly emphasized that Gibeon had been a non-Israelite population. The idea would first develop in the course of Deuteronomic-Deuteronomistic theology that the land of Canaan was inhabited by Israel alone, because the Canaanites had been annihilated (cf. Deut 7:1-6 and 20:10-18). At the end of the monarchic period, the fact of a Canaanite population in Gideon required explanation, which was provided in Josh 9:3-7, 9a, 11-15a. The story about the deceit of the Gibeonites subsequently became expanded not only by the element of the discovery of the deception along with its consequences (Josh 9:16, 17, 22-26) but also by a skillful revision in Josh 9:8, 9b, 10 in order to anchor the continuation of the narrative. Finally, a post-Priestly document redactor inserted the sections in 9:1, 2 and 15b, 18-21 in order to explain certain circumstances in the cultic purview. By considerable expansions, the foundational character of the original narrative was further reinforced.

Joshua 10 contains the two narratives regarding the battle at Gibeon (10:1-15) and the demise of the kings in the cave at Makkedah (10:16-27); the two are interconnected and reference one another.[11] The story of the victory of Israel at Gibeon cites a fragment of an old hymn of praise (10:12b, 13a).

---

10. Jörn Halbe, "Gibeon und Israel," *VT* 25 (1975): 613-41; Baruch Halpern, "Gibeon: Israelite Diplomacy in the Conquest Era," *CBQ* 37 (1975): 303-16; Menahem Haran, "The Gibeonites, The Netinim and the Sons of Solomon's Servants," *VT* 11 (1961): 159-69; Peter J. Kearney, "The Role of the Gibeonites in the Deuteronomistic History," *CBQ* 35 (1973): 1-19; Jacob Liver, "The Literary History of Joshua IX," *JSS* 8 (1963): 277-43; A. D. H. Mayes, "Deuteronomy, Joshua 9, and the Place of the Gibeonites in Israel," in *Das Deuteronomium: Entstehung, Gestalt und Botschaft* (ed. Norbert Lohfink; BETL 68; Leuven: University Press, 1985), 321-25; James B. Pritchard, "Gibeon's History in the Light of Excavation," in *Congress Volume: Oxford, 1959* (VTSup 7; Leiden: Brill, 1960), 1-12; Christa Schäfer-Lichtenberger, "Das gibeonitische Bündnis im Lichte deuteronomistischer Kriegsgebote," *BN* 34 (1986): 58-81. See now also John Day, "Gibeon and the Gibeonites in the Old Testament," in *Reflection and Refraction: Studies in Biblical Historiography in Honour of A. Graeme Auld* (ed. Robert Rezetko, Timothy H. Lim, and W. Brian Aucker; VTSup 113; Leiden: Brill, 2007): 113-37.

11. Martin Noth, "Die fünf Könige in der Höhle von Makkeda," *ABLAK* 1 (1971): 281-93; David A. Dorsey, "The Location of Biblical Makkedah," *Journal of the Tel Aviv University Institute of Archaeology* 7 (1980): 185-93.

This fragment was possibly the point of departure for the narrative, although the place of the events described might not necessarily have been connected with the taking of the land. The current continuation in Josh 10:16–27 was originally an independent tradition, "which accounted for a cave closed with large stones in the area of the meadow of the place Makkedah and the five trees standing in front of it" ("die an einer mit großen Steinen verschlossenen Höhle im Bereich der Flur des Ortes Makkeda und an fünf davor stehenden Bäumen haftet" [Noth, *ABLAK* 1 (1971): 282]).

However the prehistory of the piece may have come about, a land-taking tradition taken from the monarchic period was inserted into the foundational layer along with the transition in Josh 10:16; the same was the case with Josh 2 and 8. The narrative can lay no claim to a historical kernel. In the local shaping, only the death of some Canaanite kings was brought into connection with particular conditions of the mountain region in the territory of Makkedah (Ḫirbet el-Qōm). The idea of the land acquisition, as it would develop over the course of the monarchic period, is all that is presupposed. The conquest of additional cities in the Shephelah (Josh 10:28–43) was conveyed in stereotypical, formulaic repetition. Since the adoption of an older tradition is ruled out by virtue of this formulation, the section can only be a creation of the Deuteronomistic Historian so as to conclude the land acquisition in the southern half of the land.

The narrative about the battle at the waters of Merom (Josh 11:1–15) divides into a report about the victory over a coalition of Canaanite kings in the upper Jordan Valley (11:1–9) and a communication about the conquest of Hazor (11:10–15). In structure and vocabulary the first narrative agrees strongly with the corresponding piece about the victory at Gibeon (10:1–15), although it also shows differences in details. In any case, the linguistic agreement may imply the same author (DtrH). The adoption of a local tradition is also not discernible for the second part (11:10–15); instead, the battle action closely follows the distinctive terminology. As in Josh 10, the names of the cities participating in the coalition can be taken over from the list included in Josh 12. As in the south, so also in the north, the land is treated in summary fashion. With the concluding comment in 11:16–20, the author emphasizes the conquest of the entire land. A redactor expanded and clarified this outline through additional statements in 11:21–23.

The list of the defeated kings in Josh 12 was originally introduced only with verse 1aα*; the additional expositions concerning the regions on both sides of the Jordan in 12:1aβ–6 represent a redactional revision. The stereotypical enumeration of Canaanite kings (12:7–24) goes back to a document that was originally independent and was only subsequently inserted into the current context. However, the original list can hardly be considered a historical source, since the named cities would have existed at no contemporary point in time. It is possibly a literary creation of unknown origin, whose intention was to provide a summary of all the Canaanite cities in the western Transjordan. This list was inserted as a conclusion to the land-acquisition narrative in order to establish the total defeat of the Canaanite city-states and thereby to establish the claim to the acquired region.

I.2.2.2. Allocation of the Land (Josh 13–19)

Aharoni, Yohanan. *The Land of the Bible: A Historical Geography* (trans. Anson F. Rainey; 2nd ed.; Philadelphia: Westminster, 1979). **Bächli**, Otto. "Von der Liste zur Beschreibung," *ZDPV* 89 (1973): 1–14. **Kallai**, Zecharia. *Historical Geography of the Bible: The Tribal Territories of Israel* (Jerusalem: Magnes, 1986). Na'aman, Nadav. *Borders and Districts in Biblical Historiography: Seven Studies in Biblical Geographic Lists* (Jerusalem Biblical Studies 4; Jerusalem: Simor, 1986). **Noth**, Martin. "Studien zu den historisch-geographischen Dokumenten des Josuabuches," *ABLAK* 1 (1971): 229–80. See now also: **Hess**, Richard S. "Asking Historical Questions of Joshua 13–19: Recent Discussion Concerning the Date of the Boundary Lists," in *Faith, Tradition, and History: Old Testament Historiography in Its Near Eastern Context* (ed. A. R. Millard, James K. Hoffmeier, and David W. Baker; Winona Lake, Ind.: Eisenbrauns, 1994), 191–205.

Prior to the land distribution in the western Transjordan as the second part of the land acquisition in Josh 15–19, Moses' bestowal of land to Reuben and Gad is repeated in Josh 13. The explanations are revised by heavy redaction; the foundational element of Josh 13:1abα, 7, 15–20, 23, 24–26, 27aα*, 28 is oriented toward Num 32. In distinction to the narrative where Moses performs the land grant, which is not to be reckoned to the pre-Priestly historical writings (cf. §I.2.1.3), the tribal regions in the eastern Transjordan are (in Josh 13) constituted by border descriptions rather than by city lists (as in Num 32).

By redaction, the distribution of Hebron to Caleb in Josh 14 is added by reverting to the story of the spies in Num 13; 14. The resumption of this tradition ruptures the framework of the distribution of the tribal regions. The purpose of the inclusion is the establishment of a promise made by Moses.

For Judah, the land grant in Josh 15 comprises a border description (15:1–12) and a place list (15:20–63). The special tradition about Caleb in 15:13–19 represents a supplement. If the border description reproduces real circumstances and does not merely represent a type of utopian design, it can only stem from the time of the height of power of the Davidic-Solomonic kingdom. The city list in 15:20–63 is divided into ten districts and goes back in all probability to an administrative measure whose historical and administrative anchoring in the monarchic period certainly cannot be closely determined.

Presumably the place list organizing Judah into ten groups belongs together with the place list of Benjamin in Josh 18:21–28, such that both texts evince a register of originally twelve districts, which was created for the raising of taxes and corvée by the monarchy according to the division of the kingdom. An exact dating of this document in the ninth or eighth century is not possible.[12]

For the tribes Ephraim and Manasseh, only border descriptions are found in Josh 16 and 17, because no place lists were available to the author. In this case, 16:9 and 17:9aβ still indicate that the system of the series of fixed boundary points was originally calculated with an entire region for the house of Joseph, in which then a special place for Ephraim was inserted so that the rest remained for Manasseh (Noth, *ABLAK* 1 [1971]: 243–46). The text was worked over significantly. One narrative is dependent on a border description, which, according to the instruction of Joshua, culminates in the clearing of additional parts of the mountain (Josh 17:14–18). This points to a solution to the problem of insufficient settlement areas by taking over previously unsettled regions. As such, the piece evinces a complicated literary development: a tradition about the promise of the mountain Ephraim to the house of Joseph (17:14, 17, 18a) was reorganized by 17:15 as an establishment of the settlement of part of the eastern Transjordan by Manasseh and is then inserted into the context by further additions (17:16 and 18b). The etiological character of the piece is clear: it should justify the magnitude of the settlement for the house of Joseph.

After an extensive secondary introduction in Josh 18:1–10, a border description and city list of Benjamin follow in 18:11–28, but the place list possibly goes back to a common literary *Vorlage* along with the one of Judah (Josh 15:20–63). The six tribes of Simeon, Zebulun, Issachar, Asher, Naphtali, and Dan follow in Josh 19. For the Galilean tribes there is perhaps no series of fixed border points, and so parts of the place list were reconfigured into border descriptions (cf. Fritz, *Josua*, 188–97). The origin of this place list can no longer be determined. It possibly stems from an administrative classification of the northern kingdom that was still oriented toward the tribal regions, or the enu-

---

12. See Albrecht Alt, "Judas Gaue unter Josia," in idem, *Kleine Schriften zur Geschichte des Volkes Israel* (3 vols.; Munich: Beck, 1953–59), 2:176–288; idem, "Bemerkungen zu einigen judäischen Ortslisten des Alten Testaments," in ibid., 289–305; Frank Moore Cross and G. Ernest Wright, "The Boundary and Province Lists of the Kingdom of Judah," *JBL* 75 (1956): 202–26; Zekharyah Kallai-Kleinmann, "The Town Lists of Judah, Simeon, Benjamin and Dan," *VT* 8 (1958): 134–60; 11 (1961): 223–27; Yohanan Aharoni, "The Province List of Judah," *VT* 9 (1959): 225–46; Anson F. Rainey, "The Biblical Shephela of Judah," *BASOR* 251 (1983): 1–22; Nadav Na'aman, "The Kingdom of Judah under Josiah," *Tel Aviv* 18 (1991): 3–71.

meration goes back to an inventory at the beginning of the Assyrian hegemony in the second half of the eighth century. A later dating is ruled out, since after 700 the majority of the named settlements were destroyed and deserted.

The narrative of the distribution of the land originally comprised the lists in Josh 15; 18; and 19, with introductory comments and few narrative passages. This second part of the book of Joshua was thus essentially considerably less than the preceding land-acquisition narrative, which would conclude with the note in 19:49a. This conclusion was then expanded by the redaction of 19:49b, 50, and 51.

I.2.2.3. Joshua's Farewell Speech (Josh 24)

McCarthy, Dennis J. *Treaty and Covenant: A Study in Form in the Ancient Oriental Documents and in the Old Testament* (AnBib 21; Rome: Pontifical Biblical Institute, 1963). **Mölle**, Herbert. *Der sogenannte Landtag zu Sichem* (FB 42; Würzburg: Echter Verlag, 1980). **Perlitt**, Lothar. *Bundestheologie im Alten Testament* (WMANT 36; Neukirchen-Vluyn: Neukirchener, 1969). **Schmitt**, Götz. *Der Landtag von Sichem* (Arbeiten zur Theologie 15; Stuttgart: Calwer Verlag, 1964). **Sperling**, S. David. "Joshua 24 Reexamined," *HUCA* 58 (1987): 119–36. **Van Seters**, John. "Joshua 24 and the Problem of Tradition in the Old Testament," in *In the Shelter of Elyon: Essays on Ancient Palestinian Life and Literature in Honor of G. W. Ahlström* (ed. W. Boyd Barrick and John R. Spencer; JSOTSup 31; Sheffield: JSOT Press, 1984), 135–58.

The final action of Joshua is the covenant of the people with Yahweh as the only God, to whom alone worship is due. This act was prepared for by a long passage of a speech between Joshua and the people (24:2–24), which exceeded by far the extent and weight of the frame of the plot (24:1, 25–28). The piece is therefore not actually a narrative but rather a literary composition of its own kind that is most suitably described as a "fictive covenant scene" ("*fiktive Verpflichtungsszene*" [Perlitt, *Bundestheologie*, 269]) and has clear precedence over the speech in Josh 23. The piece is not a unity insofar as the speech of Joshua was reworked through additions (24:2aβ, 5aα, 6aαb, 7aα, 9, 10, 11a*, 12, 13b) and underwent a considerable expansion with Josh 24:19–24. In addition, 24:26, 27 was added to the narrative framework. The original text thus consisted merely of the covenant scene in Josh 24:2aβγb, 3, 4, 5a*b, 6aβ, 7aβb, 8abα, 11a*b, 13a, 16–18, 25, 28.

Shechem is surprising as a place of the event insofar as the city in the land-acquisition narrative has played no role up to this point. Shechem is mentioned in Josh 17:7 as a near destination from Michmethath and in 20:7 as well as in 21:21 in the framework of the later supplements to the book. Even without the supposition of a "*Landtag*" (legislative assembly) at Shechem, Josh 24:1–28* could go back to a local tradition. At this point, though, the conscious formation of the piece rules out the adoption of an older narrative of the contents, given that the stone located in the vicinity of a cult site at Shechem has been brought into connection with a particular action by Joshua; in particular, 24:26 and 27 represent a literary addition. Thus, no old oral tradition underlies the covenant scene, the one time this particular stone was explained. The connection of Joshua with Shechem can therefore be explained only as a literary combination. Tradition-historically, the cultic sites of Shechem went back to Abraham (Gen 12:6, 7) and Jacob (Gen 33:18–20). The particular significance of the city shows up also in the traditions in Gen 34 and Judg 9, according to which Shechem is the location of happenings set in the premonarchic era, but which stem from the monarchic period at the earliest.[13] Hence, inevitably Shechem alone came into consideration as the location of an event involving all Israel in the premonarchic period.

As a conclusion to the narrative about the conquest and allocation of the land (Josh 1–12 and 13–19), the covenant scene appears unusual, since the preceding events are thematized or reflected on no further. However, in God's speech in Josh 24:2–13*, the course of history was completed with the allusion to the successful acquisition of the land, which corresponds practically to the date presumed. Nevertheless, 24:1–28* represents an adequate conclusion to the land-acquisition narrative, since at this point the theme corresponding to Deuteronomy can be resumed, namely, that Yahweh is the one and only God. After the conclusion of the military processes was already summarized in Josh 12, and Yahweh appears in the wider course of the land acquisition in Josh 13–19 as the giver of the landed property, a reflection on Yahweh as the God of Israel was especially demanded as a conclusion to the land acquisition, because the preservation of the landed property is bound to the exclusive worship of the God who conferred the land.

Like the exodus under the leadership of Moses, so the taking of land under the leadership of Joshua is a constitutive element for Israel. Considering those holy deeds will in 24:1–28* determine exclusive worship of Yahweh. The residence in the land begins amid the danger to the cult because the other people do not take part in the adoration of Yahweh but rather worship foreign gods. Thus the speech betrays the standpoint of the author at the end of the monarchic period or the beginning of the exile. The covenant scene at Shechem is not a historical event but rather literary fiction. It has to do with the future salvation of Israel, whichi is inextricably connected with the land. The confession of Yahweh as the only God is anchored in history just as is the covenant of the people to adhere to that confession so as not to lose the holy gift of the land.

---

13. See Volkmar Fritz, "Abimelech und Sichem in Jdc IX," *VT* 32 (1982): 129–44.

I.2.3. Judges and Deliverers (Judg 1–21)

Bartelmus, Rüdiger. "Forschung am Richterbuch seit Martin Noth," *TRu* 56 (1991): 221–59. **Becker**, Uwe. *Richterzeit und Königtum: Redaktionsgeschichtliche Studien zum Richterbuch* (BZAW 192; Berlin: de Gruyter, 1990). **Halpern**, Baruch. *The First Historians: The Hebrew Bible and History* (San Francisco: Harper & Row, 1988). **Richter**, Wolfgang. *Traditionsgeschichtliche Untersuchungen zum Richterbuch* (BBB 18; Bonn: P. Hanstein, 1963). **Soggin**, J. Alberto. *Judges: A Commentary* (trans. John Bowden; OTL; Philadelphia: Westminster, 1981). See now also: **Gunn**, David M. *Judges* (Blackwell Bible Commentaries; Oxford: Blackwell, 2005). **Niditch**, Susan. *Judges: A Commentary* (OTL; Louisville: Westminster John Knox, 2008).

The book of Judges is conceived as an ongoing narrative that connects to the death of Joshua (Josh 24:29–31). After the death of Joshua, another era begins insofar as the acquisition of the land comes to an end and life in the land begins. This new episode of history certainly required new leading figures—on the one hand, to defeat Israel's threatening enemies and, on the other hand, to hold the necessary office for the tribes' coexistence. The latter function is described by שפט ("to judge"), whereas the act of salvation is designated by ישע (hiphil "help, save"). Such is the distinction between judge and savior.

Despite the linear construction, the individual pieces are relatively dissimilar in their material as well as in their formal shaping. After the summary of individual messages (Judg 1) there are different kinds of connecting pieces (Judg 1:1–3:6), followed by narratives about the judges Othniel and Ehud (3:7–11, 12–30), on which a short notice about Shamgar is dependent (3:31). The victory of the tribes over a Canaanite coalition is conveyed in double versions of narrative and hymn of praise in Judg 4 and 5; in content these versions offer more than the individual deed of a hero. For Gideon (Judg 6–8), Jephthah (10:17–12:6), and Samson (Judg 13–16), a whole series of narratives are collected into a large complex. Between them are found the Abimelech episode (Judg 9) and the lists of "minor" judges (10:1–5 and 12:8–15) as well as a historical-theological summary (10:6–16).

In Judg 17–21, the hero narrative, the predominant form up to this point, is left behind. The first part narrates the establishment of a shrine in Dan and the journey of the Danites to a new residence (Judg 17; 18), whereas the last three chapters (Judg 19–21) tell of a confrontation of the Benjaminites with the rest of the tribes. According to content and formation history, there are two narrative complexes that were originally independent and only subsequently became attached.

The beginning of the book (Judg 1; 2) is a conglomeration of additions. The summary of different notes in Judg 1 with the enumeration of the cities not conquered is an insertion, which almost represents a revision to the picture of the land acquisition in the book of Joshua (cf. §I.2.3.3.). There is a narrative about the appearance of the messenger of Yahweh in Judg 2:1–5; the contents are determined by Deuteronomistic theology and amount to an explanation of the name Bochim. The etiological character proves the piece to be a supplement that by no means contains older material but rather was developed out of the place name.

The conclusion to the book of Joshua in 24:29–31 is revised in Judg 2:6–10. The repetition of the section in this place is possibly necessitated by the insertion of Judg 1. In the summary overview of Judg 2:11–23, both 2:13, 17 and 2:20–23 represent supplements: Judg 2:13 repeats the statement of 2:12, giving the gods' names. Judges 2:17 interrupts the schema of the generations of judges, and after the actual conclusion in 2:19, 2:20–23 takes up and further expands the conception of 2:14. The historical-theological program thus originally contained only Judg 2:11, 12, 14–16, 18, 19; this program goes back to the historical-theological reflection of a redactor. An additional piece of this kind is found in Judg 10:6–16.

Thus, the book of Judges opens only in 3:1, and its kernel comprises only Judg 3–16. This foundational element indeed shows no clear construction with respect to the arrangement of the material but is held together by theological and chronological frameworks. Both elements have been constructed by literary summaries of various traditions that give the book a connecting principle. As a general rule, the theological frame that shapes each narrative consists of the phrase עשה רע בעיני יהוה ("to do what displeased Yahweh"; 2:11; 3:7, 12; 4:1; 6:1; 10:6; 13:1). Additional formulaic phrases appear as well: עבד את בעלים ("serving the Baals"; 3:7; 10:6, 10); חרה אף יהוה ("the anger of Yahweh was kindled"; 3:8; 10:7); מכר qal ("to sell" with Yahweh as subject; 3:8; 4:2; 10:7); זעק ("cry out" with Israel as subject; 3:9, 15; 4:3; 6:6, 7; 10:10, 12); כנע niphal or hiphil ("to humble"; 3:30; 4:23; 8:28; 11:33); שקט ("have rest" with the land as subject; 3:11, 30; 5:31; 8:28). These speech usages show a conscious shaping of the book, at least up to the Jephthah story.

The chronological frame not only specifies the respective years of the "minor" judges in their post (Judg 10:2, 3; 12:7, 9, 11), but also records the idle periods after Othniel, Ehud, Barak, and Gideon (3:11, 30; 5:31; 8:28) as well as the respective periods of oppression (3:8, 14; 4:3; 6:1). Samson constitutes an exception; as a "major" judge he held office for twenty years (15:20; 16:31). The possible calculations can be left off here;[14] the statements form a structure

---

14. Cf. G. Sauer, "Die chronologischen Angaben in den Büchern Deuteronomium bis 2. Könige," *TZ* 24 (1968): 1–14; Werner Vollborn, "Die Chronologie des Richterbuches," in

to connect the various units into a unified work, which is indeed made up of individual traditions but really forms a whole in view of the course of history.

I.2.3.1. History of the Deliverers (Judg 3–16)

The introduction in Judg 3:1-6 is not unified, since the stocks of peoples enumerated in verses 3 and 5 differ from one another and thus stem from different traditions. Presumably even the list originally introduced in 3:1a was lost, since the naming of the peoples who actually appear in the following narratives as opponents of Israel would be expected. The opening of a book or a section with a pure list is not exceptional (cf. Exod 1:1-4 and 1 Chr 1:1-28). The original list could have been replaced by the secondary insertion of 3:1b-6.

Concerning the first three judges, there are three traditions of various length and shaping. The narrative concerning Othniel (3:7-11) is fully embedded in the historical-theological schema of the book of Judges and proves to be a formation by the Deuteronomistic Historian. The historian incisively set the story he had fashioned at the beginning in order to emphasize the schema that would be followed in the remaining materials. In this way, he shaped the whole era uniformly. The name Othniel for the first "judge" is adopted from the literary tradition, as it is in Josh 15:17 = Judg 1:13, but the name of the opponent "Cushan-rishathaim" can no longer be verified. In any case, the name—like the entire narrative—is fictional.

The narrative about the murder of the Moabite king Eglon by the left-handed Ehud (Judg 3:12-30) is likewise included in the framework but goes back to an older tradition, but the individual features suggest a longer time frame of oral tradition.[15] The age and origin of this material are neverthe-

---

Festschrift Friedrich Baumgärtel zum 70. Geburtstag 14. Januar 1958 (ed. Leonhard Rost; Erlangen Forschungen, Reihe A, Geisteswissenschaften 10; Erlangen: Universitätsbund Erlangen, 1959), 192–96; Seán M. Warner, "The Period of the Judges within the Structure of Early Israel," *HUCA* 47 (1976): 57–79; idem, "The Dating of the Period of the Judges," *VT* 28 (1978): 455–63. See also David L. Washburn, "The Chronology of Judges: Another Look," *Bibliotheca Sacra* 147 (1990): 414–25; Mark Leuchter, "'Now There Was a [Certain] Man': Compositional Chronology in Judges–1 Samuel," *CBQ* 69 (2007): 429–39.

15. Ferdinand Dexinger, "Ein Pladoyer für die Linkshänder im Richterbuch," *ZAW* 89 (1977): 268–69; Ulrich Hübner, "Mord auf dem Abort? Überlegungen zu Humor, Gewaltanwendung und Realienkunde in Ri 3,12–20," *BN* 40 (1987): 130–40; Emil Gottlieb Heinrich Kraeling, "Difficulties in the Story of Ehud," *JBL* 54 (1935): 205–10; Hartmut N. Rösel, "Zur Ehud-Erzählung," *ZAW* 89 (1970): 270–72; J. Alberto Soggin, "'Ehud und 'Eglon: Bemerkungen zu Richter III 11b–31," *VT* 39 (1989): 95–100. See also Lowell K. Handy, "Uneasy Laughter: Ehud and Eglon as Ethnic Humor," *SJOT* 6 (1992): 233–46.

less indeterminable; all that is presupposed is an enemy relationship to the neighboring state Moab, as existed in the entire course of Israel's history. The express mention of the expansion of Moabite claim to power in the region of Jericho presupposes developments that could have taken place only after the conquest of Mesha in the ninth century (see *TUAT* 1:646–50). Even if the tradition-historical confinement and the formation history of the underlying narrative cannot be determined precisely, the shaping of this tradition is nevertheless not to be reckoned to the premonarchic period. It is a heroic story without witnesses, one whose origin is ultimately to be sought in a glorification of the heroic deed. Since the capability of extraordinary deeds by a left-handed person is also widely disseminated elsewhere as a literary motif (cf. J. A. Soggin), the narrative of Ehud is not based on a historical event but rather can go back to the narrative tradition of the monarchic period. However the narrative of Ehud emerged, it was first put into the historical context of the premonarchic period by the Deuteronomistic Historian.

Shamgar, son of Anath, is presented in the short note in Judg 3:31 as the third of the first three judges and the one who slew six hundred Philistines with a staff. More precise circumstances are not conveyed. The place and time remain in the dark; the verse merely refers briefly to his role as savior of Israel. Shamgar only appears as a figure of the premonarchic period based on the context. Presumably the author of the book of Judges adopted his name and deed from a source and reformulated the text, without leaving off the form of the list from the presumed *Vorlage*. The note in Judg 3:31 and its *Vorlage* respectively have a parallel in the communication of the heroic deeds that were attached by the list of David's heroes in 2 Sam 21:15–22 and 23:8–22. In those comments, there is a short mention of an extraordinary action that the particular hero accomplished. The event is not fleshed out any further, but rather is reduced to the kernel of the matter in the form of a bare message. The special deed is practically the mark of the individual soldier. A note such as Judg 3:31 is conceivable only based on a literary *Vorlage*, or—and this is the only alternative—it springs from pure fantasy. Since there is no reason to count it as a bare fiction, one must assume in the case of Shamgar that the name was adopted from the literary tradition. Nothing with regard to age or provenance can be determined precisely, and the relation of such a tradition to a certain historical background cannot be assumed. Indeed, its origin prior to the monarchic period appears extremely improbable.

There is a double tradition for the battle with a Canaanite coalition: after the narrative of Judg 4 comes the song of Judg 5, in which the same event is recounted again. Since there are different traditions concerning the same event, one must inquire as to the literary relationship. Because the song in Judg 5 departs from the prose description in many details, and furthermore the construction of the narrative follows the prefigured individual scenes of the song, the literary development can be determined only to the extent that Judg 4 represents the version of the Deuteronomistic Historian based on Judg 5.

In Judg 4, the Deuteronomistic framework of verses 1–3 and 23, 24 is first and foremost to be distinguished from the narrative in verses 4–22, which represents a self-contained literary unit.[16] With regard to content, the author altered the material insofar as Sisera is now the field captain of Jabin of Hazor, who was taken up as the opponent of Israel from Josh 11:1. In Judg 4:4–22, verse 7 represents an insertion that anticipates verse 9; furthermore, verses 11 and 17b constitute an addition in order to clarify the presence of Heber from the clan of the Kenites in the tribal region of Naphtali. The course of the narrative in Judg 4:4–6, 8–10, 12–17a, 18–22 is fashioned largely on the basis of the demise of Sisera in Judg 5:24–27; it shows, however, an essential difference from the song of Judg 5 in that in Judg 4:6 only Naphtali and Zebulun are named as the tribes who participated in the battle. This contradiction to the enumeration of the mobilized tribes in Judg 5:14, 15 (Ephraim, Benjamin, Machir, Zebulun, and Issachar) can be explained on the assumption that the author made an oversimplification in which he reduced the participants to the two tribes whose regions bordered Mount Tabor.

The song in Judg 5 is by no means a unified whole but rather is determined by two different levels of statements. Verses referring to the glorification of Yahweh as the God of Israel, such as 5:3–5 and 31a, stand over against those with definite profane content, such as the description of the battle in 5:19–22. The observation follows that in 5:3 and 13 the prelude to the song is found twice. Based on this distinction, a theologically shaped portion (5:2–11, 31a) can be distinguished from a historically determined portion (5:12–31). A precise date is lacking, but the hymn of praise could stem from the premonarchic period (cf. §III.1). This indicates above all the role of the charismatic leading figures, which is sensible only in the time before the formation of the monarchy.

---

16. Yairah Amit, "Judges 4: Its Contents and Form," *JSOT* 39 (1987): 89–111; Athalya Brenner, "A Triangle and a Rhombus in Narrative Structure: A Proposed Integrated Reading of Judges IV and V," *VT* 40 (1990): 129–38; A. D. H. Mayes, "The Historical Context of the Battle against Sisera," *VT* 19 (1969): 353–60; P. Weimar, "Die Jahwekriegserzählungen in Exodus 14, Josua 10, Richter 4, 1 Sam 7," *Bib* 57 (1976): 38–73. See now also Volkmar Fritz, "The Complex of Traditions in Judges 4 and 5 and the Religion of Pre-State Israel," in *"I Will Speak the Riddles of Ancient Times": Archaeological and Historical Studies in Honor of Amihai Mazar on the Occasion of His Sixtieth Birthday* (ed: Aren M. Maeir and Pierre de Miroschedji; 2 vols.; Winona Lake, Ind.: Eisenbrauns, 2006): 2:689–98.

The tradition about Gideon in Judg 6–8 is extremely complex.[17] The difficulties begin already with the names, since in 6:32; 7:1; and 8:29, 35 Gideon is given the name Jerubbaal, which appears as well in Judg 9:16, 19 and in 1 Sam 12:11, but then appears in the form Jerubbesheth in 2 Sam 11:21. Indeed, one person could have been subsequently renamed, but here the different names appear originally to have indicated different persons. It is clear, however, that the equivalence of the two names is meant to be achieved by the narrative in Judg 6:25–32. Therefore this piece is to a certain extent a literary shaping out of different traditions that grew together in order to harmonize existing discrepancies and balance tensions.

At this point Jerubbaal is considered the father of Abimelech according to Judg 9:1, 5, 16, 18, 28, 57; by his character, then, the Gideon traditions (Judg 6–8) and the events concerning Abimelech (Judg 9) are combined with each other. The emphasis on fatherhood has the significance of bringing the Abimelech story, which had fallen from the framework of the judges stories, into the narrative context. Since an original tradition about Jerubbaal in Judg 6–8 is nevertheless indiscernible, the name can only have been forced in from Judg 9. The equivocation of Gideon with Jerubbaal thus goes back to redaction-historical work in order to weave the different materials together by means of filiation. As the final consequence of this redactional work, Gideon himself finally becomes the father of Abimelech in Judg 8:31.

The Gideon narrative constitutes a conglomeration of various materials that grew to its current size only gradually. Based on the literary framework, Judg 6:1 and 8:28 are considered a narrative about the battle against the Midianites. At this point, two battle narratives are found in Judg 6–8, ones that differ fundamentally regarding the names of the opponents and the location. The one takes place in En-Harod ('Ēn Ğālūd) at the southern edge of

---

17. A. Graeme Auld, "Gideon: Hacking at the Heart of the Old Testament," *VT* 39 (1989): 257–67; Walter Beyerlin, "Geschichte und Heilsgeschichtliche Traditionsbildung im Alten Testament," *VT* 13 (1963): 1–25; John A. Emerton, "Gideon and Jerubbaal," *JTS* 27 (1976): 289–312; Herbert Haag, "Gideon – Jerubbaal – Abimelech," *ZAW* 79 (1967): 305–14; Ernst Kutsch, "Gideons Berufung und Altarbau Jdc 6,11–24," in *Kleine Schriften zum Alten Testament: Zum 65. Geburstag Ernst Kutsch* (ed. Ludwig Schmidt and Karl Eberlein; BZAW 168; Berlin: de Gruyter, 1986), 99–109; Hartmut N. Rösel, "Studien zur Topographie der Kriege in den Büchern Josua und Richter IV," *ZDPV* 92 (1970): 10–24; Ludwig Schmidt, *Menschlicher Erfolg und Jahwes Initiative: Studien zu Tradition, Interpretation und Historie in Überlieferungen von Gideon, Saul und David* (WMANT 38; Neukirchen-Vluyn: Neukirchener, 1970), 5–53; Charles Francis Whitley, "The Sources of the Gideon Stories," *VT* 7 (1957): 157–64. See now also Eliyahu Assis, *Self-Interest or Communal Interest: An Ideology of Leadership in the Gideon, Abimelech and Jephthah Narratives (Judg. 6–12)* (VTSup 106; Leiden: Brill, 2005).

the Valley of Jezreel and depicts the flight up to the Jordan (6:2–6, 33–40; 7:1–25). The other appears as a continuation of that event, accounting for Succoth and Penuel in the land east of the Jordan (8:4–21). Despite certain commonalities, both originally go back to independent traditions, having no demonstrably long history of tradition. The first narrative is an artistic construction out of several individual scenes, whereas the climax with the raid on the camp shows marvelous characteristics. The continuation by a second piece presents more of the conflict with the cities Succoth and Penuel—which apparently were seen as non-Israelite cities—as the battle against the Midianites, whose "kings" Zebah and Zalmunna are named only here. Despite numerous geographic statements, the adoption of older material is not discernible; on the contrary, the piece evinces literary shaping by the colloquialisms of borrowed figures of speech such as "then I will thrash your flesh with wild thorns and briers" and "as the man is, so is his strength." The naming of Karkor (8:10) could be an allusion to the conquest of Qarqar by Shalmaneser III in the year 853, especially given that the participation of King Ahab of Israel is explicitly attested in the anti-Assyrian coalition (*TUAT* 1:361). Even if the author of the book of Judges could have already encountered a tradition with details concerning Gideon's actions as judge, the artistic decoration of the narratives, by means of various motifs, appears most likely to be the work of a relatively late author. In addition, the numerous names of people and places as well as the high figures for the army point to a late composition. Because of that, A. Graeme Auld (*VT* 39 [1989] 267) even holds that Judg 6–8* represents only a supplement to the Deuteronomistic book of Judges. In it Gideon was designated as an army leader like Joshua; Gideon really descended from the clan of Abiezrite in Ophrah, but he summoned the tribes Asher, Zebulun, and Naphtali for his military expeditions.

With regard to content, the additional pieces place the character of Gideon in the center and comprise literary insertions, which were added to the foundational layer by redactors. The piece in Judg 6:7–10 is omitted in a fragment from Qumran (4QJudg^a [4Q49]) and is probably a very late addition (cf. Robert G. Boling, *Judges: Introduction, Translation, and Commentary* [AB 6; Garden City, N.Y.: Doubleday, 1975], 40). In Judg 6:11–24, a narrative about the construction of the altar in Ophrah was connected to the story of the commission. The episode about the destruction of the altar to Baal (Judg 6:25–32) assumes the motif of cultic zeal and presupposes the name Jerubbaal from Judg 9 being forced into the Gideon complex; it can thus only be a late development without the assumption of older traditions. The inquiry scene in 6:36–40 is indebted to theological reflection and is clearly an insertion. The motif of the discontented tribe in 8:1–3 appears to be woven out of the proverb, "Is not the gleaning of the grapes of Ephraim better than the vintage of Abiezer?" The refusal to become king in 8:22, 23 points ahead to Judg 9 and goes back to an antimonarchic redaction. The story about the golden ephod (8:24-27) superimposes a negative aspect on the portrait of Gideon and ruptures the framework of the stories of the judges; the section was perhaps created in analogy to Exod 32. The various notes in Judg 8:29-35 are supplements concerning the wider fate of Gideon and of Israel after Gideon's death, which correspond in part to the notes about Joshua (Josh 24:29-31). Judges 8:30, 31 were formulated according to the judges schema in Judg 10:1-5 and 12:8-15, serving as a literary transition to Judg 9.

Originally only the war narratives of Judg 6:2-6, 33-35; 7:1-25; 8:4-21 were connected with Gideon. These judge stories were shaped very elaborately and in each case comprise several scenes, in which the marvelous aspect of the event should be further enhanced. The individual scenes were artfully interwoven with one another, which suggests a conscious literary shaping. There is evidence neither of a historical kernel nor of the adoption of older, oral tradition. Presumably the descriptions of the pursuit and annihilation of Succoth and Penuel (8:4-21) represent a subsequent addition. In any case, there is in Judg 7 and 8 no credible report concerning warfare in the premonarchic period.

The story of the deliverance from the Midianites by Gideon is supplemented by further additions of several individual pieces (Judg 6:11-24, 36-40; 8:24-27, 29-31) in which Gideon appears as the contender of exclusive worship of Yahweh and the benefactor of an offering site; he will later, however, be guilty of cultic transgression. These expansions represent additions for the biography of the judge figure. The life of the hero was characterized by the framework of the connection between deed and consequence: human success is based on the work of Yahweh, and Yahweh's gift of success is dependent on the good behavior of the humans. The actual story of the judge has thus taken on a biographical framework, which is clearly subject to a qualified point of view.

The narrative about the monarchy of Abimelech in Shechem (Judg 9) is not unified literarily.[18] The expansion of the reign of Abimelech over all Israel

---

18. Thomas Arthur Boogaart, "Stone by Stone: Retribution in the Story of Abimelech and Shechem," *JSOT* 32 (1985): 45-56; Lawrence E. Toombs et al., "The Fourth Campaign at Balâṭah (Shechem)," *BASOR* 169 (1963): 1-60, esp. 27-32; Robert J. Bull and James F. Ross, "The Biblical Traditions of Shechem's Sacred Area," *BASOR* 169 (1963): 27-32; Edward F. Campbell Jr., "Judges 9 and Biblical Archaeology," in *The Word of the Lord Shall Go Forth: Essays in Honor of David Noel Freedman in Celebration of His Sixtieth Birthday*

in 9:22, 55 owes to redactional revision, but 9:16–19a, 24, and 57 also represent subsequent additions. The integration of the Jotham Fable of 9:7–15 necessitates the inclusion of the comments in 9:5b, 16a, 19b–21, 49–59. As such, the Jotham Fable was originally an independent piece that had nothing to do with the incidents concerning Abimelech.[19] In the arranged text, two narratives were assimilated:

— the Gaal episode, in which Abimelech, the ruler of Arumah, successfully beat down a revolt from Shechem, over which he ruled (9:26–41)

— the narrative about the monarchy of Abimelech over Shechem, over the course of which the city was destroyed and in the end, Abimelech meets his death in Thebez (9:1–5a, 6, 23, 25, 42–45, 50–54, 56).

Tradition-historically, the Gaal episode is the oldest piece, on which the narrative about the monarchy of Abimelech in Shechem is literarily dependent. Thus, the latter does not go back to an old tradition but rather represents a new version, which emphasizes the connection between the manner of attaining rule and the ignominious demise of the king who attains rule in such a way. This didactic character was further strengthened by the integration of the Jotham Fable and expanded to a fundamental confrontation with the character of the king: Abimelech therefore becomes the cautionary example, as the choice of the wrong person led to the downfall of those who chose this king. Whereas the later narrative concerning the connection between deed and consequence only referred to Abimelech, this was widened to the inhabitants of Shechem by the expansion of the Jotham Fable in order to establish the

---

(ed. Carol L. Meyers and M. O'Connor; Winona Lake, Ind.: Eisenbrauns, 1983), 263–71; Volkmar Fritz, "Abimelech und Sichem in Jdc IX," *VT* 32 (1982): 129–44; Hanoch Reviv, "The Government of Shechem in the El-Amarna Period and in the Days of Abimelech," *IEJ* 16 (1966): 252–57; Hartmut N. Rösel, "Überlegungen zu 'Abimelech und Sichem' in Jdc IX," *VT* 33 (1983): 500–503; Herbert H. Schmid, "Die Herrschaft Abimeleks (Jdc 9)," *Judaica* 26 (1970): 1–11; J. Alberto Soggin, "Bemerkungen zur alttestamentlichen Topographie Sichems mit besonderem Bezug auf Jdc 9," *ZDPV* 83 (1967): 183–98.

19. Rüdiger Bartelmus, "Die sogenannte Jothamfabel: Eine politisch-religiöse Parabeldichtung," *TZ* 41 (1985): 97–120; Frank Crüsemann, *Die Widerstand gegen das Königtum* (WMANT 49; Neukirchen-Vluyn: Neukirchener, 1978), 19–42; Barnabas Lindars, "Jotham's Fable: A New Form-Critical Analysis," *JTS* 24 (1973): 355–66; Eugene H. Maly, "The Jotham Fable: Anti-monarchical?" *CBQ* 22 (1960): 299–302; Ronald J. Williams, "The Fable in the Old Testament," in *A Stubborn Faith: Papers on Old Testament and Related Subjects Presented to Honor William Andrew Irwin* (Dallas: Southern Methodist University Press, 1956), 3–26. See now also Silviu Tatu, "Jotham's Fable and the *crux interpretum* in Judges IX," *VT* 56 (2006): 105–24.

fate of the city as well. In the redactional work of Judg 9:16b–19a, 24, 57, the responsibility of the Shechemites was further emphasized. The growth of the tradition clearly owes to theological signs.

The Gaal episode presupposes the circumstances of local rule as it existed during the Late Bronze Age (1550–1200) in the city-states of Canaan. However, the tradition hardly reaches back to the time before the land acquisition of the Israelite tribes. A formation in the premonarchic period is even less possible, given that Shechem was not settled from approximately 1150 to 975. The shaping of this episode could thus at the earliest have taken place only after the reestablishment of Shechem in the early monarchic period. At this point, knowledge of the later version will be presupposed, with the ignominious end of Abimelech serving as an allusion to 2 Sam 11:21, which is part of the framework of the event concerning Bathsheba. This expansion shows that the material from Judg 9 was already known in the composition of this note. Since the narrative of 2 Sam 11 cannot have been formed prior to the tenth century, the reference provides an indication that the tradition about Abimelech was already extant in the early monarchic period, although its formation in the premonarchic period is not demonstrable. The Gaal episode, on the contrary, can reflect interpolitical confrontations in the city of Shechem after the founding of the state in the tenth century, whereas Abimelech appears as a figure who intervenes in the event from outside. Only in the wider shaping of the tradition does Abimelech become the ruler of the city, though his claim to power fails miserably because a monarchy established by murder cannot survive. The character of the king here undergoes a negative assessment, which was probably only developed since the ninth century in the framework of the change of dynasty in the northern kingdom. The revision of the narrative with the Jotham Fable brings a further reinterpretation of the material insofar as now the fate of the Shechemites is established. This expansion by means of the integration of the Jotham Fable comes from a redactor. The later version of the narrative about Abimelech perhaps goes back to the Deuteronomistic Historian as the author of the Deuteronomistic History, whereas the Gaal episode is in the process of tradition in the monarchic period.

Judges 10:1–5 is the first part of the judges schema, whose resumption is found in 12:8–15.[20] The two parts of the enumeration of the minor judges

---

20. Alan J. Hauser, "The 'Minor Judges': A Reevaluation," *JBL* 94 (1975): 190–200; Hans-Wilhelm Hertzberg, "Die kleinen Richter," *TLZ* 79 (1954): 285–90; Tomoo Ishida, "The Leaders of the Tribal Leagues: 'Israel' in the Pre-monarchic Period," *RB* 80 (1973): 514–30; Niels Peter Lemche, "The Judges—Once More," *BN* 20 (1983): 47–55; E. Theodore Mullen Jr., "The 'Minor Judges': Some Literary and Historical Considerations," *CBQ* 44 (1982): 185–201; Martin Noth, "Das Amt des 'Richters Israel,'" in *Festschrift, Alfred Ber-*

probably belonged together originally, and they serve the literary framework of historical-theological reflection in 10:6–16 and the narratives about Jephthah in 10:17–12:6.

In contradistinction to the remaining composition, Judg 12:7 cannot be reckoned to the list of judges, since the verse diverges so strongly from the remaining schema. Instead, it is the conclusion of the Jephthah complex, which was shaped by redaction in the style of the formula. The burial place is lacking, however, since none was named in the tradition of Judg 10:17–12:6.

The enumeration of the "minor" judges follows a fixed schema, comprising the name together with the name of the father, the judge's place of origin and place of burial, and the years of activity. In total, only the judges Tola, Jair, Ibzan, Elon, and Ebron are included in the list of judges. Corresponding to the place of their burials, they are divided into different parts of the land; their tribal affinity is determined likewise. The place of their graves can thereby be considered the city of their work:

Tola: Shamir in Mount Ephraim
Jair: Kamon (Qamm) in Gilead
Ibzan: Bethlehem (Bēt Laḥm) in Zebulun
Elon: Aijalon in Zebulun
Ebron: Pirathon (Ferʿata) in Ephraim

Some of the names also appear elsewhere in the tradition: Tola is named in Num 26:23 in a clan list of the tribe of Issachar and could have been taken up from there along with the name of the father Puva. Jair was a son of Manasseh according to Num 32:41, and the "tent villages of Jair" (cf. the Eng. transliteration "Havvoth-jair") in the eastern Transjordan were named after him. Elon is also mentioned as the eponym of a clan of Zebulun in Num 26:26. The two names Ibzan and Ebron are unattested elsewhere in the biblical tradition. If the names do not simply stem from the literary tradition, they are most likely

---

tholet zum 80. Geburtstag (ed. Walter Baumgartner et al.; Tübingen: Mohr Siebeck, 1950), 404–97; Wolfgang Richter, "Zu den 'Richtern Israels,'" *ZAW* 77 (1965): 40–72; Hartmut N. Rösel, "Die 'Richter Israels': Rückblick und neuer Ansatz," *BZ* 25 (1981): 180–201; Klaus-Dietrich Schunck, "Die Richter Israels und ihr Amt," in *Volume du Congrès: Genève 1965* (VTSup 15; Leiden: Brill, 1966), 252–62; idem, "Falsche Richter im Richterbuch," in *Prophetie und geschichtliche Wirklichkeit im alten Israel: Festschrift für Siegfried Herrmann zum 65. Geburtstag* (ed. Rüdiger Liwak and Siegfried Wagner; Stuttgart: Kohlhammer, 1991), 364–70; J. Alberto Soggin, "Das Amt der 'Kleinen Richter' in Israel," *VT* 30 (1980): 245–48; Zeev Weisman, "Charismatic Leaders in the Era of the Judges," *ZAW* 89 (1977): 399–411. See now also Richard D. Nelson, "Ideology, Geography, and the List of Minor Judges," *JSOT* 31 (2007): 347–64.

to be thought of as important local people who were adopted into the tradition due to their effect.

At this point, the schema of the lists of judges, with their stereotypical phrases, corresponds to the form that exists for Saul in 1 Sam 13:1, for David in 1 Kgs 2:10–12, for Solomon in 1 Kgs 11:41–43, and for the additional kings of Israel and Judah; according to the seminal analysis of Wolfgang Richter, this correspondence is referred to again and again in the literature. In addition, the schema for the kings conveys, "similar to the (list) of the judges, statements about the duration of the reign in the ruling city, statements about the realm of the ruler, about death and burial as well as the succession formula" ("ähnlich wie die [Liste] der Richter Angaben zur Regierungsdauer in der Regierungsstadt, Angaben des Herrscherbezirks, zu Tod und Grab sowie die Sukzessionsformel" [Rösel, *BZ* 25 (1981): 189]). The literary shaping of the judges schema thus presupposes the formulaic summary for the kings. The composition of the judges schema thus took place in the monarchic period at the earliest, but the list was presumably already available in the composition of the Deuteronomistic History. An office of significance to all Israelites, one that preceded the monarchy, was postulated with this list by projecting the circumstances of the monarchic period back to the time before the formation of the state. The names were presumably adopted from the literary tradition.

The five figures cannot be verified historically, and not until their placement in the judges schema did they have any significance as nationwide officeholders. The office of the judges over all Israel is thus a fiction from the monarchic period. Corresponding to the range of meaning of שפט ("to judge") holding the office of the judge comprises not only the preservation of justice but also the preservation of rule. The "minor judges" were also described according to the meaning of the verb used for their activity as leader and ruler in Israel. In this extensive function, they precede the monarchy. The judges schema thus indicates a certain historiographic shaping: even before the monarchy, an office over all Israel evolved out of the charismatic figures of the great judges, whose job cannot be closely described but was outlined by the range of meaning of the name of the office itself.

The narratives concerning Jephthah (Judg 10:17–12:6) were framed by the two sections of the list of judges in 10:1–5 and 12:8–15.[21] As such, the work is a

---

21. Wolfgang Richter, "Die Überlieferung um Jephtah, Ri 10,17–12,6" *Bib* 47 (1966): 485–556; Manfried Wüst, "Die Einschaltungen in die Jiftachgeschichte, Ri 11:13–26," *Bib* 56 (1975): 464–79. See now also L. Juliana M. Claassens, "Notes on Characterisation in the Jephtah Narrative," *JNWSL* 22 (1996): 107–15; idem, "Theme and Function in the Jephtah Narrative," *JNWSL* 23 (1997): 203–19; Naomi Steinberg, "The Problem of Human Sacrifice in War: An Analysis of Judges 11," in *On the Way to Nineveh: Studies in Honor of*

conscious composition. Despite the different formulation of the judges schema with ויקם ("he stands up") (10:1, 3) and וישפט ("he judges"; 12:8, 11, 13), it is to be concluded that the two pieces originally constituted a unity; the original unit was torn apart only by the insertion of the Jephthah complex, especially the formulation of 12:7, presuming that the list of judges was already available to the author of the Deuteronomistic History. Even the division of the judges schema explains the difference in vocabulary: "Apparently the Deuteronomistic Historian, when he pushed the Jephthah tradition within the list of judges, reworked the second part of the list" ("Offenbar hat DtrH, als er die Jiftach-Überlieferung in die Richterliste schob, den zweiten Teil der Liste umgearbeitet" [Becker, *Richterzeit*, 225]). With the verb שפט ("to judge") he trenchantly expressed his conception of the presumed office over all Israel.

By means of the concluding comment in Judg 12:7 and the cessation of the narratives between the two sections of the judges schema, Jephthah, whose actions had been those of a savior character, was made into a "judge." Consequently, for Jephthah the formula "the land had rest for forty (eighty) years" (Judg 3:11, 30; 5:31; 8:28) is lacking; in its place is the statement about the duration of his term of office. In a way, the preceding conception was broken by the inclusion of the Jephthah complex, namely, that periods of oppression (3:8, 14; 4:3; 6:1) alternated with periods of salvific actions and rest. Only in 13:1 is the thought of oppression taken up once again in the introduction of the Samson narrative. With Jephthah, a reorientation was thus perfomed: the major judges were at this point to be regarded no longer as saviors from the distress brought on by enemies, but rather as judges and therefore as ones who held an office. The Deuteronomistic Historian thus used the notes about the "minor" judges to identify even the savior figures Jephthah and Samson as judges. No longer a charismatic leader but rather the holder of an office guaranteed the security necessary for the life in the cultivated land.

At this turning point of reinterpretation, the Deuteronomistic redactor inserted a new summary to his historical-theological program in Judg 10:6–16. The necessity of the transition from the ideal savior to the officeholder was prepared for by the events connected to Abimelech (Judg 9): internal conflicts, as were presumed in the oldest piece of the tradition in the Gaal episode (9:26–41), were now to be managed by an officeholder and not by a charismatic

---

George M. Landes (ed. Stephen L. Cook and S. C. Winter; ASOR Books 4; Atlanta: Scholars Press, 1999): 114–35; Heinz-Dieter Neef, "Jephta und seine Tochter (Jdc XI 29–40)," *VT* 49 (1999): 206–17; Renate Jost, *Gender, Sexualität und Macht in der Anthropologie des Richterbuches* (BWANT 164; Stuttgart: Kohlhammer, 2006), esp. 164–207; Dieter Böhler, *Jiftach und die Tora: eine intertextuelle Auslegung von Ri 10,6–12,7* (Österreichische Biblische Studien 34; Frankfurt am Main: Lang, 2008).

leader. Therefore, the second part of the book of Judges (chs. 10–16) takes place against the backdrop of the office of the judge, although on top of that the narrative substance of individual savior figures was also taken up. The insertion of judges having official powers over all Israel on the part of the Deuteronomistic Historian ultimately serves to prepare for the institution of the monarchy. The final judge, Samuel, prepares the way for the first king, Saul, in 1 Sam 8–11, in order to allow the new form of the state, the monarchy, to appear as an unbroken transition from the premonarchic to the monarchic period.[22]

The centerpiece of the Jephthah complex in Judg 10:17–12:7 is the narrative about the warfare in 11:29–40, which is nevertheless tightly interwoven with the description of the events connected to the fulfillment of the vow. Indeed a war report can easily be dissolved out of the context (Judg 11:19, 32, 33), but this report is much too sparse and stereotypical to lead back to an older tradition. However, the events concerning Jephthah's daughter are too tightly connected to a certain location in the mountains at Mizpah in Gilead to be considered only a literary decoration.

On the contrary, the foundational narrative for a particular but no longer precisely understandable custom of young women in connection with the end of youth was transferred to Jephthah and joined together with the war narrative. In any case, the custom is older than the narrative; but if the practice itself should reach back to the premonarchic period, still nothing indicates that the foundational story is older than the monarchic period. By contrast, the narrative offers no evidence at all of the temporal circumstances, and by means of the oath the narrative assumes a universally disseminated motif that is also commonly encountered elsewhere in the literature.[23] The adoption of the material by the Deuteronomistic Historian presupposes that in its original form it was already connected with Jephthah. In the present version, the war report and the narrative about the vow and its consequences cannot be separated from each other, since Jephthah's success in the military expedition constitutes the necessary precondition for the progression of the narrative. The narrative was framed by the postscript in 12:7 and probably also by the exposition in 10:17, 18. The original Jephthah narrative thus comprised only Judg 11:29–40.

---

22. See Volkmar Fritz, "Die Deutungen des Königtums Sauls in den Überlieferungen von seiner Enstehung 1 Sam 9-11," *ZAW* 88 (1976): 346–62.

23. Wilbur Owen Sypherd, *Jephthah and His Daughter: A Study in Comparative Literature* (Newark: University of Delaware, 1948); David Marcus, *Jephthah and His Vow* (Lubbock: Texas Tech Press, 1986); Ulrich Hübner, "Hermeneutische Möglichkeiten," in *Die Hebräische Bibel und ihre zweifache Nachgeschichte: Festschrift für Rolf Rendtorff zum 65. Geburtstag* (ed. Erhard Blum, Christian Macholz, and Ekkehard W. Stegemann; Neukirchen-Vluyn: Neukirchener, 1990), 489–501.

The remaining sections grew from this center piece. The negotiation of Jephthah with the elders of Gilead (Judg 11:1-11) is a subsequent addition for the purpose of constructing the material into a biography. The negotiation with the Ammonites in 11:12-28 in the conclusion to its story presupposes the Tetrateuch narrative and owes to a redactor. The section concerning the war with Ephraim in 12:1-6 takes up again from 8:1-3 the motif of the discontentment of Ephraim and is likewise a redactional insertion. Like 8:1-3, 12:1-6 was first composed and inserted in the postexilic period. That is, the confrontation with the Ephraimites probably reflects the confrontations with the inhabitants of the former northern kingdom, who pursued their own path in the Hellenistic period as Samaritans, having cultic practices at Gerazim that were not oriented toward the temple of Jerusalem. All three pieces appear to have been put in only after the conclusion of the Deuteronomistic History.

In the Samson complex of Judg 13-16, the building up of the material progressed the furthest toward a biography of the hero. The beginnings of this process were already discernible with Gideon and Jephthah. The framing comments in 13:1 and 16:31a show that in the book of Judges an extensive text complex was incorporated, one whose literary formation was already largely finished when it was placed after the second list of judges in Judg 12:8-15. The literary complex consists of a series of individual narratives, which were put together without additional back references and connecting links.[24]

---

24. Joseph Blenkinsopp, "Structure and Style in Judges 13-16," *JBL* 82 (1973): 65-76; James L. Crenshaw, "The Samson Saga: Filial Devotion or Erotic Attachment?" *ZAW* 86 (1974): 470-504; J. Cheryl Exum, "Promise and Fulfillment: Narrative Art in Judges 13," *JBL* 99 (1980): 43-59; eadem, "Aspects of Symmetry and Balance in the Samson Saga," *JSOT* 19 (1981): 3-29; Hermann Gunkel, "Simson," in idem, *Reden und Aufsätze* (Göttingen: Vandenhoeck & Ruprecht, 1913), 38-64; Othniel Margalith, "Samson's Foxes," *VT* 35 (1985): 224-29; P. Nel, "The Riddle of Samson," *Bib* 66 (1985): 534-45; Joshua Roy Porter, "Samson's Riddle: Judges XIV 14,18," *JTS* 13 (1962): 106-9; Adrianus van Selms, "The Best Man and the Bride: From Sumer to St. John with a New Interpretation of Judges, Chapters 14 and 15," *JNES* 9 (1950): 65-75. See now also Carol Smith, "Samson and Delilah: A Parable of Power?" *JSOT* 76 (1997): 45-57; Jichan Kim, *The Structure of the Samson Cycle* (Kampen: Kok Pharos, 1993); Eliyahu Assis, "The Significance of the Narrative Concerning the Annunciation of Samson's Birth (Judg 13)," *Shnaton* 15 (2005): 21-38; Phina Galpaz-Feller, *Samson: The Hero and the Man: The Story of Samson (Judges 13-16)* (Bible in History 7; Bern: Lang, 2006); Markus Witte, "Wie Simson in den Kanon kam: Redaktionsgeschichtliche Beobachtungen zu Jdc 13-16," *ZAW* 112 (2000): 526-49; Bernhard Lang, "The Three Sins of Samson the Warrior," in *Berührungspunkte: Studien zur Sozial- und Religionsgeschichte Israels und seiner Umwelt; Festschrift für Rainer Albertz zu seinem 65. Geburtstag* (ed. Ingo Kottsieper, Rüdiger Schmitt, and Jakob Wöhrle; AOAT 350; Münster: Ugarit-Verlag, 2008), 179-92.

The concluding formula "Samson was a judge in Israel for twenty years" is found in Judg 15:20 as well as in 16:31b, each time at the end of a literary unit. The repetition of the formula is therefore a clue that the three episodes of Judg 16—Samson in Gaza (16:1–3), Samson's capture (16:4–22), and Samson's death (16:23–31a)—represent a literary supplement by which the biography of the hero could be rounded off up to his historic end. As such, Judg 16:1–3 represents an individual tradition with the character of an anecdote in order to demonstrate Samson's extraordinary strength. The piece presumably stemmed from oral tradition and was inserted in this position in order to amplify the heroic deeds. By contrast, the narratives about the capture and death of Samson in Judg 16:4–22 and 23–31a are artistic literary formations to report the additional fate of the hero. The assumption that an old song is taken up in the twice-cited sentence, "Our god has given Samson our enemy into our hand," appears improbable insofar as this would have had to be adopted from the Philistines. Instead, it appears to be shaped by the author to give the narrative a lively visualization. From the given tradition, the author of these sections took up the literary motifs of weakness in the face of the tears of a woman and extraordinary strength connected with long hair. Additionally, the birth story in Judg 13 is to be considered a literary formation in which the motif of childlessness was connected with the motif of transferring the requested child to Yahweh; the same connection is carried out also in the birth story of Samuel in 1 Sam 1. The narrative of Samson's birth in Judg 13 is the only subsequent addition to the rest of the complex.

The sections about Samson freeing himself at Ramath-lehi (Judg 15:9–17) and about the origin of the spring at Lehi (15:18, 19) have an etiological character and already presuppose the portrait of the violent Samson. Both pieces are more likely late formations to build up the portrait of the hero than old traditions. Nevertheless, since Samson first became a savior figure in the narrative in Judg 15:9–17, liberating Judah from the threat by the Philistines, this piece must have already been included in the narrative complex when the Samson material was inserted in the book of Judges.

The tradition in Judg 14:1–15:8 basically conveys events of Samson's personal life. He stands out in two respects: he marries a Philistine woman and has unbridled power, which he thoughtlessly employs against his personal enemies or against whatever he wants. These two extraordinary "qualities" are the actual theme of the tradition and have apparently produced the tradition. Thus, the actions of Samson are by no means in connection with acts of war, but rather with rash revenge that shows personal courage but does not consider the additional consequences. The interconnections of the individual events—marriage, riddle wager, loss of the woman, and destruction of the harvest—into an enclosed whole may very well imply a longer developmental history, but this idea cannot be developed any more precisely.

According to the geographic statements, Samson is a figure from the border region between Judah and Philistia, but he cannot be classified temporally due to the paucity of references. To be sure, the characteristics of extraordinary love and outstanding strength do not yet give Samson the characteristics of the hero, but they do allow him appear as an excellent human who recklessly executes his personal will based on his physical ability. A historical person thus appears to stand behind the tradition, one who lived in the premonarchic or even in the early monarchic period. As an agent of the law of the jungle, he indeed bore the traits of a berserker but hardly corresponded to the ideal hero in ancient Israel. Therefore, the tradition complex of Judg 14:1–15:8 could have been incorporated into the book of Judges only after saving actions (15:9–17) could be narrated about Samson, although these cannot be regarded as historical. The further expansion of Samson's biography in Judg 13 and 16 indeed includes the trait of his personal weakness with respect to women but at the same time emphasizes his God-given strength, which was included to correspond to the divine instruction to annihilate the enemies so that Israel could triumph over the Philistines. Thus, the tradition about the mighty man Samson was expanded on two levels, first as a savior and then as a contender for God.

The Samson narratives hark back to an existing tradition that at least comprised Judg 14:1–15:8. It cannot be determined whether the piece in 15:9–17, which reinterpreted Samson as a savior figure, was likewise already existent. In any case, the Deuteronomistic Historian shaped the formulas in Judg 13:1 and 15:20 in order to insert the Samson material into the book of Judges. Except for the late insertion in 15:18, 19, the complex was expanded around 13:2–25 and 16:1–31 and so was converted into a biography of the hero. The question of which redactor is responsible for that arrangement can remain open. In any case, the expanded Samson narrative concluded the Deuteronomistic book of Judges.

I.2.3.2. The Appendices (Judg 17–21)

Two themes were connected in Judg 17–18: the migration of the Danites and the construction of a shrine in Dan.[25] "The main theme is ultimately about

---

25. Yairah Amit, "Hidden Polemic in the Conquest of Dan: Judges XVII–XVIII," *VT* 40 (1990): 4–20; Abraham Malamat, "The Danite Migration and the Pan-Israelite Exodus-Conquest: A Biblical Narrative Pattern," *Bib* 51 (1970): 1–16; Hermann Michael Niemann, *Die Daniten: Studien zur Geschichte eines altisraelitischen Stammes* (FRLANT 135; Göt-

the cultic symbol installed in the city of Dan" [("Das Hauptthema handelt von dem schließlich in der Stadt Dan aufgestellten Kultbild" [Noth, "Der Hintergrund von Ri 17–18," 134]). The narrative thus represents a foundation story of the shrine in Dan. The existence of a cultic site in Dan was presupposed also in 1 Kgs 12:28–30, when the installation of the shrine in Dan as a shrine for the kingdom and its furnishing with a golden calf as a cultic object by Jeroboam I were reported. Nevertheless, no tradition-historical connection between the two traditions can be determined.

The motif of the acquisition of a new residence by the tribe of Dan in the upper Jordan Valley is connected with the main theme. In that context the city Laish is acquired and renamed Dan. That relocation of the tribal region was not at first a topic in the sources. According to Judg 13:25, the border region between the mountain and the coastal plains in the vicinity of Zorah (Ṣarʿa) and Eshtaol (ʿArṭūf) was considered the residence of the tribe of Dan. Through considerable expansion, the tribal territory was established in this region during the land allocation of Josh 19:41–46. Since the monarchic period, the place Dan (Tell el-Qāḍī) was nevertheless known to one of the Jordan sources (cf. 1 Sam 3:20; 2 Sam 3:10; 1 Kgs 12:28–32; 15:20; 2 Kgs 15:29). However the acquisition of the city Dan may have happened, the motif of an expansion of the settlement area does not necessarily have to stem from an old tradition, but rather can be a later creation to clarify the fact that the Danites had settled in two regions so far removed from each other. The narrative in Judg 17; 18 thus reflects a historical reality of the monarchic period and thus corresponds to the explanation given but not necessarily to historical facts.

The implementation of the main topic points to the erection of a cultic site in Dan. At this point, though, the narrative contains a series of strokes that allow the cult symbol of Dan and the officiating priests to be cast in an unfavorable light, actually betraying outright contempt. The text reads as a scandalous chronicle. The origin of the wealth remains unclear, and the institution of the household cult happens apart from the legitimation of a theophany. The officiating Levite is a chance acquaintance and is not shown further; he remains nameless and changes employers without scruples. By ruthlessly revealing the dubious circumstances of its formation and installation, the narrative does not exactly show Micah's cult symbol as a praiseworthy cultic artifact. This subliminal rejection makes it improbable that the narrative is based on an old tradition from Dan. Instead, the detailed description of a less-than-favorable

---

tingen: Vandenhoeck & Ruprecht, 1985), 61–147; Martin Noth, "Der Hintergrund von Ri 17–18," *ABLAK* 1 (1971): 133–47. See now also A. D. H. Mayes, "Deuteronomistic Royal Ideology in Judges 17–21," *BibInt* 9 (2001): 241–58.

prehistory produces an effective, biting criticism aimed at the center of the cult at Dan. The report has the intention not only "to represent the cult symbol from the beginning in an unfavorable light" ("Absicht, das Kultbild von vorn herein in einem ungünstigen Licht darzustellen" [Noth, "Der Hintergrund von Ri 17-18," 137]), but also fundamentally to expose it as a human work. Not legitimation but disqualification is the intention of the author, whose exilic standpoint is unmistakably pronounced in Judg 18:30.

The appendix in Judg 17; 18 proves to be a late creation with the intention of mocking cultic institutions as purely human work. Since the exile of the institutional priesthood is presupposed, the narrative can have emerged only after the Assyrian conquest in the second half of the eighth century. "Its ridicule, its irony, and its polemic are after all only possible and understandable in a particular literary-historical phase" ("Ihr Spott, ihre Ironie und ihre Polemik sind überhaupt erst in einer bestimmten literaturhistorischen Phase möglich und verstandlich" [Becker, *Richterzeit*, 254]). Since it fits well in the Deuteronomistic temple theology, it would not have been composed prior to the seventh century in the circle of Deuteronomistic theology. Its insertion in the Deuteronomistic book of Judges is not to be reckoned before the postexilic period. This polemical piece with its discriminatory *Tendenz* is ruled out as a possible source for the early history.

The text complex about the tribal war against Benjamin (Judg 19–21) represents a self-contained literary unit, in which the individual parts, for all their independence, nevertheless refer to one another.[26] It is thus not a collection of independent stories but rather a conscious literary conception that, because of its length, is to be designated as a novella. The individual parts are narrated in extensive detail by "Lust zum Fabulieren" ("an inclination to make up stories," J. A. Soggin), although the acting characters oddly remain nameless. After the trespasses against hospitality and custom on the part of the men of Gibeah, the further event proceeds in a fixed order and ultimately leads to a good end.

---

26. Otto Eissfeldt, "Der geschichtliche Hintergrund der Erzählung von Gibeas Schandtat (Richter 19–21)," in idem, *Kleine Schriften II* (Tübingen: Mohr Siebeck, 1963), 64–80; Hans-Winfried Jüngling, *Richter 19, ein Plädoyer für das Königtum: Stilistische Analyse der Tendenzerzählung Ri 19,1–30a;21,25* (AnBib 84; Rome: Biblical Institute Press, 1981); Stuart Lasine, "Guest and Host in Judges 19: Lot's Hospitality in an Inverted World," *JSOT* 29 (1984): 37–59; E. J. Revell, "The Battle with Benjamin (Judges 20:29–48) and Hebrew Narrative Technique," *VT* 35 (1985): 417–33; Klaus-Dietrich Schunck, *Benjamin: Untersuchungen zur Entstehung und Geschichte eines israelitischen Stammes* (BZAW 86; Berlin: Töpelmann, 1963), 57–79; Shemaryahu Talmon, "'In Those Days There Was No מלך in Israel (Judges 18–21)," in idem, *King, Cult, and Calendar in Ancient Israel: Collected Studies* (Jerusalem: Magnes Press, 1986), 39–52.

Not only the entire course but also the individual scenes are extensively stylized, in that a series of literary motifs was adopted. The criminal disregard of the right to hospitality in Judg 19:16–26 is found also in Gen 19:1–11. The dismemberment of a human in Judg 19:29 is without example but has a parallel in the dismemberment of oxen by Saul to announce the army levy in 1 Sam 11:4. Setting up the ambush to overcome a superior enemy (Judg 20:29–48) was extensively described in Josh 8. Finally, the rape of women is a universal motif that is found outside the Bible in numerous variations, of which the Rape of the Sabines on the part of the Romans according to Livy and Plutarch represents the best-known version in antiquity (cf. Elisabeth Frenzel, *Motive der Weltliteratur: Ein Lexikon dichtungsgeschichtlicher Längsschnitter* [3rd ed.; Stuttgart: Kröner, 1988], 170–85). Materially it is thus a conglomeration of various topoi, but the geographic framework is not specific and is adopted from the biblical tradition. Indeed, the designation Sela-rimmon ("rock of Rimmon") is found only in Judg 20:45, 47; 21:13, but the remaining place names Gibeah (Tell el-Fūl), Mizpah (Tell en-Naṣbe), Bethel (Bētīn), and Jabesh-gilead are well attested elsewhere in the tradition and are taken up from there. The warfare against an individual tribe has a model in Judg 12:1–6. The motifs and the geographic framework of Judg 19–21 were thus prefigured by the biblical literature. The numerical statements turn out to be unrealistic exaggerations. Accordingly, this complex can only be a relatively late creation, which deals with the fate of Benjamin for reasons no longer ascertainable. At no place are the adoption and revision of older traditions discernible; therefore this novelesque composition is ruled out as a source for the history of Israel in the premonarchic period. As an additional reference to the premonarchic era, material was added to the book of Judges; by the repetition of the formula from Judg 17:6 and 21:25, "in those days there was no king in Israel; all the people did what was right in their own eyes," the redactor produced the necessary literary and temporal reference.

I.2.3.3. The Prologue (Judg 1; 2)

Auld, A. Graeme. "Judges 1 and History: A Reconsideration," *VT* 25 (1975): 261–85. **Mullen**, E. Theodore, Jr. "Judges 1:1–36: The Deuteronomistic Reintroduction of the Book of Judges," *HTR* 77 (1984): 33–54. **O'Doherty**, Eamonn. "The Literary Problem of Judges 1:1–3:6," *CBQ* 18 (1956): 1–7. **Smend**, Rudolf. "Das uneroberte Land," in idem, *Zur ältesten Geschichte Israels: Gesammelte Studien II* (BEvT 100; Munich: Kaiser, 1987), 217–28. **Weinfeld**, Moshe. "The Period of Conquest and of the Judges as Seen by the Earlier and the Later Sources," *VT* 17 (1967): 93–113. See now also: **Fritz**, Volkmar. "Das 'negative Besitzverzeichnis' in Judicum 1," in *Gott und Mensch im Dialog: Festschrift für Otto Kaiser zum 80. Geburtstag* (ed. Markus Witte; 2 vols.;

BZAW 345; Berlin: de Gruyter, 2004), 1:375–89. **Kallai**, Zecharia. "Joshua and Judges 1 in Biblical Historiography," in idem, *Biblical Historiography and Historical Geography: Collection of Studies* (Beiträge zur Erforschung des Alten Testaments und des antiken Judentums 44; Frankfurt am Main: Lang, 1998), 243–60.

As a compilation of different materials, the only organizational principle of Judg 1 is a division between the southern tribes Judah and Simeon (1:1–21) and the northern tribes, of which Manasseh, Ephraim, Asher, Naphtali, and Dan were named (1:22–36). The entire chapter therefore stands in decided contradiction to the land-acquisition narrative of the book of Joshua, according to which the whole land west of the Jordan was conquered and allocated under the leadership of Joshua. By contrast, Judg 1 mentions individual actions on the part of various tribes and, most notably, lists the cities that could not have been taken by the conquest of the land. There is therefore, prior to the transition to the era of the judges, a decided correction to the historical picture of the book of Joshua. Such a corrective supplement proved essential, for in the wider course of history there were two inconsistencies that urgently required an explanation. On the one hand, in the book of Judges Israel was plagued by enemies even after the acquisition of the land; on the other hand, the history of individual cities appears differently in the historical description of 1–2 Kings. These discrepancies between the program contained in the book of Joshua and the facts of the monarchic period longed for an explanation, which Judg 1 gave in the form of short announcements. One part of these notes, therefore, depends on the summary of corresponding passages from the book of Joshua. The intention of this redactional summary is thus always certain: to summarize the historically reliable data concerning the wider history of the people, insofar as it is of significance for the monarchic period, and therefore to eliminate possible contradictions and to avert the doubts that would arise from them.

The sources and the conception of the author of Judg 1 can be established for the most part, given that the language is largely shaped in Deuteronomistic fashion. The opening of the book in Judg 1:1 gives the impression that each tribe must again conquer the regions allotted to them in Josh 13–19. Thus a fictional second land acquisition is presumed, but essentially the chapter communicates only the sequence of this second conquest. The introduction refers to the land distribution by Joshua. The first action of the united tribes of Judah and Simeon aims at the conquest of Jerusalem in order to secure Judah's claim to the later capital city and cultic center point (Judg 1:2–10). The contradiction to historical reality thus remains irresolvable: according to 2 Sam 5:6–10, Jerusalem was first conquered by David and, as the property of the king, had at first belonged to no tribal region, which is also why the city is carefully ignored in the description of the boundaries between Judah and

Benjamin (cf. Josh 15:9; 18:16). This section of Judges reflects no old tradition but instead reveals a strictly theological intention: Judah had seized the place that later became the political and cultic focal point of the people. The most significant city thus belongs to the most significant tribe.

A similar *Tendenz* underlies the claim to the acquisition of Hebron; Judg 1:11 thus also has to do with a subsequent change to existing circumstances by means of a new legitimation. The claim to Hebron by Caleb was already established in the pre-Priestly spy story of Num 13, 14*, and the clan of Caleb also receives the city in Josh 15:13–14, granted expressly by Joshua. The explicit mention of Cain in Judg 1:16 remains enigmatic, even though the Kenites were only mentioned on the margins of the wider history (cf. Judg 4:11, 17; 5:24; 1 Sam 15:6), as their own group within Judah, they nevertheless appear to have played such an important role that their explicit naming was necessary in this place.[27] In Judg 1:17 there is an additional etiological explanation for the place name Hormah, which is probably later tradition-historically than the narrative of Num 21:1–3. This comment is perhaps determined by the necessity to communicate in at least one place the fulfillment of the ban commandments in Deut 7:2 and 20:16–18. The seizure of three of the five Philistine cities in Judg 1:18 should attest to the acquisition of the entire coastal plain. By leaving the city of Gath unmentioned, the account suggests that this Philistine city never belonged to Judah. As such, the redactor here supports an expansion of the region, which perhaps owed to the addition of Josh 15:46–47, where the Philistine city was reckoned to Judean territory contrary to the historical facts. In Judg 1:19 Judah's land acquisition was then summarized in analogy to Judg 1:9; in 1:20 and 21 there are corrective supplements by a later redactor.

The taking possession of Bethel by the House of Joseph in Judg 1:22–26 is just as emphatic for the northern tribes as the acquisition of Jerusalem by Judah in Judg 1:8. The particular emphasis on Bethel is justified insofar as a cultic site was located in Bethel, which was raised to a state shrine by Jeroboam I (cf. Gen 28:10–22; 31:13; 35:7; 1 Kgs 12:28–29; Amos 3:14; 4:4–5).

From Judg 1:27 on, then, lists of the unconquered cities are mentioned, the statements for the individual cities having been taken up from the literary tradition. The names given for Manasseh—Beth-shean, Taanach, Dor, Ibleam, and Megiddo—appear also in Josh 17:11–13, but these are subsequent redactions and thus cannot have served as a *Vorlage*. With the exception of Ibleam, which is cited again in 2 Kgs 9:27 in connection with Megiddo, all the names are found in the list of Solomonic provinces (1 Kgs 4:11, 12), where they des-

---

27. See Siegfried Mittmann, "Ri 1,16f und das Siedlungsgebiet der kenitischen Sippe Hobab," *ZDPV* 92 (1973): 212–35.

ignate the fourth and fifth provinces. The classification of Solomon's provinces does not explain when these cities came to Israel; however, the juxtaposition of provinces with tribal names and the like, which were named after cities, indicates the coexistence of both Canaanite and Hebrew people groups during the early monarchic period. The majority of the names from Judg 1:27–28 thus could have been adopted from this document of the monarchic period by logical deduction: the cities mentioned in 1 Kgs 4:11, 12 as having the Canaanite population in the premonarchic period still did not belong to Manasseh and consequently could not have been conquered by Manasseh. The comment about the unconquered cities was thus deduced from the historical narrative of 1–2 Kings; at the same time, the notion of compulsory labor was also adopted (cf. 1 Kgs 9:15, 21). Since Ibleam is not named in 1 Kgs 4:11, 12, the name must either have been taken up from another place or have fallen out of its original position.

A similar method of adoption can be postulated also for Gezer in Judg 1:29. The repetition of the text in Josh 16:10 is a redactional insertion and cannot have served as a *Vorlage*. The conquest of the city by Joshua in Josh 10:33 is a redactional addition and need not be considered here, and Gezer is mentioned in Josh 12:12 among the conquered Canaanite cities. The statement about Gezer thus cannot stem from the book of Joshua. At this point, there is in 1 Kgs 9:16 the curious note about the conquering of Gezer by an unnamed pharaoh and the presentation of the city to Solomon as a dowry. Although this statement cannot be verified historically, it can nevertheless be recognized that the city cannot have belonged to the tribal region of Ephraim up until the early monarchic period. The comment of Judg 1:29 is thus to be understood solely as a logical consequence from 1 Kgs 9:16.

In the wider text of Judg 1:30–36, verses 31b and 36 represent additions from a later hand. For the tribes Zebulun, Asher, Naphtali, and Dan, the names stem from the place lists for these tribes in Josh 19, whereas the names Kitron and Acco were mistakenly corrupted in the *Vorlage*. The individual cities were adopted from the following places:

Kitron and Nahalol (Judg 1:30)	Josh 19:15
Sidon and Acco (Judg 1:31–32)	Josh 19:28, 30
Beth-shemesh and Beth-anath (Judg 1:33)	Josh 19:38
Aijalon and Shaalbim (Judg 1:34–35)	Josh 19:42

The basis for the selection of these cities can no longer be determined. At this point, Aijalon and Shaalbim were mentioned in the second Solomonic province in 1 Kgs 4:9, so ultimately their naming can go back to that citation.

On the whole, Judg 1 proves to be a summary of different materials that was created in view of the wider process of the historical narrative. For the time of the judges as well as for the time of the kings, the existence of the Canaanites as a population element in the land was not to be denied, such that the portrait of the land acquisition outlined in the book of Joshua required correction at least on individual points. The necessary correction by a redactor was created by stringing together different materials as an introduction to the book of Judges. The insertion at this position owes to the break that is marked off by the death of Joshua at the end of the era of land acquisition. Prior to the beginning of life in the land, some cities' property relationships were rectified by this addition, whereas the distribution of the land in tribal territories is presupposed. Thus, there is no older tradition having a different conception of the land acquisition underlying the concept of Judg 1; on the contrary, it is a literary summary devoid of historical value. "The materials are not in any historical sequence, nor do they attempt to portray a sequential history of the conquest" (Mullen, "Judges 1:1–36," 53). With the establishment of the particular successes of Judah and the failures of the northern tribes, the land acquisition was updated in view of the circumstances of the monarchic period in order to rule out contradictions and to establish the claim of Judah.

The self-contained piece in Judg 2:1–5 is stylized as an etiological narrative. The place name Bochim appears only here and cannot be located without any additional clue, if it is not an altogether fictive formation. With the additional naming of Bethel, the Septuagint has the place located in the vicinity of that city, which probably owes to the name Allon-bacuth (אלון בכות), literally "the weeping oak," in the proximity of Bethel in Gen 35:8. Naming Gilgal produces a connection with the book of Joshua, since Gilgal was the garrison of the camp according to Josh 4:19, 20; 5:9, 10; 9:6; 10:6, 7, 9, 15, 43; 14:6. The content has to do with the transgression of the confederation through disregard for the will of God: "They have not obeyed my voice." The accusation is treated without reference to concrete circumstances or facts. As a result of the covenant federation's transgression, the land acquisition remains incomplete: as such, Israel remains tempted by foreign gods and falls into worship of them. The piece is thus determined by Deuteronomistic theology (cf. Josh 23). At this point, Judg 2:1–5 belongs together with Judg 1 insofar as it virtually represents a sort of commentary on the partial failures of the land seizure. In the short narrative, the events of Judg 1 were interpreted historical-theologically: with the Canaanites remaining in the unconquered cities as a population in the land, their gods would prove to be Israel's undoing; that is, worshiping Canaanite deities becomes the basis for threat and for oppression of Yahweh's own people. The piece therefore points ahead to the wider history in which the book of Judges becomes the exemplary narrative for the later monarchic period: only fidelity to the federation provides protection from enemies, and disobediently breaking the federation leads necessarily to destruction. The passage in Judg 2:1–5 possibly stems from a redactor of Deuteronomy, as there is only one redactor oriented toward a federation charter.

The death of Joshua in Judg 2:6–10 repeats the text of Josh 24:29–31 with certain changes.[28] The resumption is required by the insertion of Judg 1:1–2:5. The most significant difference from the *Vorlage* is the explicit statement in Judg 2:10 that in the progress of the story, the memory of the divine salvific deeds will be forgotten by the descendants. According to the opinion of the author, the story remains oriented toward the salvific appointment of Yahweh, in which the foundational saving act of Yahweh, the giving of the land, began at the march through the sea under Joshua.

Judges 2:11–23 offers a historical-theological summary of the time of the judges; the original text (2:11–16, 18, 19) was supplemented secondarily by 2:17 and 20–23.[29] As with the summary of Judg 10:6–16, the piece probably stems from the Deuteronomic-oriented redactor. In terms of the connection between deed and consequence, the fate was represented as self-blame; that is, by falling away from Yahweh, punishment consistently follows in the form of oppression by the enemies. The shaping of Deuteronomistic historical theology is clear, and the sole measure for the course of history is adherence to the worship of Yahweh. Israel fails by worshiping foreign gods, whereas adherence to Yahweh guarantees victory over the enemies. Only the exclusive worship of Yahweh secures salvation; falling away to foreign gods compromises the received salvific gift and leads to threat and destruction (cf. Deut 4:26; 8:19–20; 11:17; 30:18). Proper recognition of Yahweh rules out any commitment to other gods. If Israel turns to foreign deities, the ensuing historical events are a punishment for which they themselves are responsible. Thus through this passage the era of the judges takes place against the background of Deuteronomistic theology.

I.2.4. The Tribal Sayings

Gunneweg, Antonius H. J. "Über den Sitz im Leben der sogenannten Stammessprüche (Gen 49; Dtn 33; Jdc 5)," *ZAW* 76 (1964): 245–55. **Zobel**, Hans-Jürgen. *Stammesspruch und Geschichte: Die Angaben der Stammessprüche von Gen 49, Dtn 33*

---

28. Hartmut N. Rösel, "Die Überleitungen vom Josua- ins Richterbuch," *VT* 30 (1980): 342–50.

29. Walter Beyerlin, "Gattung und Herkunft des Rahmens im Richterbuch," in *Tradition und Situation: Studien zur alttestamentlichen Prophetie: Artur Weiser zum 70. Geburtstag am 18.11.1963* (ed. Ernst Würthwein und Otto Kaiser; Göttingen: Vandenhoeck & Ruprecht, 1963), 1–30.

und Jdc 5 über die politischen und kultischen Zustände im damaligen "Israel" (BZAW 95; Berlin: Töpelmann, 1965).

The critical analysis of the book of Judges has come to the conclusion that the foundational element of the Song of Deborah in Judg 5 is a text from the premonarchic period. As the single historically verifiable source, this hymn of praise takes on a particular significance. The greatest value is therefore the enumeration of the tribes, which occurs in two groups; at first the participants in the battle are named, and then those absent are expressly rebuked. After removing secondary expansions, there appears in Judg 5:13–18 a list of ten tribes: Ephraim, Benjamin, Machir, Zebulun, Issachar, Reuben, Gilead, Dan, Asher, and Naphtali. These are identified in different ways in short comments.

The *Sitz im Leben* of these comments cannot have been the battle; only after the battle was the victory over the enemies assessed and probably also celebrated. The participating tribes were praised briefly for their activity, and the others were characterized as rooted in their residences. The pronounced evaluation only referred to the situation of this one concrete military expedition; this was not a general characterization of the tribes.

These comments thus differ fundamentally from the tribal sayings compiled in Gen 49 and Deut 33. Since those sayings make fundamental statements about the individual tribes, they possibly come into consideration as sources for the constitution of Israel—if their date in the premonarchic era can be secured. Therefore they must be investigated as to the time of their formation.

Based on the examination of Hans-Jürgen Zobel, the following grouping can be made regarding form and content:

1. Metaphors, according to which the tribe is compared with an animal (Gen 49:9, 14, 17, 21, 22, 27; Deut 33:22)
2. Plays on words, by which the fate of the tribe could be explained based on its name (Gen 49:13, 16, 19)
3. Direct statements about a tribe (Gen 49:10)
4. Interpretive expansions of the images (Gen 49:10–12, 15, 23–24)
5. Sayings with theophoric elements (Gen 49:25–26; Deut 33:8–10, 12, 13–16, 17, 23)
6. Forms of prayers (Deut 33:6, 7, 11, 18–19, 20–21, 24–25)
7. Sayings in which the eponyms are addressed as individual persons (Gen 49:3–4, 8)

The collection of the tribal sayings contain various pieces regarding form and content, so their formations owe to different circumstances. None of the numerous forms can lay claim to an oral tradition that reaches back to the premonarchic period. At most, the metaphors and their characteristic comparisons of the tribes presuppose an independent existence of the tribe, insofar as the metaphors at least for Judah (Gen 49:9), Dan (49:17), and Benjamin (49:27) still apparently suggest independent military actions. Yet it is by no means necessary to date this back before the formation of the monarchy, for the comparisons could express the self-consciousness of each tribe during the monarchic period. Consequently, the tribal sayings hardly originated prior to the monarchic period, at which time the community of individual tribes also demanded the establishment of their idiosyncrasies in order to distinguish themselves as independent entities. None of the sayings goes back prior to the tenth century, and they cannot be considered as sources for the history of the individual tribes prior to the institution of the monarchy.

I.2.5. Syntheses

According to the biblical portrait, the early history of Israel followed up the march through the wilderness (Exod 15–Num 20) with the conquest and allocation of the eastern Transjordan by Moses (Num 21; 32) and the conquest and allocation of the western Transjordan by Joshua (Josh 2–19). After the land acquisition, the history of the people in the land began with the period of the judges (Judg 3–16). This historical picture underlies the Deuteronomistic History and was developed in the books of Joshua and Judges. As such, the Deuteronomistic Historian consciously structured the course of history. The premonarchic period with the unification of all the tribes under one central authority precedes a premonarchic era when the tribes seized the land and lived in confrontation with the neighboring peoples.

The Deuteronomistic History was presumably first composed after the end of the monarchy in the first half of the sixth century. The shaping of the Deuteronomistic historical portrait thus only took place after the collapse of the state of Judah. The entire course of history was structured and described from reflection that must have bridged a period of more than five centuries. This means, though, that the outline of the early history of Israel provided by the Deuteronomistic Historian is not a pure fiction so long as intermediate stages can proven; to the extent that the formation of this historical portrait can be traced to intermediate stages, the rendition of historical events in the tradition is probably based on proximity to the occurrences described. The question of historical truth is thus inseparable from the question of the authenticity of the tradition.

In the shaping of the early history of Israel, the Deuteronomistic Historian adopted and partially reformulated older traditions:

- A spy story in Josh 2, which perhaps at one time contained the conquest of Jericho by treason
- A narrative in Josh 8 concerning the fate of the king of Ai, which was connected with a heap of stones at the site of the ruins at et-Tell
- The fragment of a hymn of praise in Josh 10:12b, 13a, which goes back to an event that cannot be precisely verified in the region of the mentioned places Gibeon and Aijalon
- A tradition about the demise of Canaanite kings in the cave at Makkedah in the Shephelah (Josh 10:16–27)
- The narrative about Achsah concerning landed property in Judah (Josh 15:13–19)
- A list of Canaanite cities (Josh 12:10–24)
- Border descriptions of Judah and Benjamin (Josh 15:1–12; 18:11–20)
- The place lists for the classification of the province of Judah (Josh 15:20–63; 18:21–28)
- Place lists of the northern tribes Zebulun, Issachar, Asher, and Naphtali (Josh 19:10–39)
- A place list of Dan (Josh 19:41–46)
- The Ehud narrative (Judg 3:12–30)
- The Song of Deborah (Judg 5:12–17, 18b, 19–22, 24–30)
- The narrative about Gideon's battle against the Midianites (Judg 6:2–6, 33–35; 7:1–25; 8:4–21)
- The Jotham Fable (Judg 9:8–15)
- The Gaal episode (Judg 9:26–41)
- The list of the minor judges (Judg 10:1–5; 12:8–15)
- The narrative about Jephthah and his daughter (Judg 11:29–40)
- The narrative about Samson's wedding and acts of revenge (Judg 14:1–15:8)

The Deuteronomistic Historian thus adopted extremely disparate materials into his work. Only songs and lists were taken up verbatim; the narratives are considered to have been reshaped. The songs could stem from oral or written tradition, and the explicit mention of a Book of the Upright (Book of Jashar) in Josh 10:13 suggests a collection of songs in the monarchic period. Since in the Song of Deborah in Judg 5:12–17, 18b, 19–22, 24–30, the tribes still act autonomously, this hymn of praise could stem from the premonarchic period. The same point of origin is to be presumed, but cannot be proven, for the fragment in Josh 10:12b, 13a.

The various types of lists of cities and descriptions of borders in Josh 12; 15; 18; and 19 is to be reckoned from the outset as the product of scribal recording. Such enumerations should adhere to the facts of a certain point in time. Whatever their original purpose might have been, they basically derive from the monarchic period, for in connection with taxes and military service it became necessary to enumerate the existence of the villages for the regions of individual tribes or to determine the borders by naming fixed points. The Deuteronomistic Historian was the first to project this source material back into the premonarchic period. As documents of the monarchic period, the lists are to be ruled out for the history of early Israel.

The lists of judges in Judg 10:1–5 and 12:8–15 assume a special position, given that the Deuteronomistic Historian might have found these lists already compiled. The formulation in analogy to the schema of kings reveals, though, that this note was hardly composed prior to the monarchic period. Since additional evidence is lacking for the names, the historicity of these judges can be neither proven nor disproven. Most certainly they were confined locally to the places named, which implies that these figures of otherwise limited significance were taken over from local tradition. The claim of an office over all Israel can only be understood as a projection from the monarchic period, when the office of the judge was composed in the sense of a precursor to the monarchy.

The narratives are grouped around three themes: land acquisition, battle against the enemies, and shaping local institutions and customs. The land-acquisition narratives stem from local traditions, in which particular facts were explained through events during the land seizure. At the same time, in the local preliminary stages the notion of a land acquisition by all Israel is presupposed, since this represents a constitutive element in each tradition. Even the pre-Deuteronomistic land-acquisition traditions already consider that the seizure of the land was a venture on the part of all Israel. Thus the formation of the land acquisition traditions can only have taken place when Israel had converged into a politically and militarily acting entity. At this point the Song of Deborah shows that not all the tribes participated in the battle against the Canaanites, since the participation in the military action was decided by each tribe individually; collective action was thus dependent on the individual decisions of the participating tribes. In the military sphere, an action by all the Israelites is not attested until the monarchic period. In the land-acquisition narratives, therefore, the circumstances of the monarchic period were transferred to the era prior to the settlement. The composition of a land acquisition by all the Israelites proves the narratives to be formations from the monarchic period; the narratives indeed provide a clue in certain places but by no means reach back to the premonarchic period. By using the place traditions concerning Jericho and Ai, both of which probably originated in the monarchic period, the land-acquisition narrative was first created as a historical outline in connection with the Deuteronomistic History. The narratives in the book of Joshua are ruled out as a source for the history of the seizure of the land by the Israelite tribes, since they merely reflect the historical picture of the monarchic period.

The narratives about battle against the enemies differ with respect to form and content. On the one hand, there are individual deeds, as with Ehud and Samson; on the other hand, there are expeditions against the neighboring peoples, as in the cases of Gideon and Jephthah. The Deuteronomistic Historian thus adopted and revised very disparate material, which must have already developed during the monarchic period. The necessary evidence is lacking for the assumption of a collection of these narratives of individual battle events and heroic deeds in a pre-Deuteronomistic "book of Judges"; the thesis of Wolfgang Richter, that the Deuteronomistic Historian already had the primary layer of Judg 3–9 existing as a literary composition, is therefore to be abandoned, since the individual traditions were first joined together into a major block by means of the transitions created by the Deuteronomistic Historian.

With the exception of the Song of Deborah, it cannot in any case by proved that the traditions already stemmed from the premonarchic period, since none of the traditions evinces a temporal confinement that would suggest their formation in this era. The heroic deeds of Ehud and Samson are embellishments of individual actions, the historical reality of which are indeterminable. The battles of Gideon and Jephthah against the Midianites and Ammonites were so generally narrated that an exact temporal classification and determination cannot be fixed. And with regard to the confrontations concerning the hegemony in Shechem, the concrete circumstances that would enable a historical classification are lacking.

The Deuteronomistic Historian, with his historical outline, first created the preconditions according to which the individual pieces could have been put in the context of a course of history. As such, the personal heroic action and the victory over the enemies correspond more readily to notions that are demonstrable from the early monarchic period (cf. 1 Sam 13–2 Sam 24). With the narratives about battle and war, the ideals of the monarchic period were projected back into the premonarchic period.

The few pieces with the explanations of local facts, such as Judg 9:26–41 or Josh 15:13–19, are intended to establish certain circumstances and are thus historically unverifiable.

The Song of Deborah alone in Judg 5:12–17, 18b, 19–22, 24–30, and perhaps the fragment in Josh 10:12b, 13a, can count as sources from the premonarchic period. Apart from that, the monarchic period represents the actual productive era in which the fundamental narratives of the acquisition and the contestation of the land were created. Possibly other hymns of praise were lost early on; by the time the early history of Israel faded out of sight there were apparently no longer any additional texts. The paucity of the preservation can most likely be explained by the contingency of oral tradition. This means, though, that there were hardly any fixed, written traditions.

On a larger scale, the formation of the tradition concerning the period without kings first began in the monarchic era. This is not very surprising, given that a certain tradition about the individual kings developed since the emergence of the monarchy. From the standpoint of the sovereignty instituted and the unity of all the Israelites, the question was asked concerning the prehistory and was answered by individual narratives about exemplary characters. The foundational guidelines are the unity of the people, the leadership by especially outstanding persons, and the provision of Yahweh; these basic ideas determined the formation of the tradition in the early monarchic period and might also have shaped the portrait of the early history as it appears in the individual traditions from the monarchic period, on the basis of which the premonarchic period was thematized. By means of the narratives about the great judge figures, the premonarchic period was turned into an ideal era in which Yahweh acted through the men he selected. The notion of the direct rule of God through the judges was developed and implemented in the Deuteronomistic History in a deliberate contrast to the representation of the monarchic period.

The Deuteronomistic Historian first joined the individual pieces of the tradition into a historical portrait. In this historical representation, the Deuteronomistic Historian adopted additional materials such as various lists, which originally had nothing to do with the eras described. The outline of an entire history of Israel is thus the achievement of the Deuteronomistic Historian. He converted the ideas drawn up in the individual traditions into a comprehensive representation. As the author of the history, the Deuteronomistic Historian thus not only collected the materials but also generated a unified historical representation by creating additional narratives as well as forming literary transitions and a chronological framework. Therefore, the entire course of history takes place against the background of the will of God as determined in Deuteronomy. God's rule over the people takes place in history, and the events of salvation or disaster happen according to the standard of carrying out divine statutes.

The historical portrait of the Deuteronomistic Historian is therefore governed by the guiding principle of fidelity to Yahweh as the God of Israel. At the same time, the author is oriented by the ideals of the monarchic period:

one land, one people, one king. The concept of the unity of the people under one leadership was given already by the pre-Priestly historical writings with the representation of the exodus under the leadership of Moses (Exod 1–14) and could thus be presupposed. The actual theme of the early history in the Deuteronomistic History is therefore the land. The Deuteronomistic Historian converted the conquest and allocation of the promised land under the leadership of Joshua into a fundamental salvific event. The wider inhabitation in the land takes on the point of view of continually new saving actions by individual figures according to the will of Yahweh and as self-defense against the enemies. This structuring of the early history of Israel supported not only individual traditions of the monarchic period but also the claim of Israel to the land. This historical portrait can only be overcome by reconstructing the history in its discernible and recordable developments.

The meagerness of the literary sources indeed makes the reconstruction of the era difficult but not impossible. Since the biblical texts are hardly sufficient, a representation of the historical sequence must utilize all the additional aids of historical work. To these belongs first and foremost the enlistment of the results of archaeological research. To be sure, as silent witnesses of the past the monuments cannot replace written tradition, but they do provide insight into the settlement history and the development of the material culture. Furthermore, the few extrabiblical sources can and must be analyzed to cast light on the era, even if they do not directly refer to the Israelite tribes. This brings about the possibility of grasping by way of analogy certain aspects of society and the societal development at least in outline; at the same time, the proviso that there are no unmediated statements must always remain valid. Finally, though, the biblical traditions are also to be examined as to whatever extent the circumstances of the premonarchic period have been preserved in kernel form in the texts of the monarchic period.

II. Historical Reconstruction of the Epoch

II.1. Chronological Framework

Within the Deuteronomistic History is found a fixed chronological framework that commences after the land was first conquered. Whereas the book of Joshua contains no temporal information, Judges delineates both the respective terms of office and the exact time period of the oppressions that occurred when no judge was in office. Thus, a chronological frame of the entire span of the judges can be extracted. The compilation of the time periods is as follows:

before Othniel	8 years	Judg 3:8
Othniel	40 years	Judg 3:11
before Ehud	18 years	Judg 3:14
Ehud	80 years	Judg 3:30
before Deborah	20 years	Judg 4:3
after Barak	40 years	Judg 5:31
before Gideon	7 years	Judg 6:1
after Gideon	40 years	Judg 8:28
Tola	23 years	Judg 10:2
Jair	22 years	Judg 10:3
Jephthah	6 years	Judg 12:7
Ibzan	7 years	Judg 12:9
Elon	10 years	Judg 12:11
Abdon	8 years	Judg 12:14
Samson	20 years	Judg 15:20

According to this chronology, the entire period of the judges amounts to 349 years; this information is unverifiable, however. One the one hand, some of the data leave out reference points in order to place the relative dates in an absolute chronology. On the other hand, the round numbers of twenty, forty, or eighty years represent unreliable information, being determined according to the scheme of biblical generations, according to which the lifespan of one generation lasts forty years. A historically accurate chronology thus cannot be produced for the time period of the judges. On the contrary, the statements provide a chronological framework in order to bring the different traditions into a temporal succession so that the impression of a historical course of the era emerges.

The time calculation of the Deuteronomistic History will resume with the absolute identification in 1 Kgs 6:1 that the construction of the temple began in the fourth year of the reign of Solomon, 480 years after the exodus. By synchronizing 1–2 Kings, the fourth year of the reign of Solomon can be determined with certainty as the year 961 B.C.E. The duration of 480 years reveals that the whole history of early Israel comprises twelve generations of forty years, which is thus useless for writing history. Even in the chronological framework of the Deuteronomistic History, the number can be made consistent only if one inserts a large variable for the time of the conquest of the land under Joshua, for which no chronological data are explicitly provided. The following information can be added to sum up the time between Samson and Solomon:

Eli	40 years	1 Sam 4:18
Saul	2 years	1 Sam 13:1
David	40 years	1 Kgs 2:11
Solomon	4 years	1 Kgs 6:1

Thus, another eighty-six years must be added to the 349 years of the time of the judges. Adding the forty years of the sojourn in the wilderness (Deut 2:7; 8:2; 29:4; Josh 5:6) this amounts to 475 years. The difference in the sum of 480 years in 1 Kgs 6:1 can be overcome by setting the unreported chronology of the land conquest at five years. The Deuteronomistic History thus establishes a chronology free of contradictions, which nevertheless cannot be utilized historically since a part of the data is based on the idealized concept of a succession of generations. A chronology of the premonarchic period according to the Deuteronomistic History cannot be recovered.

Numbers 13:22b merely fabricates the necessary reference to Egyptian chronology: "Hebron was built seven years before Zoan in Egypt." Certainly the note in this context is useless on several grounds. First, the Deuteronomistic History stands in a completely different context. Second, the statement does not refer to any nearly certain date of the city's foundation. Third, the statement of seven years does not exactly make for a reliable impression. Thus,

Num 13:22 is to be discarded for establishing a chronological link to the history of Egypt.

As opposed to the monarchic period, there are no fixed dates for the premonarchic period; nevertheless, Egyptian chronology can assist in determining a fixed point in time. Up to the beginning of the monarchy, given its system of synchronization, a solid chronology remains uncertain at every temporal reference. Each date can be determined only within a margin of several decades based on archaeological findings or general observations. Thus, for the early history of Israel an actual chronology cannot be extracted from the biblical texts. For the establishment of temporal events and developments, there remains the possibility of only a relative classification. The succession of the pharaohs of the New Kingdom (Eighteenth to Twentieth Dynasties) serves as the sole chronological frame, given that their dates in office can be determined with absolute certainty. The yearly specification of Egyptian chronology is based on two assumptions, but any emerging difficulties and uncertainties are at this point of no consequence. On the one hand, the pharaohs of each dynasty, including the duration of their rule, are listed in two sources: the tradition of the Hellenistic historian Manetho and the papyrus of the Turin King List. As such, the succession and relative chronology can be determined. On the other hand, various astronomical data from the New Kingdom enable the calculation of an absolute chronology, since the observation of the stars can be calculated exactly. As such, there is a chronological frame on which datable findings outside Egypt can be hung. A chronology for the second half of the second millennium in the region of Syria-Palestine can therefore be achieved by connecting other findings to these data. For the pharaohs of the Nineteenth and Twentieth Dynasties there are the following dates from Erik Hornung (*History of Ancient Egypt: An Introduction* [trans. David Lorton; Ithaca, N.Y.: Cornell University Press, 1999]):

Nineteenth Dynasty	
Ramses I	1295–1293
Seti I	1293–1279
Ramses II	1279–1213
Merneptah	1213–1203
Seti II	1203–1196
Siptah	1196–1190
Tausret	1190–1188
Twentieth Dynasty	
Setnakhte	1186–1184
Ramses III	1184–1153

Ramses IV	1153–1146
Ramses V	1146–1142
Ramses VI	1142–1135
Ramses VII	1135–1129
Ramses VIII	1129–1127
Ramses IX	1127–1109
Ramses X	1109–1099
Ramses XI	1099–1070

Concerning the classification of the eras of civilization, as is common in archaeology, the following schema is used:

Middle Bronze II	1950–1550
Late Bronze	1550–1200
Iron I (Early Iron Age)	1200–1000
Iron II	1000–587

It is gradually becoming apparent that the decisive development in the material culture between the Late Bronze Age and the Iron Age actually first occurs over the course of the twelfth century; nevertheless, for practical matters this book will stick to the traditional classification of the eras, since it is presupposed by so much of the scholarly literature. The subdivision of the Iron Age is not only an archaeological finding, but is also reflected in the trajectory of political development. The institution of the monarchy in Israel by Saul and David in the last quarter of the eleventh century marks the end of the premonarchic era and also coincides with the end of Iron Age I, that is, the Early Iron Age.

II.2 Canaan at the End of the Late Bronze Age

Buccellati, Giorgio. *Cities and Nations of Ancient Syria: An Essay on Political Institutions with Special Reference to the Israelite Kingdoms* (SS 26; Rome: Istituto di Studi Del Vicino Oriente, Università di Roma, 1967). **Dever**, William G. "The Beginning of the Middle Bronze Age in Syria-Palestine," in *Magnalia Dei, the Mighty Acts of God: Essays on the Bible and Archaeology in Memory of G. Ernest Wright* (ed. Frank Moore Cross et al.; Garden City, N.Y.: Doubleday, 1976), 3–38. **Gerstenblith**, Patty. *The Levant at the Beginning of the Middle Bronze Age* (ASOR Dissertation Series 5; Philadelphia: ASOR, 1983). **Mazar**, Amihai. *Archaeology of the Land of the Bible* (2 vols.; AB Reference Library; New York: Doubleday, 1990, 2001), 1:174–294. **Helck**, Wolfgang. *Die Beziehungen Ägyptens zu Vorderasien im 3. und 2. Jahrtausend v.Chr.* (2nd ed.; ÄA 5; Wiesbaden: Harrassowitz, 1971). **Mazar**, Benjamin. "The Middle Bronze Age in Palestine," *IEJ* 31 (1981): 172–85. **Tubb**, Jonathan N. "The MB II A Period in Palestine: Its Relationship with Syria and Its Origin," *Levant* 15 (1983): 49–62. **Weinstein**, James M. "The Egyptian Empire in Palestine: A Reassessment," *BASOR* 241 (1981): 1–28. **Weippert**, Helga. *Palästina in vorhellenistischer Zeit* (Handbuch der Archäologie,Vorderasien 2/1; Munich: Beck, 1989), 200–343. See now also: **Ilan**, David. "The Dawn of Internationalism—The Middle Bronze Age," in *The Archaeology of Society in the Holy Land* (ed. Thomas E. Levy; New York: Facts on File, 1995): 297–319. **Bunimovitz**, Shlomo. "On the Edge of Empires—Late Bronze Age (1500–1200 BCE)," in *The Archaeology of Society in the Holy Land* (ed. Thomas E. Levy; New York: Facts on File, 1995), 320–31. **Finkelstein**, Israel. "The Territorial-Political System of Canaan in the Late Bronze Age," *UF* 28 (1997): 221–55. **Na'aman**, Nadav. "The Network of Canaanite Late Bronze Kingdoms and the City of Ashdod," *UF* 29 (1998): 599–626.

After a nonurban intermediate stage, numerous new cities were founded in the southern Levant over the course of several centuries from the beginning of the second millennium. The first phase of this urbanization began in the twentieth century, and a second phase followed in the eighteenth century. Despite numerous destructions with constant reconstruction, most of the cities existed in the eras of the Middle Bronze Age II (1950–1550 B.C.E.) and the Late Bronze Age (1550–1200) up to around 1200 B.C.E. Characteristic of these cities were colossal fortifications that enclosed and protected the inhabited area. Many of these cities covered a wide expanse; Megiddo had an average norm of 5 hectares (12 acres), but the city called Laish in Dan covered an expanse of 20 hectares (49 acres), and Hazor, having 80 hectares (198 acres), was the largest city that ever existed in the western Transjordan. The cities were located in close succession in the plains on account of the favorable conditions for agriculture; by contrast, only isolated urban centers existed in the mountains, and the fringes of the steppe belt in the south and east were not settled at all. In many cases the reestablishment of cities occurred in places that were already settled in the preceding eras of the Early Bronze Age II and III (2950–2350) owing to their favorable locations near springs and arable land. Thus, the Middle Bronze Age city layouts were established on the old settlement hills of Dan, Hazor, Megiddo, Beth-shean, Shechem, Aphek, Jericho, and Gezer. In addition, however, places without a prehistory such as Acco, Bethel, and Beth-shemesh were involved in the Middle Bronze Age urbanization.

Each city, together with the surrounding land, constituted an autonomous region that was governed by a local ruler. Each of these city-states was independent, since a majority of the inhabitants were farmers who cultivated the surrounding land. In addition, there were the necessary artisans such as potters and blacksmiths and also merchants, who conducted flourishing and productive long-distance trade with the Aegean region in particular. At the pinnacle of the societal order stood one ruler who exerted oversight; it is unknown whether the majority of inhabitants belonged to additional classes. The underclass comprised the slaves, and the priests assumed a special position. This social differentiation is evident also in the appearance of the city, where in addition to the extended residential area, there always was a palace of the ruler and a temple for various gods, together with their adjacent buildings.

The nearness of the cities to one another brought them into mutual rivalry, since every expansion of urban land—and so also the sphere of power—could only come at the expense of a neighbor. The coexistence of the cities is also therefore marked by constant conflict and battle, as emerges especially from the so-called Amarna letters. The extension of the ruling area by a city prince over other regions of another ruler was only ever for a short duration, because no such continuance could last, given the balanced match of mutually limited powers.

This situation of rivaling city-states did not change with the conversion of the region to the Egyptian province of Canaan. After the conquests of Thutmose III (1479–1425), the city-states were subject to Egyptian hegemony, which the pharaoh could nevertheless exert only nominally for the most part. Although Egyptian troops were stationed in some places such as Beth-shean, this presence had little influence on the political and cultural development of the individual cities during the Late Bronze Age.

II.2.1. The Collapse of the Canaanite City-States

Fritz, Volkmar. "Das Ende der spätbronzezeitlichen Stadt Hazor Stratum XIII und die biblische Überlieferung in Josua 11 und Richter 4," *UF* 5 (1973): 123–39. **Gonen**, Rivka. "Urban Canaan in the Late Bronze Period," *BASOR* 253 (1984): 61–73. **Kempinski**, Aharon. *Megiddo: A City-State and Royal Centre in North Israel* (Materialien zur allgemeinen und vergleichenden Archäologie 40; Munich: Beck, 1989). See also now: **Ussishkin**, David. "Levels VII and VI at Tel Lachish and the End of the Late Bronze Age in Canaan," in *Palestine in the Bronze and Iron Ages: Papers in Honour of Olga Tufnell* (ed. Jonathan N. Tubb; London: Institute of Archaeology, 1985), 213–28. **Ussishkin**. "The Destruction of Megiddo at the End of the Late Bronze Age and Its Historical Significance," *Tel Aviv* 22 (1995): 240–67 = *Mediterranean Peoples in Transition: Thirteenth to Early Tenth Centuries BCE* (ed. Symour Gitin, Amihai Mazar, and Ephraim Stern; Jerusalem: Israel Exploration Society, 1998), 197–220.

An immense general decline took place during the Late Bronze Age. To be sure, new settlements were established also in the fourteenth and thirteenth centuries, but generally these are very small. Numerous cities diminished or were abandoned. The quality of the pottery and the intensity of the long-distance trade in the Aegean were diminishing. In many places, the fortifications were not rebuilt after destruction. At the same time, there is a decrease in population. The reasons for this general drop are unknown and are not ascertained from the archaeological data. In view of the general situation, there are several prevailing factors that could have caused a diminution of the former size; most likely the combination of various causes effected the generations-long process of the loss of power and prosperity. These factors include war, epidemics, famines, and tribute payments.

Wars were an unalterable and inevitable part of life. The warlike confrontations must have been very numerous and gruesome, as shown by the scope of destruction in the unearthed cities. Thus, in the period from 1950 to 1130 B.C.E. Megiddo was completely destroyed and rebuilt no fewer than eight times. Since not every campaign ended with the destruction of the city, the number of military expeditions was considerably higher. In the Late Bronze Age their number continued to increase since, in addition to the cities' conflicts with each other, the numerous campaigns of the pharaohs of the New Kingdom ensued at this point. The pharaohs maintained their hegemony by numerous campaigns to Syria and Palestine. Thus Tuthmose III, after the decisive defeat of the Syrian and Palestinian cities in the year 1468 B.C.E., still undertook sixteen additional campaigns in the region to secure his rule. Even if these campaigns affected only parts of the region, they nevertheless represented a considerable disruption of the land and presumably also of agriculture and trade, since peace is the *sine qua non* for the prosperity of agricultural production and economic transactions. Additionally, there were wars among the city-states. Even if precise information is lacking concerning confrontations among the individual cities, the complaints of individual rulers about raids and conquests of neighboring principalities indicate that such attempts at extending one's own territory at the expense of the bordering regions were by all means the order of the day. In addition, between their expeditions the pharaohs exerted their dominion only nominally, such that ultimately there existed no control over the local rulers' claims to power. To be sure, the loss due to wars is not measurable, but in any case it is to be considered a disturbance.

We cannot obtain information concerning epidemics, but we can assume that they occurred on account of the given circumstances of life with their lack of hygienic conditions; as such, epidemics periodically decimated the population again and again. The extent cannot be assessed, but each diminution of the population also diminished the military and economic strength of the city. An epidemic therefore had devastating consequences because it weakened the community's continued existence.

Annual rainfall would have varied, and not only did the rains need to begin at the right time, but the harvest could also be diminished by pests or storms. Since grain was the main foodstuff, deficient supply led immediately to famine because the uncovered demand could not be compensated for adequately by other foodstuff or by trade. In addition, there is presently no evidence of stockpiling provisions. Lack of nutrition always leads to a weakening of the population.

To be sure, nothing is known concerning tribute to the Egyptian occupying power, but neither can it be ruled out that the city-states had to fulfill certain obligations to the pharaoh. These could have consisted of paying tribute in the form of precious metals or even obligation to maintain the troops stationed in the land. In any case, Egyptian dominance involved contributions and economic burdens. Each payment or supply had to be produced, which thus meant an economic loss, since the goods they handed over were no longer available to cover their own needs.

The city-states thus stood not only in competition with each other and in confrontation with the great power of Egypt but also with the unpredictable facts of nature. The size of the cities required, moreover, a minimum number of inhabitants in order to guarantee their defense in instances of raid or siege. The example of the siege of Megiddo by Thutmose III shows the relative strength of the fortified cities; in 1468 Thutmose could force the surrender of the city only after seven months. Each city was self-sufficient, since the occupants produced the necessary foodstuff and goods themselves. This independence of the city-states with respect to their supply determined their strength, which had ensured their continued existence for centuries. Only for the metals did there exist an absolute dependence on commercial trade with the Aegean and the Mesopotamian area; yet in the absence of a delivery they could get by temporarily by melting down. The military campaigns and small catastrophes apparently weakened the system of city-states again and again until the system became extinct in the decades after 1200.

The destruction of numerous cities at the end of the period of the Middle and Late Bronze Age is extremely difficult to date, since apart from the pottery, clearly datable findings turn up in a only few places. The best temporal classification offers artifacts with names of the Egyptian pharaohs, but the Mycenaean pottery also facilitates a chronological reference. Since the Mycenaean wares are also well-represented by imported goods in Egypt, the transition from the Mycenaean III B era to the Mycenaean III C era can be fairly certainly determined at 1190 B.C.E. For all the places in which the Mycenaean III B wares are still represented, the year 1190 indicates a *terminus ad quem* for their existence.

The Canaanite cities Hazor (stratum XIII) and Shechem were definitely destroyed a few years before this time. In Shechem the settlement was only restored in the tenth century, whereas in Hazor—prior to the reestablishment of the city by Solomon (stratum X B)—two sparse settlement layers are proven (strata XII and XI); based on their expanse and their findings, though, these cannot be considered a continuation of the Canaanite city. At about the same time, Aphek in the coastal plains (stratum X 12) was destroyed, and the city was only sporadically settled up to the eleventh century.

The cities that demonstrably became extinct after 1190 are the ones in which were found Mycenaean III C wares or artifacts having cartouches of the pharaohs after Ramses II (1279–1213). Thus in Beth-shean and in Lachish, the existence of the cities during the first half of the twelfth century is attested by the cartouches of Ramses III (1184–1153). In Megiddo, there is a chest that bears the cartouche of Ramses VI (1142–1135), although it stems from no clear discovery context. Thus the last Canaanite city (stratum VII A) cannot have perished before 1135, because it had already been destroyed once around 1200 (stratum VII B). Gezer was also settled during the entire twelfth century, since the names of several pharaohs of the Ramessides are attested; Ramses III, Ramses IV (1153–1146), Ramses VIII (1129–1127), and Ramses IX (1127–1109) are mentioned on various objects. According to the pottery evidence, the Canaanite city still continued to exist in the eleventh century. Gezer came to Israel only under Solomon, as stated in the note in 1 Kgs 9:17.

A continuity of the settlement history is established after the end of the Canaanite city in Megiddo. The development of the settlement layers of strata VI B and VI A are indeed fundamentally differentiated from the preceding Canaanite city (stratum VII A), but the material culture clearly stands in the Canaanite tradition up to the end of the eleventh century. Accordingly it can thus be concluded that this settlement continued to be inhabited by Canaanites. A similar continuation of settlement histories having constant inhabitation has been proved also for Beth-shean and Achshaph (Tell Kesān in the valley of Acco).

The collapse of the Canaanite cities thus did not occur at the same time or conclusively. On the contrary, the destruction of the city-states extended over a longer period of time during the twelfth century. After the destruction, which is characterized most of the time by a large burned layer, there was in some cities such as Hazor, Shechem, Aphek, and Lachish, a break in the settlement history insofar as these places were not built again except for sporadic settlements. By contrast, Megiddo, Gezer, Beth-shean, and Achshaph show a continuation of the city culture—albeit with certain losses—in unbroken succession up to the beginning of the monarchic period. This continuation of the settlement history is comprehensible only on the presupposition of a continuation of the population. The few excavated settlement hills thus indicate that the number of city-states after 1200 reduced considerably but that in individual cities the Canaanite culture and the previous population continued on uninterruptedly even if the former position of power no longer existed.

II.2.2. The Canaanites

Astour, Michael C. "The Origin of the Terms 'Canaan', 'Phoenician', and 'Purple.'" *JNES* 24 (1965): 346–50. **Lemche**, Niels Peter. *The Canaanites and Their Land: The Tradition of the Canaanites* (JSOTSup 110; Sheffield: JSOT Press, 1991). **Mazar**, Benjamin. "Canaan and Canaanites," in idem, *Biblical Israel: State and People* (Jerusalem: Magnes, 1992), 16–21. **Van Seters**, John. "The Terms 'Amorites' and 'Hittite' in the Old Testament," *VT* 22 (1972): 64–81. See now also: **Killebrew**, Ann E. *Biblical Peoples and Ethnicity: An Archaeological Study of Egyptians, Canaanites, Philistines, and Early Israel, 1300–1100 B.C.E.* (SBLABS 9; Atlanta: Society of Biblical Literature, 2005).

"Canaanites" is a collective term for the autochthonous population of the southern Levant in the second millennium. The name is derived from כנען ("Canaan") the general designation for the land west of the Jordan. Canaan is presumably a derivation from the word כנע, which in Hebrew is used with the meaning "to subdue," "to humble." As such, Canaan signifies a humiliated, lowly land, thus the "depression" or the "lowland." Considering the fact that this land is mostly made up of mountains, only two conclusions can be drawn regarding this designation: it originated apart from the land and above all has the coastal plains in view. Accordingly, the derivation from the word *kinaḫḫu* for the color purple is to be given up. The name Canaan is found in numerous scribal variations in the cuneiform texts of the second millennium from Mari, Alalakh, Nuzi, Ugarit, and Amarna (evidence in M. Weippert, *RlA* 5:352–55). Since it is a general designation, a clear boundary of the region is not presupposed. In Egyptian, the designation Canaan (*p₃ Knʿn*) then replaced all the other names of the land such as Retenu, Dahi, and Horu (*Rtnw, Ḏ₃hj,* and *Ḥ₃rw*). In the Bible, Canaan was adopted as the term for the settlement region of the Israelite tribes.

In contrast to the term "Canaan," however, the *nomen gentilicium* "Canaanites" is only sparsely attested in the sources of the second millennium (see Lemche, *Canaanites*, 28–52). At the same time, a pejorative undertone in some of the sources is not to be ignored. The term "Canaanites" denoted the people who stood outside of the society of the respective scribe. Already before 1200 "Canaanite" was a vague circumlocution for people from the geographic region "Canaan," lacking any further determination of their background and position or their belonging to an ethnic group or social class. In this sense "Canaan" was used in extrabiblical sources to designate the pre-Israelite population.

At least a part of the Canaanite population survived the collapse of the system of city-states in the first half of the twelfth century. This emerges clearly from the continuity of the settlement history in the twelfth and eleventh centuries in places such as Beth-shean, Megiddo, Achshaph, and Gezer. By contrast, the definitively abandoned cities such as Hazor, Shechem, Aphek, and Lachish guaranteed the continuity of Canaanite culture in a reduced area and the survival of the indigenous population.

The special position of the city centers is in any case still clear at the beginning of the monarchy. In the division of the state into administrative regions by Solomon in 1 Kgs 4:7–19, some provinces were named after Israelite tribes and the rest according to the enumeration of cities.[1] This combination from two different principles for the enumeration of provinces is clearly conditioned historically: in addition to the tribal territories, there were regions having cities that were regarded as the successive settlements of the city-states. In the Solomonic reign, two different groups were still identifiable: the new element of Israelite tribes and the old element of Canaanite cities. Despite their ethnic affiliation, both population elements were enclosed in the state established by Saul and David. This means, though, that the population of the former Canaanite cities must have been considered in the premonarchic period an independent entity, which according to the use of the extrabiblical collective concept could be designated as Canaanites. The antithesis between the old and new population was thus maintained until the monarchic period.

Even in biblical parlance, "Canaanites" designates the inhabitants of the land of Canaan before the seizure of the land by the Israelite tribes. Yet the Canaanites normally appear in a series along with other peoples such as the Amorites, Hittites, Perizzites, Jebusites, Hivites, and Girgashites (cf. Gen 10:15–18a; 15:19–21; Exod 3:8, 17; 13:5; 23:23, 28; 33:2; 34:11; Num 13:29; Deut 7:1; 20:17; Josh 3:10; 9:1; 11:3; 12:8; 24:11; Judg 3:5; 1 Kgs 9:20; 1 Chr 8:7; Ezra 9:1; Neh 9:8). Considering the late time of composition for these

---

1. See Albrecht Alt, "Israels Gaue unter Salomo," in idem, *Kleine Schriften zur Geschichte des Volkes Israel II* (2nd ed.; Munich: Beck, 1959); G. Ernest Wright, "The Provinces of Solomon," *Eretz Israel* 8 (1967): 58–68; Yohanan Aharoni, "The Solomon Districts," *Tel Aviv* 3 (1976): 5–15; Hartmut N. Rösel, "Zu den 'Gauen' Salomos," *ZDPV* 100 (1984): 84–90; Nadav Na'aman, *Borders and Districts in Biblical Historiography: Seven Studies in Biblical Geographic Lists* (Jerusalem Biblical Studies 4; Jerusalem: Simor, 1986), 167–201; Volkmar Fritz, "Die Verwaltungsgebiete Salomos nach 1 Kön 4,7–19," in *Meilenstein: Festgabe für Herbert Donner zum 16. Februar 1995* (ÄAT 30; Wiesbaden: Harrassowitz, 1995), 19–26. See also Paul S. Ash, "Solomon's? District? List," *JSOT* 67 (1995): 67–86.

texts, none of which can be dated prior to the late monarchy, it is nevertheless improbable that a historical reality stands behind this stark differentiation of the population of the land in the premonarchic period. The origin of this series is unknown, but its meaning is explicit and clear: with a greater number of enemies, the miracle of their defeat grows.

Even if some of the names go back to ancient designations of ethnic groups, in the context of the books of Joshua and Judges they offer no proof at all of the different population elements of the land. The linguistic usage at most reflects the consciousness and the notions of the exilic and postexilic periods and not the real circumstances for the time of the land acquisition. Because of the lack of concrete statements of self-identification from the inhabitants of the land, the collective term "Canaanites" adheres to the designation of the city inhabitants and their descendants during the twelfth and eleventh centuries.

Analogous to the Canaanites, the remaining peoples were also designated by reverting to the past, without characterizing the actual circumstances. The different enumerations of the pre-Israelite inhabitants of Canaan are a projection to draw the picture of a complex population structure. The various enumerations of the original inhabitants should represent a comprehensive inventory of the non-Israelite residents of Canaan, but in fact they offer no historical information concerning the composition of the population. Only in some cases can the derivation of the names still be ascertained.

The designation "Amorites" is not to be separated from the Akkadian *Amurru*, by which is designated the population west of the Euphrates that invaded the Mesopotamian cultivated land in the second millennium. To be sure, the kingdom of Amurru in northern Syria disappeared after 1200 in connection with the Sea Peoples movement, but the designation of the northern Syrian areas as Amurru was nevertheless retained in the Assyrian sources. In the biblical writings, the designation Amorites is used synonymously with Canaanites to a great extent, but it predominantly indicates the inhabitants of the eastern Transjordan (see Num 21:13; Josh 2:10; 9:10; 24:8; Judg 10:8; 11:20). Presumably, the concept was adopted from Assyrian or Babylonian linguistic usage at the end of the monarchic period as a general identification of former inhabitants of the land; it is not the correct designation of a definite population group.

"Hittites" are a people of Indo-Germanic origin who immigrated to Asia Minor at the beginning of the second millennium. The empire constituted around 1600 became extinct prior to 1200 in connection with the Sea Peoples movement. In 1 Kgs 10:29 and 2 Kgs 7:6, in addition to the Aramean kingdom the Hittite kingdom denotes Syria, which has to do with successive states of former vassals of the empire. The Hittites were clearly differentiated from the

Phoenicians in 1 Kgs 11:1, and occasionally individual persons were designated as Hittites (cf. 1 Sam 26:6; 2 Sam 11:3–24). The concept thus names a population element in addition to the Arameans and Phoenicians in Syria, but does not mean the direct descendants of the population of the Hittite heartland.

The "Hivites" are not attested outside the Bible; the designation is found in Gen 43:2; 36:2; Josh 9:7; 11:3, 19; Judg 3:3 outside the summaries for a population group in the land. Since the equation with another ethnic group is ruled out,[2] it can only refer to a small minority group of non-Israelites who are otherwise completely unknown and cannot be determined precisely.

Outside of the enumerations, the "Perizzites" were still named in Gen 13:7; 34:30; Judg 1:4, 5 alongside the Canaanites; in Josh 17:15 they are mentioned alongside the Rephaim as inhabitants of the east Jordanian forest regions. The word is not to be separated from the biblical term פְּרָזִי, which probably designates "a class of the population ousted from the cities and living in the open land" ("eine aus den Städten verdrängte, im offenen Land lebende Bevölderungsschicht" [*HAL*, 909]). Perizzites could originally have been the technical term for the relatives of a definite social class, which became obsolete in its original meaning.

The designation "Jebusites" is from the place or territory name Jebus, which was located in the vicinity of Jerusalem (cf. Josh 15:8; 18:16). Based on the equation of Jebus with Jerusalem (Josh 15:63; 18:28; Judg 1:21; 1 Chr 11:4) the pre-Israelite inhabitants of the city became Jebusites.

The "Girgashites" were only occasionally named and in Gen 10:16 are differentiated from the Canaanites. The name is not attested elsewhere and is perhaps a population element analogous to the Hivites that was confined to a definite region.

For the designations of the prior inhabitants of the land, along with Canaanites, Hittites, and Amorites, old names of the second millennium were adopted that were wrested from their original location. The other names are developments of unknown origin and significance. As with the Jebusites, they are most likely linguistic developments that have their point of departure in different concepts and ultimately reflect no historical reality. For the pre-Israelite population of the land, a terminology was created that at no point in time corresponded to the historical facts. On the contrary, the occasionally

---

2. See the various attempts by Manfred Görg, "Hiwiter im 13. Jh.v.Chr.," *UF* 8 (1976): 53–55; Othniel Margalith, "The Hivites," *ZAW* 100 (1988): 60–70; George E. Mendenhall, *The Tenth Generation: The Origins of the Biblical Tradition* (Baltimore: Johns Hopkins University Press, 1973); 154–63; Robert North, "The Hivites," *Bib* 54 (1973): 43–62.

varied compilation of names was no longer connected with a notion of ethnic affiliation.

II.2.3. Israel and the Merneptah Stele

Ahlström, Gösta W. *Who Were the Israelites?* (Winona Lake, Ind.: Eisenbrauns, 1986). **Engel**, Helmut. "Die Siegesstele des Merneptah," *Bib* 60 (1970): 373–99. **Fecht**, Gerhard. "Die Israelstele, Gestalt und Aussage," in *Fontes atque Pontes: Eine Festgabe für Hellmut Brunner* (ed. Manfred Görg; ÄAT 5; Wiesbaden: Harrassowitz, 1983), 106–38. **Hornung**, Erik. "Die Israelstele des Merneptah," in Görg, *Fontes atque Pontes*, 224–33. **Otto**, Eckart. "Erwägungen zum Palästinaabschnitt der 'Israel-Stele' des Mernepta," *ZDMG* Supplement IV (1979): 131–33. **Redford**, Donald B. "The Ashkelon Relief at Karnak and the Israel Stela," *IEJ* 36 (1986): 186–200. **Sachsse**, E. "Die Etymologie und älteste Aussprache des Names ישראל," *ZAW* 34 (1914): 1–15. **Singer**, Itamar. "Merneptah's Campaign to Canaan," *BASOR* 269 (1988): 1–10. **Stager**, Lawrence E. "Merneptah, Israel and Sea Peoples," *Eretz Israel* 18 (1985): 56*–64*. See now also: **Freedman**, David Noel, and David **Miano**. "'His Seed is Not': 13th-Century BCE Israel," in *Confronting the Past: Archaeological and Historical Essays on Ancient Israel in Honor of William G. Dever* (ed. Seymour Gitin, J. Edward Wright, and J. P. Dessel; Winona Lake, Ind.: Eisenbrauns, 2006), 295–301. **Hasel**, Michael G. "Merenptah's Inscription and Reliefs and the Origin of Israel," in *The Near East in the Southwest: Essays in Honor of William G. Dever* (ed. Beth Alpert Nakhai; AASOR 58; Boston: ASOR, 2003), 19–44. **Kitchen**, Kenneth A. "The Victories of Merenptah, and the Nature of Their Record," *JSOT* 28 (2004): 259–72. **Yurco**, Frank J. "Merenptah's Canaanite Campaign and Israel's Origins," in *Exodus: The Egyptian Evidence* (ed. Ernest S. Frerichs and Leonard H. Lesko; Winona Lake, Ind.: Eisenbrauns, 1997), 27–55.

The only extrabiblical mention of the name Israel is found in the victory stele of Merneptah of Thebes. On the reverse side of an older stele there is a chiseled hymn dated to the fifth year of the pharaoh (1208) that describes a victory of Egypt over the Libyans. Only at the conclusion does the Near East come into view:

> The princes are prostrated and say, šlm; no one among the nine bows raises his head any more.
> Ṯḥnw is perished, Ḫatti is peaceful,
> Canaan is conquered with (?) every bad thing,
> Ashkelon is led away, and Gezer seized; Yanoam is annihilated,
> Israel lies idle and has no seed corn.
> Ḫr is turned into a widow for Egypt.
> All the lands as a whole are in peace;
> everyone who wandered is shackled

by the king of upper and lower Egypt,
"B'-n-r' beloved of Amon," the son of Re, Merneptah,
who is endowed with life like Re every day.

Israel is named by the determinative for a people in connection with lands and cities. Apart from the Libyans (*Ṯḥnw*) the lands were enumerated by respective territories: Ḫatti for northern Syria, Canaan for southern Palestine, and *Ḫr* (= Horu), which is likewise a word used for Palestine and here perhaps labels the north in distinction to Canaan in the south. Beyond that were listed the three cities Ashkelon ('Asqalān), Gezer (Tell Abū Šūše = Tell Ǧezer), and Yanoam (Tell Nā'am). As a designation for a people, "Israel" falls out of this series of geographical terms, such that a definite region is not necessarily designated by this name. Speaking against this also is that the text knows no clear geographic boundaries, and, in addition to the territories, cities are yet named that were located in those territories. A meaningful geographic arrangement of various names is ultimately not given.

At this point, it has been debated since the discovery of the stele in the year 1896 whether the text goes back to an expedition of Merneptah to Palestine and Syria in the fifth year of his reign. In their general and stereotypical formulation according to the model of the court style, the statements by no means make the impression that such an expedition ever really took place in the first years of the reign of Merneptah. Along with this reservation regarding the inscription, there is indeed no historical verifiability of a military expedition or a conquest of the named cities; nevertheless, the naming of Israel remains a historical fact insofar as this people was assumed to be sedentary in the region outlined by the different terms. Even if Merneptah never reached the Near Eastern regions, the name of the people Israel was connected to his time in an unspecified way by the stele. As a people, Israel had their catchment area in the area of Syria and Palestine, although all further details must remain open. The settlement region cannot be precisely established, nor can the identity of this group be determined. At most, the divergence from the previous linguistic usage as the designation of a population element outside the Canaanite city-states is remarkable (cf. §§II.4.1 and 2). This alteration is a clear indication that concrete circumstances stand behind the naming of Israel. As a people, Israel is a reality at the end of the Late Bronze Age, although they are not precisely comprehensible with respect to origin, composition, and catchment area. The Merneptah Stele can attest to no more than that, even if the inscription were to go back to concrete historical events.

The equivalence of the name *j-s-r-i-r* with the Hebrew ישראל has not been contested since the discovery of the stele in the year 1896; the Egyptian transcription corresponds to the reign of the so-called group writing of the

New Kingdom. The derivation of the name is, however, just as unfamiliar as its original meaning. The two folk-etymological explanations in Gen 32:29 and Hos 12:4–5 interpret the name by means of the word שׂרה ("to contend"). These attempts are clearly determined by the tradition of the renaming of Jacob to Israel and do not indicate the original meaning. The understanding of ישׂראל as a sentence name with the theophoric element *El* ("God") as subject is indeed correct. But since the basic meaning of the verb is not established, the original meaning remains unknown.

For the premonarchic period, Israel is not attested in the biblical texts; the citations in the Song of Deborah in Judg 5:2, 3, 5, 7, 8, 9, 11 are all found only in the later hymnal additions. Even the "ark saying" in Num 10:36 cannot be considered evidence prior to the monarchic period, since it presumably stems form the Jerusalem cultic tradition and is enacted as an invocation of Yahweh in the temple (cf. Ps 6:5 [Eng. 6:4]; 90:13; 126:4).

During the monarchic period, then, "Israel" became the comprehensive self-description of the people. At the beginning of the monarchy, the name can designate the group of northern tribes delimited from Judah (1 Sam 17:52; 18:16; *inter alia*) as well as the community of all the tribes (1 Sam 2:28; 3:20; 10:20; *inter alia*). After the division of the monarchy ישׂראל will then be differentiated from Judah as the independent entity of the northern kingdom. The use of the name was prefigured already at the beginning of the monarchic period to the extent that it could be used as a designation even for the new political unity of the political agreement of the tribes under the rule of a king. In any case, the Merneptah Stele toward the end of the thirteenth century presupposes an ethnic group "Israel" in the Egyptian dominion of Syria-Palestine, even if no additional details concerning this population element emerge from the name.

II.3. The Resettlement of the Land in the Early Iron Age (1200–1000)

At about the same time as the collapse of the Canaanite city-states, a resettlement of the land ensued that extended over the entire era. The old city centers were usually avoided, and the regions outside the old conurbation were preferred. The Canaanite cities were mainly located in the plains, so the new settlements were predominantly in the mountains and on the margins. At the same time, the character of the settlement changed insofar as small and unfixed settlements clearly predominated. The changes during the Early Iron Age affected the settlement regions as well as the settlement forms and the material culture.

II.3.1. Settlement Regions

Axelsson, Lars Eric. *The Lord Rose Up from Seir: Studies in the History and Traditions of the Negev and Southern Judah* (trans. Frederick H. Cryer; CBOT 25; Stockholm: Almquist & Wiksell International, 1987). **Coote**, Robert B., and Keith W. **Whitelam**. *The Emergence of Early Israel in Historical Perspective* (Social World of Biblical Antiquity 5; Sheffield: Almond, 1987). **Finkelstein**, Israel. *The Archaeology of the Israelite Settlement* (Jerusalem: Israel Exploration Society, 1988). **Fritz**, Volkmar. "Erwägungen zur Siedlungsgeschichte des Negeb in der Eisen I-Zeit (1200–1000 v.Chr.) im Lichte der Ausgrabungen auf der *Ḫirbet el-Mšāš*," ZDPV 91 (1975): 30–45. **Gal**, Zvi. *Lower Galilee during the Iron Age* (Winona Lake, Ind.: Eisenbrauns, 1992). **Glueck**, Nelson. *Explorations in Eastern Palestine I–IV* (AASOR 14, 15, 18–19, 25–28; New Haven: ASOR, 1934–51). **Mittmann**, Siegfried. *Beiträge zur Siedlungs- und Territorialgeschichte des nördlichen Ostjordanlandes* (ADPV 2; Wiesbaden: Harrassowitz, 1970). See also: **Finkelstein**, Israel, and Nadav **Na'aman**, eds. *From Nomadism to Monarchy: Archaeological and Historical Aspects of Early Israel* (Jerusalem: Yad Izhak Ben-Zvi, 1994). **Finkelstein**, Israel, *Living on the Fringe: The Archaeology and History of the Negev, Sinai and Neighbouring Regions in the Bronze and Iron Age* (Monographs in Mediterranean Archaeology 6; Sheffield: Sheffield Academic Press, 1995).

Through surveying, the distribution of the new settlements is well understood for different parts of the land. On the one hand, there is a sharp increase in the Early Iron Age settlements compared with the number of Late Bronze Age cities; that is, at this point regions were settled in which no cities had previously existed. On the other hand, a change of structure is also discernible, since the new settlements are on average 0.5 to 1 hectare (1.25 to 2 acres) smaller than the previous city centers. Both observations can be verified in different regions.

Regarding Galilee the settlement schema clearly emerges for the eastern portion, as shown in the map by Israel Finkelstein (see fig. 1 below) based on the thoroughgoing survey conducted by Zvi Gal. During the Late Bronze Age only a few cities existed on the periphery of the plains or high plateau. In the Early Iron Age almost the entire region is covered with places. In particular, numerous new settlements were laid out in the difficult-to-access upper Galilee. According to previous findings, there were also successive settlements in the hills of ruins from the Bronze Age. In total, there are nine cities of the Late Bronze Age as opposed to fifty-one settlements of the Early Iron Age, of which forty-two were newly established outside the previous settlement areas. As such, the settlement density and population increased, even if the Early Iron Age places were of a substantially smaller area than the Late Bronze Age cities.

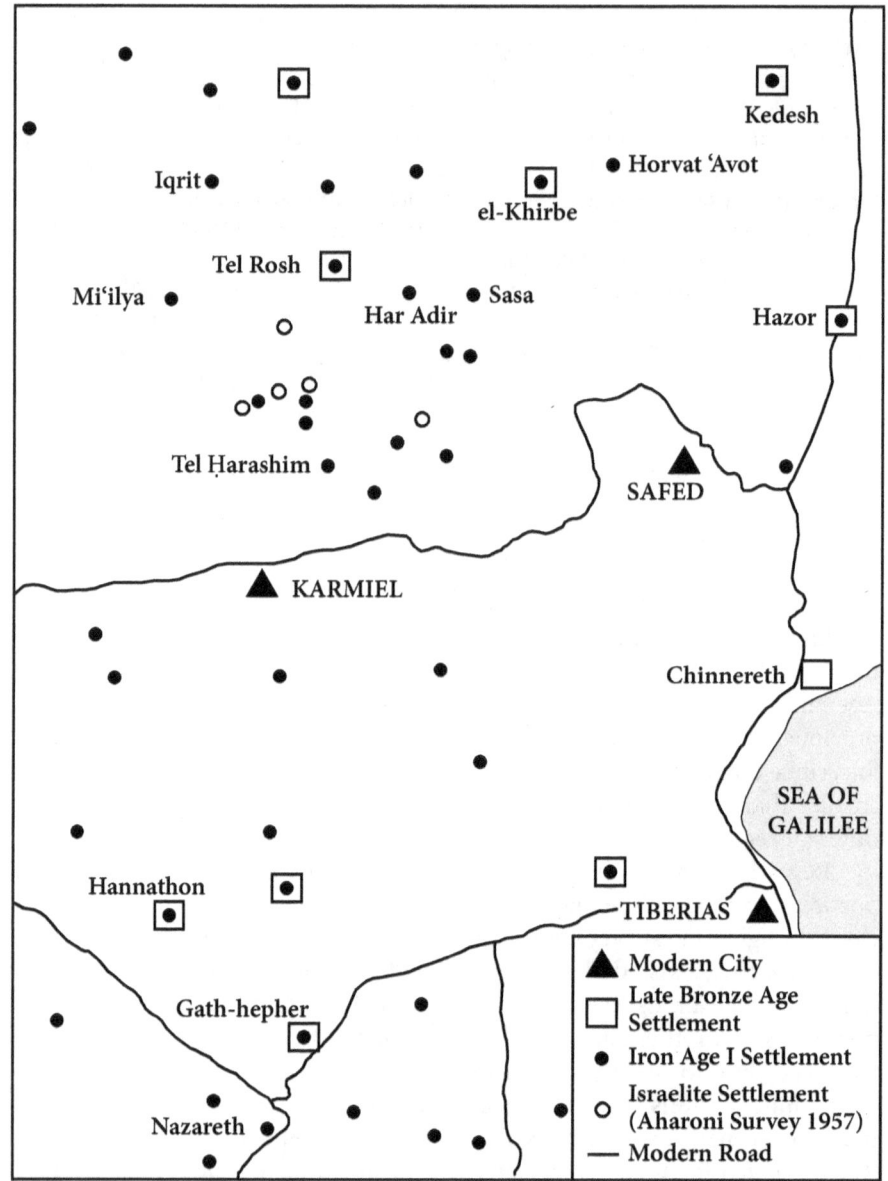

Figure 1. Map of the eastern Galilee with settlement sites of the Late Bronze Age and Early Iron Age according to Israel Finkelstein.

A similar result can be established in the eastern Transjordan based on Nelson Glueck's and Siegfied Mittmann's surveys. For the region between Jabbok and Yarmuk, excepting the Jordan rift, the number of settlement places rose from fifteen in the Late Bronze Age to seventy-three in the Early Iron Age; fifty-eight establishments occurred in previously unsettled places. In particular there was practically an explosive increase of settlements in Aǧlūn (fig. 2). In total, the number of settlement sites increased fivefold, and the new settlers pushed forward even into regions that had not previously been settled. In contrast to the limited number of city centers in the Late Bronze Age, the land was covered with a tight network of villages in the Early Iron Age.

Yet the development of Mount Ephraim dropped off radically (fig. 3). According to the survey conducted by Finkelstein between Bethel and Shechem, only six cities existed in this region during the Late Bonze Age, and all of them were in the central part of the mountains. For the Early Iron Age 115 places are proven, although many of them were inhabited only for a short time. Nevertheless, despite the relatively short duration of their existence, the increase in the number of settlement sites, which were distributed over the entire mountain at this point, is a clear indication of the increase in population and the extension of the settlement areas in the time after 1200. The high point of the settlement density was reached around the middle of the eleventh century.

For other parts of the land we do not have comparable investigations with statistical analysis. It is to be expected, however, that in the remaining regions, with the exception of the coastal plains and the Jezreel Valley, there would be a similar expansion of settlement activity. The Negeb constitutes an exception insofar as no cities were established there for the Late Bronze Age, whereas for the Early Iron Age numerous new foundations can be documented.

After 1200, the settlement of the land suddenly changed. The number of settlement sites sharply increased over the number of Late Bronze Age cities. Moreover, the new establishments came about in regions of dense forestation or arid climate and thus were far outside the sphere of influence of the city centers. Although these new villages were considerably smaller in expanse, they still took up only a fraction of the area of a Late Bronze Age city. As an additional element to the complete restructuring, a fundamental change in formation and type of construction occurs, as seen in archaeological research.

II.3.2. Settlement Form

The new settlements of the Early Iron Age not only differ in size from the Canaanite cities but also evince considerable differences in their conception. The community of a city in the Late Bronze Age indeed consisted largely of

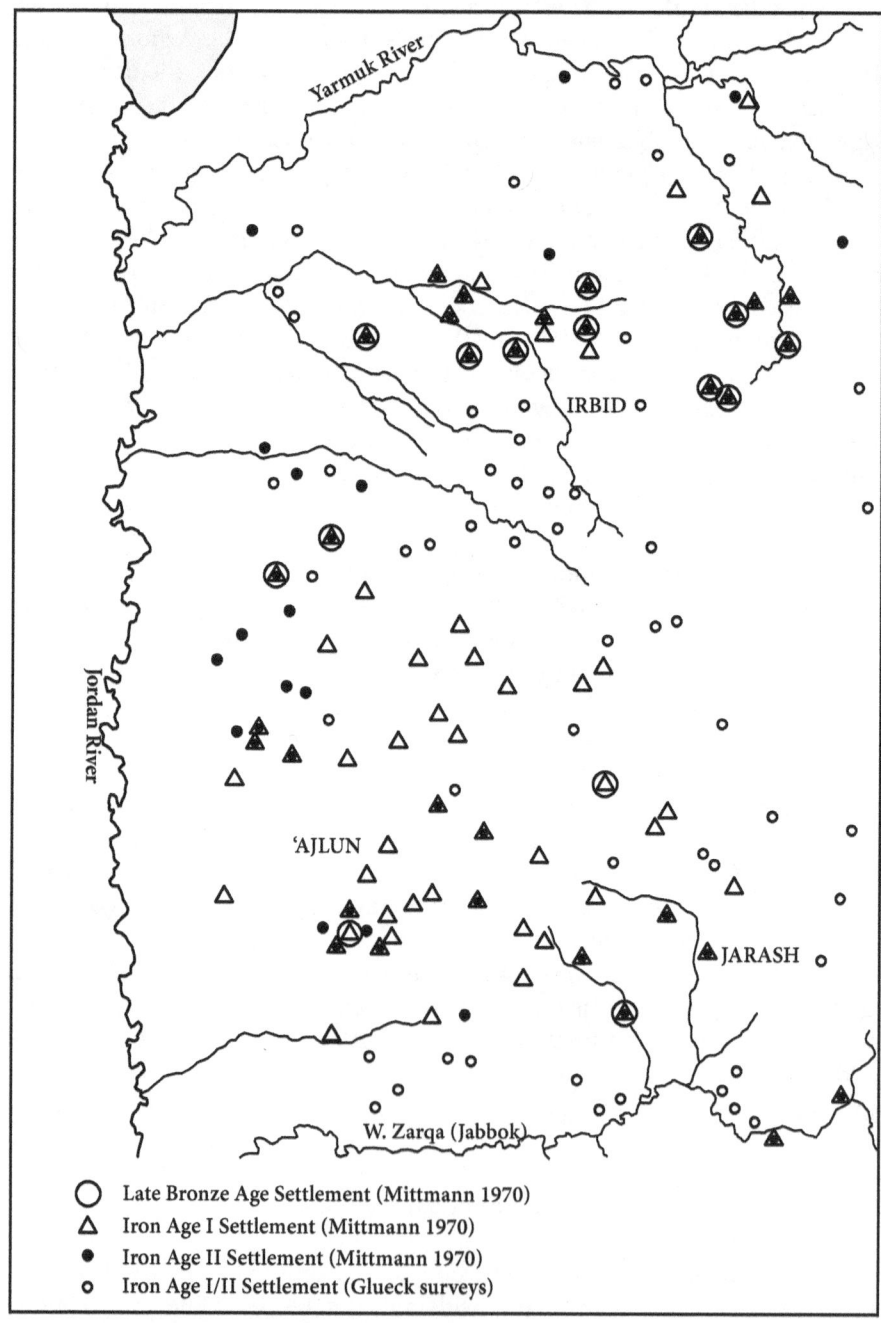

Figure 2. Map of the eastern Transjordan with the settlement sites of the Late Bronze Age and Early Iron Age according to Siegfried Mittmann.

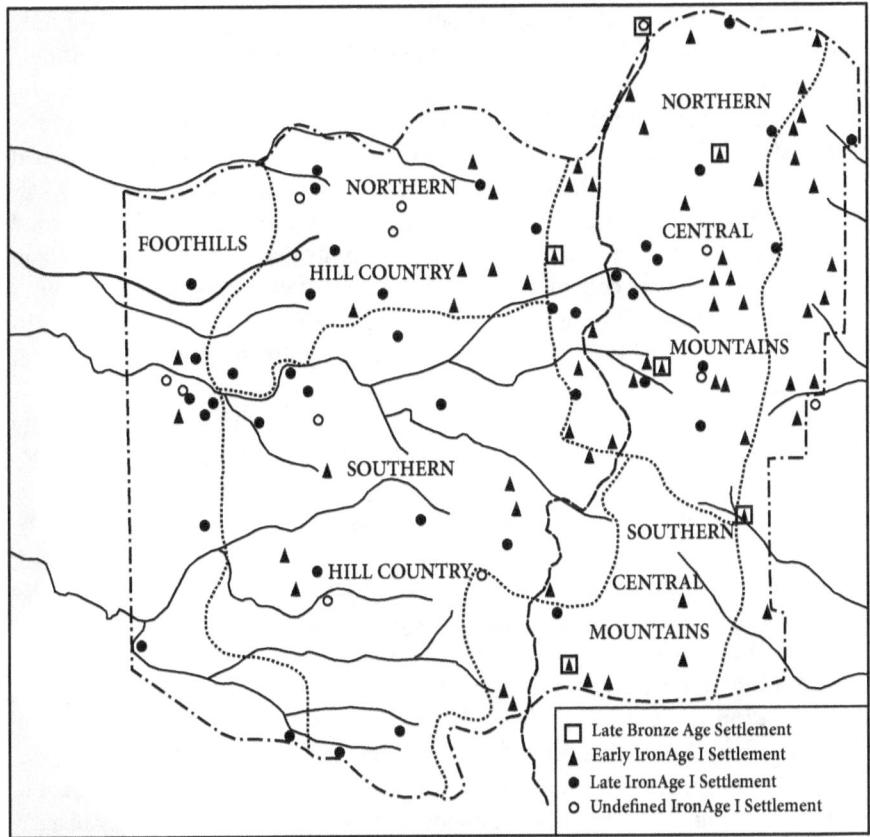

Figure 3. Map of Mount Ephraim with the settlement sites of the Late Bronze Age and Early Iron Age according to Israel Finkelstein.

residential districts, but the large building complexes of the temple and palace stand out from those. By means of the fortification, a clear boundary of the expanse was set: entrance was possible only through the city gate, where all traffic could be controlled. On the inside, the predominant construction form of the courtyard house enabled a certain regularity to the layout, such that a conscious plan is recognizable to some extent. All these elements are lacking in the villages of the Early Iron Age. As a general rule they are unfortified, indicate no public buildings, and lack every form of design.

The few excavated hamlets show a certain diversity in the layout and in the construction forms. Mostly they were established in places having no prehistory, but they could also (as in the case of Ai) be constructed on ruins from the Early Bronze Age or (as in the case of Hazor) be built on the hills of ruins from forlorn Canaanite cities. For the most part they were abandoned after the beginning of the re-urbanization in the tenth century, because only in exceptional cases, for example, in Tell es-Sebaʿ, does the city of the monarchic period stand on the remains of the village from the premonarchic era. This form of agricultural settlement is limited to the Early Iron Age and is thus a strange phenomenon that demands explanation, but the controversial question of the ethnic affiliation of the inhabitants and the historical development must be left aside in their details. In this context we are concerned with a more precise characterization of the excavated settlements. As such, only such places were considered that were adequately reconstructed through surface excavations. Dating is based on the pottery chronology. But since in the period between 1150 and 1000 the design of pottery shows an unbroken continuity and the transitions to the coterminous eras are not sharply marked, the dates are only approximate, and a margin of two to three decades must be factored in. On the whole, though, the chronology is assured by the connection of the pottery findings with datable Egyptian findings.

Hazor initially remained unsettled after the collapse of the Canaanite city. Over the course of the twelfth and eleventh centuries, however, there were two settlements on the tell, each of which existed for only a short time.[3] These two strata, XII and XI, are extremely meager and show no direct continuation of the former city settlement. The modest expanse of cleared areas allows no far-reaching claims. Stratum XII evinces only modest remains in the form of foundation walls, oven, and supply pits. In stratum XI a building was partially uncovered having a row of stone pillars typical for the era. To be sure, the expanse of this settlement site could not be determined; with reasonable certainty, though, it might have been an unfixed village of meager expanse.

Tell Qirī lies approximately 9 km northwest of Megiddo on the edge of the Jezreel Valley; the ancient name of the settlement is unknown. The Early Iron Age village was established on the remains of a city from the Middle Bronze Age IIA, which was already abandoned during the era of Middle Bronze Age IIB. The settlement history then reaches with only short breaks up to the Hellenistic-Roman period, although the place was never fortified. For the twelfth and eleventh centuries, two settlement sites were proven in strata IX and VIII, which on account of numerous successive rebuildings are nonetheless divided into three phases that differ considerably from one another.[4] In stratum VIII C the houses were built closely interlocking, whereas two follow the model

---

3. Yigael Yadin, *Hazor, with a Chapter on Israelite Megiddo* (Schweich Lectures 1970; London: Oxford University Press for the British Academy, 1972); Doron Ben-Ami, "The Iron Age I at Tel Hazor in Light of the Renewed Excavations," *IEJ* 51 (2001): 148–70.

4. Amnon Ben-Tor and Y. Portugali, "Tell Qiri: A Village in the Jezreel Valley," *Qedem* 24 (1987): 80–103.

of the three-room house. In stratum VIII B the same area evinces a series of almost square houses, which were divided by a cross wall or by a row of stone pillars into a wide room and a courtyard area. In the subsequent phase, stratum VIII A, the construction type of the three-room houses having a courtyard area is definitely maintained, but the proximity of the houses to one another changed again despite the continued use of numerous walls. As such, the path of the streets received no consideration, so these show no firmly demarcated boundaries. On account of the narrowness of the cleared areas, nothing can be said concerning the further layout of the village. The completely irregular route lacks any kind of planning; it merely maintained access to the houses. Different base types of houses could be used in the residential development; these do not stand next to each other in a discernible arrangement, but rather they are "meshed" in mutual delimitation. The great number of construction forms is noticeable: in addition to broad rooms with courtyards in front, there is also the so-called three-room house and the house divided lengthwise by stone pillars. (Since the three phases of stratum IX are largely reconstructed, they are not considered here.)

According to the biblical sources, Shiloh (Ḫirbet Sēlūn) played a significant role in the premonarchic period, since the ark was kept there until its loss to the Philistines (cf. 1 Sam 1–4; Judg 21:15–25). For the Early Iron Age settlement, though, only some houses on the western edge of the settlement hill could be uncovered thus far; these had been installed in the glacis of the Middle Bronze Age fortifications.[5] Consequently, the houses follow none of the usual construction forms but, typical of the era, show the construction with stone pillars that served to divide the relatively large construction units. The houses were secured by retaining walls downhill so as to form cellar rooms, which—as the numerous *pithoi* allow conjecture—were used for stockpiling (fig. 4). The village existed for only a short time from the end of the twelfth century to the middle of the eleventh century.

Ai lies on the hill named et-Tell on the southern edge of Wādī el-Ǧaya approximately 5 km east of Ramallah in the vicinity of Bethel, which is positioned only 3 km farther west in Betīn. The Early Iron Age settlement was laid out on the acropolis of the Early Bonze Age city, which at one time extended to the east on a sloping hill over an area of 11 hectares (27 acres).[6]

---

5. Israel Finkelstein, ed., *Shiloh: The Archaeology of a Biblical Site* (Monograph Series, Sonia and Marco Nadler Institute of Archaeology, Tel Aviv University 10; Tel Aviv: Institute of Archaeology, Tel Aviv University, 1993).

6. See Joseph A. Callaway, "Die Grabungen in Ai (et-Tell) 1964–1972," *Antike Welt* 11/3 (1980): 38–46; Ziony Zevit, "Archaeological and Literary Stratigraphy in Joshua 7–8," *BASOR* 251 (1983): 23–35.

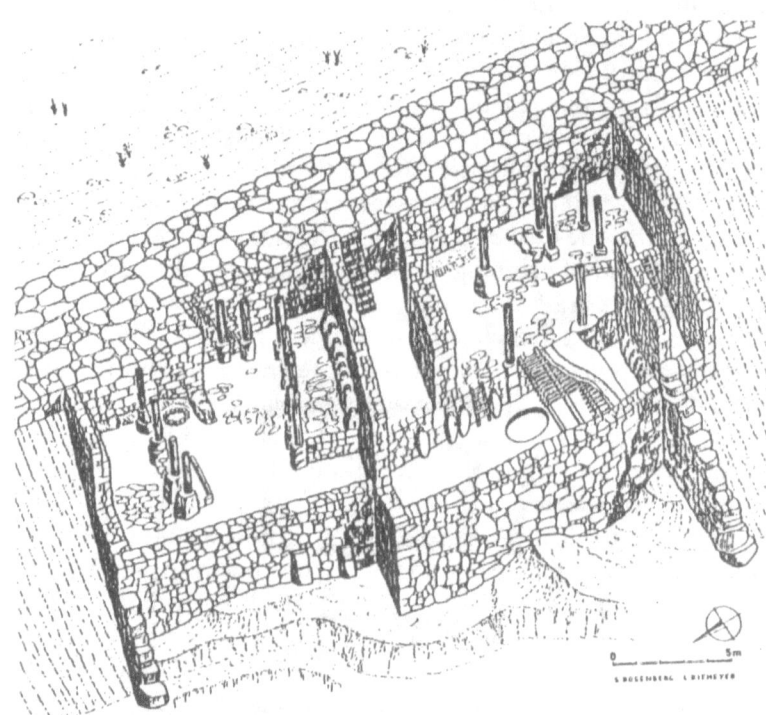

Figure 4. Isometric reconstruction of the Early Iron Age buildings in Shiloh.

It appears that the city wall from the third millennium was still visible, but with the exception of the former temple, no attempt was made to use this. The houses, despite the width of the hill, stand tightly crowded an area of roughly 1 hectare (2.5 acres) (fig. 5). Predominating is the type of long-reaching residential house, whose main room is in most cases divided by stone pillars; on the short side, which lies across from the entrance, an additional room is separated. Smaller right-angled rooms are isolated. Occasionally two rooms are connected to each other by a low passageway. For the most part the houses show considerable differences. On the northern edge of the hamlet, the houses are strung together in a way that the outer walls result in an enclosed front, by which a certain defensive position was attained. Within the houses there are cisterns in which rainwater was collected; these were bell-shaped and hewn into the limestone of the hill so that they needed no additional sealing by wall plaster. The extraordinarily irregular con-

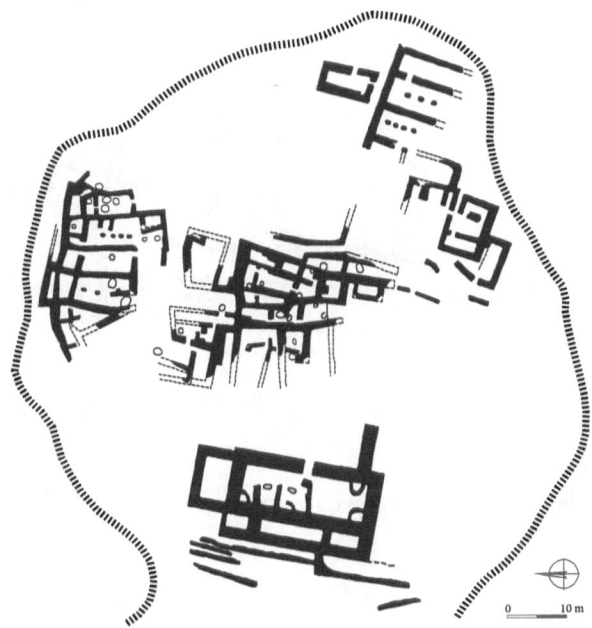

Figure 5. The Early Iron Age settlement at Ai.

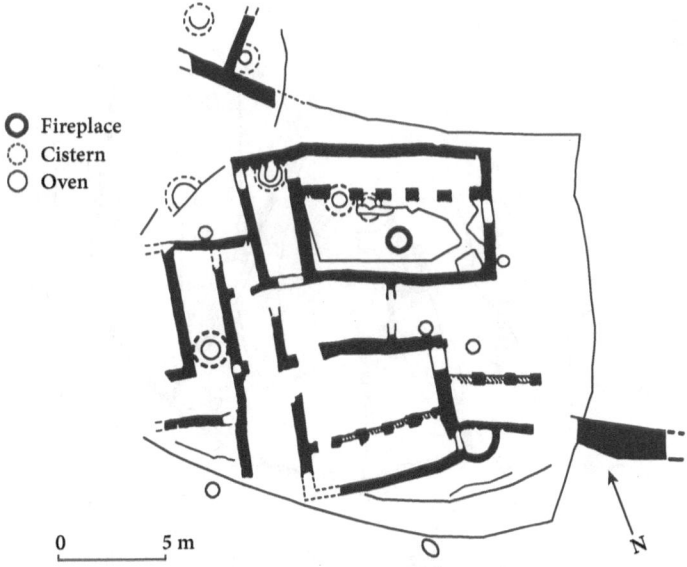

Figure 6. Three-room houses in Ḥirbet Raddāne.

92 THE EMERGENCE OF ISRAEL

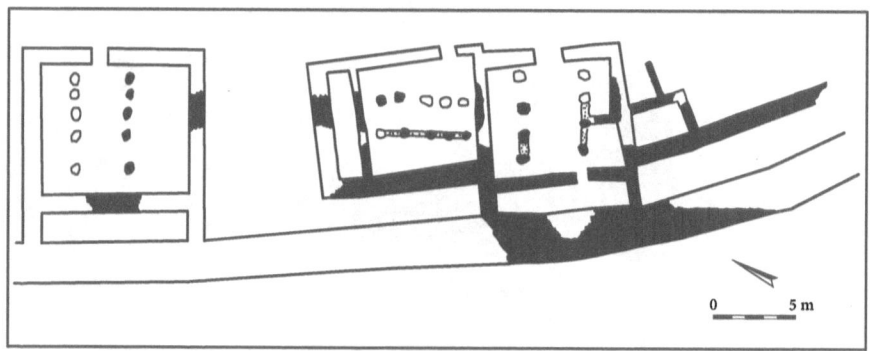

Figure 7. The development along a curtain wall in Ḫirbet ed-Dawwara.

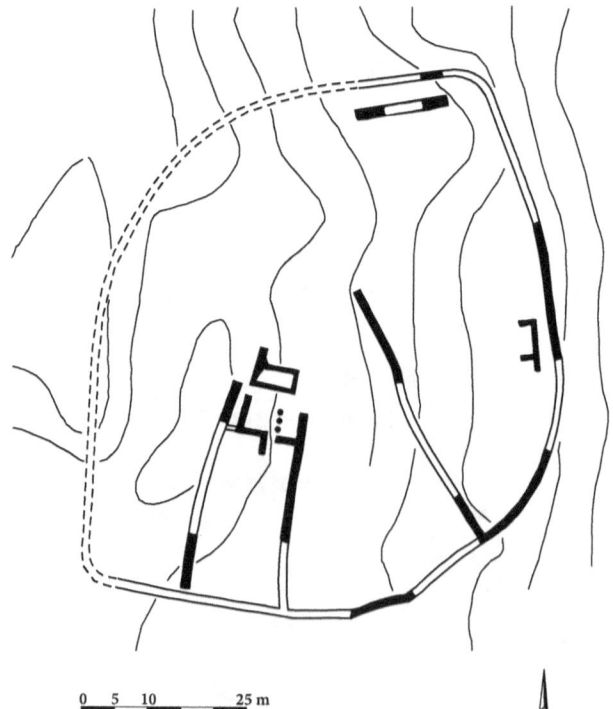

Figure 8. The farmstead at Bēt Ǧala.

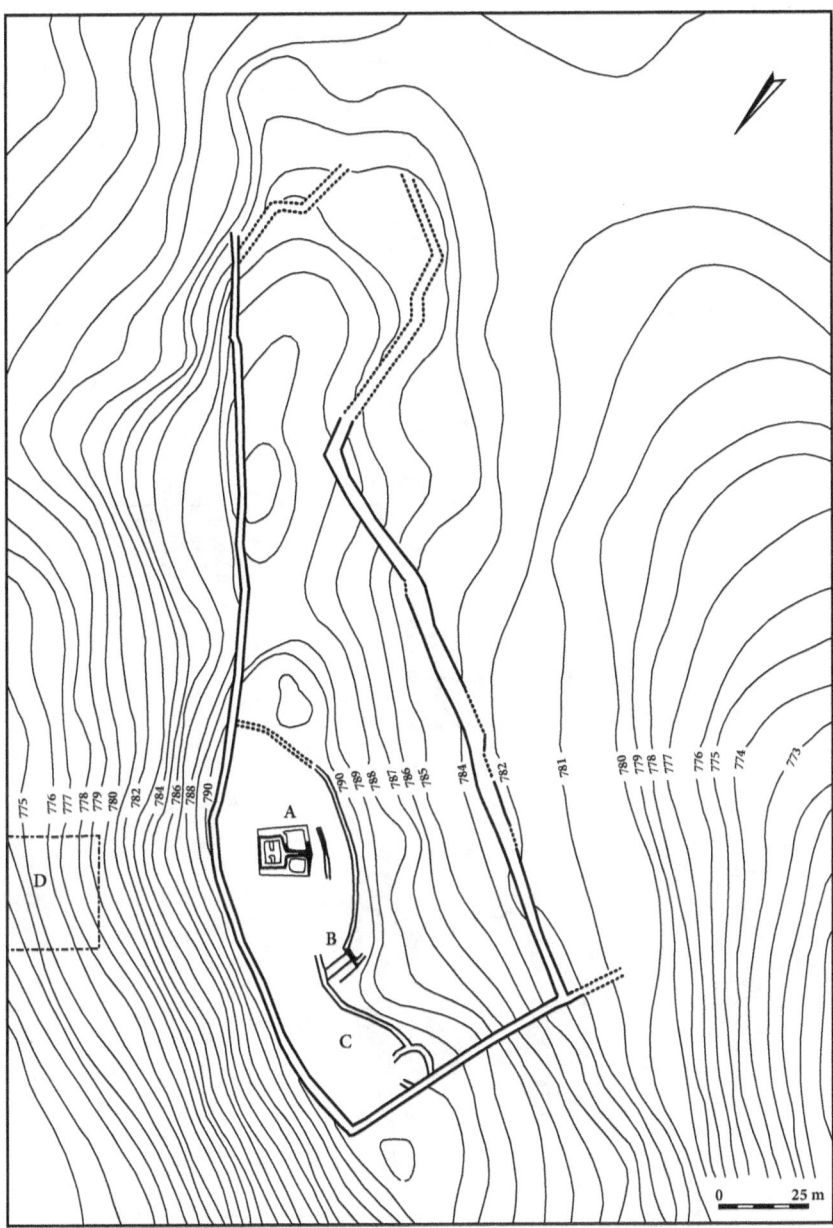

Figure 9. The farmstead on Ebal.

94   THE EMERGENCE OF ISRAEL

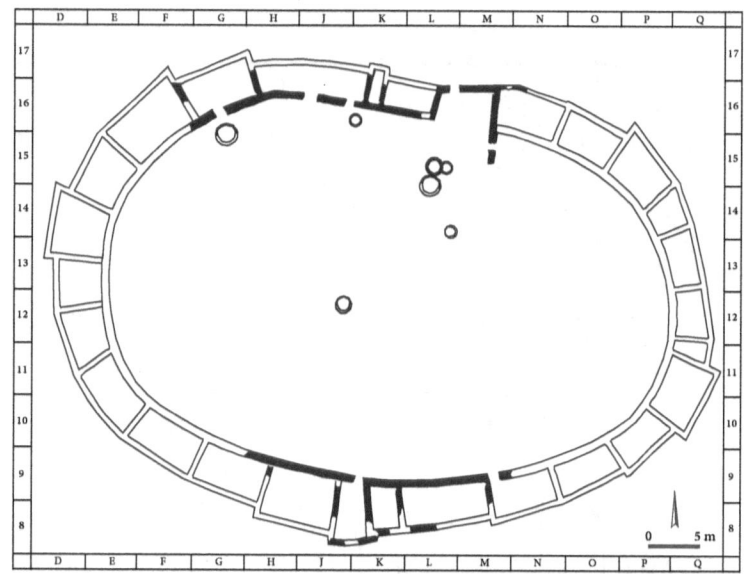

Figure 10. Plan of the circular settlement in 'Izbet Ṣarṭah, stratum III.

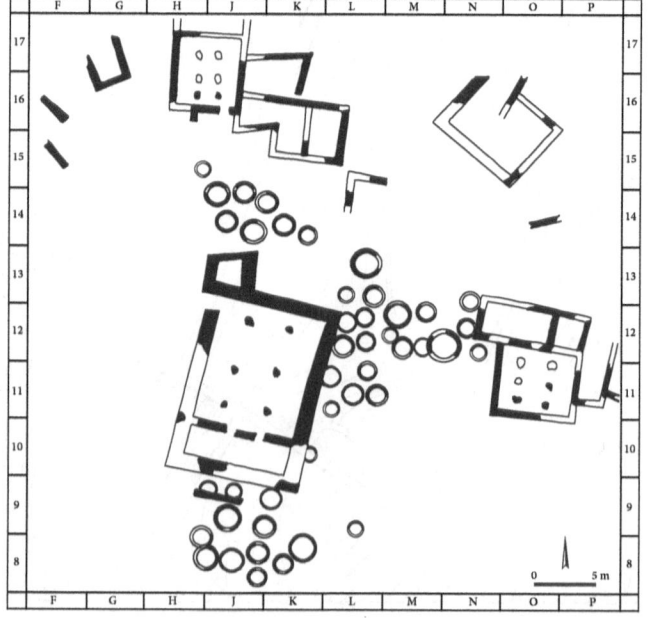

Figure 11. Plan of the settlement 'Izbet Ṣarṭah, stratum II.

HISTORICAL RECONSTRUCTION OF THE EPOCH

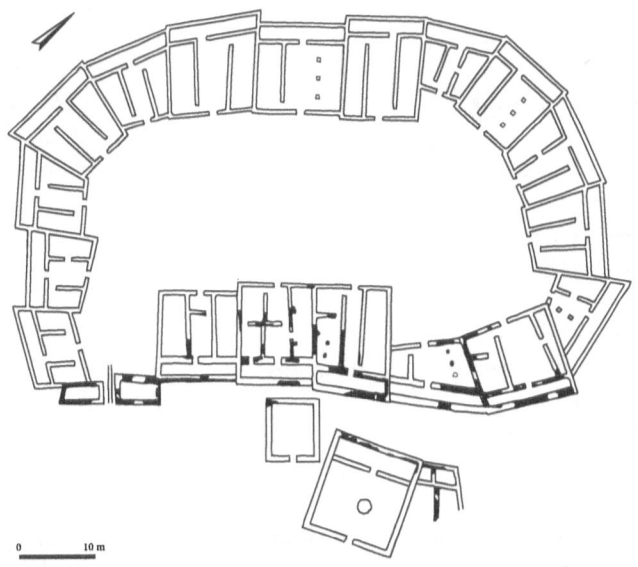

Figure 12. Reconstruction of the settlement on Tell es-Seba', stratum VII.

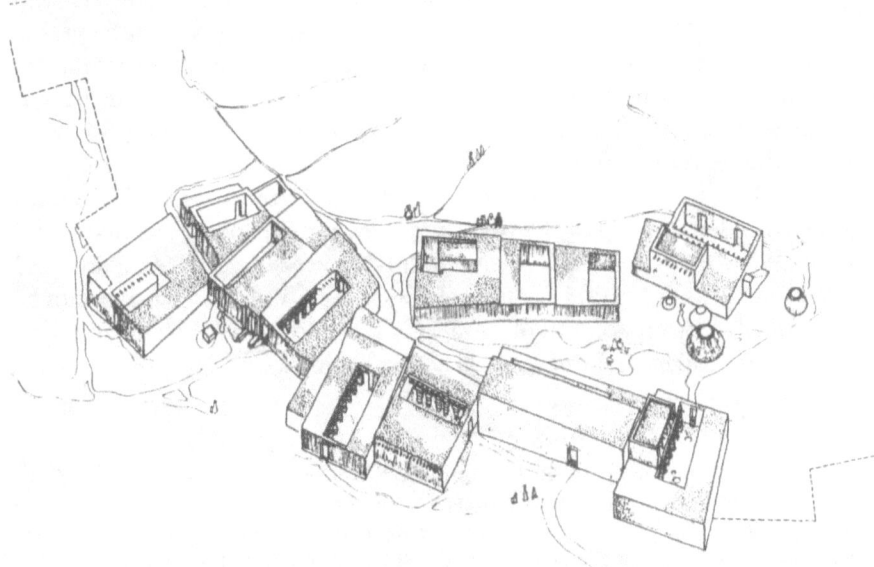

Figure 13. Reconstruction of the houses on the northern edge of the Early Iron Age settlement on Ḫirbet el-Mšāš, stratum II.

struction is noticeable, especially in the northern quarter. An alley seems to run between there and the development in the center, but not in a straight line. An irregular route is discernible also on the eastern edge of the central development. Public buildings are lacking; the one-time temple was divided by separating walls and was used as a residential house. Numerous silos, which served for stockpiling, attest the agricultural character of the settlement; bone finds indicate that small domesticated animals were kept, but the herds of sheep and goats were placed outside the residential settlement. The place was established around 1200 and existed until 1050, and two construction phases are to be distinguished. In the second phase, after 1150, room for a greater number of inhabitants was created by means of additions and partitions; the increased population also required an increase of silos. However, nothing indicates a change in the occupants. The reasons for abandoning the village are unknown.

In Ḫirbet Raddāne, immediately west of Ramallah, parts of a village were uncovered that existed about the same time as Ai.[7] In distinction to Ai, the houses are laid out very regularly according to the schema of the so-called three-room house, which generally have the opening to the underground cisterns located inside the house (fig. 6). Conversely, ovens for baking bread are mainly located outside the inhabited area in direct proximity to the outer walls.

The settlement from the end of the eleventh century at Ḫirbet ed-Dawwara in the mountains of Ephraim represents a closed layout.[8] The deteriorated condition permits no conclusive judgment concerning the development, but the principles of the design are clear. The peak of a mountain was surrounded by a wall, which is between 2.3 and 3.1 m wide and comprises an irregular oval of 90 x 70 m. The residential development follows along this wall, whereas the center remains largely open as the rock surface shows (fig. 7). In this central area, three cisterns hewn into the rock were detected. The building was founded directly in the rock, and the construction of a containment wall preceded the interior development; this proceeded very irregularly, and a gate layout is not proven. Despite the containment wall, the place cannot be spoken of as a city on account of its meager size and its lacking characteristic features. It is a village in hurdle construction having a circular wall.

---

7. Robert E. Cooley, "A Salvage Excavation at Raddana in Bireh," *BASOR* 201 (1971): 9–19; Israel Finkelstein, "Iron Age I Khirbet et-Tell and Khirbet Raddana: Methodological Lessons," in *"Up to the Gates of Ekron": Essays on the Archaeology and History of the Eastern Mediterranean in Honor of Seymour Gitin* (ed. Sidnie White Crawford; Jerusalem: W. F. Albright Institute of Archaeological Research, 2007), 107–13.

8. Israel Finkelstein, "Excavations at Khirbet ed-Dawwara: An Iron Age Site Northeast of Jerusalem," *Tel Aviv* 17 (1990): 163–208.

HISTORICAL RECONSTRUCTION OF THE EPOCH 97

Gīlō is an arbitrarily chosen name for a hamlet approximately 2 km north of Bēt Ǧala in the Judean mountains. Apart from buildings from the monarchic period, remains of an Early Iron Age development have been found.[9] In total there are three partially preserved houses and long segments of a lengthy containment wall, surrounding the largest areas (fig. 8). This wall probably served less for protection than for delimiting the settlement. Presumably the enclosure was also determined of necessity with respect to holding animals. The deteriorated condition offers little evidence of the buildings or of the surrounding wall. The meager number of buildings indicates that this is not a village settlement but rather an agricultural farmstead having adjacent buildings that were utilized for a few decades after 1200.

A comparable farmstead was discovered at Ebal, but the uncovered development was falsely interpreted by the excavators as a cultic site.[10] There are several different buildings in an area enclosed by several containment walls (fig. 9). Additional smaller adjacent buildings show the agricultural use. For the entire complex, three phases of activity can be differentiated dating to the first half of the twelfth century, but their establishment at the end of the thirteenth century is not ruled out. In any case, the farmstead was already abandoned in the middle of the twelfth century. The location at the summit of Ebal is not surprising insofar as the agricultural use of the mountain's slope is explained by the layout of terraces.

The name ʻIzbet Ṣarṭah designates a hamlet at the eastern edge of Mount Ephraim at the elevation of Aphek.[11] A hamlet was established after 1200 in this previously unsettled place, which existed in three settlement sites up to the tenth century. From the oldest settlement, in stratum III, in each of two opposite places a series of broad-roomed houses were uncovered, which can complete an oval layout (fig. 10). The circular arrangement of rooms encloses a large open area in which several silos could be identified. The reconstruction of the village into an enclosed area is supported by the fact that similar layouts have been found in the Negeb; however, those first date to the tenth century and therefore may not be adduced as a concomitant parallel.[12] The organization into an enclosed oval is clearly functionally determined, since

---

9. Amihai Mazar, "Giloh: An Early Israelite Settlement Site near Jerusalem," *IEJ* 31 (1981): 1–36.

10. Adam Zertal, "An Early Iron Age Cultic Site on Mount Ebal," *Tel Aviv* 13–14 (1986–87): 105–65.

11. Finkelstein, *Archaeology of the Israelite Settlement*, 73–80.

12. See Rudolph Cohen, "The Iron Age Fortresses in the Central Negev," *BASOR* 236 (1979): 61–79; Zeʼev Herzog, "Enclosed Settlements in the Negeb and the Wilderness of Beer-Sheba," *BASOR* 251 (1983): 41–49.

it enabled the accommodation of animals as well as serving a certain protective function against attacks. Even if the defense capability were limited, it nevertheless ruled out a sudden intrusion. The similarity of this settlement form to the organization of Bedouin, whose tents were arranged around one place, does not require the conclusion that this settlement form was adopted from a nomadic form of life and is evidence of the transition from unsettled to settled. At most it can indicate that the animals could also be brought inside the settlement were it necessary. The layout seems more like a corral than a village.

Toward the end of the eleventh century, a new settlement having a completely different character was established in ʿIzbet Ṣarṭah stratum II (fig. 11). In addition to a series of houses with two rows of stone pillars, there were various buildings of different sizes. The largest of these houses measures 16 x 12 m and was further divided across the inside by a wall, resulting in a four-room house. In this house, the entrance is in a corner of the long side. Indeed, all the houses were roughly oriented from north to south, but no planning at all is discernible. In their vicinity there were numerous silos for stockpiling. The place was unfortified and may have existed for only two to three decades.

On Tell es-Sebaʿ a settlement began in the second half of the twelfth century and extended in unbroken succession until the end of the eighth century. The founding of the fortified city in stratum V precedes a total of four settlement sites, all of which have a village character but diverge from each other sharply with respect to layout.[13] The oldest settlement of stratum IX is limited to inhabited caves in the southeastern slope of the natural hills north of Wādī es-Sebaʿ. The inhabited caves at least consisted of partially covered pits that could reach a diameter of up to 12 m. Presumably they were used over a long period of more than a hundred years by a group that was only present sporadically.

The construction of fixed houses first began in stratum VIII with a conclusive settlement of inhabitants. The transition to house construction followed in the middle of the eleventh century, but the remains are extremely sparse, since the settlement was largely destroyed with the construction of stratum VII. Only a single building can be completed with certainty; it shows, by the straight course of its wall, the construction form of the broad-roomed house with a courtyard in the front. A silo was found outside the northeastern corner of the house. Presumably a portion of the pits from stratum IX were also used. The newly established settlement in the last quarter of the eleventh

---

13. Zeʾev Herzog, *Beer-Sheba*, vol. 2, *The Early Iron Age Settlements* (Publications of the Institute of Archaeology 2; Tel Aviv: Tel Aviv University, Institute of Archaeology, 1984).

century in stratum VII, however, contains only meager remains. Although the reconstruction of individual housing units remains largely hypothetical, their juxtaposition in the form of a defensive belt seems assured (fig. 12). The entrance to the village was between two towerlike individual buildings. Additional houses were located outside the circle of houses.

After a destruction around 1000, the settlement on Tell es-Sebaʻ was reestablished in stratum VI, only to be replaced by a fortified city in 975 in stratum V. As in stratum VII, a number of houses were found all in a row, but they were not established according to a unified plan. The type of three-room house having a room separated by a stone pillar and a room on the short side is represented, but the remaining residential constructions reveal rather stark differences and no unified plan.

In Arad (Tell ʻArād) prior to the installation of a fortress by Solomon, a small village already existed during the eleventh century; its expanse, however, cannot be determined, since it was partially destroyed when another structure was subsequently built over it.[14] The remains are consequently sparse and essentially consist of a few partially preserved houses, some silos outside the residential area, and a large plastered plaza with a semicircular platform made from clay brick. The houses have partial broad rooms, and one is divided by a stone pillar, a construction that is typical of the era. The semicircle clay brick edifice was most likely a large silo. The village was apparently surrounded by a wall along the houses.

Tēl ʻIsdār is a hamlet approximately 20 km southeast of Beer-sheba, which was only sporadically settled in various eras.[15] The houses of the eleventh century from stratum III are arranged in a circle so that they enclose an open plaza having a circumference of approximately 120 m. Since the individual houses do not touch one another, there is not an enclosed circle, but the arrangement clearly had a protective function. The entire settlement consisted of more than twenty buildings. With one exception, the seven total excavated houses were extremely badly preserved; only for house 90 could the complete foundation be determined. It is a broad-roomed house measuring 12 x 6 m that was divided lengthwise into two dissimilarly wide parts by a row of five stone pillars and a wall. On the western small side, small rooms were divided crosswise by a wall. The room in front of the row of pillars was presumably not roofed and thus served as a courtyard. The settlement was probably inhabited for only a short time.

---

14. Zeʼev Herzog, "The Fortress Mound at Tel Arad: An Interim Report," *Tel Aviv* 29 (2002): 3–109.

15. Moshe Kochavi, "Excavations at Tel Esdar" (Hebrew), *Atiqot* 5 (1969): 14–48.

In the upper reaches of Wādī es-Sebaʿ lies the Early Iron Age settlement of Ḫirbet el-Mšāš, which surpasses in size all remaining villages of this era several times over.[16] For the time of its existence from the beginning of the twelfth century to the start of the tenth century, four settlement sites can be differentiated. (The further division of stratum II into two phases can be disregarded, since it only has slight structural alterations.) In the oldest site, stratum III B, only pits, an oven, and meager remains of a wall were found, which indicates an earlier sporadic presence by an unsettled population. The gradual construction of fixed houses began with stratum III A around the middle of the twelfth century. The only coherent construction complex that could be excavated shows right-angled houses having rooms on the long side and/or the small side of the courtyard as well as the use of stone pillars.

In stratum II place reaches its largest expanse, having an area of 3 hectares (7.5 acres). Although only a smaller part of the village was excavated, the development at the northern and southern edges provides good insight into its layout. In the north, several four-room houses stood next to each other in such a way that they were accessible from the eastern edge (fig. 13). The row of residential houses therefore creates no defensive belt, but instead the purpose was clearly for accessibility of fields and livestock outside the settlement. With a base area of about 120 m², the majority of houses were roughly the same size. Two of the buildings were broad-roomed houses, each one having a row of pillars but a different arrangement of rooms. In addition, a building was found that was identified as a structure that served for metallurgy. The house fronts are not in straight lines, so the streets frequently widened to small plazas. On the southern edge stands a building composed of two roughly square units. In the larger portion, different rooms were built, but the function of the layout is unclear. On the western side, a four-room house is attached that evinces a solid wall instead of two rows of pillars. North of this complex there was a fixed square building, which is very close typologically to the residential house in Amarna having a trinomial base configuration and central living room; it thus goes back to the Egyptian construction tradition.[17] About 30 m farther northwest there is an example of the courtyard house; it was divided by a stone pillar, and in one of

---

16. Volkmar Fritz and Aharon Kempinski, *Ergebnisse der Ausgrabungen auf der Ḫirbet el-Mšāš (Tēl Māśōś)* (ADPV 6; Wiesbaden: Harrassowitz, 1972–75, 1983), 7–113.

17. See Herbert Ricke, *Der Grundriß des Amarna-Wohnhauses* (Ausgrabungen der deutschen Orient-Gesellschaft in Tell el-Amarna 4; Leipzig: Hinrichs, 1932); Volkmar Fritz, "Die Verbreitung des sogenannten Amarna-Wohnhauses in Kanaan," *Damaszener Mitteilungen* 3 (1988): 27–34; see now also Kate Spence, "The Three-Dimensional Form of the Amarna House," *Journal of Egyptian Archaeology* 90 (2004): 123–52.

the western rooms there was possibly a worksite for metallurgy. The building process in stratum II is thus extremely complex. In addition to four-room houses and broad-roomed houses there were fortified kinds of buildings, the type of Egyptian residential houses, and examples of courtyard houses; the different arrangement of the quarter in the north and south is conspicuous.

The size of the place and the differentiated development distinguishes the large village on Ḫirbet el-Mšāš from the remaining settlements of the era, whose character was determined solely by the economic system of agriculture and animal breeding. The construction types show a social and also an economic differentiation, although the predominant portion of the inhabitants practiced agriculture. This discovery of an organized structure among the population, which is discernible from the building process, corresponds to long-range connections that are attested by the imported pottery; these comprised Egyptian, Philistine, and Phoenician wares as well as Midianite pottery from northwest Arabia. Contact therefore must have reached to northwest Arabia and to the Phoenician coastal cities. On account of the strong destruction by erosion, stratum I is very badly preserved, but some four-room houses are evident. Furthermore, a small fortress existed on the southern edge. Around 1000 the settlement was abandoned, probably owing to the newly established urbanization at the beginning of the monarchic period.

The Early Iron Age settlements show considerable differences in size and layout, but the common characteristic is nonetheless the lack of large buildings. There is no palace or temple here, which was the essential element of the Canaanite city. In addition, the villages are normally unfortified, although occasionally the houses on the periphery are laid out in the form of a defensive circle. Toward the end of the eleventh century in Ḫirbet ed-Dawwara and Arad stratum XII, the first walls appear, which surrounded the settlement for protection. Characteristic of the settlements is a relatively disordered type of construction as well as the layout of numerous silos and cisterns. The forms used in house construction are by no means unified, but houses constructed with pillars to block off the interior predominated. The street route is irregular, and occasionally a plaza could remain open within the settlement. The majority of the villages were established in previously unsettled places, but occasionally they also stood on sites of ruins that had long been abandoned.

All the settlements of the Early Iron Age have a clear agrarian character. The inhabitants cultivated the surrounding land and raised livestock. Conspicuous, however, is the variety of the settlement models, which cannot be explained by the number of inhabitants and economic structure alone. The settlements uncovered up to now can be divided into three groups corresponding to their layout:

Circular Villages

Characteristic of the circular village is the layout of the houses in a circle or oval, such that a plaza remains open in the center. As such, the houses can stand apart as at Tēl ʿIsdār or comprise an enclosed ring, as in ʿIzbet Ṣarṭah stratum III or perhaps at Tell es-Sebaʿ stratum VII. Presumably the settlement Arad stratum XII is also to be reconstructed in this form. The defense capability was improved by having the backs of the houses up against one another. The form of house used is of secondary significance, since all types were suitable for this arrangement. So then in ʿIzbet Ṣarṭah stratum III there were simply broad-roomed houses in a row with each other, whereas at Tell es-Sebaʿ stratum VII the four-room house predominated. The circular village corresponds to the form of Bedouin encampments, according to which the tents are grouped around an open plaza. In addition to the protective function, this arrangement has to do with the common use of an enclosed place, so the accommodation of herds is considered the most likely function.

Scattered Villages

Typical for this settlement form is the area's random building process consisting of individual buildings or building complexes of several houses. Between the individual units, streets of different widths and irregular plazas could remain open. The arrangement of the houses is completely unsystematic corresponding to the disordered development; the village remains open on the periphery. The settlements of Ai, in Ḫirbet Raddāne, ʿIzbet Ṣarṭah stratum II, Ḫirbet el-Mšāš stratum II, and at Tell es-Sebaʿ stratum VI are to be classified by this form. The inhabitants lived together in a relatively tight area and cultivated the fields located outside the village. Facilities for common use could have existed outside the place if need be.

Farmsteads

By farmsteads is to be understood individual buildings or groups of buildings that are surrounded by a wall in a more or less wide semicircle. This wall hardly serves for defense, but instead probably represents an enclosure for holding livestock. The farmstead can consist of several buildings that were established in the vicinity of the main building according to the economic necessities. The best example for one such farmstead is Gīlōh.

The layout of the settlements allows only very qualified conclusions as to the settlers. In some places such as Ḫirbet el-Mšāš or Tell es-Sebaʿ a phase preceded the construction of fixed houses, in which nomads possibly established a storehouse that was used for only a short time. Only two groups come under consideration as inhabitants of the new villages: either Canaanites from the former cities or unsettled people who had once lived in the vicinity of the cities. The assumption that there were immigrants is excluded, because the material culture clearly stands in the Canaanite tradition. It cannot be ruled out that the remainder of the city population withdrew to uninhabited regions to secure their survival. The majority of the villages explored thus far, though, were established and inhabited by previously unsettled population groups, but it is assumed that these peoples were accustomed to contact with the Canaanite city-states for a long period of time. The new settlers did not come into the land suddenly from the surrounding steppes and wilderness but rather had lived already as nomads for a part of the year in a certain dependence on and conflict with the city centers. The form of coexistence is most likely to be designated as symbiosis.

With the collapse of the Canaanite city-states during the twelfth century, the symbiosis also collapsed between various population groups having different ways of life. This resulted in inevitable alterations with respect to the cultivation of the necessary grain. Since there was no more supply of the foodstuff generated by agriculture on the part of the cities, the unsettled peoples inevitably and increasingly had to transition to agriculture. This necessity could have forced the seizure of fixed settlement places and the transition to building houses.

II.3.3. Economic System and Social Structure

Borowski, Oded. *Agriculture in Iron Age Israel* (Winona Lake, Ind.: Eisenbrauns, 1987). **Hopkins**, David C. *The Highlands of Canaan: Agricultural Life in the Early Iron Age* (Social World of Biblical Antiquity 3; Sheffield: Almond, 1985). **Thiel**, Winfried. *Die soziale Entwicklung Israels in vorstaatlicher Zeit* (Neukirchen-Vluyn: Neukirchener, 1980).

As opposed to the Late Bronze Age cities, the various villages of the Early Iron Age represent a new settlement form. To be sure, occasionally even in the old settlement hills there are establishments having the character of a village, but the majority of new foundations occurred in such regions that were hardly settled previously: the forest regions of the mountains and the steppes of the periphery. In conjunction with this new settlement, a fundamental restructuring of the preceding type of settlement ensued. In addition, some of the urban centers also continued to exist in reduced form in the valleys, given their good conditions for agriculture. The change in settlement form thus constituted less a change than an extension of the preceding economic system. Agriculture was now transferred to the regions of the land that had previously been used only sporadically or not at all. The foundations of the economy remained agriculture and livestock breeding.

Corresponding to the different geographic and climate conditions in the various regions, there were regional differences with respect to agriculture. Rain-fed agriculture was practiced exclusively; artificial watering was (yet) unknown. Grain was foundational for nourishment, and bread was baked from grain daily. The two cultivated types were barley and wheat, which are attested in the Early Iron Age settlement of Ḫirbet el-Mšāš. Barley is largely independent of climate and thrives in hot and dry climates as well as in cold regions; it produces the highest yield in loam or marlaceous loam but also grows well in loamy sand, whereas clay (or "heavy") soil is unsuitable. As such, it is the ideal type of grain for the southern Levant, since the conditions for its good growth are guaranteed everywhere. Barley (שערה) also serves as livestock fodder but is presumed to have served exclusively for human nutrition in the premonarchic era. The normal bread grain was wheat (חטה). As with barley, cultivated plants of wheat were developed already in the Neolithic Age (8000–4000 B.C.E.) in the wilderness areas. To the numerous types of wheat belong also spelt, emmer, and einkorn. The advantage of this type of grain is in the high nutrient content of 12 to 13 percent protein. It grows best in a temperate climate in wet and brittle soils. It is especially well suited for the Mediterranean climate, since wheat became rich in protein in the warm and dry summer. Like barley, wheat was ground with rubbing stones into the bread grains flour (קמח) and semolina (סלת).

Since precipitation was limited to the rainy season of October to April, the winter seed was the usual method of agriculture. Sowing took place in the rainy season from December to February, and the harvest began as early as April in the valleys, in May in the mountains, and ended in June at the latest. This rhythm for grain cultivation is attested already in the so-called farmer's calendar from Gezer, which is dated to the tenth century:

Two months to gather (the olives)
Two months for sowing
Two months for the late sowing
One month to cut the flax
One month for the grain harvest
One month for the (remaining) harvest and measuring
Two months for gathering grapes
One month for the fruit harvest

Although the inscription is dated to the tenth century, the circumstances had not changed from the previous eras. The agricultural year began in October/November, the actual time of sowing was in December and January, and the harvest was in May. Then in June the grain was threshed and measured outdoors; that is, the yield was determined in order to hand over taxes and to use the possible surplus for the purpose of trade. The grain harvest secured the food for the coming year, and a bad harvest led to famine (2 Sam 21; 1 Kgs 17:1; 2 Kgs 8:1). As such, not only could the absence of rain hinder growth, but the standing grain could also be stricken with diseases such as rust and blight (Deut 28:22; Amos 4:9; Hag 2:17) or be consumed by deer and pests. The effects of mice and locusts could be especially devastating (Amos 7:1, 2; Joel 1:2). If the harvest was annihilated, an adequate supply could not be secured in some other way. Under normal conditions, however, the yield depended on the composition of the soil. The soil weathering from Cenoman predominantly in the southern Levant was very fertile and enabled yields up to tenfold for sown wheat and fivefold for barley in the plains and valleys, but the results could fluctuate according to location and weather.

The fields were tilled by hand, which was complicated by stony ground as well as thorns and thistles (Gen 3:18). The only available mechanical tools were the hook plow to dig up the soil and the sickle to cut the stalks. For threshing, either animals were driven over the harvested goods or a threshing sled of oxen was used (Amos 1:3; Mic 4:13).

In addition to wheat and barley, fruit-bearing trees and grapevines, fig trees, pomegranates, and olives belong to the indigenous usable plants (Deut 8:8). There is evidence also of pistachio and almond trees and date palms. The olive trees assumed the highest rank (Judg 9:8–9), since the olive provides the oil necessary in all spheres of life. Viniculture also played a large role, because wine was a typical regional product (Gen 27:28, 37). Wine played an important part in daily life, and its use was by no means limited to feasts (Judg 9:13; Ps 104:15). The cultivation of lentils is also indicated. In addition, there were vegetables and spices, which were presumably cultivated in gardens. Besides the basic foodstuff of bread, there was also an abundance of fruits and vegetables. The individual family supplied itself with the produce obtained from their land. Surpluses could be bartered for consumer goods such as pottery wares or iron tools and jewelry. Although a some kind of barter is thus presupposed, this was nevertheless contained within close limits. There was no market; individual professions such as blacksmiths and potters were dependent on the supply by others, although it is not impossible that they carried on their own agriculture in small amounts.

Concerning domesticated animals, the ass used as a pack animal and for riding is to be distinguished the farm animals of cows, sheep, and goats. Cattle and small domesticated animals were kept in herds outside the villages, and they served primarily as suppliers of milk and the products produced from it. The slaughter of an animal occurred only in connection with an offering, which was performed as a communal meal (1 Sam 1). The sheep were shorn to obtain wool (1 Sam 25:2). The herds grazed apart from the tilled fields in open areas or in the forest regions and were tended by family members or herders. The ratio of cattle to sheep and goats was about 1:3, according to the analysis of bones found in the Early Iron Age settlements of Shiloh and Ḥirbet el-Mšāš. As opposed to agriculture, animal breeding was presumably of lesser significance for daily nourishment, which was based on grain and oil. To supply meat, animals were also hunted. Wild boars, the gazelle, and the Mesopotamian fallow deer are attested by bone findings. Seldom did a family have an ass as a riding or pack animal. Owning an ass could be considered a sign of a certain affluence, and the animal itself had a high value. The majority of the population traveled by foot and carried loads on their backs or on their heads.

Unlike animal breeding, the cultivation of one's own supply of vegetables clearly took priority. The short duration of the settlement of numerous villages may therefore suggest that the soil in the vicinity of the settlement was already exhausted after a few years, decreasing production and necessitating a transition to the previously unsettled regions. On the other hand, though, the number of settlements increased over the course of the eleventh century, which suggests a population growth that could have been constituted by adequate nutrition and good supply.

The excavated settlements give no information concerning the social structure. To be sure, a certain differentiation is presupposed for the settlement in Ḥirbet el-Mšāš stratum II, but precise details are not discernible. In addition, for the settlement of ʿIzbet Ṣarṭah stratum II, the different size of the houses (see fig. 11) suggests differentiated social positions of the inhabitants, but no more than that is discernible. It is merely to be assumed that, as in all agrarian societies, social position and economic strength were determined reciprocally. Thus, social rank was dependent on the amount of cultivated land. Therefore, it remains to conjecture that in addition to large groups of small farmers who tilled a share of land corresponding to the number of adult members of the family, there was also a small group of landowners who had command over a share of land so large that it could be cultivated only by means of additional employees.

The narrative in 1 Sam 25 indicates one such distinction in rank within village society. Although we do not find out about the size of Nabal's landed property, the three thousand sheep and one thousand goats belonging to him would have been impossible for the members of his family to herd and shear. The herders delegated to the task thus stand in a working relationship to Nabal, whose economic strength allowed him to produce a surplus in order to pay his workers. In addition to the herders, farmhands and housekeepers belong to the group of employees. The affluence of Nabal is evidenced not only in that his wife Abigail rides on an ass, but also in that she is accompanied by five maidens (1 Sam 25:42). The large landowner thus offers work to the unmarried sons and daughters of the small farmers, though keeping them in economic dependence. In particular, the freestanding farmsteads appear to have been inhabited by such large landowners, since they could not be cultivated by one family alone.

Yet social distinctions existed also in the villages, although the vast majority of the inhabitants stood in one rank. Most likely there was a two-class system, especially since slaves are not necessarily to be presumed for this era. The vast majority of the population, who subsisted all by themselves on their landed property, stands over against the few affluent families.

The division of society into an upper class having considerable landed property and farmers who owned a house and portion of land, as is constitutive for the monarchic period, was presumably already preset by the social order of the premonarchic period. However, the obligations connected with monarchic rule decisively intensified the division of society into two classes.[18]

The development of the society depicted in Josh 7:14–18 was projected back into the premonarchic period from the perspective of the monarchic period (cf. 1 Sam 10:19–21). An individual's affiliation presupposed the following structure: tribe (שבט), clan (משפחה), and father's house (בת אב). Accordingly, the superordinated unit of the tribe divides into individual clans, and these in turn comprised individual fathers' houses. The smallest group in the social framework was thus the house of the father, which corresponded to the family, which comprised the family's father, his wife or his wives, and the unmarried children but could also include other unmarried dependents, widows or divorcees. In any case, the core of the family was the parents and their children, and the solidarity of the group resulted from the close kinship bond. By all accounts the family was organized patrilineally and virilocally, descent and residence being oriented along the male line. Presumably the son established a new father's house after marriage, comprising immediate families (and not extended families). All the family members were subordinate to the *paterfamilias*, to whom belonged the decision-making authority in all matters. Women and children were persons having inferior rights and receiving protection and sustenance only by their familial affiliation. The families lived together

---

18. Albrecht Alt, "Der Anteil des Königtums an der sozialen Entwicklung in den Reichen Israel und Juda," in idem, *Kleine Schriften zur Geschichte des Volkes Israel* (3 vols.; Munich: Beck, 1959), 3:348–72; Frank Crüsemann, *Der Widerstand gegen das Königtum* (WMANT 49; Neukirchen-Vluyn: Neukirchener, 1978).

in residential and economic community. Each one of the individual housing units in the Early Iron Age, then, was presumably inhabited by one family.

Within the family a strict division of labor predominated. The household tasks, including the education of children, were incumbent upon the women, and the men saw to the work in the fields and went hunting. The children were also probably enlisted as herders, as is still common today in Near Eastern villages. Each family's own ground was cultivated and lay in the vicinity of the village. The next larger unit was the clan, a group connected by bloodline. The clan comprised several families related to one another, but a unified entity must not be presumed. A commitment to solidarity emerged from the kinship connection, which had to be preserved above all by exercising blood vengeance (cf. 2 Sam 14:7) and by observing the so-called levirate marriage (cf. Gen 38:6–10). The clan was thus both a social unit and a legal community.

It cannot be decided whether the clan was identical to the village community or several places belonged to a clan. Presumably there were both manifestations. For as a son established a new family upon marriage and must have owned both house and farmland, presumably the clans must have split off again and again in order to establish new settlements; thus, the individual villages and settlements were not too large. The modest dimensions of 0.5–1 hectare (1.25–2.5 acres) in the Early Iron Age settlements points directly to such separations, but the measure of growth cannot be calculated. A matter that concerned the clan in its totality was presumably discussed and decided by a committee of the families' fathers.

The tribe was the combination of several clans into an entity that must have met in action, especially in military expeditions (cf. §II.5.2). The amalgamation was supported by the assertion of the descent of all the relatives from one single tribal father. This conception of tracing back all the tribal members to one common ancestor was apparently first established after the land acquisition in order to unite the settlements of a certain region into one political entity so as to enable certain opportunities. "The tribal ancestors were nothing but personifications of the given tribal names" ("Die Stammesahnen sind nichts anderes als Personifikationen der vorgegebenen Stammesnamen" [Thiel, *Die soziale Entwicklung Israels*, 105]). Thus the individual tribes are more territorially than genealogically determined entities. Nothing is known concerning their wider organization; in military expeditions they were probably led by charismatic heroes, as they were depicted by Barak in Judg 5:12 as well as by Gideon (Judg 6–8) and Jephthah (Judg 10–13) in the narratives of the monarchic period and perhaps also by the so-called minor judges (Judg 10:1–5 and 12:8–15). In any case, on account of being sedentary, the function of a tribal leader—which is of vital significance for survival in nomadic societies—was superfluous.

Even though the social organization cannot be read immediately from the sources, this structure is nevertheless to be presumed for the premonarchic period. Families and clans are the naturally determined units by marriage. The tribe is an entity *sui generis* that is attested for premonarchic Israel by the enumeration in the Song of Deborah in Judg 5:14–18. The combination of clans into tribes suggests a cohesion of clans, which is determined not only by bloodline but also by other factors that can no longer be determined. Since the tribes of Judg 5:13 were named "the people of Yahweh," common Yahweh worship could have been a decisive factor for the constitution of the tribes. The combination of tribes into a political unit first ensued with the institution of the monarchy under Saul and David.

II.3.4. Material Culture

By material culture is understood the buildings and artifacts of human creation that were necessary to manage life and to control nature. To these belong the construction of houses and cultic sites, the use of pottery, as well as metal weapons and tools. These cultural products are the direct expression of learned capabilities, and they characterize the portrait of the era. Since they indicate characteristic features within a period, they can also be understood and valued as the expression of cultural creation.

To be sure, the Early Iron Age settlements differ considerably from one another in their layout; nevertheless, with respect to the construction forms, the distinctiveness of a few types can be established, which then continue into Iron Age II.[19]

Broad-roomed houses are found only occasionally, but by no means are they limited to the circular villages. The essential feature is the location of the entrance in the long side of the building. This type is essentially a one-room

---

19. François Braemer, *L'architecture domestique du Levant à l'âge du fer* (Prehistoire du Levant; Paris: Editions Recherche sur les civilisations, 1982); Volkmar Fritz, "Bestimmung und Herkunft des Pfeilerhauses in Israel," *ZDPV* 93 (1977): 30–45; Yigal Shiloh, "The Four Room House: Its Situation and Function in the Israelite City," *IEJ* 20 (1970): 180–90. See also Ehud Netzer, "Domestic Architecture in the Iron Age," in *The Architecture of Ancient Israel from the Prehistoric to the Persian Periods: In Memory of Immanuel (Munya) Dunayevsky* (ed. Aharon Kempinski; Jerusalem: Israel Exploration Society, 1992), 193–201; Shlomo Bunimovitz and Avraham Faust, "Building Identity: The Four-Room House and the Israelite Mind," in *Symbiosis, Symbolism, and the Power of the Past: Canaan, Ancient Israel, and Their Neighbors from the Late Bronze Age through Roman Palaestina* (ed. William G. Dever; Winona Lake, Ind.: Eisenbrauns, 2003), 411–23.

house, but it can also be divided by stone pillars lengthwise and furnished with small rooms divided by walls crosswise (fig. 14.1 and 2). The crucial question as to the use of roofing is not entirely clear for the broad-roomed house having a row of pillars, but the entrance through the broader part of the house probably led into a courtyard, since otherwise the house would lack light and ventilation for the rear rooms.

The pillared house is likewise rare; the right-angled building having the entrance in the small side is partitioned lengthwise by two rows of stone pillars. Concerning the three constructed long rooms, the middle one is wider than the two on the sides; presumably this portion was not roofed and was thus a courtyard.

The domestic architecture was defined by three-room and four-room houses (fig. 14.3 and 4), which frequently stood next to one another in a row. The four-room house denotes a building that, on the one hand, was divided by two rows of stone pillars lengthwise like the pillared house and, on the other hand, had a wider room on the back side that stretched over the entire width. The entrance was generally found in the broad room opposite the small side. The designation four-room house is misleading insofar as the central area was a courtyard that provided light and ventilation for the remaining rooms. The fundamental conception could be modified by fixtures and additions as well as by the construction, but retention of the base plan shows the firm standard of this type. With the three-room house, only a side room found in addition to the courtyard is to be seen as a minor variation of this construction form.

These three forms of domestic houses hang closely together typologically, but a clear derivation is unsuccessful as of yet. Despite having a courtyard, the Early Iron Age houses differ fundamentally from the Canaanite domestic house by use of stone pillars and by the organization of the rooms. The typical courtyard house of the Late Bronze Age had an approximately square courtyard preferably in the center of the building, and this courtyard could be surrounded by rooms on two, three, or four sides. The courtyard house was widely disseminated in the second millennium and thus does not come under consideration as a model for the house construction of the Early Iron Age. Nevertheless, in the Late Bronze Age cities, isolated buildings are also found that were partitioned by rows of stone pillars. This type of construction is attested above all by some houses in the Late Bronze Age city Timnah (Tell Batāši), but this form of room division remains an exception.[20] Even

---

20. George L. Kelm and Amihai Mazar, "Tel Batash (Timnah) Excavations: Second Preliminary Report (1981–1983)," *BASOR* Supplement 23 (1985): 93–120. See now Amihai

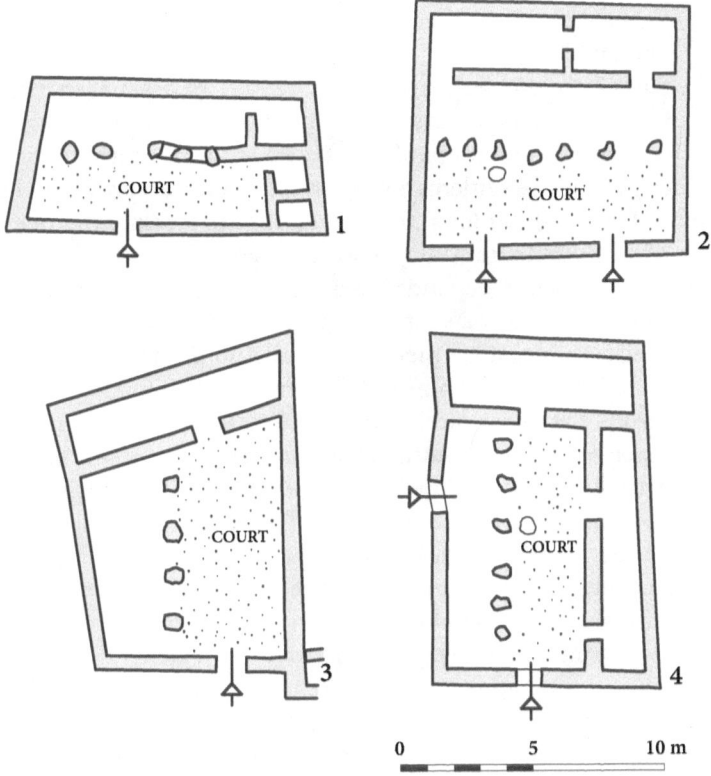

Figure 14. Construction forms of the Early Iron Age: 1 and 2. broad-roomed houses; 3. three-room house; 4. four-room house.

if the pillared type of construction was never used in the greater expanse of the Canaanite cities, this classification of right-angled buildings using rows of stone pillars, which also served to connect the roof, can go back to Canaanite culture. In any case, though, the complete distinctiveness of different construction types up to the four-room house first arose in the Early Iron Age, and the predominant use of this construction form is an indication of the new settlements. Thus, although there were predecessors for the pillared type of construction in the Late Bonze Age cities, the types of four-room houses and their derivations nevertheless developed only since the twelfth century. The

---

Mazar, *Timnah (Tel Batash). I, Stratigraphy and Architecture* (2 vols.; Qedem 37; Jerusalem: Institute of Archaeology, Hebrew University of Jerusalem, 1997).

construction forms in the different villages do not simply represent an adoption of the architecture of the Late Bronze Age, but instead definitely represent a development and innovation of the Early Iron Age.

In the Early Iron Age settlements no cultic sites have yet been discovered. This lack of altars and temples is striking and can perhaps suggest that within the settlements there were no public cultic exercises. Perhaps, though, there were shrines outside the settlements, but none have been proven definitively up to now (cf. §II.6.5). So long as the findings are lacking, the question of Early Iron Age cultic sites must be answered negatively.

The pottery evinces a dependence on Canaanite culture insofar as most forms were taken up and developed further.[21] At the same time, a decline in quality is discernible, since there is virtually no decoration of the vessels whatsoever. Concerning the bowls, the carinated bowls have disappeared completely from the repertoire, and only occasionally is a bent-rim still found. The open bowls were continued, as were the round bowls having a rim curved inwards. The chalice—bowls with a high base—developed a particular shaping of the rim with a hollow neck as well as a shaping of the base by gradation. The *kraters* diminish, but new is a particular form having numerous handles. The cooking pot remains unchanged with its oval bottom; however, they were furnished with handles, the opening was closed off further, and the overlapping rim was sharply emphasized and extended farther downward. New is the one-handled cooking pot with a rounded bottom, which nevertheless evinces no particular form of rim. The jug kept its ovoid body, but the mouth obtained a straight or slightly curved rim. The *pithos* shows a particular development that served for stockpiling and is practically a distinctive sign for the new settlements of the Iron Age. This *pithos* has a long, stretched-out body and is up to 1.5 m high; it comes to a point or semicircle at the base, the mouth evinces a sharply thickened rim, and the body has two or four handles. Its particular characteristic is a bulge under the neck, which came about by fitting the specially rotated mouth into the already constructed body by means of a smoothening rotation; the form has been given the name "collared-rim jar."[22] Regarding jugs, the double-conical forms return, and

---

21. Ruth Amiran, *Ancient Pottery of the Holy Land: From Its Beginnings in the Neolithic Period to the End of the Iron Age* (New Brunswick, N.J.: Rutgers University Press, 1969), 191–293.

22. M. M. Ibrahim, "The Collared Rim Jar of the Early Iron Age," in *Archaeology in the Levant: Essays for Kathleen Kenyon* (ed. Roger Moorey and Peter Parr; Warminster: Aris & Phillips, 1978), 116–26; Douglas L. Esse, "The Collared Rim Jar: Scholarly, Ideology and Ceramic Typology," *SJOT* 2 (1991): 99–116. See now also Eli Yannai, "The Origin and Distribution of the Collared-Rim Pithos and Krater: A Case of Conservative Pottery

those with ovoid bodies predominate. The strainer jugs are reinforced with a spout attached to the body; these were presumably used for brewing beer. With the juglets the point disappears, giving way to pieces with rounded bottoms. The two-handled water flask was likewise maintained, as was the lamp without a base stand. By contrast, the *pyxis* was adopted from Mycenaean culture, and the body was stretched farther. Despite the numerous differences in detail, the entire repertoire of the Late Bronze Age was continued; however, the cooking pot represents a separate development. In spite of certain regional differences, on the whole the pottery shows a dependence on the Late Bronze Age wares that is to be considered both direct adoption and separate continuation.

In addition, with respect to metallurgy the Canaanite tradition of handicraft was continued. The hoard finds from Megiddo, Beth-shean, and from Tell es-Saʿīdīye in the Jordan Valley nevertheless stem from the city centers in which the continuation of the Canaanite population is presumed.[23] But tools and weapons were also produced in the new settlements of the Early Iron Age. In addition to the garment clasps, knives, axes, and arrowheads and spear points were cast out of bronze—an alloy of copper and tin. The raw metal probably came from the repositories in Fēnān on the eastern edge of the Arabah. In this old mining region, the smelting of copper ore resumed during the Early Iron Age, after the long-distance trade of metals came to a halt with the collapse of the Late Bronze Age city culture.[24]

Production in the Ancient Near East from the Fourth to the First Millennium BCE," in *"I Will Speak the Riddles of Ancient Times": Archaeological and Historical Studies in Honor of Amihai Mazar on the Occasion of His Sixtieth Birthday* (ed: Aren M. Maeir and Pierre de Miroschedji; 2 vols.; Winona Lake, Ind.: Eisenbrauns, 2006): 1:89–112; Ann E. Killebrew, "The Collared Pithos in Context: A Typological, Technological, and Functional Reassessment," in *Studies in the Archaeology of Israel and Neighboring Lands: In Memory of Douglas L. Esse* (ed. Samuel R. Wolff; SAOC 59/ASOR Books 5; Chicago: Oriental Institute of the University of Chicago; Atlanta: ASOR, 2001), 377–98; Avner Raban, "Standardized Collared-Rim Pithoi and Short-Lived Settlements," in *Studies in the Archaeology of Israel and Neighboring Lands: In Memory of Douglas L. Esse* (ed. Samuel R. Wolff; SAOC 59/ASOR Books 5; Chicago: Oriental Institute of the University of Chicago; Atlanta: ASOR, 2001), 493–518.

23. Ora Negbi, "The Continuity of the Canaanite Bronzework of the Late Bronze Age into the Early Iron Age," *Tel Aviv* 1 (1974): 159–72.

24. Andreas Hauptmann, G. Weisgerber, and Ernst Axel Knauf, "Archäometallurgische und bergbauarchäologische Untersuchungen im Gebiet von Fenan, Wadi Arabah (Jordanien)," *Der Anschnitt* 37 (1985): 163–95; Volkmar Fritz, "Vorbericht über die Grabungen in *Barqā el-Hetīye* im Gebit von *Fēnān, Wādī el-ʿAraba* (Jordanien) 1990," *ZDPV* 110 (1994): 125–50. See now also Thomas E. Levy et al., "High-Precision Radiocarbon Dating

The use of iron is an innovation.[25] Although bronze was by no means completely supplanted, it did come to a gradual replacement that reached its high point in the tenth century. The origin of the new technology is still undetermined. To be sure, iron was long known in the form of meteorites, but on account of its high melting point it could not be processed. The slow advance of iron was made possible by the development of tempering. The early production of steel emerged through forging in connection with heating by charcoal fire. The amalgamation of the blazing metals by charcoal led to the necessary hardness of iron. Its greater firmness as opposed to bronze ensured sharper cutting surfaces of knives and sickles and an increased hardness for agricultural and stone masonry equipment. Iron found usefulness also for weapons and tools that required the two properties of a sharp blade and high resilience. Even if iron could never entirely replace bronze, since it was not suitable for casting, its use nevertheless signified a technological advance that was in no way limited to the new villages.

On the whole, the material culture of the Early Iron Age gives a complex picture. On the one hand, the adoption of numerous cultural goods such as pottery shows a close dependence on Canaanite culture. On the other hand, the numerous innovations are incalculable. In addition to the new settlement form, the departure from the courtyard house and the use of further developed forms of pillared houses as well as the use of iron belong to these independent developments. Despite the adoption of individual elements, the culture of the Early Iron Age is not simply a continuation of Canaanite predecessors. Nevertheless, the material legacy of the new settlements is inconceivable without a certain dependence on and orientation toward the Canaanite cities and their successive establishments. With all originality, an intensive contact of two population groups over a certain period is to be presumed. As such, this connection is considered to have taken place up until the first half of the twelfth century.

---

and Historical Biblical Archaeology in Southern Jordan," *Proceedings of the National Academy of Sciences* 105 (2008): 16460–65.

25. Theodore A. Wertime and James D. Muhly, eds., *The Coming of the Age of Iron* (New Haven: Yale University Press, 1980); Tamara Stech-Wheeler, James D. Muhly, K. R. Maxwell-Hyslop, and R. Maddin, "Iron at Taanach and Early Iron Metallurgy in the Eastern Mediterranean," *AJA* 85 (1981): 245–68; Jane C. Waldbaum, *From Bronze to Iron: The Transition from the Bronze Age to the Iron Age in the Eastern Mediterranean* (SMA 54; Göteborg: Aström, 1978).

HISTORICAL RECONSTRUCTION OF THE EPOCH   115

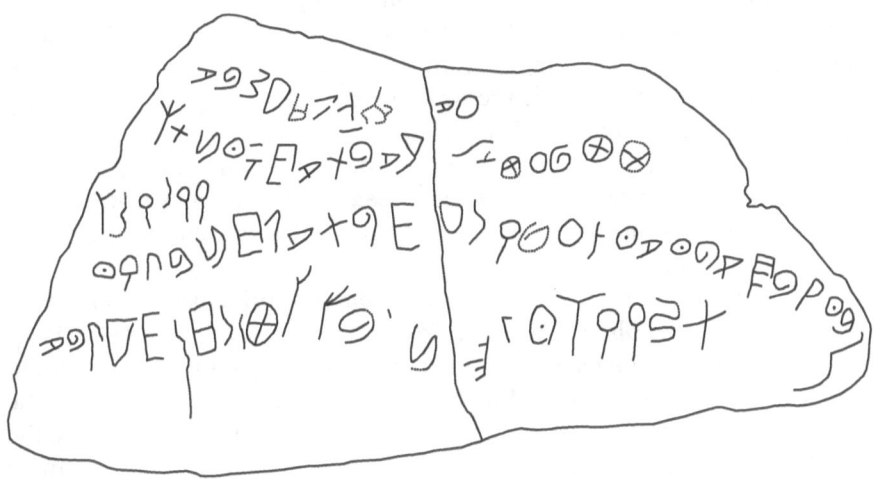

Figure 15. The ostracon from 'Izbet Ṣarṭah.

II.3.5. Alphabetic Script

Cross, Frank Moore. "Early Alphabetic Scripts," in *Symposia Celebrating the Seventy-Fifth Anniversary of the Founding of the American Schools of Oriental Research (1900–1975)* (ed. Frank Moore Cross; Cambridge, Mass.: ASOR, 1979), 97–123. **Cross**. "Newly Found Inscriptions in Old Canaanite and Early Phoenician Scripts," *BASOR* 238 (1980): 1–20. **Demsky**, Aaron. "A Proto-Canaanite Abecedary Dating from the Period of the Judges and Its Implications for the History of the Alphabet," *Tel Aviv* 4 (1977): 14–27. **Naveh**, Joseph. *Early History of the Alphabet: An Introduction to West Semitic Epigraphy and Palaeography* (2nd ed.; Jerusalem: Magnes, 1987). **Sass**, Benjamin. *Studia Alphabetica: On the Origin and Early History of the Northwest Semitic, South Semitic, and Greek Alphabets* (OBO 102; Göttingen: Vandenhoeck & Ruprecht, 1991). See now also: **Sass**, Benjamin. *The Alphabet at the Turn of the Millennium: The West Semitic Alphabet ca. 1150–850 BCE; the Antiquity of the Arabian, Greek and Phrygian Alphabets* (Tel Aviv, Occasional Publications 4; Tel Aviv: Emery and Claire Yass Publications in Archaeology, 2005).

Apart from some written finds from Egypt, inscriptions in this era are completely lacking. Nevertheless, the single and unique ostracon so far from 'Izbet Ṣarṭah attests that the alphabetic script was already fully developed in the eleventh century (fig. 15). The writing exercise evinces five lines carved on a potsherd: the first represents the letters of the alphabet except for *mem* in the sequence common in Hebrew up until today, and only ʿayin and pe are transposed with one another. The letters were written by an unskilled hand from left to right and stand in the tradition of the so-called proto-Canaanite script. Given the deficiency of the find, the development of this alphabetic script is still not completely explained, but it probably originated in the southern Levant. With alphabetic script, a new system of writing developed; based on the limited number of signs, its increased simplicity proved superior to syllabic cuneiform and Egyptian hieroglyphs, and alphabetic script gained general acceptance in the first millennium.

The alphabetic script depends on the acrophonic principle—that is, every sign reproduces the phoneme of the first letter of the depicted object. With this type of writing, the register of signs, which amounted to several hundred in a syllabic script, was reduced to the number of phonemes existing in the language. The Proto-Sinaitic and Proto-Canaanite inscriptions comprise the oldest attestation for this letter script. In the Proto-Sinaitic inscriptions there are short carvings in stone from Ṣerabit el-Ḫādem at Sinai, which stem from foreign workers in the Egyptian mines. The reading, register of signs, and date are extremely contested, but they hardly go back prior to the eighteenth century.[26] The pictographic form of the signs and the lack of vowels allow the conjecture that the development of this system is analogous to the Egyptian hieroglyphs.

The Proto-Canaanite inscriptions are likewise only short dedications or statements of names that are found on various objects; the oldest ones stem from the sixteenth century. Although the number of inscriptional finds increases sharply up to the end of the Late Bronze Age, longer texts in this script are nevertheless lacking thus far. (The texts of the thirteenth century from Ugarit were written in an alphabetic cuneiform.) The Proto-Canaanite letter script was apparently in use only locally in the second millennium and gained acceptance against the high cultural writing system only in the first millennium. Already before 1000 the alphabet having twenty-two letters was adopted from the Phoenicians into Hebrew and Aramaic, but the forms of the letters underwent certain changes despite great inertia. By the eighth century at the latest, the Phoenicians had mediated this Semitic alphabet to the Greeks; by adapting some signs for the vowels and adding a few letters as supplements for their existing sounds, the Greeks made a comprehensive system containing every sound.[27] With the adoption of the Proto-Canaanite alphabet and its continua-

---

26. William Foxwell Albright, *The Proto-Sinaitic Inscriptions and Their Decipherment* (Cambridge, Mass.: Harvard University Press, 1966).

27. Alfred Heubeck, *Schrift* (Archaeologia Homerica 3, Kapitel 10; Göttingen: Vandenhoeck & Ruprecht, 1979).

tion into ancient Hebrew writing, the foundations for the later development of intellectual culture were laid in the Early Iron Age.

II.4. THE LAND ACQUISITION

Forschungsberichte: **Herrmann**, Siegfried. "Israels Frühgeschichte im Spannungsfeld neuer Hypothesen: Studien zur Ethnogenese 2," *Abhandlungen der Rheinisch-Westfälischen Akademie der Wissenschaften* 78 (1988): 43–95. **Otto**, Eckart. "Israels Wurzeln in Kanaan," *Theologische Revue* 85 (1989): 3–10. **Weippert**, Helga, and Manfred **Weippert**. "Die Vorgeschichte Israels im neuen Licht," *TRu* 56 (1991): 341–90. **Weippert**, Manfred. *The Settlement of the Israelite Tribes in Palestine: A Critical Survey of Recent Scholarly Debate* (SBT 2/21; Naperville, Ill.: Allenson, 1971).

Select Literature: **Aharoni**, Yohanan. "New Aspects of the Israelite Occupation in the North," in *Near Eastem Archaeology in the Twentieth Century: Essays in Honor of Nelson Glueck* (ed. James A. Sanders; Garden City, N.Y.: Doubleday, 1970), 254–65. **Ahlström**, Gösta W. "The Early Iron Age Settlers at *Ḥirbet el-Mšāš (Tēl Māśōś))*," *ZDPV* 100 (1984): 35–52. **Ahlström**. "The Origin of Israel in Palestine," *SJOT* 2 (1991): 19–34. **Albright**, William Foxwell. "The Israelite Conquest of Canaan in the Light of Archaeology," *BASOR* 74 (1939): 11–23. **Alt**, Albrecht. "The Settlement of the Israelites in Palestine," in *Essays on Old Testament History and Religion* (trans. Robert A. Wilson; Garden City, N.Y.: Doubleday, 1967), 173–222. **Alt**. "Erwägungen über die Landnahme der Israeliten in Palästina," in idem, *Kleine Schriften zur Geschichte des Volkes Israel* (3 vols.; Munich: Beck, 1953), 1:126–75. **Callaway**, Joseph A. "A New Perspective on the Hill Countty Settlement of Canaan in Iron Age I," in *Palestine in the Bronze and Iron Ages: Papers in Honour of Olga Tufnell* (ed. Jonathan N. Tubb; London: Institute of Archaeology, 1985), 31–49. **Chaney**, Marvin L. "Ancient Palestinian Peasant Movements and the Formation of Premonarchic Israel," in *Palestine in Transition: The Emergence of Ancient Israel* (ed. David Noel Freedman and David Frank Graf; Social World of Biblical Antiquity 2; Sheffield: Almond, 1983), 39–90. **Coote**, Robert B. "Early Israel," *SJOT* 2 (1991): 35–46. **Finkelstein**, Israel. *The Archaeology of the Israelite Settlement* (trans. David Saltz; Jerusalem: Israel Exploration Society, 1988). **Finkelstein**. "The Emergence of Early Israel: Anthropology, Environment and Archaeology," *JAOS* 110 (1990): 617–86. **Fritz**, Volkmar. "Die Landnahme der israelitischen Stämme in Kanaan," *ZDPV* 106 (1990): 63–77. **Geus**, C. H. J. de. *The Tribes of Israel: An Investigation into Some of the Presuppositions of Martin Noth's Amphictyony Hypothesis* (SSN 18; Assen: Van Gorcum, 1976). **Gottwald**, Norman K. *The Tribes of Yahweh: A Sociology of the Religion of Liberated Israel, 1250–1050 B.C.E.* (Maryknoll, N.Y.: Orbis Books, 1979). **Halpern**, Baruch. *The Emergence of Israel in Canaan* (SBLMS 29; Chico, Calif.: Scholars Press, 1983). **Hauser**, Alan J. "Israel's Conquest of Palestine: A Peasants' Rebellion?" *JSOT* 7 (1978): 2–19. **Herrmann**, Siegfried. "Basic Factors of Israelite Settlement in Canaan," in *Biblical Archaeology Today: Proceedings of the International Congress on Biblical Archaeology, Jerusalem, 1984* (ed. A. Biran; Jerusalem: Israel

Exploration Society,1985), 47–53. **Isserlin**, Benedikt S.J. "The Israelite Conquest of Canaan: A Comparative View of the Arguments Applicable," *PEQ* 115 (1983): 85–94. **Lapp**, Paul W. "The Conquest of Palestine in the Light of Archaeology," *Concordia Theological Monthly* 38 (1967): 283–300. **Lemche**, Niels Peter. *Early Israel: Anthropological and Historical Studies on the Israelite Society before the Monarchy* (VTSup 37; trans. Frederick H. Cryer; Leiden: Brill, 1985). **Malamat**, Abraham."Israelite Conduct of War in the Conquest of Canaan," in *Symposia Celebrating the Seventy-fifth Anniversary of the Founding of the American Schools of Oriental Research (1900–1975)* (ed. Frank Moore Cross; Cambridge, Mass.: ASOR, 1979), 35–56. **Mazar**, Amihai. "The Israelite Settlement in Canaan in the Light of Archaeological Excavations," in Biran, *Biblical Archaeology Today*, 61–70. **Mazar**, Benjamin. "The Early Israelite Settlement in the Hill Country," in *The Early Biblical Period: Historical Studies* (ed. Shmuel Aḥituv and Baruch A. Levine; trans. Ruth and Elisheva Rigbi; Jerusalem: Israel Exploration Society: 1986), 35–48. **Mendenhall**, George E. "The Hebrew Conquest of Palestine," *BA* 25 (1962): 66–87 = *Biblical Archaeology Reader III* (1970), 100–120. **Miller**, J. Maxwell. "Archaeology and the Israelite Conquest of Canaan: Some Methodological Observations," *PEQ* 109 (1977): 87–93. **Noth**, Martin. "Grundsätzliches zur Deutung archäologischer Befunde auf dem Boden Palästinas," *ABLAK* 1 (1971): 3–16. **Noth**. "Der Beitrag der Archäologie zur Geschichte Israels," *ABLAK* I (1971): 34–51. **Rowton**, Michael B. "The Topological Factor of the Hapiru Problem," *Anatolian Studies* 16 (1965): 375–87. **Rowton**. "Urban Autonomy in a Nomadic Environment," *JNES* 32 (1973): 201–15. **Rowton**. "Enclosed Nomadism," *Journal of the Economic and Social History of the Orient* 17 (1974): 1–30. **Rowton**. "Dimorphic Structure and Topology," *Oriens Antiquus* 15 (1976): 17–31. **Rowton**. "Dimorphic Structure and the Parasocial Element," *JNES* 36 (1977): 181–98. **Schoors**, Antoon. "The Israelite Conquest: Textual Evidence in the Archaeological Argument," in *The Land of Israel: Cross-roads of Civilizations* (OLA 19; ed. E. Lipiński; 1985), 77–92. **Shiloh**, Yigal. "Elements in the Development of Town Planning in the Israelite City," *IEJ* 28 (1978): 36–51. **Shiloh**. "The Casemate Wall, the Four Room House, and Early Planning in the Israelite City," *BASOR* 268 (1987): 3–16. **Stager**, Lawrence E. "Merenptah, Israel and Sea Peoples: New Light on an Old Relief," *Eretz Israel* 18 (1985): 50–64. **Stager**. "The Archaeology of the Family in Ancient Israel," *BASOR* 260 (1985): 1–35. **Thiel**, Winfried. "Vom revolutionären zum evolutionären Israel," *TLZ* 113 (1988): 313–40. **Vaux**, Roland de. "The Settlement of the Israelites in Southern Palestine and the Origins of the Tribe of Judah," in *Translating and Understanding the Old Testament: Essays in Honor of Herbert Gordon May* (ed. Harry Thomas Frank and William L. Reed; Nashville: Abingdon, 1970), 108–34. **Vieweger**, Dieter. "Überlegungen zur Landnahme israelitischer Stämme unter besonderer Berücksichtigung der galiläischen Berglandgebiete," *ZDPV* 109 (1993): 20–36. **Weinfeld**, Moshe. "The Pattern of the Israelite Settlement in Canaan," in *Congress Volume: Jerusalem 1986* (ed. J. A. Emerton; VTSup 40; Leiden: Brill, 1988), 270–83. **Weinfeld**. "Historical Facts behind the Israelite Settlement Pattern," *VT* 38 (1988): 324–56. **Weippert**, Manfred. "The Israelite 'Conquest' and the Evidence from Transjordan," in Cross, *Symposia*, 15–34. **Yadin**, Yigael. "The Transition from a Seminomadic to a Sedentary Society in the Twelfth Century BCE," in Cross, *Symposia*, 57–68. **Yeivin**, Shmuel. *The Israelite Conquest of Canaan* (Uitgaven van het

Nederlands Historisch-Archaeologisch Instituut te Istanbul 27; Istanbul: Nederlands Historisch-Archaeologisch Instituut in het Nabije Oosten, 1971).

See now also: **Ben-Tor**, Amnon. "The Fall of Canaanite Hazor: The 'Who' and 'When' Questions," in *Mediterranean Peoples in Transition: Thirteenth to Early Tenth Centuries BCE* (ed. Symour Gitin, Amihai Mazar, and Ephraim Stern; Jerusalem: Israel Exploration Society, 1998), 456–67. **Dever**, William G. *Who Were the Early Israelites, and Where Did They Come From?* (Grand Rapids: Eerdmans, 2003). **Finkelstein**, Israel. "The Great Transformation: The 'Conquest' of the Highlands Frontiers and the Rise of the Territorial States," in *The Archaeology of Society in the Holy Land* (ed. Thomas E. Levy; New York: Facts on File, 1995), 349–65. **Finkelstein**. "Ethnicity and Origin of the Iron I Settlers in the Highlands of Canaan: Can the Real Israel Stand Up?" *BA* 59 (1996): 198–212. **Faust**, Avraham. *Israel's Ethnogenesis: Settlement, Interaction, Expansion and Resistance* (Approaches to Anthropological Archaeology; London: Equinox, 2006). **Herzog**, Ze'ev. "Beersheba Valley Archaeology and Its Implications for the Biblical Record," in *Congress Volume: Leiden, 2004* (ed. André Lemaire; VTSup 109; Leiden: Brill, 2006): 81–102. **Killebrew**, Ann E. "The Emergence of Ancient Israel: The Social Boundaries of a 'Mixed Multitude' in Canaan," in *"I Will Speak the Riddles of Ancient Times": Archaeological and Historical Studies in Honor of Amihai Mazar on the Occasion of His Sixtieth Birthday* (ed: Aren M. Maeir and Pierre de Miroschedji; 2 vols.; Winona Lake, Ind.: Eisenbrauns, 2006), 2:555–72. **Nakhai**, Beth Alpert. "Israel on the Horizon: The Iron I Settlement of the Galilee," in *The Near East in the Southwest: Essays in Honor of William G. Dever* (ed. Beth Alpert Nakhai; AASOR 58; Boston: ASOR, 2003), 131–51.

The book of Joshua depicted the land acquisition as a historical-theological construction. As such, the capture of the land was an event of salvation-historical significance: the entire land west of the Jordan was conquered by all the collective tribes under the leadership of Joshua. Part of the land acquisition included the expulsion of the Canaanites and the allocation of the land to the Israelite tribes. The military events are set against the background of Deuteronomistic theology, which makes compulsory from the outset an eradication of the preceding inhabitants designated as Canaanites in order to ward off any danger of *cōnūbium* with them from the outset (cf. Deut 7:1–6). According to this theological premise, the land acquisition was not only a conquering expedition but was also connected with an annihilation strategy in order to declare the land as the sole residence of the Israelite tribes. The land acquisition means taking possession of the land, leaving no other valid claim to it.

This concept was carried out in the book of Joshua by reverting to traditions corresponding to the monarchic period. The few adopted narratives about the conquest of Jericho (Josh 2) and the conquest of Ai (Josh 8) as well as about the demise of the kings in the cave of Makkedah (Josh 10:1–27) presuppose both the idea of military expulsion and also the historical entity of one Israel in the totality of all the tribes (cf. §II.2.2.1). Since the notion of a unified Israel participating in the land acquisition is constitutive for the narratives, which of course did not develop until the monarchic period, the land acquisition stories cannot reach back to the premonarchic period. The late date of the formation of the narratives of course makes it improbable that historical memories have been preserved in them or that that they reflect historical events. On the whole, the book of Joshua is to be designated as fiction on the basis of its intention and formation; it is thus useless as a historical source. A reconstruction of the expulsion, which led to the settlement of the land by the Israelite tribes, can thus at no point be supported by the book of Joshua.

How little the historical portrait agrees with reality shows in the cases of Jericho and Ai by comparing the literary tradition with the archaeological findings.[28] In Jericho a settlement break began in the fourteenth century that stretched to the twelfth century; the place was not settled in the period of the land acquisition and therefore also cannot have been explored and conquered. For Ai, every trace of a city is lacking during the second millennium. During the Early Bronze Age II (2950–2650) a city with strongly reinforced walls indeed existed on the mound of Ai, but that was already abandoned after 2650 B.C.E. As such, the place remained deserted until the establishment of an Early Iron Age village in the twelfth century. There was thus no city that could have been conquered by the Israelites in either Jericho or Ai. The report about the conquest in Josh 6 and 8 cannot refer to cities existing in the time of the land acquisition. This contradiction between the ascertainable facts and the alleged occurrences cannot be reconciled and eliminates the book of Joshua as a historical source. Since the biblical reconstruction of the early history of Israel is untenable, the historical picture of the era must be constructed another way.

II.4.1. Land Acquisition Theories

Methodologically, the result of critical analysis can deal with the occurrence of the land acquisition only according to what can be developed hypothet-

---

28. Cf. Arnulf Kuschke, "Hiwwiter in Ha-'Ai?" in *Wort und Geschichte: Festschrift für Karl Elliger zum 70. Geburtstag* (AOAT 18; Kevelaer: Butzon & Bercker, 1973), 115–19; Martin Noth, "Bethel und Ai," *ABLAK* 1 (1971): 210–28; Helga and Manfred Weippert, "Jericho in der Eisenzeit," *ZDPV* 92 (1976): 105–48; Joseph A. Callaway, "The Significance of the Iron Age Village at (Ai (Et-Tel)," in *Proceedings of the Fifth World Congress of Jewish Studies* (ed. Pinchas Peli; 4 vols.; Jerusalem: World Union of Jewish Studies, 1969), 1:56–61; Ziony Zevit, "The Problem of Ai: New Theory Rejects Battle as Described in Bible but Explains How Story Evolved," *BAR* 11.2 (1985): 58–69.

ically and represented by a model. The point of departure for such theory formation is thus, on the one hand, the given circumstances as they are represented based on archaeological research and, on the other hand, analogues to available, comparable occurrences in other times and other places. Scholars propose the following solutions for the land acquisition.

The Infiltration Model

The model was initially developed by Albrecht Alt and essentially determined the history of research in the German-speaking areas. The point of departure for this hypothesis is the conclusion that the historical picture of the book of Joshua does not stand up to critical examination. In particular, it contradicts the so-called negative list of property in Judg 1, which Alt saw as a historically reliable source. The recording of historical changes must therefore come from the ascertainable findings in the land. Thus, Alt based his historical development on two observations: (1) the historical territorial difference between the individual land areas, as they are discernible based on the settlement allocation; (2) the fluctuation of unsettled groups between the wilderness regions and the actual cultivated land, named "pasture rotation" (*Weidewechsel*) by Alt, a phenomenon that was attested in different centuries and continued into the modern era.

Assuming individual elements of the Israelite portrayal of history, Alt concluded that the Israelite tribes were originally nomads who bred livestock on the periphery. Since they were not in a position to attack the cities, they initially settled in the less-settled regions of the mountains and only afterward gained additional portions of land. Thus two phases for the settlement of the land were distinguished: the land acquisition and the land extension. The actual land acquisition was imagined as an absolutely peaceful process. At the same time, a change in the economic system was connected to the development of the settlement, since at that point agriculture was pursued in addition to breeding animals, which required staying the whole year in one place and constructing more fixed residence sites. According to Alt, the transition to agriculture practically compelled the task of pasture rotation and the continuance in the land, but Alt definitely considered intermediate stages and slow developments. "Thus the binding of the tribes to the obtained soil and thus the abandonment of the old homeland gradually result from the change in the economic system" ("So ergab sich ... aus der Veränderung der Wirtschaft allmählich die Bindung der Stämme an die gewonnene Scholle und damit der Verzicht auf die alte Heimat" [Alt, *Kleine Schriften*, 1:149]). The land acquisition was thus a process of transition from the nomadic life of livestock breeding to settled rural activity that was carried out over a long period of time, and the altered economic system involved the change in the way of life.

Further reasons are not given for this rearrangement from pasture rotation to inhabiting the cultivated land and thus from nomadism to a sedentary life. "In the majority of cases, the tribes themselves would have made alterations in their location throughout the year, and so they began to remain continually in the regions of the cultivated land previously only sought out in the summer, providing the necessary sustenance for their herds even in winter" ("In der Mehrzahl der Fälle werden es Veränderungen in der Lage der Stämme selbst gewesen sein, die sie dahin brachten, das ganze Jahr über und damit dauernd in den vorher nur während des Sommers aufgesuchten Gebieten des Kulturlandes zu bleiben, die ihren Herden ja auch im Winter die nötige Nahrung boten" [Alt, *Kleine Schriften*, 1:147]). After the initial settlement took place, the settlement region expanded to a second phase, where it also brought military confrontations with the cities who sought to reassert their spheres of influence.

Alt thus developed his thesis from the territorial-historical facts and in analogy to the transhumance of nomads who bred domesticated animals. The settling down was explained as a transition to agriculture, since this economic system necessitated ongoing residence in the area of useful fields. The groups that became settled came from the wilderness and the steppes bordering on the cultivated land, and pasture rotation presupposed a relative migration between both habitats. The process proceeded peacefully, and the acquisition of more fixed residences was established by the turn to agriculture. The Israelite tribes thus appear as having immigrated to the cultivated land and there having become settled nomads, who fundamentally and definitively abandoned their previous way of life. On the whole, a very compelling but nonetheless simplified picture of the land acquisition results.

After this peacefully proceeding first phase of the land acquisition, a second phase then began with the enlargement of the settlement areas by means of military actions. These conquests of additional regions were not endeavors by the entirety of the Israelites but instead are considered to be military expeditions by individual tribes. These were restricted locally, since they were only ever directed against individual city rulers. Alt's portrayal of the conquest of the Canaanite cities was oriented by the so-called negative property list in Judg 1, in which the various cities were listed that were not conquered by the tribes (though cf. §I.2.3.3). In any case, regardless of the peaceful infiltration in the beginning phase, Alt accounted for military confrontations in the wider course of the land acquisition.

The Revolution Model

George E. Mendenhall designed a completely different portrayal of the events that led to the constitution of a premonarchic Israel. The point of departure is the conclusion that the way of life of the settled farmers and that of the nomadic herders do not necessarily stand in contradiction. Both groups can exist not only in close economic connection with each other but can also belong to one social unit related by family ties. In the second millennium, the social distinction was not between settlers and nomads but between city and land. On this premise, the *ḫapiru* of the cuneiform sources appear as a social class outside of the cities who inhabited the open land and stood in conflict or even threatening enmity against the city-dwellers. On the premise that the later Hebrews are identical with the *ḫapiru*, the land acquisition is represented as the opposition of these groups against the city rulers. What is crucial is the social process that occurred along with it and turned into a political process: "the withdrawal, not physically and geographically, but politically and subjectively, of large population groups from any obligation to the existing political regimes" (Mendenhall, "Hebrew Conquest," 107). The land acquisition is thus turned into a revolt of underprivileged classes of ancient city-dwellers against the cities and their ruling area. The new unity of these groups consolidated in the land outside the cities was understood as "tribes," and their binding power was a new religious conviction.

According to Mendenhall, the land acquisition was a local development that had its origin in the cities and finally led to a new settlement structure, a new social structure, and a new religion. The new settlements were established by the *ḫapiru*, after these ancient city-dwellers abandoned their loyalty to the city-state and its ruler and congregated into a newly structured society of independent tribes.

The two theories stand irreconcilably opposed, since they come from different sociopolitical premises. Both also leave numerous questions open that cannot be addressed further here. In the immigration model, neither the destruction of the city-states nor the necessity of settlement was adequately explained. That the new settlements of the Early Iron Age cannot be explained simply as the continuation of Late Bronze Age urban culture sets the archaeological findings in opposition to the revolution model. Although none of the hypotheses can adequately explain the complex upheaval during the twelfth and eleventh centuries, understanding the era depends on developing theories. The models developed by Alt and Mendenhall were also then developed in several variations. In view of the social circumstances, two opposing positions can be distinguished. On the one hand, the inhabitants of the Early Iron Age settlements are seen as descendants of the Canaanites, and, on the other hand, they are classified as a nonurban population element with their own ethnic identity. The first version was advocated most notably by C. H. J. de Geus, Norman K. Gottwald, and Niels Peter Lemche, and the second position is identified with Israel Finkelstein. Since an immigration from outside the land cannot be taken into account, the origin of the inhabitants can only be sought in the land.

C. H. J. de Geus understands premonarchic Israel as an ethnic group. The social structure does not suggest a nomadic past. The most significant unit was the clan united by intermarriage, and the tribes were geographically determined amalgamations of kindred clans. Since the clan was the actual seat of political power, the transition to state formation can only be seen as a development coming from the clans. In premonarchic Israel there existed neither a cultic-shaped coalition of tribes (amphictyony) with a central shrine nor the national office of a judge. The political organization rather had its starting point in the cities and was continued by the clans; early Israel thus grew out of the urban centers of Canaan.

Norman K. Gottwald understands the emergence of Israel as a process of liberation, in which the religion of Yahwism played a decisive role. As opposed to the Canaanite feudal society, lower-class groups rose up and established new settlements outside the cities. It was not nomads breeding small domesticated animals who carried out the process of the land acquisition but rather a socially oppressed class of the city population. After seizing the new settlement places, a tribal formation became a form of political organization. Premonarchic Israel is thus not the result of land-seeking nomads settling down but rather an event of social changes by which the lower classes not only triggered a coup but also were its sole survivors.

Niels Peter Lemche also rules out a nomadic past for early Israel but likewise rejects the revolution hypothesis. The reasons for the collapse of Canaanite city culture cannot be found in the social circumstances alone; instead, they are far more complex. After the end of Egyptian hegemony, political and economic factors certainly played a decisive role. Even if all the details are no longer discernible from the paucity of sources, early Israel still must have developed out of the remnant of Canaan. The decline of Late Bronze Age cities triggered a movement that led to the establishment of new settlements outside the former city-states. At the beginning of that process stands not a revolution but an evolution. As such, the occupants of the new settlements gradually outgrew the society of the Late Bronze Age city-states. The new form of organization into tribes was not established in a nomadic past, but is based rather on the voluntary loyalty of different groups, who developed a new sense of community based on their new situation and common experiences. Premonarchic Israel, with its new settlement form and societal structure, is thus to be understood as an evolution from the Canaanite population of the former city-states. In that regard, this model is a decisive modification of the revolution hypothesis.

In contrast to these hypotheses, which are oriented by social models, Israel Finkelstein proceeds from the archaeological findings. This is noteworthy in two respects. On the one hand, a change in the settlement regions is discernible, and, on the other hand, the number of settlements increased rapidly. The establishment of numerous new settlements outside the sphere of influence of Canaanite cities goes back to nomadic elements in the southern Levant. To be sure, this unsettled population ultimately stemmed from the Middle Bronze Age cities, but they lived for a century outside of urban culture. The settlement emerged as the inevitable consequence of the collapse of the Late Bronze Age city-states. Along with the end of the urban centers, the symbiosis between nomads and cities also came to an end. Foundational for this form of coexistence was the nomads' supply of necessary grain. The decline in grain cultivation forced the nomads to pursue agriculture themselves and to adopt a sedentary way of life with its economic system. That the inhabitants of the new settlements must have lived in such economic symbiosis with the Canaanites prior to their settlement is also evident in the continuation of the material culture, which presupposes a longer contact that involved cultural exchange. In continuation of the foundational work by Alt and on the assumption of the symbiosis theory of Fritz, the thesis of the nomadic past of the inhabitants is established not only from the dissemination and installation of new settlements but also from the economic circumstances.

A decision concerning the historical course of the land acquisition thus can be made only after a renewed examination of the circumstances existing around 1200. Since the direct sources for this time are lacking, the methodological presuppositions must first be discussed for any further clarification of the process.

1. The extrabiblical sources are very sparse for the entire time of the second millennium, and a major portion of this material is extremely thin and only partially meaningful. The Amarna letters, named after their place of discovery in Egypt, give the best insight into the political circumstances of the time around the middle of the fourteenth century. The Amarna letters are the diplomatic correspondence written in cuneiform between the city ruler in Syria and Palestine and Pharaohs Amenhotep III (1391–1353) and Amenhotep IV (1353–1336). The writings give a certain insight into the relationship of individual city-states to their Egyptian overlords.[29]

---

29. Text editions: Jørgen Alexander Knudtzon, *Die El-Amarna Tafeln* (2 vols.; Vorderasiatische Bibliothek; Leipzig: Hinrichs, 1908, 1915; repr., Aalen: O. Zeller, 1964); Anson

2. The Bible is ruled out as a historical source for the era of the land acquisition. The book of Joshua merely offers a portrayal of the process as it developed at the end of the monarchic period; this has nothing to do with the historical sequence but instead merely concretizes a historical-theological construction on the basis of a Deuteronomistic conception. Only the foundational element of the Song of Deborah gives a snapshot of the circumstances of the land acquisition. Accordingly, a total of ten tribes are to come out of the land, being connected to each other by a yet to be determined form of communal action. Nothing is reported about the origin and means of their settlement.

3. Archaeological research has in the past decades uncovered numerous settlements of the era and thus constructed a picture of the settlement structures after 1200 (cf. §II.3.2). This picture is in no way complete and evinces a variety that is difficult to systematize. However, we now have real data that must be interpreted as events of a complete restructuring of the settlement form. The findings do not indicate under what conditions these changes took place, but the formation of any additional theory must be consistent with the diverse aspects of Early Iron Age culture. From the archaeology, then, a kind of touchstone is obtained for the various hypotheses.

4. Sociology and ethnology have sharpened the view for the societal relationships and changes. In particular, nomadism has undergone numerous investigations, such that the different manifestations have emerged clearly. As a result of this improved state of research, the interaction between social and economic structures can indeed be grasped, but the variety of phenomena constitutes a warning, since the experiences and behaviors based on a certain group cannot be transferred to another society arbitrarily. All endeavors to record the social form of premonarchic Israel remain hypothetical, and all analogies are always to be scrutinized critically.

II.4.2. The Ḫapiru

Bottéro, Jean. *Le problème des Ḫabiru* (Cahiers de la Société asiatique 12; Paris: Impr. nationale, 1954). **Greenberg**, Moshe. *The Ḫab/piru* (AOS 39; New Haven: American

---

F. Rainey, *El Amarna Tablets 359–379: Supplement to J. A. Knudtzon, Die E.-Amarna Tafeln* (2nd ed.; AOAT 8; Neukirchen-Vluyn: Neukirchener, 1978). Cited as EA with tablet number and line number; William L. Moran, ed., *The Amarna Letters* (Baltimore: Johns Hopkins University Press, 1992); see now also Yuval Goren, Israel Finkelstein, and Nadav Na'aman, *Inscribed in Clay: Provenance Study of the Amarna Tablets and Other Ancient Near Eastern Texts* (Monograph Series 23; Tel Aviv: Emery and Claire Yass Publications in Archaeology, 2004).

Oriental Society, 1955). **Loretz**, Oswald. *Habiru-Hebräer: Eine sozio-linguistische Studie über die Herkunft des Gentiliziums 'ibrî vom Appellativum ḫabiru* (BZAW 160; Berlin: de Gruyter, 1984). **Na'aman**, Nadav. "Ḫapiru and Hebrews: The Transfer of a Social Term to the Literary Sphere," *JNES* 45 (1986): 271–88. **Weippert**, Manfred. *The Settlement of the Israelite Tribes in Palestine: A Critical Survey of Recent Scholarly Debate* (SBT 2/21; Naperville, Ill.: Allenson, 1971), 63–102.

The basis for the livelihood of the city during the Late Bronze Age was the surrounding land that was used for agriculture. Since villages are unknown in this era, there was presumably no country population and thus no opposition between city and country. The southern Levant was here completely different from other regions in the Near East; in the case of Ugarit, for example, a majority of the population belonging to the city-state lived in the numerous villages in the surrounding land.[30] This lack of a country population in Canaan is of great significance for the later development. The farmers resided in the cities and constituted the majority of its inhabitants. Only the ḫapiru and the nomads lived outside the cities.

The word ḫapiru appears in different spellings and in numerous texts of the second millennium, originally designating a particular class of people. The common characteristic of this group is the status as refugees: they left their traditional way of life and so gave up their previous social position and then belonged to a marginal class of society. Depending on the circumstances, the people designated as ḫapiru lived outside of the control of the city-state or even within a city-state in a special legal position.

The Amarna letters allow a certain insight into the real circumstances of these people. In these letters, the rulers of various cities in Canaan again and again assure the pharaoh of their loyalty, whereas they do not fail to acknowledge the same shortcoming on the part of their opponents nor to black them out accordingly. The threat on the part of the ḫapiru runs like a red thread through a majority of the correspondence. However, the concept has undergone an extension insofar as ḫapiru now designates the political adversary who stands in opposition to the pharaoh and to his loyal governor on the ground. The designation signifies the opposition apart from their rank and social affiliation, such that one could formulate pointedly: ḫapiru is whoever stands up against Egyptian hegemony.

The accusations frequently remain unclear, since specific names and concrete terms are avoided. As examples, there are several expressions compiled by Abdiḫiba of Jerusalem, but the chronological sequence is no longer discern-

---

30. Michael Heltzer, *The Rural Community in Ancient Ugarit* (Wiesbaden: Reichert, 1976).

ible and is also meaningless in this context. In general he raises the accusation, "The ḫapiru plunder all the lands of the kings" (EA 286,50) or "but now the ḫapiru take the cities of the king" (EA 288,36–38). The immediate territory of Abdiḫiba is not exempt from charge: "The land of the king has fallen away to the ḫapiru, and now as well a city of the land of Urusalim, whose name is Bêt-Ninib, a city of the king, has gone away to there, where the people of Kilti are" (EA 190,12–18). Occasionally it is clear that other royal cities served the ḫapiru in order to become liberated from the dominion of the pharaoh. One of the strongest opponents of the Egyptian claim to power was Labaya of Shechem, and apparently his sons continued the politics of independence: "See, this deed is the deed of Milkili and the deed of the sons of Labaya, which have given the land of the king to the ḫapiru" (EA 287,29–31; cf. 289,18–24). Abdiḫiba of Jerusalem did not have his land under control, and his rule is constantly threatened by the ḫapiru and by those who serve as their instruments of power. So that he could be master of the situation, Abdiḫiba incessantly asked his overlords about sending troops.

Behind the ḫapiru thus stands a group of people outside the city's social system, who lived on the periphery of the city and sought out the fringes and forests as places of refuge from pursuit. Since they were not farmers or herders, they had no fixed residence and did not strive for landed property. Their only concern was the exertion of power in order to secure sustenance for themselves out of the cities' provisions. As marginal groups of society, they terrorized the land with brutal force in order to remain alive by means of extorted contributions. Their social position outside of city society determined their behavior, which perhaps is most likely to be understood as blackmailing robbery. By their incessant disruption of the economic foundations of the city, they brought the land to the brink of chaos by interfering with agriculture and trade and by making the ruler of the city aware of the limits of his power again and again. The ones excluded from society grew in number, became a threat to the social order, and slowly but surely destroyed the economic foundations of those on whom they depended.

Since no additional sources are available beyond this insight into the circumstances before and during the Amarna age, the question of the extent to which this conflict contributed to the collapse of the city rulers cannot be pursued further. To guarantee their own supply, the people named ḫapiru were dependent on the cities. Therefore, it is not unthinkable that this group established settlements after the collapse of the city-states in order to pursue agriculture themselves. Although the ḫapiru were an unattached group with no intention of settling down, it cannot be ruled out that in the changes after 1200, such groups turned into peaceful and settled inhabitants of the land. In any case, the phenomenon appears to have disappeared after 1200 since the term *ḫapiru* does not show up anymore in the Egyptian sources. Accordingly, it can thus be reckoned that the *ḫapiru* element arose in the population during the Early Iron Age and took up residence in the newly established settlements outside the former cities.

Although numerous cities were not rebuilt following their destruction, some additional cities continued to exist. Thus, in Megiddo and Gezer, Bethshean and Achshaph (Tell Kesān), settlement is discernible up to the tenth century. To be sure, the question arises as to the whereabouts of the population from places such as Hazor or Lachish, which were left behind during the Early Iron Age, but clearly their survival in the traditional settlement places is not ruled out. This continuation of the settlement history during the Early Iron Age in individual cities makes it improbable that the new settlements were established as alternatives for the former cities. Even after the great catastrophe in the twelfth century, which is constituted by the collapse of Egyptian rule in Canaan, some cities existed on, such that one cannot speak of a general withdrawal of the former city dwellers to the land. Indeed, it cannot be ruled out that even former city inhabitants settled outside the city catchment areas, but the reestablishment of numerous villages far from the former city centers during the twelfth and eleventh centuries can hardly be reasonably understood as a restructuring of the mode of settlement. The difference between the city-states and the village settlements is too great to assume the same population for both.

The possible equivalence of the term *ḫapiru* with the designation of the group "Hebrews" (*'ibrî*) does not contribute to the resolution of this question. It is possible that the terms are related, but functionally the biblical linguistic usage does not relate to the groups designated as *ḫapiru* in the second millennium.[31] With few exceptions, the biblical references to "Hebrews" are found in the Joseph story (Gen 39:14, 17; 40:15; 41:12; 43:32), in the pre-Priestly exodus narrative (Exod 1:15, 19; 2:7, 13; 3:18; 5:3; 7:16; 9:1, 13; 10:3), and in 1 Samuel (1 Sam 4:6, 9; 13:3, 19; 14:11, 21; 29:3). According to these references, the word serves predominantly as a designation of Israelites in the mouths of their enemies. This linguistic usage probably reflects the fact that during the monarchic period, Israelites were designated as Hebrews by the neighboring peoples, whereas the word did not occur as national self-identification. Similar to *ḫapiru*, "Hebrew" (*'ibrî*) was thus a term for a particular group outside one's own society, a term that did not carry with it an ethnic or

---

31. Klaus Koch, "Die Hebräer vom Auszug aus Ägypten bis zum Großreich Davids," *VT* 19 (1969): 37–81; Niels Peter Lemche, "'Hebrew' as a National Name for Israel," *ST* 33 (1979): 1–23; David Noel Freedman and B. E. Willoughby, "עִבְרִי," *TDOT* 10:430–45.

a national determination. Both concepts thus indicate a certain commonality, but the identity of the groups cannot be derived out of that.

II.4.3. Nomads in the Second Half of the Second Millennium

Giveon, Raphael. *Les bédouins Shosou des document égyptiens* (Documenta et monumenta Orientis antique 18; Leiden: Brill, 1971). **Görg**, Manfred. "Zur Geschichte der Šꜣśw," *Bib* 45 (1976): 424–28. **Helck**, Wolfgang. "Die Bedrohung Palästinas durch einwandernde Gruppen am Ende der 18. und am Anfang der 19. Dynastie," *VT* 18 (1968): 472–80. **Henninger**, Joseph. *Über Lebensraum und Lebensformen der Frühsemiten* (Arbeitsgemeinschaft für Forschung des Landes Nordrhein-Westfalen: Geisteswissenschaften 151; Cologne: Westdeutscher Verlag, 1968). **Klengel**, Horst. *Zwischen Zelt und Palast: Die Begegnung von Nomaden und Sesshaften im alten Vorderasien* (Vienna: Schroll, 1972). **Staubli**, Thomas. *Das Image der Nomaden im Alten Israel und in der Ikonographie seiner seßhaften Nachbarn* (OBO 107; Göttingen: Vandenhoeck & Ruprecht, 1991). **Weippert**, Manfred. "Semitische Nomaden des zweiten Jahrtausends," *Bib* 55 (1974): 265–80, 472–83. See now also: **Meshel**, Zeev. "Wilderness Wanderings: Ethnographic Lessons from Modern Bedouin," *BAR* 34.4 (2008): 32–39. **Rainey**, Anson F. "Whence Came the Israelites and Their Language?" *IEJ* 57 (2007): 41–64. **Levy**, Thomas E., Russell B. **Adams**, and Adolfo **Muniz**. "Archaeology and the Shasu Nomads: Recent Excavations in the Jabal Hamrat Fidan, Jordan," in *Le-David Maskil: A Birthday Tribute for David Noel Freedman* (ed. Richard Elliott Friedman and William H.C. Propp; Biblical and Judaic Studies 9; Winona Lake, Ind.: Eisenbrauns, 2004), 63–89.

Nomadism is a complex phenomenon. As modern field research has shown, despite similarities among unsettled groups, there are great differences with respect to economic foundations, family structures, and tribal organization. Such differences are already to be presumed for the nomads of the third and second millennia. However, the form of Bedouin life first began with the domestication of camels after 1000.[32] The attested nomads in the texts of the third and second millennia were not camel breeders and thereby were not familiar with the possibilities given for transhumance over vast distances. On the contrary,

---

32. On the domestication of camels, see Reinhard Walz, "Neue Untersuchungen zum Domestikationsproblem der altweltlichen Cameliden," *ZMDG* 104 (1954): 45–87; Burchard Brentjes, "Das Kamel im alten Orient" *Klio* 38 (1960): 23–52; Richard W. Bulliet, *The Camel and the Wheel* (Cambridge: Harvard University Press, 1975); Ernst Axel Knauf, "Supplementa Ismaelitica 11: Ex 4,24–26, Philo Byblius 2,33 und der kanaanäisch-städtische Hintergrund 'jahwistischer' Überlieferungen," *BN* 40 (1987): 16–23, esp. 20–22 on the archaeological evidence for camels in Late Bronze and Iron Age Jordan.

HISTORICAL RECONSTRUCTION OF THE EPOCH   131

these groups bred small domesticated animals and are falsely designated as "half-nomads." Characteristic of this form of life is the transmigration called pasture rotation, which conforms to the time period. In the months of the rainy season, the nomads let their herds of sheep and goats graze on the fringes of the cultivated land, since this offered sufficient nourishment for the animals. In the dry season, the pasture was shifted to the cultivated land, since here even in the summer months there is enough vegetation available to supply the animals. Since the small animals must be watered daily, a spring or a well in proximity to the pasture is the *sine qua non* for the sojourn in a certain region.

The grain necessary for the nourishment of the family was either grown by the nomads themselves in the plains regions or acquired in the cultivated land by bartering. The supply of basic foodstuff required either the attachment to fixed regions on the fringes of the cultivated land during the winter months or the dependence on the agriculture practiced by the inhabitants of the cultivated land. The economic system of the unsettled people presupposes in any case a certain proximity to the cultivated land and along with that a constant contact with the inhabitants of the city.

The nomads are differentiated from the townspeople not only by their alternative economic system. The different living conditions resulted in a social structure that varied from that in the city centers. Moreover, the acquisition of city culture was unfamiliar to the nomads at least in part, which accounts for the fashioning of different forms of material culture. In particular, every form of house construction is lacking. Since no sources are available, the social structure of the nomads of the second millennium can be described only hypothetically and represented in outline.

    1. Characteristic of nomadism is the tent, which can be erected in any place and broken down again and moved at any time.[33] The form of the tent in the second millennium is unknown, since the black tent used currently by the Bedouins, with its construction of long strips on numerous posts, presumably originated only in the first millennium. Still, in the Assyrian reliefs of the eighth century, the tents of the nomads and those of the Assyrians were represented in the same way; their characteristic is a single post or a single row of middle posts, on each of which an additional rafter-like connecting piece branches off. The question as to the type of tent used in the second millennium thus cannot be answered. Apart from the tent, the movable possessions were modest, since at most a donkey was available as a pack animal. In any

---

    33. See Carl Gunnar Feilberg, *La tente noire: Contribution ethnographique à l'histoire culturelle des nomades* (Nationalmuseets Skrifter: Etnografisk Raekke 2; Copenhagen: I kommission hos Gyldendal, 1944); Torvald Faegre, *Tents: Architecture of the Nomads* (Garden City, N.Y.: Doubleday, 1979).

case, the baggage had to contain little in terms of size and weight in order to ensure the maneuverability of the migration. The nomads had no houses, no fixed places, and—apart from their herds—no great property.

2. As a general rule, the tents stood at a wide distance from each other. Since the herds took up a large area in order to have adequate provisions, there was inevitably a loose mode of settlement, so the individual dwellings were scattered over a wide area.

3. As a tent community, the family constitutes the smallest social unit. The common bond of several families to a larger connection owed solely to descent. Descendants of the same ancestors formed an overall unity of individual families, which is designated as a clan. The common bond of the clan members shows most of all in blood vengeance and marriage. All the clans that go back to one ancestor belong to a tribe. This largest unit is chiefly manifested in the action of military expeditions.

4. The social classification makes the formation and exertion of power difficult for individuals within the ranks of clans and tribes. Only within the family is the supremacy of the *paterfamilias* evident. As a rule, in marriage the woman transitions into the family of the man—although it also occurs among nomads that the man moves to the family of the woman, which family is left again by divorce (uxorilocal residence). Blood vengeance, to which the male clan members were bound in instances of murder of a next of kin, meant a strong protection for the life of the individuals; however, already early on there were provisions for compensation.

5. Apart from interpersonal conflicts that were regulated within the society, the way of life appears to have been connected with a certain peaceable nature, which was necessitated by the circumstances. To be sure, there were invasions and robbery as well as battles over watering holes and pastures, but the economic system and order of society hardly permitted long military expeditions, which presuppose a high degree of planning and direction. Even if there were limited confrontations, the livestock breeding half-nomads lacked the warlike character of the later full nomads. "The smaller the group and the tighter their symbiosis with the settled population, the sooner the relations could be peaceful" (Henninger, *Über Lebensraum*, 31: "Je kleiner die Gruppe und je enger ihre Symbiose mit den Seßhaften war, desto eher konnten die Beziehungen friedlich sein"). This fundamentally peaceful coexistence with the city-states does not rule out, though, that the nomads became involved in military confrontations with various powers in matters of political hegemony.

6. The individual tribes or subgroups presumably adopted fixed settlement regions over long periods of time. The change back and forth from the steppe to the cultivated land took place within certain borders that were set by the neighboring of other tribes and their regions. The steppes area bordering

HISTORICAL RECONSTRUCTION OF THE EPOCH 133

to the south and east of the cultivated land were delineated relatively in such a way that dissemination and the manner of rotation of a tribe or its subgroups must have proceeded according to given courses.

There is textual evidence of individual nomadic tribes of the second millennium who lived in the vicinity of particular city-states. Thus, Jaminites, Haneans, and Suteans are mentioned in the archive of Mari in the central Euphrates from the eighteenth century, according to which there were numerous conflicts. On the whole, though, a balanced relationship seems to have predominated, especially because the nomads were dependent on the stronger economic city for their grain supply.

Toward the end of the second millennium, after the collapse of Hittite rule, from 1200 on Aramean tribes pushed to the front of northern Syria and there built a series of small states with a tribal ruler at the head who resided in a newly established capital city. The transition of these tribes to settled life brought about a reurbanization of the land, which was a lengthy process stretching over several centuries. From the region of the upper Euphrates, the following principalities with city centers are known from the tenth century:

Bīt ʿAdini	Til Barsip (Tell el-Aḥmar)
Bīt Baḫiāni	Guzana (Tell Ḥalāf)
Jaʿudi	Samʾal (Zincirli)
Bīt Agusi	Arpad (Tell Rifʿat)

The establishment of these small states was carried out by the Semitic tribes designated as Arameans, who stemmed from the steppes regions on both sides of the Euphrates. Additional establishments of states came as well in the area of the Orontes, in southern Syria, and in southern Mesopotamia by former nomadic groups. The entire movement of these numerous tribes toward the end of the second millennium is designated as the Aramean migration. The Aramean states existed as independent principalities until the eighth century, when they were conquered by the Assyrians and integrated into the empire as provinces. This transition of nomadic tribes to settlement and the formation of city-states having their own character within the prevailing zone of a certain people group lies mostly in the dark due to the paucity of sources but without a doubt is analogous to the processes in the southern Levant. This process of the land seizure by the unsettled peoples was facilitated or even necessitated on the basis of changing power dynamics. Presumably, following the collapse of the numerous city-states in the Syrian region after 1200, a power vacuum existed, which the groups united as Arameans penetrated in order to assume the inheritance of the city rulers thus far.

Of the nomads in the region of Palestine from the second half of the second millennium, the Shasu (*š3św*) in particular are known from Egyptian sources; but other groups were also mentioned occasionally. These Shasu are attested for the entire region from Sinai and northwest Arabia as far as Kadesh at the Orontes (Tell Nebī Mend); this word refers to a large population group with the same way of life in the entire catchment area. Since prior to 1200 they are occasionally connected with the rebellious city-states, the Shasu also prove to be enemies of the Egyptians. As such, they were controlled by the pharaohs and repeatedly listed in the booty lists as prisoners. Pharaoh Ramses III (1184–1153) reports a successful expedition against the nomadic inhabitants of Seir, which unfortunately cannot be dated: "I destroyed the people of Seir among the Bedouin [Shasu] tribes. I razed their tents: their people, their property, and their cattle as well, without number, pinioned and carried away in captivity, as the tribute of Egypt. I gave them to the Ennead of the gods, as slaves for their houses" (*ANET*, 262).

On the whole, the Shasu were described negatively in the Egyptian sources as disastrous inhabitants of the already dangerous wilderness: "As highwaymen they upset the Asiatic trade routes; they are giants who secretly watch the unsuspecting travelers in order to attack them at the right moment; yes, they are unpredictable anarchists who not only cause unrest and confusion among the Egyptians but also massacre each other" (Staubli, *Das Image der Nomaden,* 37). However, the Shasu were illustrated in the reliefs of the Eighteenth Dynasty analogous to the other enemies of Egypt but were differentiated from the remaining Asiatic peoples by their hair, style of beard, and a tasseled loincloth down to the knee. As a general rule, all the hair on the head was curly and held together by a headband. This stylization was maintained also in the later representations under Seti I, Merneptah, and Ramses III. Despite the standardization, the members of the Shasu can always be recognized in Egyptian representations by their characteristic hair and beard style (Staubli, figs. 15–48).

Based on the form of representation, the two prisoners in the ivory carvings from Megiddo stratum VII A can be identified as Shasu. The piece stems from the twelfth century and shows a throne scene, whose various figures are depicted differently; the two prisoners paraded before the enthroned ruler are indeed naked—and are therefore recognizable as circumcised men—but their hair and beards show the same characteristic style familiar from the Shasu in the Egyptian reliefs (fig. 16). The scene thus depicts the local ruler in a reception provided with wine and entertained by lyre players, with the procession of prisoners from an expedition. This suggests military confrontations between the Canaanite city ruler and the Shasu. Even if the carvings were not manufactured in Megiddo, they still must reflect a historical reality. Besides the punitive expeditions of the pharaohs, there were probably also such expeditions by the Canaanite city-states against the Shasu. Apparently the Shasu did not play

HISTORICAL RECONSTRUCTION OF THE EPOCH   135

a more important political role in the structure of city rule, and their social membership and organization are unknown. In times of trouble they were permitted to go beyond the borders to Egypt in the Delta region in order to secure the necessary provisions for their families and herds. The Shasu who served as soldiers in the Egyptian army were presumably prisoners of war (Staubli, 41–44 with figs. 25–27). After Ramses III they were not named in the sources. Since they hardly just disappeared as a population group, it is thought that their designation was replaced by other terms.

II.4.4. The New Settlement Form and the Origin of Its Inhabitants

The settlements of the twelfth and eleventh centuries were the result of a change in the political population; they cannot be understood as the continuation of the Late Bronze Age city culture. Instead, they mark a new type of settlement. Some resettled hills such as Megiddo and Gezer have modest continuations under the city rulers, but the settlements represent a new phenomenon with respect to their spread and architectural installations. This development came to an end in the tenth century with the reurbanization of the land under Kings David and Solomon. The new settlements are thus the immediate consequence of a regrouping of the prevailing structures in the land's population until approximately 1200. As such, the obvious connection of the commodities of daily life with Canaanite culture shows that the settlers could not have been immigrants from other regions of the Near East. The new population continued a cultural inheritance that had developed in the land. Thus only the population elements proven in the land previously can be considered as founders and inhabitants of the numerous settlements; they are therefore either to be considered as descendants of the former city inhabitants or as coming from groups outside the societal order of the city, as the social classes of the ḫapiru and the nomadic Shasu arose. The answer to this alternative is disputed in the

Figure 16. Ivory carvings from Megiddo stratum VII A.

research and can only be resolved by further investigation of the settlement history and structure.

The comparison of construction forms in the Early Iron Age settlements shows that the four-room house stands at the end of a line of development on account of its sophisticated plan. The other two types of buildings must therefore be the older forms in terms of the history of construction (see fig. 14). At this point, broad-roomed houses and pillared houses have a common characteristic in the partition of a courtyard by means of stone pillars inside of a rectangular building, but they differ in the location of the courtyard, which limited the location of the entrance. Despite this difference, the common features suggest that both types go back to the base form of a house subdivided by pillars in the courtyard and having covered rooms. Indeed, the development of this form of construction can be traced back to a few examples at the Late Bronze Age; the wide dissemination of this type into various characteristics emerges only from the twelfth century in the Early Iron Age settlements. The different location of the courtyard in the various types is determined in each case by the necessary accessibility to the rooms, which may reflect a different use. Presumably the three-room house and four-room house go back to the extension of the pillared houses with an additional room in which the small side is opposite the entrance.

Since the predecessors of the design appeared occasionally already in Late Bronze Age cities, these construction forms cannot have developed from the structure of nomads' tents. Even if the types of houses cannot be derived from the tent construction, their accumulation in the Early Iron Age settlements is a new phenomenon. With the dissemination of these forms of construction, as already in its arrangement, the new settlement form is decidedly distinguished from the Late Bronze Age city. The predominant use of the new house-type and the avoidance of the previously customary form of the courtyard house can suggest changes in the needs of the occupants in the way the houses were used. The courtyard house in all its characteristics comprises a self-contained zone that protects the family in every relationship; the necessary exposure and ventilation comes from the central courtyard, and apart from the door, there were windows in addition to the inner courtyard. Even the broad-room house and the three- and four-room houses constitute self-contained units and have an available courtyard. As a general rule, this courtyard occupies a larger area given its long-stretching rectangular form. Moreover, the rooms lying lengthwise are usually separated with stone pillars so as to form a half-open room. This construction type is distinguished from the courtyard house by a greater integration of covering the open areas of the house. Presumably, the different mode of construction reflects a difference in the way of life, since the house construction would apparently fulfill other needs. The development of the new house type is thus rooted in an area outside the Late Bronze Age city.

Yet even the layout of the settlements indicates that they were not established by the inhabitants of the former cities. Except for the few farmsteads, which can be disregarded in this context, the new settlements are structured completely differently. In the circular areas, an open space was created in the middle, which regulated communication. In this way all were members of the settlement, each part of the whole maintaining its independence. This hurdle-shaped arrangement is designed to form a common storage area, as is still customary by nomads today. The circular area thus reflects a tradition that had been more indigenous to unsettled people than to settled city-dwellers.

Yet the village, with its unplanned mode of construction, is not completely different from the layout of a city, since a city can show the same irregularity in development. In many cases of the Late Bronze Age city, a right-angled alignment of the construction units can be discerned that was furthered by the form of the courtyard house. Thus, the formation of *insulae* is perhaps recognizable in the tight development of Megiddo stratum VIII, although this principle decreases in the ensuing strata VII B and VII A. In contrast, the Early Iron Age villages are a conglomeration, whereas occasionally, as in Ai and Shiloh, buildings still available from past eras could be used. The construction of settlements in the Early Iron Age does not show evidence of knowledge for the layout of an organized community or adherence to an organizing principle.

Although neither the constructions forms nor the layour of the area is conclusive to indicate the origin of the new settlers, both innovations speak against the establishment of the settlements by former city-dwellers. The inhabitants during the entire Late Bronze Age always rebuilt their cities after their destruction, as the continuity of the settlement history emerges in numerous settlement hills. "The continual rebuilding of Late Bronze Age towns on their earlier scale clearly shows that the former population of these towns was in fact unwilling to withdraw from urban society and that they actually returned to their hometowns" (Na'aman, "Ḫapiru and Hebrews," 277). If the establishment of new settlements by former city-dwellers is improbable based on the discernible facts, only the groups in the vicinity of the cities come into question as builders—those who lived outside the city on account of their social position or their way of life. From the sources, two of these groups are known: the people of lesser rights and unfamiliar way of life called Hapiru (*ḫapiru*) and the nomads designated as Shasu (see §§II.4.1 and 2). In all probability, then, the resettlement of the land does not go back to the former city population but rather is the result of groups settling down, those who had previously persisted outside the city in an unsettled way of life.

The reason for the transition of these groups to settlement can only be conjectured. Over the course of the decline of Egyptian dominion, after 1200 the system of Canaanite city rulers also collapsed. The detailed causes are unknown, but in any case the balance of power that previously existed dropped off. Along with the tight network of Canaanite cities, the earlier symbiosis between the nomads and the city centers also lapsed. The necessary grain supply was no longer available, and there were presumably further breakdowns in other foodstuffs and consumer goods. Thus, these groups who had previously pursued agriculture only a little or not at all were forced into farming in order to supply their food.

The new settlements manifest the development of new regions for agriculture by previously unsettled parts of the population. That both *ḫapiru* and previous city-dwellers could have been located within the new settlements should not be ruled out. It is improbable, though, that these settlements were laid out only or predominantly by the former city population. The new mode of settlement does not trace back to a relocation of the way of life from the city to the land, but rather marks the transition of people from nomadism to settlement by expanding their economic system and maintaining their social structure.

From the view of the monarchic period, these new settlers comprise the Israelite tribes. Despite their origin, the inhabitants of the Early Iron Age settlements were designated as Israelites. This view of the written sources combined with the archaeological findings makes it probable that the population elements named Hapiru and Shasu in the various sources are connected with these newly designated groups. Moreover, the Canaanites lived on in the successive settlements of the former city centers. The renaming of the non-Canaanite population brings a self-identity to expression that owes at least in part to the new way of life. As evidence that the identity expressed in the names corresponds to the historical reality, the Merneptah Stele attests to the name of Israel (see §II.2.3). Indeed this ethnic entity cannot be delineated closely with respect to residence and political organization, but the Merneptah Stele documents the only extrabiblical reference to Israel as a group in addition to other peoples and the Canaanite cities. The land acquisition was thus not only the settlement of different population elements outside the cities but also the formation of a people; now, based on the common way of life, groups of different origin congregated into a community, which then during the monarchic period led to the idea of a single people. However different the origin of the new settlers might have been, after the land acquisition the common way of life led to cohesion as a tribe and then to the amalgamation of the tribes into one Israel.

II.5. The Life of the Tribes in the Cultivated Land

II.5.1. The System of the Tribes

Bächli, Otto. *Amphiktyonie im Alten Testament: Forschungsgeschichtliche Studie zur Hypothese von Martin Noth* (TZ Sonderband 6; Basel: Friedrich Reinhardt, 1977). **Fohrer**, Georg. "'Amphiktyonie' und 'Bund'?" in idem, *Studien zur alttestamentlichen Theologie und Geschichte* (BZAW 115; Berlin: de Gruyter, 1969), 84–119. **Geus**, C. H. J. de. *The Tribes of Israel: An Investigation into Some of the Presuppositions of Martin Noth's Amphictyony Hypothesis* (SSN 18; Assen: Van Gorcum, 1976). **Herrmann**, Siegfried. "Was bleibt von der Jahwe-Amphiktyonie?" *TZ* 48 (1992): 304–14. **Mayes**, A. D. H. "Israel in the Pre-monarchy Period," *VT* 23 (1973): 151–70. **Namiki**, Koichi. "Reconsideration of the Twelve-Tribe System of Israel" *AJBI* 2 (1976): 29–59. **Noth**, Martin. *Das System der zwölf Stämme* (BWANT 52; Darmstadt: Wissenschaftliche Buchgesellschaft, 1930). **Seebass**, Horst. "Erwägungen zum altisraelitischen System der zwölf Stämme," *ZAW* 90 (1978): 196–220. **Smend**, Rudolf. "Gehörte Juda zum vorstaatlichen Israel?" in idem, *Gesammelte Studien II: Zur ältesten Geschichte Israels* (BEvT 100; Munich: Kaiser, 1987), 200–209. **Weippert**, Helga."Das geographische System der Stämme Israels," *VT* 23 (1973): 76–89. See now also: **Gottwald**, Norman K. *The Tribes of Yahweh: A Sociology of the Religion of Liberated Israel, 1250–1050 BCE* (The Biblical Seminar 66; Sheffield: Sheffield Academic Press, 1999). **Scheffler**, Eben. "Beyond the Judges and the Amphictyony: The Politics of Tribal Israel (1200-1020 BCE)," *Old Testament Essays* 14 (2001): 494–509. **Bienkowski**, Piotr and Eveline van der **Steen**. "Tribes, Trade, and Towns: A New Framework for the Late Iron Age in Southern Jordan and the Negev," *BASOR* 323 (2001): 21–47. **Kallai**, Zecharia. "A Note on the Twelve-Tribe Systems of Israel," *VT* 49 (1999): 125–27. **Steen**, Eveline J. van der. "Tribes and Power Structures in Palestine and the Transjordan," *NEA* 69 (2006): 27–36.

The history of Israel pertaining to the land acquisition lies largely in the dark, since for the premonarchic period almost no sources are available. The only datable text in this era is the Song of Deborah in its original version, Judg 5:12–17, 18b, 19–22, 24–30. Although clear criteria for an exact temporal classification are lacking, according to all appearances the hymn of praise was composed prior to the formation of the monarchy under Saul and David toward the end of the eleventh century. The single applicable piece of evidence for the historical classification is the mention of Taanach and Megiddo in Judg 5:19. According to the text, the battle occurred at the southeastern edge of the Valley of Jezreel, when both cities existed. Megiddo was settled after the collapse of the last city of stratum VII A around 1130 and thereafter until the annexation of the Canaanites into the state territory under David and Solomon (strata VI B–V A). In distinction to this continued settlement history, in Taanach, according to the preliminary findings of the settlement sequence, there was a discontinuous settlement; after the destruction of the city around the middle of the twelfth century, the resettlement first began over the course of the eleventh century. As such, the second half of the twelfth century is ruled out for the date of the battle sung about in the Song of Deborah. The starting point of these events in the first half of the twelfth century is excluded because the dissemination of new settlements first reached its high point in the eleventh century, and thus a conflict between new settlers and the remaining inhabitants of the Canaanite city is probable. The Song of Deborah presumably reflects the relationships of the eleventh century; apart from that a more exact date of the text and the events it relates is not possible.

In the hymnic framework, the name Israel appears in Judg 5:2, 7, 8, 11, but the name does not occur in the oldest element of the song. Instead, a total of ten tribes are enumerated: the participants in the battle are named first (Judg 5:14, 15a), and then the missing tribes are established (5:15b–17, 18b). The enumeration was thus determined by this subdivision into two groups: the tribes of Ephraim, Benjamin, Machir, Zebulun, and Issachar participated; the tribes of Reuben, Gilead, Dan, Asher, and Naphtali were blamed for their absences.

The context permits no other conclusion than that with this number of ten all the tribes who were called to participate in war against the enemies were named. The enumeration thus indicates a historical quantity, namely, those tribes that were covenanted together to take part in military expedition. This covenant presupposes a commonality that can only be inferred. The basis for this common action would have been the consciousness of solidarity that was socially and religiously rooted. This is not at all to say that this point comes from mere suppositions, for at the very least one can assume common elements such as the same social structure of small village communities and the same connection to a form of religion apart from the Canaanite religion with its pantheon.

With respect to the ten named tribes there are at this point two notable aspects: (1) the southern tribes are lacking, and (2) some of the names deviate from later conventions. Particularly noticeable is the absence of Judah; the two tribes farthest to the south are Benjamin and Dan, so habitations in the region of the coastal plains are still presumed for the latter. Furthermore, the tribe of Simeon is not named as in the later enumerated twelve-tribe system. Apparently Judah and Simeon did not yet belong to premonarchic Israel. However the federation of tribes may have been organized, the two southern tribes were not included in it. This exceptional position of Judah apart from the remaining tribes is reflected also in the early history of the monarchy. After the death of Saul, the Judeans chose David to be their king, whereas Abner made Ishbaal, the surviving son of Saul, to be king in Mahanaim over

"Gilead, Asher, Jezreel, Ephraim, Benjamin, and over all Israel" (2 Sam 2:8–9). The northern tribes twice separated from the south and dissolved the personal union created by the person of the king (2 Sam 20:1; 1 Kgs 12:16):

> We have no portion in David,
> no share in the son of Jesse.
> Everyone to your tents, O Israel!

Prior to the formation of the state, Israel did not include Judah (and Simeon), and conditions apparent even before the institution of the monarchy led ultimately to the dissolution of the united monarchy into two states: Israel and Judah. The grounds for tensions existing between the north (including the land east of the Jordan) and the south are unknown; it is only clear that the differences were already given in the time before the institution of the monarchy.

Of the names called in Judg 5:14–17, 18b, Ephraim, Benjamin, Zebulun, Issachar, Reuben, Dan, Asher, and Naphtali also appear in the later texts, as opposed to Machir and Gilead, who are not later used as names of tribes. Both were counted as sons of Manasseh in the wider tradition (Num 26:28–37; 32:39–42, cf. Deut 3:13–15), so both designations are subordinated to the name of Manasseh. The later enumerations of the tribes also show an essential difference from the names given in Judg 5, since additional tribes would be named besides Judah and Simeon. The compilation of tribal sayings in Gen 49 and Deut 33 as well as the numerous lists of tribes are *sui generis* literary traditions; these enumerations require their own investigation and do not necessarily reflect historical reality, although they have usually been consulted for wide-ranging constructions of the early history of Israel. At the same time, it should be noted from the outset that the significance of individual tribes as independent outstanding figures goes back to the period of the monarchy. Only in the arrangement of the state territorial provinces under Solomon (1 Kgs 4:7–19) were the tribal names Naphtali, Asher, Issachar, and Benjamin used once each in an administrative document to designate the eighth to eleventh provinces, and Ephraim and Gilead are clearly counted as names of territories in the first and twelfth provinces.

Apart from minor variants in the sequence of individual names, two systems of tribal lists can be differentiated: the genealogical system and the geographic system. To the first schema belong Gen 29:31–30:12 with 35:16–20; 35:22–26; 46:8–25; 49:1–27; Exod 1:2–4; 1 Chr 2:1, 2; 27:16–22. The second schema is found only in the Priestly writings or in the texts associated with P: Num 1:5–15, 20–47; 2:3–31; 7:12–83; 10:14–28; 13:4–15; 26:5–51. The principal difference is that in the genealogical system Levi is named as a tribe, whereas this name is missing in the geographic system, according to which

Joseph's two sons Ephraim and Manasseh were named instead of Levi in order to complete the number twelve. The comparison of the names in both systems makes the differences clear:

Geographical system according to Num 26:5–51	Genealogical system according to Gen 29:31–30:12; 35:16–20
Reuben	Reuben
Simeon	Simeon
Gad	Levi
Judah	Judah
Issachar	Dan
Zebulun	Naphtali
Manasseh	Gad
Ephraim	Asher
Benjamin	Issachar
Dan	Zebulun
Asher	Joseph
Naphtali	Benjamin

The genealogical system is firmly anchored in the pre-Priestly historical writings and can be considered the older of the two. This priority does not only establish that the older historical representation is to be fixed earlier temporally than the Priestly Document, but there are also practical grounds for this designation. According to the position of the order of the Priestly Document, the Levites belong to the descendants of Levi as cult personnel along with the priests. They perform service in the shrine around which the people camp, and therefore the Levites can no longer constitute a "worldly" tribe (cf. Num 1). The Priestly Document has thus altered the tribal system according to its idea of the tabernacle as the center point of the people; thus, the name Levi was removed and Joseph became included through his sons Ephraim and Manasseh.

In the pre-Priestly historical writings, the genealogical system is anchored in the patriarchal history, in which the twelve eponyms of the tribes were made to be sons of Jacob (Gen 29:31–30:12 and 35:16–20). In this way the unity of Israel was established: every tribe had its tribal father, and every tribal father was a son of the patriarch Jacob; as such, all of Israel is the progeny of Jacob. It is unknown to what extent the attribution of different tribal ancestry to different wives and concubines of Jacob should reveal a hierarchy of tribes. In addition, it is completely unknown from where, via the names removed from Judg 5, the tribal designations Levi, Gad, and Simeon stem. It remains merely conjectural that they were not adopted from a pure literary tradition but rather reflect a historical reality even if this can no longer be determined. Only the relationships for Judah are clear, since this has to do with an important figure who began to play a different role in the early monarchy with David's elevation to king (cf. 2 Sam 2:1–4a).

At this point the formation of the pre-Priestly historical writings cannot be dated with certainty. The dating to the time of Solomon in the early monarchic period stands up against doubts and misgivings insofar as the fashioned theology involving God's acts of blessing and humanity's responsibility for their actions first developed in the wider course of the monarchic period. In any case, the composition of this historical representation is attributed to the period of the monarchy. This "national epic" was created in order to establish the unity of the people by proving a common origin and facilitating the understanding of a common history. Since even older traditions are adopted and utilized in this historical work, it cannot be ruled out that the tribal system was inherited in whole or in part from the tradition. Even if it should be older than the written record in Genesis, it still cannot reach back to the premonarchic period, since there was no manifest awareness then of a twelve-tribe system. On the contrary, the Song of Deborah clearly verifies that the tribe called Judah was not included. A system of twelve tribes was nonexistent and unknown in the premonarchic period; it was probably under David that Judah first became a part of the unified state, which replaced the federation of tribes from the premonarchic period.

The genealogical system of the twelve tribes is thus a literary design. A historical reality underlies this insofar as the named tribes—or at least the majority of them—constituted the kingdom ruled by David and Solomon. The extent of this kingdom exceeds the tribal regions covered in the enumeration of Judg 5:14–17, 18b; the genealogical system was thus further developed with respect to the historical reality of the premonarchic period. At the same time it is a piece of fiction, since the Davidic-Solomonic kingdom covered even the regions of the ancient Canaanite city-states. In any case, the twelve-tribe system is no inventory of historical facts, but rather a programmatic design by which the unity and solidarity of the people could be established and mediated. Despite all the differences among the individual tribes, Israel is one people because all the tribal fathers descended as sons from one patriarch. Tracing Israel back to twelve tribes each of which is descended from an ancestor who was a son of the one father Jacob "constituted Israel, the community held together by the band of blood-relationship, as related from the tribal father" and thus constituted Israel as *one* people (Fohrer, "Amphiktyonie," 103: "konstituiert die durch die Bande der Blutsverwandtschaft zusammengehaltene Gemeinschaft Israel als vom Stammvater her verwandt").

Since the system of twelve tribes includes Judah, this historical-theological construction can be no older than the monarchic period. As grounds for the unity of the people, the schema of twelve reaches back only to the era of the united monarchy. The dating in the early monarchic period is not too certain, since the design could have been developed as a restoration program even after the division of the kingdom into Israel and Judah. In any case, the genealogical system is ruled out as a source for the early history of Israel. Nor can the geographic system in the book of Numbers be enlisted for the reconstruction of a connection of tribes in the premonarchic period, since it was literarily dependent on the older genealogical system. All further variants in Josh 21; 1 Chr 6 and 12; as well as Deut 33 are later still and thus cannot be used for historical analysis.

This determination of the system of tribes as a historical-theological program for establishing the unity of Israel renders Martin Noth's thesis of an amphictyony of tribes in the premonarchic period inapplicable, since its foundation in the sources is undone. For the time before the institution of the monarchy, Noth posited an analogy to the Greek and Italian amphictyonies having a sacral tribal confederation that fundamentally constituted its members by the number twelve. The main point of this tribal community was a common shrine in which individual members cared for the cult, each one in turn for one month of the year. Connected with the supposition of a central shrine was the notion of a common law and a central court.

Thus, Noth understood premonarchic Israel as a sacral and judicial community that originated by voluntary covenant and was held together by the preservation of legal order, but Yahweh war receded as a binding element. Georg Fohrer had already rejected this model of a tribal confederation on the basis of evidence that no central cult existed in the premonarchic period, but this was based on sparse evidence rather than the juxtaposition of numerous shrine locations. Since the lists of judges in Judg 10:1–5 and 12:8–15 represent late formations analogous to the king schema (see §I.3.2.1), the assertion of an office over all Israel is understood only as a projection from the monarchic period to the premonarchic era so that the office of the judge appears as the preliminary stage of the monarchy. There is just as little evidence for a central office prior to the formation of the state as there is for a central shrine. Since the remaining presuppositions also do not withstand a critical examination, the thesis of a sacral tribal confederacy for premonarchic Israel must be given up. The idea of a premonarchic Israel as a particular community through the common cult, which already had the essential central authorities for coexistence available prior to the monarchic period, was first developed when Israel constituted a significant political force during the monarchy, through which all the tribes were integrated in the unity of one state.

Prior to their unification under the institution of the monarchy by Saul and David, the different tribes constituted no amphictyony but instead led independent lives for the most part. Common action was—as the Song of Deborah verifies—apparently compelled only by the necessity of defense against a common enemy. Against the background of common religion, Yahweh war was probably the only institution for common action.

II.5.2. Yahweh War

Rad, Gerhard von. *Holy War in Ancient Israel* (trans. and ed. Marva J. Dawn; Grand Rapids: Eerdmans, 1991). **Smend**, Rudolf. *Yahweh War and Tribal Confederation: Reflections upon Israel's Earliest History* (trans. Max Gray Rogers from 2nd German ed.; Nashville: Abingdon, 1970). **Stolz**, Fritz. *Jahwes und Israels Kriege: Kriegstheorien und Kriegserfahrungen im Glauben des alten Israel* (ATANT 60; Zurich: Theologischer Verlag, 1972). **Weippert**, Manfred. "'Heiliger Krieg' in Israel und Assyrien," *ZAW* 84 (1972): 460–93. See now also: **Thompson**, Thomas L. "Holy War at the Center of Biblical Theology: Shalom and the Cleansing of Jerusalem," in *Jerusalem in Ancient History and Tradition* (ed. Thomas L. Thompson; JSOTSup 381 = Copenhagen International Seminar 13; London: T&T Clark, 2003), 223–57. **Klingbeil**, Martin. *Yahweh Fighting from Heaven: God as Warrior and as God of Heaven in the Hebrew Psalter and Ancient Near Eastern Iconography* (OBO 169; Fribourg: Universitätsverlag; Göttingen: Vandenhoeck & Ruprecht, 1999).

Since nothing of the war narratives of the book of Judges can be dated to the premonarchic period with certainty, the Song of Deborah remains, in its earliest form (Judg 5:12–17, 18b, 19–22, 24–30), the only description of a military campaign in that era. Even if the song intoned by Deborah depicts only individual scenes in meager form, the sequence of events still develops clearly from the song. To begin with, every military campaign needs a competent leader, who in this case is named Barak son of Abinoam. Nothing is reported regarding his competency; his personality must have established the necessary qualifications. To mobilize the army levy, all the community of enlisted tribes were requested, but the dispatch of armed men apparently depended on the decision of the individual tribes; after all, five of the ten requested tribes were blamed for being absent in the battle of "the people of Yahweh." The five tribes who participated in the battle achieved the victory against "the kings of Canaan, at Taanach, by the waters of Megiddo," with cooperation from the forces of nature (Judg 5:20–21):

> The stars fought from heaven,
> > from their courses they fought against Sisera.
> The torrent Kishon swept them away,
> > the onrushing torrent, the torrent Kishon.

A description of the battle is lacking. The mention of horses indicates the use of chariots on the part of the Canaanites. These were not at the disposal of the Israelite tribes, so the Canaanites had the tactical advantage of quicker maneuverability in open terrain. Regardless of whether the name of God was pronounced in connection with the battle events, Yahweh was nevertheless presupposed as the God of the tribes because they were the "people of Yahweh" (Judg 5:13). The forces of nature, which intervene in favor of the people and ultimately decide the battle in their favor, are perhaps represented as independent cosmic powers, since the discourse does not say a word about Yahweh's action. These mighty acts are juxtaposed with the deed of Jael, which does not really have as much to do with the outcome of the battle but is of crucial significance for the wider fate of the people. It is her determination that brings about the death of the enemy leader Sisera, after he had arrived from the battle unhurt and on foot. With the triumph in mind, the song comes to a close by taunting the enemies.

Despite the intervention of the cosmic powers, Yahweh war is completely within the realm of human action. Only where humans withstand the challenge by the enemy do other powers take effect in the event in favor of the people of Yahweh. To be sure, the victory owes to supernatural help, but the annihilation of the enemy is by no means the work of God alone. According to the understanding of the Song of Deborah, Yahweh war is thus a war that Israel leads with help from Yahweh and not a war that Yahweh leads for Israel.

Since the view of Yahweh war changed drastically over the course of Israel's history, statements in later texts cannot simply be transferred to the premonarchic period. It is assumed that the army congregated in an army camp, but particular regulations do not appear to be connected with it.

In the Deuteronomistic History, war was a proof of the power of Yahweh, with Israel participating only in the consecration to destruction as instrument and executioner (cf. Josh 6). In the Chronicler's History, Yahweh war finally became "a great cultic venture operated according to strict regulations" (Smend, *Yahweh War*, 36), in which Israel participated only by fasting and prayer (cf. 2 Chr 20).

In the Song of Deborah, however, Yahweh war is still not a sacral institution; the embeddedness of preparation and development of military undertakings in cultic actions first accrues to Yahweh war over the course of the tradition. This cultic shaping also prohibits any inference from the later texts to circumstances in the premonarchic period. Yahweh war did not establish the unity of Israel, and such a unity is not even assumed. Prior to the formation of the state, there was merely the foundation in the obligation to conduct combat against a common enemy under a common leader and under the protection of a common God. This essential condition notwithstanding, the tribe could still be absent from the event by refusing to follow. Given the possibility of this decision, the tribe definitely had a certain sphere of action and proved to be an autonomous and independent entity. Not until the formation of the state did there exist the unification of the tribes as a political entity under the rule of a king.

II.5.3. The Tribes' Habitations

Fritz, Volkmar. *Das Buch Josua* (HAT 1/7; Tübingen: Mohr Siebeck, 1994). **Kallai**, Zecharia. *Historical Geography of the Bible: The Tribal Territories of Israel* (Jerusalem: Magnes, 1986). **Lindars**, Barnabas. "The Israelite Tribes in Judges," in *Studies in the Historical Books of the Old Testament* (ed. J. A. Emerton; VTSup 30; Leiden: Brill, 1979), 95–112. **Noth**, Martin. "Studien zu den historisch-geographischen Dokumenten des Josuabuches," *ABLAK* 1 (1971): 229–80. **Schunck**, Klaus-Dietrich. *Benjamin: Untersuchungen zur Entstehung und Geschichte eines israelitischen Stammes* (BZAW 86; Berlin: Töpelmann, 1963).

Although the understanding of all Israel as one community of twelve tribes first developed over the course of the monarchic period, the tribe nevertheless represented a firmly defined social entity. Indeed, the concept was not used in the Song of Deborah, yet the names of ten tribes were given. Thus, for early Israel the tribe was the form of organization of the people of Yahweh insofar as it represented a significant social unit. The tribe (שבט) was divided into individual clans (משפחה), which in turn comprised different families (בית אב). As a historical entity, the tribe thus included a series of connected groups. Nevertheless, whereas the families belonging to a clan were connected to one another by ancestry, the amalgamation of clans to a tribe could also owe to other factors besides blood relation. The tribe could likewise be constituted by a common history or a common settlement region. In any case, each tribe had its own history, even if this can be illuminated in no further detail owing to the paucity of sources. A "tribe" thus does not necessarily refer to a form of organization that already existed for individual groups prior to taking the land. On the contrary, individual tribes were first constituted out of different portions of populations in the land. Even if the question about the formation of different tribes cannot be clarified further, the possibility of the development in the cultivated land must remain open. Not until the monarchic period, with the plan of the twelve-tribe system, were all the tribes traced back to a tribal father, thus carrying out the principle of blood relation completely (cf. §II.5.1). All the members of a tribe derive from one eponym, such that the connection to a tribe establishes the families' history. The determination that the tribe comes from the lineage of a first ancestor is in any case not to be assumed for the early history of Israel. On the contrary, a tribe in the premonarchic period could indicate a regional incorporation of different clans and families. All that can be asserted is that each tribe, at whichever point it was established, constituted a relatively fixed entity.

In the enumeration of the Song of Deborah, no particular order or structure is discernible. The division into two groups results from their response to the call to participate in the planned military expedition. One can wonder, nevertheless, whether placing Ephraim first in one group and Reuben in the other reflects a special significance of these two tribes. In the later lists of the twelve-tribe system, the succession of tribes is subject to great variation, yet Reuben always stands first in the genealogical system, whereas in the geographic system even Judah can be named in the first position. At this point, the subsequent initial placement of Judah reflects the special position of this tribe in the monarchic period; accordingly, a historical role could be hidden behind the naming of Reuben in first position in the twelve-tribe system. This cannot be verified further by the sources, though, and thus lies hidden in the darkness of the early period.

For the individual tribes, the attempt should at least be made to ascertain what is discernible for the early history. The most important source is shown in the lists made in Josh 15–19. These contain descriptions of borders based on the basis of border check points and place lists. To be sure, this documentary material stems from the monarchic period at the earliest; however, since the cultivated land was a very limited area and the settlement regions were already occupied in the premonarchic period, the tribal regions were already determined at the beginning of the monarchic period. The circumstances put narrow limits on any change, such that the borders may hardly have changed at all over the course of the monarchic period. At most, alterations can be considered on the periphery where two tribes ran up against one another, but for the most part there were stable relationships. Regarding this stability, the settlement areas presumed for one time did not change at all through the transition from village to city at the beginning of the monarchic period. Even the establishment of new cities, which began under the influence of the monarchy in the tenth century, was carried out within the framework of the residential areas presumed at a given time. So with respect to the place names, it is to be emphasized at the outset that the lists in Josh 15–19 reflect the situation of the monarchic period, and a name can only then stem from the premonarchic period if the settlement of the place shows a corresponding continuation for the entire era of the Iron Age.

The division of the kingdom into twelve provinces shows just how strong the inertia of settlement regions of individual tribes must have been. In the document 1 Kgs 4:7–19, the eighth to eleventh provinces were simply designated by the name of the tribe. By and large this administrative installation marks the end of the exclusive validity of the tribal regions. Since the kingdom encompassed even the territories of the former Canaanite city-states, a restructuring was unavoidable, such that the remaining provinces no longer corresponded with the residences of individual tribes. The Solomonic era thus suggests a juxtaposition of different territorial demarcations.

Ephraim (אפרים) is probably originally the name of a territory that was constructed by the locative affix out of אפר "fruitful land." The name is connected to the central part of the central Palestinian mountains, the traditional name being הר אפרים, "mountains of Ephraim" (see, inter alia, Judg 7:24; 17:8; 18:2; 19:1, 16, 18). The name was thus transferred from the region to the group of inhabitants, who came to be understood as a tribe. Accordingly, Ephraim was also the name of one of the tribal fathers, but he is counted along with Manasseh as the son of Jacob's son Joseph. Given his identification in the Song of Deborah, it is unclear why Ephraim was not placed in the number of the sons of Jacob. The relation first comes about by adoption (Gen 48:1–20). Ephraim, like Manasseh, was presumably connected too closely with Joseph in the tradition to be counted in the succession of Jacob's biological sons. Consequently, the brotherhood of the two tribes Ephraim and Manasseh constitutes the "House of Joseph" (בית יוסף; see Gen 43:18, 19; 50:8; Josh 17:17; 18:5; Judg 1:22, 23, 35; 2 Sam 19:21; 1 Kgs 11:28; Amos 5:6; Obad 18; Zech 10:6). This summary under a common generic name shows a close connection between the two tribes. At this point, from the fact that Manasseh is not mentioned in the Song of Deborah, it can only be concluded that a tribe by that name did not exist at the time of the events described. As such, Manasseh can be designated among the tribes only as one born out of season, one who was first constituted in the monarchic period. Such a development could have taken place in one of two ways: either some parties of the tribe of Ephraim split off and additional parties settled in the mountain, or certain regions that did not belong to premonarchic Israel were distributed as a region of this tribe.

According to the tradition, the tribe of Manasseh at one time comprised the northern regions of the central Palestinian mountains from the summit of Tappuah (Tell Šeḫ Abū Zarad) to the ridge at the edge of the Jezreel Valley (see Josh 17:7–13). In addition, the northern east Jordanian land between Jabbok and Yarmuk was also attributed to Manasseh (see Josh 13:29–31; Num 32:39–

42). That allocation of regions on both sides of the Jordan—probably under the influence of the tribe named Machir in the Song of Deborah—was first attested in late (postexilic) texts and probably does not reflect a real historical process. This means, though, that a tribal territory of Manasseh was formed not by expanding the settlement but by allotment of additional regions. In the system of the tribes, Manasseh is at the earliest a construction from the monarchic period that was designed to seize areas that did not belong to tribal regions in the premonarchic period as now belonging to all Israel.

However, Ephraim is the designation for a region in the premonarchic period, whose name was transferred to the entirety of its inhabitants. According to Josh 16:5–9, the property of Ephraim inside the northern border of Benjamin, which is slightly south of present-day Ramallāh, extended at least to the summit of Tappuah. Therefore the tribal region should not be identified with the area of the "mountains of Ephraim," which could definitely stretch farther to the north and at least have encompassed the area of Shechem. According to 1 Kgs 4:8, the mountains of Ephraim constituted the first Solomonic province, which was apparently larger than the original tribal region. In any case, in the Song of Deborah Ephraim signifies the heartland of the mountains, which, according to the preliminary report, was densely settled in the Early Iron Age.

According to Judg 5:14, Benjamin (בנימין) takes a preeminent position, insofar as this tribe preceded all the other tribes. It is unknown to what extent the succession of the tribes participating in the expedition corresponded to a rank in status. In the metaphor of Gen 49:27, Benjamin appears to be an especially militaristic tribe, but the distribution of booty from a successful raid assumes a provenance in a foreign region. The saying possibly alludes to an independent military endeavor by the tribe in the premonarchic period. Therefore, it is hardly accidental that Saul, the first king, stemmed from Benjamin, since the formation of the monarchy was closely connected to military success. Still under David dangerous opponents grew out of this tribe, e.g. Shimei (2 Sam 16:5–14) and Sheba (2 Sam 20). The wider prehistory of the tribe lies in darkness. Even if the narrative of the Benjaminite Ehud (Judg 3:15–30) cannot be verified historically and cannot be interpreted in the sense of an oppression by Moab, it nevertheless indicates the ideal of fearless heroes in the context of war. The narrative of the tribal war against Benjamin (Judg 19–21) goes back just as little to a historical kernel (see §I.2.3.2); at most the piece reflects the wish to break forcefully the special prestige of this tribe by an action on the part of all Israel.

The name *Benjamin*, having the signification "son of the right side = the south" can have been conceived only after the tribe had a settled existence in the cultivated land, since it presupposes residence in the extreme south of the

Ephraimite mountains. The second millennium cuneiform expression *mārū yamīna'i* ("south people") has nothing to do with Benjamin either ethnically or historically.

According to the division of the kingdom in 927, Benjamin was caught between the fronts in a particular way, since the region between Israel and Judah was contested. Despite belonging to the southern kingdom, the northern border of Benjamin shifted multiple times as a result of confrontations with the neighboring states (see Schunck, *Benjamin*, 140ff.). The original settlement region therefore cannot be uncovered either from the description of the borders in Josh 18:11–20 or from the list of cities in Josh 18:21–28, since both stem first from the monarchic period. The list of the places of Benjamin in Neh 11:31–35 probably first arises from the postexilic period and can be left aside here. Nevertheless, in spite of minor differences, the core region of Benjamin is laid out in this document. The description of the borders of Benjamin is a combination of the southern border of Ephraim (Josh 16:2, 3a) and the northern border of Judah (Josh 15:5b–9), but the territory to the mountains and the western edge of the Jordan Valley remains restricted. Despite the partially detailed data in the description in Josh 18:11–20, the exact course of the borders remains vague. From the vicinity of Jericho (Tell es-Sulṭān) the border advances up to Bethel (Bētīn) and ends around Beth Horon (Bēt 'Ūr et-Taḥta). The southern border leads from Kiriath-jearim (Dēr el-Azhar) to Jerusalem (although the city is omitted), through the mountains east of Jerusalem back to the Jordan Valley. The region included in the place list of Josh 18:21–28 corresponds largely to what is described by the fixed border points. The territory of Benjamin was thus in the southern part of the Ephraimite mountains roughly between Jerusalem in the south and Bethel in the north. Since the place list stems from an independent source in the monarchic period, it clearly attests the use of tribal names to describe and determine certain regions. Yet under Solomon, the tribal region constituted its own province (1 Kgs 4:18).

Machir (מכיר) was equated with the remaining tribes in Judg 5:14. In all further texts that stem from the postexilic period, Machir is listed as a son of Manasseh and also as a clan within this large association. In the later systematization of the tribes during the monarchic period, Manasseh turned into a generic name for numerous groups named after their settlement regions; in the premonarchic period a tribe of Manasseh does not appear. Thus presumably even the northern part of the mountains of Ephraim, more particularly to the hills of Tappuah that belonged to Ephraim, did not belong to the territories of premonarchic Israel. In fact, not until the notion of the land acquisition by all Israel was the region of Manasseh added, which included territory on the eastern and western sides of the Jordan. In the tradition, the number of clans allotted to Manasseh fluctuates considerably. According to Num 32:39–

42, the clans Machir, Jair, and Nobah inhabited the northern east Jordanian land; for Machir there was an explicit claim to Gilead, the land on either side of the Jabbok. The original settlement region was nevertheless probably north of the territory of Gilead, since Gilead is named in Judg 5:17 as its own tribe. In Deut 3:13–14 only Machir and Jair were named; in Josh 13:30–32 and 17:1 Machir assumes a special position as the firstborn of Manasseh.

In the monarchic period, Machir appeared to be the most significant group east of the Jordan, having a far-reaching settlement region. The region belonging to Manasseh west of the Jordan was, in the postexilic texts of Num 26:30–32 and Josh 17:2, named after clans and cities that are known from the ostraca of Samaria: Abiezer, Helek, Asriel, Shechem, Hepher, and Shemida.[34] It is unknown why these cities and clans were not added to the tribe of Ephraim in the fictive distribution of the whole land. In any case, the assumption of a west Jordanian tribe of Manasseh and its expansion into the land east of the Jordan should be given up. Manasseh was first included as a tribe in the schema during the monarchic period, and then the parts of the mountains located between Ephraim and the Galilean tribes Issachar and Zebulun were subsumed under its name. The northern land east of the Jordan at most constituted an independent entity under the name Machir, which was probably north of Gilead geographically; the region was added to the new entity Manasseh by the change of the tribal system. That the name Machir means "one who sells oneself for payment" is not to be considered historical.

Concerning Zebulun (זבולן) little is known. In Judg 5:18a the name was transferred in order to produce the agreement with Judg 4:6. (The naming of Naphtali and Zebulun as participants in the battle in the prose report of Judg 4 was probably determined on the basis that the territories of both tribes bordered Mount Tabor, the place where the narrator shifted the action of the battle.) In the later tribal sayings of Gen 49:13 and Deut 33:13–14, Zebulun was connected with the sea, which presupposes an access to the coast. The resonance of a possible cultic practice at Tabor cannot be verified precisely,

---

34. See Yohanan Aharoni, *The Land of the Bible: A Historical Geography* (trans. Anson F. Rainey; 2nd ed.; Philadelphia: Westminster, 1979), 356–68; André Lemaire, *Les ostraca* (vol. 1 of *Inscriptions hébraïques*; Littératures anciennes du Proche-Orient 9; Paris: Cerf, 1977), 23–65; Benjamin Mazar, "The Historical Background of the Samaria Ostraca," in idem, *The Early Biblical Period: Historical Studies* (ed. Shmuel Ah[ituv and Baruch A. Levine; trans. Ruth and Elisheva Rigbi; Jerusalem: Israel Exploration Society, 1986), 173–88; Martin Noth, "Der Beitrag der samarischen Ostraka zur Lösung topographischer Fragen," *PJ* 28 (1932): 54–67; idem, "Das Krongut der israelitischen Könige und seine Verwaltung," *ABLAK* 1 (1971): 159–82. See now also Hermann Michael Niemann, "A New Look at the Samaria Ostraca: The King-Clan Relationship," *Tel Aviv* 35 (2008): 249–66.

but there may have been a shrine in the region of this massive towering mountain. The meaning of the name is unclear; the possible derivation from the word זבל ("lift up") offers no insight whatsoever. According to the description in Josh 19:10–16, the tribal region may have comprised a part of southern Galilee and the northern Jezreel Valley. Since the border description given in Josh 19:10–16 was first created by the Deuteronomistic Historian, the basis for the named section must have been a list of the places of Zebulun. According to the original place list, in which admittedly only a few places can be identified, Zebulun inhabited a region east of Tabor that in the north reached up to the southern end of the valley Sahl Baṭṭōf, and in the south was probably marked off by the edge of the mountain. Its extension to the east is not clear, especially since a connection to the sea must be assumed. The tribal region of Zebulun possibly even included the southern part of the Valley of Acco.

The tribe Issachar (יששכר) still had an enclosed region at the time of Solomon, since it constituted its own province in the division of the land. The prehistory of the tribe is unknown, given that nothing can be assumed historically from the metaphor in Gen 49:14. The comparison with the ass could transfer the preference for this riding and pack animal to the tribe and probably points out cleverness and care, patience and contentedness. In the poetic literature, the wild ass signified the desire for freedom and independence (cf. Job 6:5; 11:12; 39:5–8). Issachar should thus be assessed positively by the tribal saying. The tribal region is determined in Josh 19:18–20 by a place list, according to which it comprised the lower Galilee east of Tabor up to the hills of the southern edge of Lake Genessaret; the bay of Beth-Shean was not included, however. The point in time and the circumstances of the development of the settlement are unknown, which is the case with all the Galilean tribes. Like Zebulun, Issachar bordered in the south the territories of the former Canaanite city-states, whereas in the northern Upper Galilee the tribes of Naphtali and Asher were settled.

Reuben (ראבן) stands at the top of the tribal lists according to both the genealogical and geographic system; accordingly, he is the first ancestor of the tribe, as the eldest son of Jacob. The basis for this preeminence is unknown. According to the narrative of the allocation of the land east of the Jordan by Moses (Num 32) Reuben belonged to the east Jordanian tribes, which had possibly carried out their land acquisition independent of the west Jordanian tribes (see §I.2.1.3). By no means did Reuben stem from the land west of the Jordan; instead Reuben was indigenous to the strip of cultivated land and the steppe regions bordering it in the southern east Jordanian land. According to the city list in Josh 13:15–23, which is partially identical to that in Num 32:34–38, the settlement region of Reuben extended over the entire east Jordanian high plateau up to the Arnon River. Since the area east of the Dead Sea was lost to King Mesha of Moab in the ninth century, this list could convey the relationships of the tenth or even the eleventh century. Reuben is thus the tribe farthest south in the land east of the Jordan, and Reuben's land acquisition probably took place prior to the formation of the Ammonite and Moabite states. Apparently Reuben had become insignificant in the early monarchic period, and his role in the early history lies in darkness.

Gilead (גלעד) turned from a territory name into a tribal designation. The name was preserved in Ḫirbet Ǧelʿad in the central land east of the Jordan, and originally Gilead designated the area south of Jabbok (Arḍ el-ʿArḍe), but the concept was also transferred to the region north of Jabbok (Ǧebel ʿAǧlūn). With the introduction of the tribal names Manasseh and Gad, northern Gilead was attributed to Manasseh, whereas southern Gilead was added to Gad (cf. Josh 13:24–31). As long as the names Manasseh and Gad were still uncommon, Gilead served as a collective designation for the inhabitants of the central land east of the Jordan and also as the name of a tribe. Already in the Solomonic period Gilead was used as an identification of the central land east of the Jordan (1 Kgs 4:19); the name gained acceptance as a territorial designation.

Dan (דן) was probably a relatively smaller tribe (see Judg 13:25), originally indigenous to the vicinity of Zorah (Ṣarʿa) and Eshtaol (Ḫirbet Dēr Sūbēb). This region is also mentioned along with foreign ships (Judg 5:17), which presumes a proximity in the coastal plains. By contrast, the saying in Gen 49:17 shows the strategic location of habitation to be at the edge of the mountain, with its important ascent in the central Palestinian mountain area. In the place list of Josh 19:41–46, the region of Dan reaches to the coastal plains between Sorek and Yarqon; however, this list hardly dates before the seventh century and reflects relationships that do not correspond to the premonarchic period. In the eleventh century the tribe of Dan was probably exposed in a particular way to the pressure of the Philistines and therefore sought out new settlement places toward the end of the premonarchic period; the city of Laish is attested in the Jordan sources and was made into the center of a new tribal region. In any case, the new name of the city Dan and the tradition in Judg 17–18 (see §I.2.3.2) assumes such a change. In addition, the reference to the area Bashan in the saying in Deut 33:22 already has in mind the new territory in the north of the land.

Asher (אשר) constituted a province by the division of state regions under Solomon (1 Kgs 4:16) and was thus an enclosed settlement region available still in the tenth century and whose vicinity on the coast clearly developed from Judg 5:17. Additional information concerning the early history is lacking; the statements of the tribal sayings in Gen 49:20 and Deut 33:24 at least attest economic prosperity. The name is formed from the word אשר, "happy blessededness," but the precise meaning cannot be ascertained. The name is not attested outside the Bible, since the reading *i-ś-r in the lists of Pharaohs Seti I and Ramses II refer to Assyria.[35] In the description of the settlement from the monarchic period in Josh 19:24–31, an extensive place list was reorganized, with the help of additional geographic landmarks, into a description of borders. At the same time, however, inconsistencies in the groups of names remained such that a meaningful series of border points cannot be formed. The place of the original list that could be located was in the western Upper Galilee on the coast and in the northern part of the Valley of Acco. In the south, the tribal region bordered on the region of Zebulun, and in the north it would not cross the hills of Rās en-Nāqūra.

The tribe of Naphtali (נפתלי) was under Solomon likewise identified as its own province (1 Kgs 4:15). The meaning of the name is not certain, but it probably has to do with a tribal designation. In the tribal saying of Gen 49:21, Naphtali is compared to a hind, a doe, but the meaning of this image is unclear. By then the Mesopotamian fallow deer, which were earlier indigenous to the Galilean wilderness, were already extinct, having been hunted for their delicious meat. The comparison perhaps alludes to the secluded way of life and sudden appearance from the wild, as is typical of all species of deer. In any case, the metaphor draws on Galilean fauna. A place list underlies the description of the tribal region in Josh 19:32–39. The territory encompassed the eastern Galilee; the upper Jordan Valley was largely an unsettled marshland. In the north it reaches to Kadesh (Qedes) and in the south to the end of Lake Genessaret; in the west it included the eastern part of the Sahl Baṭṭōf. The region of Naphtali bordered in the east on Lake Genessaret and on the Jordan Valley, in the south on the regions of Issachar and Zebulun, and in the west on the region of Asher.

The tribes named in the Song of Deborah thus comprise three groups corresponding to their geographic division:

(1) The central Palestinian tribes: Ephraim; Benjamin; Dan
(2) The Galilean tribes: Zebulun; Issachar; Asher; Naphtali
(3) The east Jordanian tribes: Reuben; Machir; Gilead

Based on this division, three historical conclusions are possible:

(1) The southern Palestinian tribes were not named and thus did not participate in the events of Judg 4–5. Thus it follows clearly that Judah and the

---

35. Jan Jozef Simons, *Handbook for the Study of Egyptian Topographical Lists Relating to Western Asia* (Leiden: Brill, 1937), nos. XVII,4 and XXV,8.

additional groups subsumed under this name did not belong to premonarchic Israel but rather constituted an independent entity with an independent history.

(2) The northern tribes occupied settlement regions enclosed only in the area of Galilee and in the southern part of the central Palestinian mountainous land. Not only did the coastal plains and the wider parts of the Jezreel Valley lay outside the tribal region, but the greater part of the central Palestinian mountains was not the territory of a tribe but rather was only added to the tribe of Manasseh in the subsequent construction of the monarchic period.

(3) In addition to Reuben, the east Jordanian tribes were named Machir and Gilead. The designations Gad and Manasseh first became transferred to the east Jordanian tribes during the monarchic period, and then they appear in the different systems of the tribes. Since there is no description of the territories for the three tribes Machir, Gilead, and Reuben, the tribal territories cannot be precisely delineated; instead, their location can only be approximated. These three groups probably did not acquire a closed settlement of the entire east Jordanian land in the eleventh century. In any case, the Jordan Valley was not included.

According to this analysis, in the eleventh century the settlement by the tribes was limited to only parts of the land. There are two factors to explain this. First, the valleys were still entirely or partly occupied settlements that succeeded the Canaanite city-states; second, the individual groups were numerically small units that could occupy only a limited settlement area.

The entire land was not allocated according to tribes until the monarchic period with the "system of tribes." To be sure, this distribution had a beginning point in the data of the early period, but by no means did this correspond with reality prior to the formation of the state. Not until the monarchy, with its claim to a territorial state, did the idea of a settlement of the entire land by Israelite tribes take shape. This conception of one Israel "from Dan to Beer-sheba" then became projected back to the prehistory. Indeed, the majority of tribes had already constituted their territories already in the eleventh century, but they inhabited only a meager portion of the later state organization. Still under Saul the monarchy appears not to have had an enclosed state territory. Instead, the state was composed of individual tribal regions, as the list of regions controlled by Ishbaal in 2 Sam 2:9 still indicates. Perhaps the reported inheritance of Ishbaal, the king of Abner's favor, was smaller than the kingdom ruled by Saul; however, it was still constituted according to tribes and territories. The concluding phrase "and over all Israel" is clearly a subsequent interpretation. As such, Ishbaal ruled over Gilead, Asher, Jezreel, Ephraim, and Benjamin. The names of the four tribes were already named in the Song of Deborah; by Jezreel only the

Jezreel Valley can be meant, which at least partially belonged to the region of Zebulun and Issachar. Even if, by the designation Jezreel, the region of these two tribes was intended, the named tribes of 2 Sam 2:9 still lack those of Judg 5:14–17, 18b, namely, Naphtali, Dan, Machir, and Reuben; as such, Ishbaal exerted rule over only a part of the Israelite tribes and hardly over an existing enclosed state territory. By his military expeditions and conquests, David was the first to create a territorial whole in which the remaining regions of the land were enclosed in addition to the tribal regions.

The naming of numerous tribes after territory names shows that they could not have constituted a social entity until they were in the land. The tribes thus hardly immigrated to the land as a closed group, but rather first consolidated after conquering certain settlement regions. Their prehistory is unknown, but it must have had one or even several common characteristics as prerequisite to having achieved such an amalgamation. Each or even several tribes could have had in common the same economy, ancestry, or even religion.

II.6. The Religion of Yahweh

In the law collection of Deuteronomy, which is stylized as a speech by Moses, monotheism became presupposed as historical reality. The Deuteronomistic History followed on this programmatic proclamation of Yahweh as the one and only God of the pre-Priestly historical writings according to which the worship of Yahweh had begun in the time before the flood with Enosh, the grandson of Adam (Gen 4:26). According to the biblical view, monotheism belonged to Israel from the beginning: Yahweh is the creator of the world, the God of the patriarchs, and the God who brought Israel out of Egypt. The confession to the one God found its binding formulation in Deut 6:4: יהוה אלהינו יהוה אחד. According to Hebrew grammar, there are different opinions on the syntax of the sentence,[36] and thus different translations are possible:

---

36. See Eduard Nielsen, "Weil Jahwe unser Gott ein Jahwe ist" (Dtn 6:4f.), in *Beiträge zur alttestamentlichen Theologie: Festschrift für Walther Zimmerli zum 70. Geburtstag* (ed. Herbert Donner et al.; Göttingen: Vandenhoeck & Ruprecht, 1977), 288–301; Timo Veijola, "Höre Israel! Der Sinn und Hintergrund von Deuteronomium VI 4-9," *VT* 42 (1992): 528–41; Georg Braulik, "Das Deuteronomium und die Geburt des Monotheismus," in idem, *Studien zur Theologie des Deuteronomiums* (Stuttgarter biblische Aufsatzbände 2; Stuttgart: Katholisches Bibelwerk, 1988), 257–300. On the Samaritan view of the proclamation, see Rudolf Macuch, "On the Pre-history of the Credal Formula 'There Is No God but God,'" in *The Development of Islamic Ritual* (ed. Gerald Hartwing; article trans. A. Gwendolin Goldbloom; Burlington, Vt.: Ashgate, 2006); trans. of "Zur Vorgeschichte der Bek-

Yahweh, our God, Yahweh (is) unique.
Yahweh, our God, (is) one Yahweh.
Yahweh (is) our God, Yahweh (is) unique.

The translation of יהוה אחד as "Yahweh alone" is simply ruled out, since the Hebrew numeral "one" cannot be used adverbially. Despite the finding that אלהינו frequently appears in apposition to יהוה, it is syntactically more likely that two parallel statements are present, having either similar or complementary content. The two parts of the statement are thus to be understood each time as nominal sentences, "which, according to the rule of parallelism, express approximately the same thing concerning Yahweh." The meaning of both sentences is, then, not to be found in a statement about the essence of Yahweh. On the contrary, Yahweh is solely and exclusively the God of Israel: "Yahweh is our God, Yahweh is unique." The formulation after the imperative "Hear, O Israel" proves to be "a confession to Yahweh as the unique God of Israel,"[37] which was probably first developed in connection with Deuteronomistic theology. This understanding of the sentence is supported by the formulation in Deut 4:35 (cf. 4:38), where the uniqueness of Yahweh is emphasized once again: "Yahweh is God and no one else besides him." According to this statement, Yahweh is not only the single God, but in fact even the existence of other gods is ruled out. Since Deuteronomistic theology first originated toward the end of the monarchy in Judah, the proclamation in Deut 6:4 was formulated initially in the seventh century under particular historical conditions and cannot be assumed in this form in the preceding eras. The form of monotheism so expressed can by no means be transferred to the early history of Israel. Monotheism thus entails the exclusive acknowledgment and worship of a single deity. This monotheistic level of understanding God was not attained until during the exile with the preaching of Deutero-Isaiah. According to Isa 44:6; 45:5, 6, 18; and 46:9, Yahweh, as the sole God, is the God of the entire world and its creator and sustainer; all other gods are as such nonexistent.

So, then, the monarchic period shows itself to be an era of debate concerning Yahweh as the only God.[38] Besides Yahweh, numerous other god-

---

enntnisformel lā ilāha illā llāhu," *ZDMG* 128 (1978): 20–38. See also Oswald Loretz, *Des Gottes Einzigkeit: Ein altorientalisches Argumentationsmodell zum 'Schma Jisrael'* (Darmstadt: Wissenschaftliche Buchgesellschaft, 1997).

37. Timo Veijola, "Höre Israel! Der Sinn und Hintergrund von Deuteronomium vi 4–9," *VT* 42 (1992): 531: "die nach den Regeln des Parallelismus ungefähr dasselbe über Jahwe aussagen"; and 536: "ein Bekenntnis zu Jahwe als dem einzigen Gott Israels."

38. See Bernhard Lang, *Der einzige Gott: Die Geburt des biblischen Monotheismus* (Munich: Kösel, 1981); Othmar Keel, ed., *Monotheismus im alten Israel und seiner Umwelt*

desses and gods are attested, so that a pluralism in the worship of the God of Israel is inferred that can be characterized as polytheism. As distinguished from Yahweh, these other divinities are attested in the environment, and it is assumed that they were the subjects of religious ideas and practices. In contrast, in the biblical tradition, Yahweh appears as the genuine God from the beginning of history on; therefore, the question as to the origin and rootedness of Yahweh worship in the early history must be examined specifically. Since written sources are lacking for the era before 1000, every examination relies on inference. One must be explicitly cautious before projecting back an inference, given that the relationships of the early period could in no way correspond to those of the monarchic period and its completely different conditions. Additionally, the designed portrait of Yahweh's progressive revelation that appears in Israel's historical writings cannot be enlisted for the reconstruction of ancient Israelite religion, since this concept was first developed during the monarchic period.

II.6.1. The Name of Yahweh

Abba, Raymond. "The Divine Name Yahweh," *JBL* 80 (1961): 320–28. **Astour,** Michael C. "Yahweh in Egyptian Topographical Lists," in *Festschrift Elmar Edel: 12 März 1979* (ed. Manfred Görg and Edgar Pusch; ÄAT 1; Bamberg: Görg, 1979), 17–33. **Brownlee,** William Hugh. "The Ineffable Name of God," *BASOR* 226 (1977): 29–46. **Cross,** Frank Moore. "Yahweh and El," in idem, *Canaanite Myth and Hebrew Epic: Essays in the History of the Religion of Israel* (Cambridge, Mass.: Harvard University Press, 1973), 44–75. **Delekat,** Lienhard. "Yāhō-Yahwáe und die alttestamentlichen Gottesnamenkorrekturen," in *Tradition und Glaube: Das frühe Christentum in seiner Umwelt: Festgabe für Karl Georg Kuhn zum 65. Geburtstag* (ed. Gert Jeremias et al.; Göttingen: Vandenhoeck & Ruprecht, 1971), 23–75. **Freedman,** David Noel. "The Name of the God of Moses," *JBL* 79 (1960): 151–56. **Görg,** Manfred. "Jahwe—ein Toponym?" *BN* 1 (1976): 7–14. **Görg.** "Anfänge israelitischen Gottesglaubens," *Kairos* 18 (1976): 256–64. **Herrmann,** Siegfried. "Die alttestamentliche Gottesname," in idem, *Gesammelte Studien zur Geschichte und Theologie des Alten Testaments* (TB 75; Munich: Kaiser, 1986), 76–88. **Knauf,** Ernst Axel. *Midian: Untersuchungen zur Geschichte Palästinas und Nordarabiens am Ende des 2. Jahrtausends v.Chr.* (ADPV 10; Wies-

---

(Biblische Beiträge 14; Fribourg: Verlag Schweizerisches Katholisches Bibelwerk, 1980); Walter Dietrich and Martin A. Klopfenstein, eds., *Ein Gott allein? JHWH-Verehrung und biblischer Monotheismus im Kontext der israelitischen und altorientalischen Religionsgeschichte* (OBO 139; Göttingen: Vandenhoeck & Ruprecht, 1994). See now also Othmar Keel, *Die Geschichte Jerusalems und die Entstehung des Monotheismus* (2 vols.; Orte und Landschaften der Bibel 4.1; Göttingen: Vandenhoeck & Ruprecht, 2007).

baden: Harrassowitz, 1988), 43-63. **MacLaurin,** E. C. B. "YHWH: The Origin of the Tetragrammaton," *VT* 12 (1962): 439–63. **Mayer,** Rudolf. "Der Gottesname im Lichte der neueren Forschung," *BZ* n.F. 2 (1958): 26–53. **Mowinckel,** Sigmund. "The Name of the God of Moses," *HUCA* 32 (1961): 121–33. **Rose,** Martin. *Jahwe: zum Streit um den alttestamentlichen Gottesnamen* (ThSt 122; Zurich: Theologischer Verlag, 1978). **Schmid,** H. "JHWH, der Gott der Hebräer," *Judaica* 25 (1969): 257–66. **Schleif,** A. "Der Gottesname Jahwe," *ZDMG* 90 (1936): 679–702. **Soden,** Wolfram von. "Jahwe, 'Er ist, Er erweist sich,'" *WO* 3 (1964–66): 177–87. See now also: **De Troyer,** Kristin. "The Names of God: Their Pronunciation and Their Translation—A Digital Tour of Some of the Main Witnesses," *lectio difficilior* 2 (2005); online: http://www.lectio.unibe.ch/05_2/troyer_names_of_god.htm. **Kooten,** George H. van, ed. *The Revelation of the Name YHWH to Moses: Perspectives from Judaism, the Pagan Graeco-Roman World, and Early Christianity* (Themes in Biblical Narrative 9; Jewish and Christian Traditions; Leiden: Brill, 2006).

According to Deuteronomistic theology, Yahweh is the only God and as such the only God to whom worship is due, since he is the creator of the world and the lord of history. Over the course of the monarchy, this form of monotheism clashed with the claims of other gods that developed and gained acceptance in the exilic period. Yahweh is considered the God from the very beginning of the world, and he approaches Israel through history. The origin of Yahweh worship cannot be verified by means of sources. At this point, though, Yahweh was used as the proper name of God from the early monarchic period in the biblical literature, such that the ideas connected to the name predate the monarchic period. The designation of the tribes as "people of Yahweh" in Judg 5:13 is regarded as the only example from the premonarchic period.

Although the original vocalization of the name of God יהוה (*Yhwh*) is not handed down, the pronunciation "Yahweh" can be considered definite. The long form, the Tetragrammaton, as opposed to the short form, יהו (*Yhw* = *Yahû*), represents the original spelling. The short form can be shortened further still as יה (*Yh* = *Yah*) and יו (*Yw* = *Yô*) (evidence in M. Weippert, *RlA* 5:246–53). All these spellings are also supported by inscriptions outside the Bible: the Tetragrammaton is found since the ninth century on the Mesha inscription, in the tomb inscriptions of Ḫirbet el-Qōm and Ḫirbet Bēt Lēy, as well as in the ostraca of Arad and Lachish (evidence by D. N. Freedman, *ThWAT* 3:535–39). Analogous to the ancient Semitic one-sentence names, Yahweh is to be regarded as a finite verbal form: third person masculine singular imperfect of the verb *h-y-h* ("to be"). The nearest parallels show that names of God were formed in the same way in Old Arabic: *Yaʿūq*, "he protects"; *Yaʿbūb*, "he sprouts up here"; *Yaġūt*, "he helps" (evidence in Knauf, *Midian*, 44). Since a hiphil form of *h-y-h* is not supported, the only remaining view is that of the meaning "he is" in the sense of "he proves himself" (W. von Soden). This essential designation of Yahweh as developed from the name, however, gives no indication at all concerning the origin and form of early Yahweh worship.

A folk-etymological interpretation of the name of Yahweh is found in Exod 3:14 in the self-introduction אהיה אשר אהיה. The context of Exod 3:9–14 is generally attributed to the Elohist, but the designation of the source to which it belongs is irrelevant for understanding the passage.[39] It is a play on words with the finite verbal form first person singular imperfect of the verb היה (h-y-h). The interpretation of the sentence must therefore come from the basic meaning of היה (h-y-h). The meaning of the word is to be understood as "to be" or "to become" in the sense of an event (cf. Ps 89:37 [Eng. v. 36])), and the verb is defined as a dynamic and not a static concept. Thus, there are resonating nuances such as "existence" (*Dasein*) or "presence," and the word is always directed toward effectiveness. By no means can h-y-h be understood in the sense of an ontological expression, as the Septuagint suggests with the translation ὁ ὤν. The verbal form shows an unfinished action, and the duration is expressed at most through the future. The sense of the sentence is therefore not grasped correctly by the Septuagint, but rather through the future translation by Luther: "I will be who I will be" ("Ich werde sein, der ich sein werde"). The element of the effectiveness of God that is contained in the word's meaning is then emphasized even more strongly by Martin Buber: "I will exist as who I will exist" ("Ich werde dasein, als der ich dasein werde"). The sentence thus makes no statement concerning the manner of being or the essentiality of Yahweh, but rather it comprises the offer of divine presence as the existence of God in

---

39. On Exod 3:14, see Th. C. Vriezen, "'*Ehje 'ašer 'ehje*," in *Festschrift, Alfred Bertholet zum 80. Geburtstag* (ed. Walter Baumgartner; Tübingen: Mohr Siebeck, 1950), 498–512; Johannes Lindblom, "Noch einmal die Deutung des Jahwe-Namens in Ex 3,14," *ASTI* 3 (1964): 4–15; W. H. Schmidt, "Der Jahwename und Ex 3,14," in *Textgemäss: Aufsätze und Beiträge zur Hermeneutik des Alten Testaments. Festschrift für Ernst Würthwein zum 70. Geburtstag* (ed. A. H. J. Gunneweg and Otto Kaiser; Göttingen: Vandenhoeck & Ruprecht, 1979), 123–38; Hans-Peter Müller, "Der Jahwename und seine Deutung Ex 3,14," *Bib* 62 (1981): 305–27; Magne Saebø, "Offenbarung oder Verhüllung? Bemerkungen zum Charakter des Gottesnamens in Ex 3:13–15," in *Die Botschaft und die Boten: Festschrift für Hans Walter Wolff zum 70. Geburtstag* (ed. Jörg Jeremias and Lothar Perlitt; Neukirchen-Vluyn: Neukirchener, 1981), 43–55. See now also William M. Schniedewind, "Explaining God's Name in Exodus 3," in *"Basel und Bibel": Collected Communications to the XVIIth Congress of the International Organization for the Study of the Old Testament, Basel 2001* (ed. Matthias Augustin and Hermann Michael Niemann; BEATAJ 51; Frankfurt am Main: Lang, 2004), 13–18; Cornelis den Hertog, "The Prophetic Dimension of the Divine Name: On Exodus 3:14a and Its Context," *CBQ* 64 (2002): 213–28; Anthony Phillips and Lucy Phillips, "The Origin of 'I Am' in Exodus 3.14," *JSOT* 78 (1998): 81–84; Vladimir Orel, "The Words on the Doorpost," *ZAW* 109 (1997): 614–17.

the sense of future presence. The name will be interpreted to the effect that the nearness of God was declared for the future. In Exod 3:14 there is thus no statement concerning the original meaning, but rather an interpretation of the name that comes from reflection. Yahweh proves himself to be the God of Israel by his existence, which his action in history in support of his people guarantees. The name is not deciphered, but is interpreted in the sense of a theology of presence. By this disclosure of God's continuing works in history, the meaning of the name of Yahweh is, however, not illuminated but rather further obscured.

Therefore, there is no possibility that deciphering the name of Yahweh will lead to the origins of Yahweh worship. There is even less chance of working back to the beginnings of ancient Israelite religion. Since Yahweh is not named in the Canaanite pantheon, it must be concluded that the Israelite tribes did not adopt their God from the realm of the gods of Canaan. On the contrary, a particularity exists with the worship of Yahweh that constitutes a critical distinction between early Israel and its environment. Furthermore, יהוה (*Yhwh*) is not attested as a name of a god in either Akkadian or Egyptian sources. The single comparable piece of evidence is found in the geographic list of Amenhotep III (1391–1353) from Soleb; it was copied under Ramses II in ʿAmarah (see Astour, "Yahweh," 19). Altogether, six of the listed places begin with the phrase *tꜣ šꜣsw*, "land of Shasu." The Shasu were a nomadic group from the steppes region of the Near East (see §II.4.2), and the name following the phrase "land of Shasu" is clearly to be understood as a designation for a territory. Under this register there is also found the connection *tꜣ šꜣsw yhwꜣ*, "Land of Shasu of Yahu." From the preceding context it is thus clear that *yhwꜣ* designates a region, which then appears also in the shortened form *yh* in lists of Ramses III. The identified region cannot be located precisely, but based on the name Shasu in this context it is at least to be found in the east and south in the cultivated land of Syria-Palestine bordering the steppes region. From the rest of the geographic names listed in the writing, perhaps *sʿrr* can be identified with the biblical Seir (שעיר) and thus be found in the region of Edom. Nevertheless, the establishment of the region named *yhwꜣ* in northwest Arabia is still not certain.

Without reservation or difficulties, the consonants *yhwꜣ* permit comparison with the Tetragrammaton *Yhwh*. The equation of *yhwꜣ* with יהוה *Yhwh* can nevertheless be claimed only by qualifying that the name of the territory turned into the name of the God. Such a transference is in no way ruled out from the outset, since one name can definitely represent the deity, the land, and the inhabitants, as is perhaps the case with Ashur. Thus, it may be that Yahweh signifies the name of a region and at one time was considered its God. This thesis at least needs to be examined with regard to its probability. The thesis then proves correct if it can be demonstrated or at least maintained with some certainty that originally Yahweh was confined to a region in the south of Palestine bordering the west.

On this point, in the depictions of the theophanies there are explicit descriptions of Yahweh's arrival from southern lands in three places:

> Yahweh, when you went out from Seir,
> when you marched from the region of Edom. (Judg 5:4)

> Yahweh came from Sinai,
> and lighted upon us from Seir
> He appeared from Mount Paran
> and came to Meribath-kadesh. (Deut 33:2)

> God came from Teman
> and the Holy One from Mount Paran. (Hab 3:3)

All three statements put Yahweh in connection with regions far to the south at Sinai or near northwest Arabia. However, none of the three passages can lay claim to a great age, so the question whether these passages preserve older traditions must be examined in each individual case.

Judges 5:4 belongs to the hymnic framework of the Song of Deborah and was composed at the earliest in the monarchic period, alluding to Seir and Edom, which are east of the Arabah. Both are names of territories, with Edom "the Red" designating the narrow strip of cultivated land at the drop-off of the eastern Jordanian high plateau, and Seir "the hairy" designating the mid-level of the mountains of Nubian sandstone. The name refers to the former woodlands of this mountain drop-off. Both names are already attested in Egyptian sources of the New Kingdom (see Manfred Weippert, "Edom und Israel," *TRE* 9:291–99). The name Edom was then transferred to the inhabitants of the mountains. These probably merged for the first time in the eighth-century state formation, whereas in the tenth century Edom was ruled by the kings in Jerusalem. Yahweh's actual place of residence before his theophany is thus clearly delineated: it was outside the settlement territories of the Israelite tribes in the district in whose proximity the land named *yhwꜣ* is also to be found. This location is not derivable from the wider biblical tradition and stands in contrast to the view borrowed from Canaanite mythology that Yahweh's place was in Mount Zaphon in the north (cf. Ps 48:3 [Eng. v. 2]; Isa 14:13).[40] This notion of an arrival of Yahweh out of Edom and Seir can only stem from a tradition in

---

40. See Otto Eissfeldt, *Baal Zaphon, Zeus Kasios und der Durchzug der Israeliten durchs Meer* (Beiträge zur Religionsgeschichte des Altertums 1; Halle: Niemeyer, 1932); William Foxwell Albright, *"Baal-Zaphon,"* in *Festschrift, Alfred Bertholet zum 80. Geburtstag* (ed.

which a causal connection existed between the God and his "residence." The name Yahweh thus definitely could have been confined to a particular territory in northwest Arabia, albeit one that is no longer to be delimited.

Deuteronomy 33:2 and Hab 3:3 point in the same direction. Both passages stem from the end of the monarchic period at the earliest and already evince a certain literary tradition by their geographic terms: Sinai is the name of the mountain of God (Exod 19:18); Paran is a desert mountain in the region of the present-day Sinai Peninsula (Num 10:12; 12:16), whose exact location is indeed unknown but must be found in Sinai. The name still adheres today to Wādī Fērān in the south of the peninsula. According to the Deuteronomistic History, Meribath-kadesh is the place of the sojourn of Israel at the end of the wandering in the wilderness (Deut 1:2, 19, 46; 2:14; 9:23); the place can be identified with Tell el-Quḍērāt on the eastern edge of the Sinai Peninsula. Place designations concerning the wilderness tradition from the pre-Priestly writings and the Deuteronomistic History are thus forced into Deut 33:2; as such, the formula of the appearance of Yahweh with respect to the place statements would be brought into harmony with the biblical tradition.

In Hab 3:3 there is a mixture of geographic terms. Teman is a common synonym for Edom (cf. Amos 1:12; Jer 49:7, 20; Ezek 25:13; Obad 1:9) and refers to the place east of the (Arabah. However, the naming of Paran refers at the same time to the mountain of the Sinai Peninsula. The old tradition about the arrival of Yahweh from Edom thus appeared alongside the location from the literary tradition of the Tetrateuch.

In the historical narrative of the pre-Priestly writings, Sinai is the mountain of the theophany (Exod 19); the Deuteronomistic History borrowed the idea of the mountain of God but named the place of the event Horeb (Deut 1:2, 6, 19; 4:10, 15 *inter alia*). As one station in the wandering in the wilderness, Sinai was in the region of the present-day Sinai Peninsula, and without an exact location, the mountain is possibly one within the mountain mass; the determination at the Ǧebel Mūsa in the vicinity of St. Catherine's Monastery goes back demonstrably to the Christian anchorites of the fourth century at the earliest.[41] The description of the theophany in Exod 19 with the imagery of fire and smoke makes Yahweh appear as a storm and tempest god; these images correspond to the ideas of the appearance of Yahweh as they would develop in the Jerusalem temple (cf. Pss 18:8–16 [Eng. vv. 7–15]; 50:3; 97:2–5;

Walter Baumgartner; Tübingen: Mohr Siebeck, 1950), 1–14; H. Schmid, "Jahwe und die Kulttraditionen von Jerusalem," *ZAW* 67 (1955): 168–98.

41. See Paul Maiberger, *Topographische und historische Untersuchungen zum Sinaiproblem: Worauf beruht die Identifizierung des Ǧabal Mūsā mit dem Sinai* (OBO 54; Göttingen: Vandenhoeck & Ruprecht, 1984).

104:32).⁴² In any case, the view is untenable that the transference in Exod 19 used images of the phenomena of a volcanic eruption and so established the transfer of Sinai to northwest Arabia (see Knauf, *Midian*, 56–60).

In confining the theophany to Sinai, the pre-Priestly history did not simply abandon the geographic framework of the exodus and wandering in the wilderness and fall back on cultic-shaped figurative speech, as is also evidenced in the theophany descriptions of Psalms. As artistic as the literary compilation was, the keyword connection of סיני (*syny*) to סנה (*snh*) also shows that the revelation at Sinai was prepared for intentionally by the call of Moses at the thornbush in Exod 3. In any case, nothing indicates that the view of the theophany description refers back to an old tradition of a mountain of God. An assimilation of elements, such as resonates in Judg 5:4, is not given in Exod 19. Instead, with the Sinai narrative it is a literary construction of the monarchic period.

That Sinai appears as the divine mountain in Exod 19 must be strictly separated from Yahweh's possible land of origin east of the Arabah (Judg 5:4). The narrative of the revelation of God at Sinai, by its position in connection to the exodus tradition, is certainly and completely independent of the expression of Yahweh's homeland in the south of the eastern Jordanian highlands and mountains. Since the geographic location of the mountain of the theophany can be explained by its literary frame within the pre-Priestly historical writings, the statement of Yahweh's arrival from Edom and Seir has to have an independent tradition history. The age of the tradition underlying Judg 5:4 is not discernible but goes back at least to the tenth century, when Edom was under the rule of David and Solomon. The origin of Yahweh worship cannot be traced back further historically.

If, however, according to the identification of the Egyptian sources, the name of Yahweh was attached already in the fourteenth century to a certain region east of the Arabah that was inhabited by the Shasu, then in the course of the population's political changes the homophonic name of God could already have been known prior to 1000 in the wider vicinity of this region. To be sure, there is no certainty to be had in this matter, but there is every indication that Yahweh was already worshiped as God in the early history, at least by

---

42. Jörg Jeremias, *Theophanie: Die Geschichte einer alttestamentlichen Gattung* (WMANT 10; Neukirchen-Vluyn: Neukirchener, 1965); Frank Schnutenhaus, "Das Kommen und Erscheinen Gottes im Alten Testament," *ZAW* 76 (1964): 1–21. See also Nicholas Freyer Schmidt and P. J. Nel, "Theophany as Type-Scene in the Hebrew Bible," *Journal for Semitics* 11 (2002): 256–81; Baruch J. Schwartz, "The Priestly Account of the Theophany and Lawgiving at Sinai," in *Texts, Temples, and Traditions: A Tribute to Menahem Haran* (ed. Michael V. Fox et al.; Winona Lake, Ind.: Eisenbrauns, 1996): 103–34.

some of the tribes. It was not until the incorporation of the Canaanite population in the unified state under David and Solomon that Israel first entered into conflict with the gods of the Canaanites and had the opportunity to adopt these deities. At the beginning of Israelite religion probably stands the one God Yahweh, who in contestation with the gods of the Canaanites during the monarchic period was first turned into the only God of Israel.

It is unknown how Yahweh came to be liberated from the region after which he is named. Since the worship of God nevertheless cannot be separated from its adherents, there is definitely the possibility that Yahweh was introduced by a group within the Israelite tribes who at one time had been residing in the region of the God. In any case, Yahweh was so strongly bound to this region that he even remained confined there when the group of his worshipers had long since deserted this area in order to adopt other settlement places. Therefore he had to leave from there every time that he appeared in order to operate elsewhere. Although the worship of Yahweh in the premonarchic period can be postulated with some probability, it cannot be assumed that Yahweh had become the only God. Other gods from the time before 1000 in Israel are not known by name, but additional deities could have played a role in this era next to Yahweh. Moreover, the Canaanite population had their own pantheon.

II.6.2. Local Deities

The different settlement areas suggest that the population elements in the newly established settlements and the inhabitants in the succession of Canaanite cities lived relatively detached from one another. Not until the founding of a territorial state under Saul and David were the descendants of the Canaanites annexed into one empire; this brought about the intermingling of the population as well as conflict and influence among different forms of religion. The intense adoption of mythological ideas and divine figures from the world of the Canaanites over the course of the monarchic period is reflected in the Psalms and cannot be pursued further at this point. Even if the Israelite tribes had already come into contact with divinities of the Canaanite pantheon in the early period, that contact found no literary expression. By contrast, in the monarchic period the integration of different religions was requisite for the assimilation of different populations of the land into a state, and Jerusalem was doubtlessly the center of this unification and amalgamation.[43]

---

43. See J. Alberto Soggin, "Der offiziell geförderte Synkretismus in Israel während des 10. Jahrhunderts," *ZAW* 78 (1966): 179–204; Fritz Stolz, *Strukturen und Figuren im*

At the very least, the time had come for an encounter with individual elements of Canaanite religion. Until the time before the formation of the state, based on the naming of local deities appearing in the patriarchal narratives of Israel, several deities prefixed by the designation "El-" were familiar to the early Israelites and were also worshiped. Numerous such local gods were named in the framework of individual narratives in the pre-Priestly historical documents, but it is necessary to examine whether those writings actually have to do with local deities. The examination of this thesis concerning the history of the religion of the early period can take place only by questioning the origin and age of the respective tradition.

אל ראי (*'l r'y*): Genesis 16:14

In the Hagar narrative of Gen 16:1b, 2, 4–7a, 8, 11–14, toward the end the narrator consciously digresses from the consistent use of the name of God by having Hagar address the God who appeared to her as אל ראי: "But she called Yahweh, who had spoken to her, by the name: You are the God who sees me." At this point a folk etymological explanation follows for this identification of God. The designation of the place was then derived from the name of God, reading באר לחי ראי. The derivation of the place name is of no consequence, but it is crucial that that narrator includes ראי along with the same element as the name of God and that this can be understood as a participle from the root ראה with the first-person singular suffix. Tradition-historically, the place name precedes the narrative. Hagar's appellation of her God as אל ראי can thus be understood as a development from the place name and does not have to stem from an old local tradition. In the framework of the narrative, it is not a local El-deity but rather Yahweh who is addressed as "God seeing me." In this context אל cannot be a proper name but only an appellative, and אל ראי is consequently in the context of the narrative a circumlocution created for the deity Yahweh. For the narrator, there is no doubt that the acting God is Yahweh, but Yahweh does not reveal himself as such, so that Hagar can speak only of "God seeing me." This avoids putting the name of Yahweh in the mouth of Hagar, because Hagar's son Ishmael is the progenitor of the Ishmaelites. They do not belong to the Israelite tribes and therefore also could not be worshipers of Yahweh. By avoiding the name of God, the narrator, on the one hand, protected the claim of Yahweh as the only God and, on the other hand, took into account the facts of the environment. In this context there can be

---

Kult von Jerusalem (BZAW 118; Berlin: de Gruyter, 1970); Eckart Otto, "El und JHWH in Jerusalem," *VT* 30 (1980): 318–29.

no question of blending a local El-deity with Yahweh. On the contrary, as the only God, Yahweh can also be called by other names.

אל עולם (*'l 'wlm*): Genesis 21:33

Genesis 21:33 stands at the end of the narrative about the formation of the covenant of Abraham with Abimelech, the king of Gerar, concerning the well rights in Beer-sheba (Gen 21:22–34). The narrative contains an etiological explanation of the name Beer-sheba and is actually concluded in Gen 21:32. The note about the establishment of a cultic site comes after, and its affinity to the preceding narrative thus cannot be discerned with ultimate certainty. With ויקרא בשם יהוה, "he called on the name of Yahweh," a fixed phrase exists that is also frequently used elsewhere (Gen 4:26; 12:8; 13:4; 26:25). However, the phrase following "Yahweh" causes difficulty: אל עולם (*'l 'wlm*). Since the view that this title is in as apposition to Yahweh has to be ruled out, the occurrence of the name אל עולם in this syntactic context can only mean that Yahweh was worshiped by this name. Thus the question arises whether this is a proper name or a designation of God by use of אל as an appellative. Because the inclusion of an ancient cultic tradition in the vicinity of Beer-sheba cannot be demonstrated within the narrative, the assumption has to be ruled out that אל עולם reflects the name of a place inhabited by an El-divinity. In the context of the story, אל עולם is a manifestation of Yahweh and not a divine proper name. An independently acting god is not named here and identified with Yahweh; instead, Yahweh is given an epithet that signifies his divinity. Accordingly, אל עולם is translated "the eternal God," and perhaps a phrase used in religious language was adopted. In any case, the equivalent to עולם is found in Ugaritic texts as an epithet for El, but also for other gods,[44] and the parallelism of the epithet must not tempt one to bring the Canaanite god El into this passage of the text.

אל בית אל (*'l byt 'l*): Genesis 35:7

For reasons unknown to us, the narrative of Jacob's dream in Bethel (Gen 28:11, 12, 17, 18, 20, 21a, 22) actually ends with the erecting and anointing of a stone monument, but it lacks a comment on the invocation of God. In this history of the foundation of the cult in Bethel, the narrative represents a variant of the erecting of the altar in Bethel according to Gen 35:1–5, 7. The variation is not unimportant, as the altar first makes the cultic site serve also as a place

---

44. Evidence in Frank Moore Cross, *Canaanite Myth and Hebrew Epic: Essays in the History of the Religion of Israel* (Cambridge: Harvard University Press, 1973), 17–18.

for sacrifice. After the discourse had stressed מזבח לאל, "altar for El," twice, it says at the end of the narrative, "He [Jacob] built there an altar and named the place El (of) Bethel." El is actually superfluous in this context since it is part of the name of the place; the Septuagint and Vulgate present the text as lacking the initial אל. Nevertheless, the connection אל בית אל is verified by Gen 31:13 and is supported as original. Since Bethel is to be viewed as a place name, El is qualified by the name of the place. It does not clearly emerge from the context whether El is used here as a proper name for the god El or as an appellative denoting God. In his address, God (אלהים) speaks of "the God who appeared to you" (אל הנראה אליך; Gen 35:1), and furthermore a "God who answered me" (אל העונה אתי) is named in Jacob's address (Gen 35:3). Since the view that different gods with the name El are meant by אלהים cannot be maintained, the only remaining assumption is that the God dealing with Jacob and the God who is each time named El as well as El (of) Bethel are identical. This means, however, that אל is to be viewed as an appellative and that אל בית אל is to be understood as God (of) Bethel. With the word choice אל instead of the usual אלהים the narrator again identified God in his personal appearance and not as universal divine essence.

אל אלהי ישראל (*'l 'lhy yśr'l*): Genesis 33:20

The comment in Gen 33:20 is the conclusion of a short note concerning Jacob's arrival to Shechem: "He [Jacob] built there an altar and named it 'El, God of Israel.'" The syntagm אל אלהי ישראל is largely understood to mean that the God El is identified as the God of the people of Israel; Yahweh is addressed as such in Josh 8:30, יהוה אלהי ישראל (*yhwh 'lhy yśr'l*). The proclamation of El as the God of Israel would run counter to the entire intention of the pre-Priestly historical narrative; furthermore, this interpretation is not supported syntactically. The formula has a parallel in Ps 50:1 and Josh 22:22, אל אלהים יהוה (*'l 'lhym yhwh*), which is understood variously by the Masoretes: "God, God, Yahweh." This has to do with a ceremonial invocation that is probably rooted in the cult and does not indicate the equation of El and Yahweh. One such proclamation could also be evinced in אל אלהי ישראל, so that an understanding of אל as a proper name is not compelling. It cannot be determined whether a cultic-shaped formula was included in Gen 33:20. In any case, El can be understood here as an appellative in the sense of emphasizing the designation of Jacob's personal God; as such, the view of El as a proper name is unnecessary. The phrase is accordingly to be understood as "God, God of Israel." The formula used by the narrator, "God of Israel," is anachronistic, given that the name Israel cannot be applied to the patriarch but rather only to the people.

אל אלהי אביך (*'l 'lhy 'byk*): Genesis 46:3

This syntagm is found in Gen 46:3 in a speech of God to Jacob as a self-introductory formula אנוכי האל אלהי אביך,, "I am God, the God of your fathers." Here the given manner of speaking about the God of the fathers is incorporated, so the formula is shaped by the narrator. Since אלהים (*'lhym*) speaks of himself as אל (*'l*), the deity El cannot be intended here. By conscious word choice אל is the designation of the personhood of the acting God; he accompanies Jacob on the way to Egypt and will be explicitly equated with the God of the fathers. By this determination, God is characterized as an intimate God in his dealings with the fathers.

Only in a few places in the narratives of Genesis, by the conscious use of אל (*'l*) rather than אלהים (*'lhym*), is God named in a way that represents direct speech to or by humans. By the predications included with אל, simply different aspects of the one God are expressed. By no means is El to be understood as a proper name, but rather it represents an appellative for God. Each time a particular aspect of God is expressed by the precise designation. The narrator thus did not conflate different El-deities with the one God, but rather created the possibility of personal address to one God. The names of local deities in the religion of Israel are not included by this linguistic usage. On the contrary, the claim was preserved that God is one.

II.6.3. The God of the Ancestors

Alt, Albrecht. "The God of the Fathers," in idem, *Essays on Old Testament History and Religion* (trans. R. A. Wilson; Garden City, N.Y.: Doubleday, 1967), 1–100. **Vorländer,** Hermann. *Mein Gott: Die Vorstellungen vom persönlichen Gott im alten Orient und im Alten Testament* (AOAT 23; Kevelaer: Butzon & Bercker, 1975). **Albertz,** Rainer. *Persönliche Frömmigkeit und offizielle Religion: Religionsinterner Pluralismus in Israel und Babylon* (Calwer theologische Monographien A, Bibelwissenschaft 9; Stuttgart: Calwer, 1978; repr., Atlanta: Society of Biblical Literature, 2005). **Köckert,** Matthias. *Vätergott und Väterverheissungen: Eine Auseinandersetzung mit Albrecht Alt und seinen Erben* (FRLANT 142; Göttingen: Vandenhoeck & Ruprecht, 1988). See now also : **Toorn,** Karel van der. "Ancestors and Anthroponyms: Kinship Terms as Theophoric Elements in Hebrew Names." *ZAW* 108 (1996): 1–11.

Not until Albrecht Alt was "God of the fathers" considered as an apparent form of Israelite religion in the premonarchic period that was fundamentally different from Yahweh worship. Indicative of this religion is the idea of each worshiper is in a particular way connected to the deity, who can be present everywhere and at all times to protect in a particular way the life and well-being of the family and clan. It was not the connection to a place but the relatedness to a particular person or group that constituted the way of the God of the fathers. The worship of each deity goes back to a particular revelation of God, and the revelation was personally granted to each worshiper, who in turn named the deity.

This hypothesis of Alt was generally accepted in the history of religion in Israel and designated its own type of religion alongside the worship of Yahweh. On the contrary, Hermann Vorländer and Rainer Albertz have demonstrated, based on ancient Near Eastern parallels, the phrase "my God" or "God of my father" as a personal and familial mode of speech; they attempt to understand the phrase as an expression of individual piety. The acceptance of an independent religion of the patriarchs is thus rejected; rather, this address is aimed at a personal God, from whom care and defense are expected in a particular way, and basically all deities can be presumed to be personal gods. In the framework of ancient Near Eastern polytheism, one must establish a particular relationship to a single god from the multitude of gods, such that the well-being of the worshipers results from being with this one god.

Bound to the *paterfamilias,* each family had a certain god to whom they committed and from whom they sought help. In light of this approach, Matthias Köckert refuted the hypothesis of a separate religion of the God of the fathers conflated with the worship of Yahweh. Drawing tradition-historical conclusions about the circumstances of the premonarchic era from the sources of the monarchic period works against Alt methodologically. Nevertheless, the possibility remains that the pre-Priestly historical document recorded a definite mode of speech from the religious tradition and emphasized it in the patriarchal narratives of Gen 12–36. Therefore the question as to the *Sitz im Leben* of the formulas of the God of the fathers remains for further examination.

According to Köckert the literary findings for the designations of God can be classified as follows:

"the God (of) NN"
— the God of Abraham (Gen 31:42, 53; cf. Ps 47:10 [Eng. v. 9])
— the God of Nahor (Gen 31:53)
— the God of Abraham, Isaac, and Jacob (Exod 3:6, 15–16; 4:5; cf. 1 Kgs 18:36; 2 Chr 30:6)
— the God of Shem (Gen 9:26)
— cf. the God of Jacob (2 Sam 23:1; Isa 2:3 = Mic 4:2; Pss 20:1; 46:8 [Eng. v. 7]; 75:10 [9]; 76:7 [6]; 81:2, 5 [1, 4]; 84:9 [8]; 94:7; 114:7)
— cf. the God of Elijah (2 Kgs 2:14)

- cf. the God of Hezekiah (2 Chr 32:17)
- cf. the God of Daniel (Dan 6:27 [Eng. v. 26])
- cf. the God of Shadrach, Meshach, and Abednego (Dan 3:28)

"the God (of the) fathers + suffix"
- the God of my father (Gen 31:5, 42; cf. Exod 15:2; 18:4)
- the God of your (sg.) father (Gen 31:29 LXX; 46:3; 50:17; Exod 3:6; cf. 1 Chr 28:9)
- the God of your (pl.) father (Gen 31:29; 43:23)
- the God of their father (Gen 31:53)
- cf. the God of his father (2 Chr 17:4)

Combinations
Gen 25:24; 28:13; 32:10; Exod 3:6, 15, 16; 4:5; cf. 2 Kgs 10:5 = Isa 38:5; 1 Chr 29:10; 2 Chr 21:12; 34:3

Appellative + NN
- *pḥd* of Isaac (Gen 31:42a, 53b)
- the Mighty One of Jacob (Gen 49:23-24)

"the God of the fathers (or [of the] fathers + suffix) Abraham, Isaac, and Jacob"
(Exod 3:6, 13, 15f.; 4:5; cf. Dan 11:37 as well as eleven attestations in the Deuteronomistic History and twenty-eight attestations in the Chronicler's History)

The wide distribution of linguistic usage precludes the reduction of the formula to a certain situation or institution within the cult. Rather, it is a phrase that can vary and change according to the context. From the outset the phrase is meant to equate the God of the fathers with Yahweh. Already in the primeval history Yahweh was named explicitly "the God of Shem" and so the continuation of Yahweh worship in the primeval history was emphasized (cf. Gen 4:26). In the patriarchal narratives, the first two names given as self-introductions by Yahweh are, "I am the God of Abraham, your father" (Gen 26:24) and "I am Yahweh, the God of Abraham, your father, and the God of Isaac" (Gen 28:13). The narrator thus does not intend to characterize a particular worship of God by the patriarchs; on the contrary he emphasizes the continuation of Yahweh worship. At no place is a particular God of the fathers introduced; "God of the fathers" is always a circumlocution for Yahweh. This holds also for the *locus classicus,* Gen 31:53, where the formulation "God of Nahor" appears next to the God of Abraham. The narrator avoided the name of God with this formulation since it would have made Yahweh not just the God of the kinsfolk but the God of foreign clans as well.

The speech of the God of the fathers emerges from the literary composition of the pre-Priestly historical work without having to assume a fixed formula. It is not absolutely ruled out that phrases such as "God of my father" or "God of Abraham" were used in the realm of personal piety. By no means, however, can *pḥd Yiṣḥāq* (Gen 31:42a, 53b) count as an old designation for God; the phrase instead displays an old use of the oath performance involving the reproductive organ (cf. Gen 24:27; 47:29).[45] In any case, such fixed invocations of God permit no inference of a particular form of religion in the premonarchic period. The discussion of the God of the fathers as a separate form in the frame of ancient Israelite religion is not tenable and is thus to be given up.

II.6.4. Cultic Artifacts

The cultic practice prior to the formation of the state is not known from direct sources. Yet there are several cultic artifacts that still play a role in the early monarchic period and were inherited from the preceding era. To those belong the ark, the teraphim, and the ephod. However, an ancient Israelite tabernacle for the premonarchic period still cannot be established.[46]

II.6.4.1. The Ark

For the history of research, see **Schmitt,** Rainer. *Zelt und Lade als Thema alttestamentlicher Wissenschaft* (Gütersloh: G. Mohn, 1972). Select literature: **Budde,** Karl. "Ephod und Lade," *ZAW* 39 (1921): 1–42. **Dibelius,** Martin. *Die Lade Jahves: Eine religionsgeschichtliche Untersuchung* (FRLANT 7; Göttingen: Vandenhoeck & Ruprecht, 1906). **Gressmann,** Hugo. *Die Lade Jahves und das Allerheiligste des salomonischen Tempels* (BWAT n.F. 1; Berlin: W. Kohlhammer, 1920). **Haran,** Menahem. "The Ark and the Cherubim: Their Symbolic Significance in Biblical Ritual," *IEJ* 9 (1959): 30–38, 89–94. **Hartmann,** Richard."Zelt und Lade," *ZAW* 37 (1917–18): 209–44. **Maier,** Johann. *Das altisraelitische Ladeheiligtum* (BZAW 93; Berlin: Töpelmann,

---

45. See Klaus Koch, "*pḥd jiṣḥaq*—eine Gottesbezeichnung?" in *Studien zur alttestamentlichen und altorientalischen Religionsgeschichte: Zum 60. Geburtstag von Klaus Koch* (ed. Eckart Otto; Göttingen: Vandenhoeck & Ruprecht, 1988), 206–14; Meir Malul, "More on *pḥd jiṣḥaq* (Genesis XXXI 42–53) and the Oath on the Thigh," *VT* 35 (1985): 192–200.

46. See Volkmar Fritz, *Tempel und Zelt: Studien zum Tempelbau in Israel u. zu d. Zeltheiligtum d. Priesterschrift* (WMANT 47; Neukirchen-Vluyn: Neukirchener, 1977).

1965). **Morgenstern,** Julian. "The Ark, the Ephod, and the 'Tent of the Meeting,'" *HUCA* 17 (1942–43): 153–266; 18 (1943–44): 1–52. See now also: **McCormick,** C. Mark. "From Box to Throne: The Development of the Ark in DtrH and P," in *Saul in Story and Tradition* (ed. Carl S. Ehrlich; FAT 47; Tübingen: Mohr Siebeck, 2006), 175–86.

The ark is a wooden chest that was put in the innermost chamber of the temple by Solomon (1 Kgs 8:1–11) and was interpreted here in connection with the notion of the throne as the footstool of the one in heaven or that God was enthroned over the cherubim (cf. Pss 99:5; 132:7; 2 Chr 28:2). The fate of the ark before its transport to Jerusalem by David is presented at length in the so-called ark narrative (1 Sam 4–6; 2 Sam 6).[47] According to the narrative, the ark originally stood in the temple of Shiloh (Ḥirbet Sēlūn) but went missing in the battle against the Philistines at Ebenezer in the vicinity of Aphek (Rās el-ʿĒn). The war booty was nevertheless sent back by the Philistines and, after a stopover in Beth-shemesh, was finally located in the house of Abinadab in or by Kiriath-jearim (Dēr el-Azhar). From there it was brought by David to Jerusalem in order to be preserved in a tent in a new location.

Since the later notions of the Deuteronomistic History and the Priestly Document may not be projected back to the premonarchic era, the original significance of the ark can be reconstructed only from the ark narrative. According to this account, the ark was a noumenal artifact with which the presence of God was connected in a particular way. The ark manifests God's power, closeness, and holiness. The holiness of the artifact required its location in sacred space, the temple or a tabernacle. In military expeditions it was stationed in the army camp (see 2 Sam 11:11). At the very least it is described as a symbol for the presence of God, but one whose origin is unknown. Even if it were proven that the ark is connected to various things that are attributed a noumenal power by the nomadic Arabs (cf. J. Morgenstern), the ark by no means necessarily stems from a nomadic past; it could definitely have been created in cultivated land (see Dibelius, *Die Lade Jahves*, 111–19; Hartmann, "Zelt und Lade," 236–37).

---

47. Hermann Timm, "Die Ladeerzählung (1 Sam 4–6; 2 Sam 6) und das Kerygma des deuteronomistischen Geschichtswerks," *EvT* 26 (1966): 509–26; Klaas A. D. Smelik, "The Ark Narrative Reconsidered," *OtSt* 25 (1989): 128–44. See now also Erik Eynikel, "The Relation Between the Eli Narratives (1 Sam. 1–4) and the Ark Narrative (1 Sam. 1–6; 2 Sam. 6:1–19)," in *Past, Present, Future: The Deuteronomistic History and the Prophets* (ed. Johannes C. de Moor and Harry F. van Rooy; Oudtestamentische Studiën 44; Leiden: Brill, 2000), 88–106.

The worship befitting this symbol initially was limited to the tribe of Ephraim, in whose territory Shiloh lay. It is unknown whether already in the premonarchic period the name of Yahweh became connected with the ark. David was the first to give the ark significance to all Israel by making it the most important article in the framework of Yahweh worship and stationing it in a tabernacle in the capital, so a conscious institution of premonarchic cult tradition is to be assumed.[48] Although the ark did not actually become an image of God, it nevertheless took on a particular quality by belonging to the sphere of the divine. Since it was connected with the presence and effect of God, it guaranteed the domain of the holy in strict separation from the profane.

II.6.4.2. The Teraphim

Draffkorn, Anne E. "Ilâni/Elohim," *JBL* 76 (1957): 216–24. **Greenberg**, Moshe. "Another Look at Rachel's Theft of the Teraphim," *JBL* 81 (1962): 239–48. **Hoffner**, Harry A. "Hittite *Tarpiš* and Hebrew *Terâphîm*," *JNES* 27 (1968): 61–68. **Jirku**, Anton. "Die Mimation in den nordsemitischen Sprachen und einige Bezeichnungen der altisraelitischen Mantik," *Biblica* 34 (1953): 78–80. **Labuschagne**, C. J. "Teraphim: A New Proposal for Its Etymology," *VT* 16 (1966): 115–17. **Rouillad**, Hedwige, and Josef **Tropper**. "*Trpym*, rituals du guérison et culte des ancêtres d'après 1 Samuel XIX 11–17 et les texts parallèles d'Assur et de Nuzi," *VT* 37 (1987): 340–61. **Schroer**, Silvia. *In Israel gab es Bilder: Nachrichten von darstellender Kunst im Alten Testament* (OBO 74; Göttingen: Vandenhoeck & Ruprecht, 1987), 136–54. See now also: **Heltzer**, Michael. "New Light from Emar on Genesis 31: The Theft of the Teraphim," in *"Und Mose schrieb dieses Lied auf": Studien zum Alten Testament und zum Alten Orient* (ed. Manfried Dietrich and Ingo Kottsieper; AOAT 250; Münster: Ugarit-Verlag, 1998), 357–62. **Toorn**, Karel van der. "The Nature of the Biblical Teraphim in the Light of the Cuneiform Evidence," *CBQ* 52 (1990): 203–22.

Teraphim (תרפים) is a singular with mimation at the end, as is common with loanwords. The word was thus taken up into Hebrew from another language, but the derivation from the Hittite-Hurrite *tarpiš*, "(evil) spirit," "demon," is by no means necessary. The appearance and function of the teraphim do not

---

48. See Otto Eissfeldt, "Silo und Jerusalem," in idem, *Kleine Schriften III* (Tübingen: Mohr Siebeck, 1966), 417–25; Martin Noth, "Jerusalem and the Israelite Tradition," in idem, *The Laws in the Pentateuch and Other Studies* (trans. D. R. Ap-Thomas; London: Oliver & Boyd, 1966), 132–44; Eckart Otto, "Silo und Jerusalem," *TZ* 32 (1976): 65–77; Jörg Jeremias, "Lade und Zion," in *Probleme biblischer Theologie: Gerhard von Rad zum 70. Geburtstag* (ed. Hans Walter Wolff; Munich: Kaiser, 1971), 181–98; Martin Noth, "Samuel und Silo," *ABLAK* 1 (1971): 148–56.

clearly emerge from the evidence (Gen 31:19, 34–35; Judg 17:5; 18:14, 17–18, 20; 1 Sam 15:23; 19:13, 16; 2 Kgs 23:24; Ezek 21:26; Hos 3:4; Zech 10:2).

Their existence in the premonarchic period is probable, insofar as at the beginning of the monarchic period, Michal quite naturally had one available (see 1 Sam 19:13, 16). According to the narratives in Gen 31 and 1 Sam 19, the artifacts are slightly large but are light enough to pick up and hide and could also serve for deception. In the search for the teraphim that Rachel stole without Jacob's knowledge, Laban called them "my god(s)" (Gen 31:30); and the enormous but futile expenditure to recover them shows not only the grievousness of the loss but also the great significance of the lost pieces. The teraphim is thus an idol of unknown material that had its place in the house and held an indeterminable cultic function. As the narrative of Michal's deceit in 1 Sam 19 appears to suggest, the figure of this idol was a small image of a god in the form of a statuette and not a mask. The teraphim was thus a type of household god to guard the property and the family; the meaning of the name is unknown, however. The teraphim constituted the most important part of the movable property of the house, and its loss took the divine blessing and assistance from the house. By the theft of the teraphim, Rachel not only stole from her father but also robbed him of the divine image that secured his well-being and prosperity.

Since it could not be identified with Yahweh, this household god diminished to the point of rejection with increasing Yahweh worship in the monarchic period, since it could not be identified with Yahweh (see Exod 21:26; Zech 10:2). For the premonarchic period there are no statuettes identified as teraphim that have been proven thus far; possibly they were made out of perishable material. Comparable to the teraphim are the *ilāni* in the texts from Nuzi (see Draffkorn); these also had the task of tutelary deities and, within the family, were bequeathed to the eldest son. A similar function is attributed in Roman religion to the *penates* (household gods), which were worshiped in a particular place within the house, especially at the hearth. The *di penates* belong together with the *paterfamilias* and give the household *dominium* (dominion) and *potestas* (power). In this regard they may be comparable to the teraphim: "There are those deities who watch over the reserve and so the prosperity of the house; consequently, the actual tutelary gods of the economy are the family (or household) gods."[49] For Israel, the texts that mention the teraphim give at least a faint indication of a possible household cult in premonarchic Israel.

---

49. Georg Wissowa, *Religion und Kultus der Römer* (2nd ed.; Munich: Beck, 1912), 145.

II.6.4.3. The Oracle by Casting Lots

Dommershausen, Werner. "Das 'Los' in der alttestamentlichen Theologie," *TTZ* 80 (1971): 195–200. **Friedrich,** Ingolf. *Ephod und Choschen im Lichte des Alten Orients* (Wiener Beiträge zur Theologie 12; Vienna: Herder, 1968). **Lipiński,** Eduard. "Urim and Tummīm," *VT* 20 (1970): 495f. **Maier,** Johann. "Urim und Tummim," *Kairos* 11 (1969): 22–38. **Preuss,** Richard. "Das Ordal im alten Israel," *ZAW* 51 (1933): 121–40, 227–55. **Robertson,** Edward. "The 'Ūrīm and Tummīm: What Were They?" *VT* 14 (1964): 67–74. **Sellin,** Ernst. "Efod und Terafim," *JPOS* 14 (1934): 185–93. See now also: **Van Dam,** Cornelius. *The Urim and Thummim: A Means of Revelation in Ancient Israel* (Winona Lake, Ind.: Eisenbrauns, 1997).

In the books of Samuel there are multiple reports about obtaining oracles, and in the books of Joshua and Judges this practice of inquiring of God is naturally presupposed. The oracle was considered a legitimate form of inquiring of the deity, so it is less concerned with determining the future than with ascertaining the will of God in order to conform to the divine will when facing decisive action. The oracle is to be distinguished from the ordeal, which always applies to human action in the past and thus makes the omniscient God the guarantor of finding out the truth (see Josh 7:13–14).

Two different practices of the oracle are to be distinguished by name: the ephod and the Urim and Thummim. In completely different ways, both served to obtain Yahweh's answer with regard to a difficult decision. Although precise details are not conveyed, it clearly emerges from the context of the text that the respective question must be put in an either-or form in order to obtain an answer by the oracle of lots.

The word ephod (אפוד) is ambiguous; it can designate the garment of the priest (1 Sam 2:18; 22:18; 2 Sam 6:14), and it is used in the Priestly Document as the term for the vestments of the high priest (Exod 25:7; 28:4–30, 31–35; 35:9, 27; 39:1–21, 22–29). In 1 Sam 23:9–12 and 30:7–9, however, the ephod appears is a means of obtaining an oracle that was brought over and operated by the priest Abiathar (see 1 Sam 2:28; 14:3, 18; 21:10). According to this, the ephod was a transportable object by which Yahweh's decision was clearly discernible. As the text indicates, the question must be formulated for a yes-or-no answer. "David asked, 'Will the citizens of Keilah deliver me and my men into the hand of Saul?' Yahweh said, 'Yes'" (1 Sam 23:12). The manner of the oracle is not illuminated further. Since the question was addressed directly to the ephod, the answer also must have come immediately from it. The ephod was the medium for connecting to the divine will. The inquiry of the ephod indeed took place through the priest, but it was not restricted to a shrine. Not until the late narrative of Judg 17–18 (see §I.2.3.2) was the ephod included along with teraphim and idols in the inventory of a cultic site.

One additional means of inquiring of God was the oracle of casting lots, Urim and Thummim (אורים ותמים). The etymology of the words is unclear; both are formed by ultimate mimation, so they are actually singular terms. The phrase is contained only in late texts (Exod 28:30; Lev 8:8; Deut 33:8; Ezra 2:63; Neh 7:65), but the concepts are found as *pars pro toto* in 1 Sam 28:6 and Num 27:21 as well as in the oracle of 1 Sam 14:41 LXX. The Priestly Document actually has this lot oracle placed in the breastplate (חשֶׁן) of the high priest (Exod 28:30); the object probably goes back to an old custom. The way of inquiring of God is not really conveyed in 1 Sam 23:2 and 2 Sam 5:19, but if there is no additional way of granting an oracle then only the use of Urim and Thummim can be meant.

Like the ephod, this oracular device answered only yes-or-no questions. Presumably Urim and Thummim were two stones of different material and different colors, but they also could have been marked sticks. To obtain a decision of the divine will, these would be cast or drawn, and each one was connected to an answer—one positive and the other negative. Even if the custom is no longer attested for the wider monarchic period, the late connection of the oracle stones with the vestments of the high priest in the Priestly Document nevertheless reflects a long-standing practice. There is an analogous practice attested in Assyria of the use of a white and a black stone in inquiring about the future (Lipiński, *VT* 14 [1964]: 496). Since the performance by a priest was not mentioned specifically, the question arises whether this form of oracle could be practiced by anyone. Presumably Urim and Thummim, apart from priestly mediation for obtaining the will of God by question, were at the disposal of whoever wanted or needed to secure divine assistance. The independence from cult personnel could constitute the exception to this form of oracle and illustrate the coexistence of two different practices for the same process of securing God's will.

Both forms evince a mantic practice in premonarchic Israel. With respect to the outcomes of an action, the deity conveyed the decision. The divine answer came about through a sign. The prerequisite for this practice is the conviction that all future fate is preordained by God. By obtaining the oracle, humans thus attained access to hidden knowledge concerning the future. As such, an unmediated and unbroken connection of humans to God is presupposed, one that does not require further mediation or cultic regulation. Since only a yes-or-no answer can be expected from the ephod and from the Urim and Thummim, the possibilities of closely ascertaining important and crucial situations of present actions remain limited. So ultimately God's will remains unavailable, and human responsibility then becomes apparent.

II.6.5. Cultic Sites

The books of Joshua and Judges presuppose a series of shrines whose existence can no longer be determined on account of the layers of sources. In the Jephthah narrative, the phrase "before Yahweh in Mizpah" (Judg 11:11) suggests a cultic site at Mizpah in Gilead. In Josh 24:26 a temple is presupposed for Shechem. According to Josh 3:4, in the context of crossing the Jordan, in Gilgal a memorial site was erected that represents a cultic site. Additionally, the narrative complexes of Judg 17–18 and 19–21 include Israelite shrines in Dan (Tell el-Qāḍī) as well as in Bethel (Bētīn) and Mizpah in Benjamin (Tell en-Naṣbe). Reliable information cannot be inferred from these projections backward, but from the viewpoint of the Deuteronomistic History, a multitude of cultic sites in different places are attributed to the premonarchic period. The notes concerning altars built by Moses in Exod 17:15, Joshua in Josh 8:30, Gideon in Judg 6:24, and Samuel in 1 Sam 7:17 all point in the same direction. These are not historical reports, but merely the documentation of the naturalness of sacrificial practices apart from priestly mediation in the premonarchic period. Still yet, building an altar can also be reported as a natural action for Saul (1 Sam 14:35) and David (2 Sam 24), and 2 Sam 24 apparently also furnishes a report of a cultic site in Jerusalem prior to the construction of the temple by Solomon.

The numerous notes and narratives about cultic actions on the part of the patriarchs are to be classified as something else. Since they are very frequently connected with a self-revelation from God, they clearly have the intention of legitimating existing cultic sites as shrines to Yahweh. According to Gen 12:7–8; 13:3, 4, 18, Abraham erected an altar in Shechem, at Bethel, and in Mamre; according to Gen 21:33 Abraham planted a tamarisk in Beer-sheba. Jacob is also brought into connection with Beer-sheba in Gen 46:1b–4. Furthermore, Isaac built an altar in Beer-sheba (Gen 26:23–25). In Gen 28:18; 35:14, the *maṣṣēbâ* in Bethel is ascribed to Jacob, and Jacob also erected altars in Shechem and in Luz at Bethel (Gen 33:18–20; 35:7). The patriarchs appear in the pre-Priestly historical work as the ones who established numerous cultic sites. The different narratives thus presuppose the existence of numerous shrines in the premonarchic period.

Based on the layers of sources, only the shrines of Shiloh and Nob can be dated with certainty to the premonarchic era. The temple of Shiloh (Ḫirbet Sēlūn) is explicitly named היכל (*hykl*) in 1 Sam 1:9 and 3:3, but this was destroyed by the Philistines in the second half of the eleventh century (cf. Jer 7:12, 14; 26:6, 9; Ps 78:60). The temple of Nob was destroyed by Saul in connection with the pursuit of David, whereby the cult tradition ended (1 Sam 21:2–10; 22:6–23). The references from the monarchic period allow the conclusion that some temples existed in the premonarchic period.

Bethel and Dan were installed by Jeroboam I (926–907) as imperial shrines after the founding of the northern kingdom Israel (1 Kgs 12:26-32) in order to establish a state cult independent of Jerusalem. The shrines of Gilgal and Bethel are polemicized against in the book of Hosea (Hos 4:15; 10:5; 12:12). The cultic sites in Bethel, Gilgal, Beer-sheba, and Dan were still named in the book of Amos (Amos 4:4; 5:5; 8:14). As such, alongside Shiloh and Nob, at least Dan, Bethel, Gilgal, and Beer-sheba are to be counted among the existent shrines in the early period.

None of these cultic sites has yet been established archaeologically. However, even the excavated structures of the Early Iron Age that are claimed as cultic sites cannot count as such, since the findings are insufficient for the proof of cultic practice. These alleged cultic sites must undergo separate examinations.

Parts of a house were exposed in Hazor stratum XI, and according to the pits of stratum XII, an active building is proven once again.[50] The extant remains allow no reconstruction of the design; based on a series of stone pillars, though, it could be considered a residential house typical of the era. In a small annex 3.2 m wide, next to a hoard of bronze objects, multiple fragments of a so-called incense stand were found. Under them in a chamber were found collected objects, including the figurine of a seated goddess. In addition to pottery for normal use, the great number of basalt vessels is conspicuous.[51] The cultic interpretation is established mostly on the basis of the hoard, which was described as an offering. The artifacts of bronze are nevertheless so different that this interpretation is hardly tenable. In addition to the goddess figurine, in the chamber were found a small axe, a hilt, the point of a sword, lance shoes, two arrowheads, two fibula, a bangle, a needle, a piece of wire, and clumps of metal. This mixture is grounds for the assumption that these metal objects were collected and deported in order to melt them down. The discovery of this deposit by no means yields evidence for a cultic site.

On Ebal, remains of a building from the Early Iron Age were uncovered, in an area surrounded by a wide-ranging curtain wall at the peak of the mountain.[52] Multiple building phases are differentiated for the building, but they are not clearly demarcated from one another. Based especially on the bone

---

50. Yigael Yadin et al., *Hazor III–IV Text* (Jerusalem: Mosad Bialik, 1989), 80–81, pl. XVIII.

51. Yigael Yadin et al., *Hazor III–IV Plates* (Jerusalem: Mosad Bialik, 1961), pls. CCIII–CCVI.

52. Adam Zertal, "An Early Iron Age Cultic Site on Mount Ebal: Excavation Seasons 1982-1987," *Tel Aviv* 13–14 (1986–1987): 105–65. Cf. Volkmar Fritz, "Open Cult Places in Israel in the Light of Parallels from Prehistoric Europe and Pre-Classical Greece," in *Bibli-*

discoveries, the excavators suggested that the entire enclosure was a cultic site, and consequently they reconstructed it as an altar for burnt offerings. Examination of the architectural findings shows that such an interpretation does not stand; instead, the findings have to do with an agricultural settlement in the form of a farmstead, as is also known elsewhere in this era (see §II.3.2). The accumulation of bones of sheep, goats, and fallow deer is likewise a universal phenomenon in farm estates. The pottery and the rest of the findings indicate nothing of a particularly cultic character. The cultic interpretation of the ruins of Ebal is thus to be given up.

An additional cultic site was assumed in the so-called bull site south of Ǧenīn in the Samaritan mountains.[53] It is a circular plaza with a diameter of about 21 m, which was surrounded by a cobblestone wall that is not completely extant. The entrance lies in the west, where there was a gateway. No structural remains were found within this area. Near the entrance merely an upright stone was found, which was referred to as a stele. The sparse pottery fragments stem from the Early Iron Age. The cultic interpretation of the place is based most of all on the find of a bronze bull. This find is only 12.4 cm high and is ultimately unable to bear the burden of proof. Indeed it probably was a cultic artifact, but the piece could have been deposited there for other reasons or could have gone missing. This round enclosure could also have had an agricultural use, for example, as a pen for animals or a threshing place. In any case, proof is lacking for an interpretation as a shrine at a high place (במה) or a burnt offering site. Since the evidence of cultic use has not been proved from the available remains and the one finding, the possibility must remain open that it was an enclosure for a profane purpose.

In Arad, in stratum XII under the courtyard of the temple from the monarchic period, remains of a plastered plaza and a semicircular brick platform were uncovered.[54] In addition, a stone platform in the vicinity of the altar from Iron Age II was assigned to this Early Iron Age layer. The entire area was covered with a massive layer of ash in which a great number of bones were

---

cal Archaeology Today, 1990: Proceedings of the Second International Congress on Biblical Archaeology (ed. Avraham Biran et al.; Jerusalem: Israel Exploration Society, 1993), 183–87.

53. Amihai Mazar, "The 'Bull Site'—An Iron Age I Open Cult Place," BASOR 247 (1982): 27–42; Robert Wenning and Erich Zenger, "Ein bäuerliches Baal-Heiligtum im samarischen Gebirge aus der Zeit der Anfänge Israels," ZDPV 102 (1986): 75–86.

54. Yohanan Aharoni, "Nothing Early and Nothing Late: Rewriting Israel's Conquest," BA 39 (1976): 55–76; Miriam Aharoni, "The Pottery of Strata 12–11 of the Iron Age Citadel at Arad," Eretz Israel 15 (1981): 181–204. See now Ze'ev Herzog, "The Fortress Mound at Tel Arad: An Interim Report," Tel Aviv 29 (2002): 3–109; Lily Singer-Avitz, "Arad: The Iron Age Pottery Assemblages," Tel Aviv 29 (2002) 110–214.

found. It appears that the whole section was surrounded by a wall. West of this plaza, the remains of residential houses were uncovered, and several pits were located farther south. The complete findings from this settlement site have still not been published fully, so the data must remain open. The findings up to now, however, do not support an interpretation of the plaza as a cultic site; instead, they are the remains of a residential building from the Early Iron Age.

At Tell el-Mazar in the Jordan Valley, an Early Iron Age construction complex has been interpreted as a shrine.[55] The construction complex is only partially preserved and was surrounded by an open courtyard; on its northern side are three fairly large rooms. Neither the construction nor the pottery indicates a cultic function.

II.7. The Philistines

Dothan, Trude. *The Philistines and Their Material Culture* (New Haven: Yale University Press, 1982) (with a bibliography to 1980 on pp. 297–303). **Brug,** John F. *A Literary and Archaeological Study of the Philistines* (BAR International Series 265; Oxford: B.A.R., 1985). **Bunimovitz,** Shlomo. "Problems in the 'Ethnic' Identification of the Philistine Material Culture," *Tel Aviv* 17 (1990): 210–22. **Dothan,** Moshe. "Archaeological Evidence for Movements of the Early 'Sea People' in Canaan," in *Recent Excavations in Israel: Studies in Iron Age Archaeology* (ed. Seymour Gitin and William G. Dever; AASOR 49; Winona Lake, Ind.: Eisenbrauns, 1989), 59–70. **Dothan,** Trude. "The Arrival of the Sea Peoples: Cultural Diversity in Early Iron Age Canaan," in *Recent Excavations in Israel: Studies in Iron Age Archaeology* (ed. Seymour Gitin and William G. Dever; AASOR 49; Winona Lake, Ind.: Eisenbrauns, 1989), 1–14. **Lehmann,** Gustav Adolf. "Die 'Seevölker': Herrschaften an der Levanteküste," in *Jahresbericht des Instituts für Vorgeschichte der Universität Frankfurt am Main 1976* (Munich: Beck, 1977), 78–111. **Mazar,** Amihai. "The Emergence of the Philistine Culture," *IEJ* 35 (1985): 95–107. **Mazar,** Benjamin. "The Philistines and the Rise of Israel and Tyre," in *The Early Biblical Period: Historical Studies* (ed. Shmuel Ah[ituv and Baruch A. Levine; trans. Ruth and Elisheva Rigbi; Jerusalem: Israel Exploration Society, 1986), 63–82. **Mazar.** "The Philistines," in *Biblical Israel: State and People* (Jerusalem: Magnes, 1992), 22–41. **Noort,** Edward. *Die Seevölker in Palästina* (Palaestina antique 8; Kampen: Kok Pharos, 1994). See now also: **Ehrlich,** Carl S. *The Philistines in Transition: A History from ca. 1000–730 B.C.E.* (SHANE 10; Leiden: Brill, 1996). **Gitin,** Seymour, Amihai **Mazar,** and Ephraim **Stern,** eds. *Mediterranean Peoples in Transition: Thirteenth to Early Tenth Centuries BCE* (Jerusalem: Israel Exploration Society, 1998). **Oren,** Eliezer D., ed. *The Sea Peoples and Their*

---

55. Khair N. Yassine, "The Open Court Sanctuary of the Iron Age I Tell el-Mazar Mound A," *ZDPV* 100 (1984): 108–15.

World: A Reassessment (University Museum Monograph 108; Philadelphia: University Museum, University of Pennsylvania, 2000). **Killebrew**, Ann E. *Biblical Peoples and Ethnicity: An Archaeological Study of Egyptians, Canaanites, Philistines, and Early Israel (ca. 1300–1100 B.C.E.)* (SBLABS 9; Atlanta: Society of Biblical Literature, 2005).

II.7.1. Name and Origin

In the Bible, the inhabitants of the southern coastal plains were identified as "Philistines" (פלשתים); their centers were the five cities Ashdod, Ashkelon, Gaza, Ekron, and Gath, the so-called Pentapolis. (From the Philistines the name "Philistia" is derived for the entire coastal plains and also the name "Palestine" for the entire land.) In the second half of the eleventh century, the Philistines were menacing adversaries to the Israelite tribes; the monarchy in Israel was established decidedly as a defense against Philistine dominance since only a strong central authority could break the Philistine's claim to power. Whereas Saul failed in military confrontation with the Philistines, David ultimately eliminated the threat (see 2 Sam 8:1). The Philistine cities then continued on as independent city-states up to the Assyrian conquest in the eighth century, from which point on they were annexed in the provinces of different empires.

Originally the term "Philistine" represented a self-identification by the members of this ethnic group. The derivation of the name is as yet unsuccessful, which is not surprising given the extremely sparse sources. These people are first mentioned by Ramses III (1184–1153) as the Sea Peoples. The designation Sea Peoples refers to a consolidation of those peoples and groups who appear as enemies of Egypt during the reigns of Ramses II (1279–1213) and Merneptah (1213–1203).[56] These groups undertook a great migration through Egyptian regions and, in their search for land, also threatened the Egyptians. Presumably the Hittite Empire became extinct as a result of this migration in the last decade of the thirteenth century; furthermore, numerous city-states in Syria and the southern Levant were destroyed by the Sea Peoples.[57]

---

56. Wolfgang Helck, "Die Seevölker in den ägyptischen Quellen," in *Jahresbericht des Instituts für Vorgeschichte der Universität Frankfurt am Main 1976* (Munich: Beck, 1977), 7–21; idem, *Die Beziehungen Ägypens zu Vorderasien im 3. und 2. Jahrtausend v.Chr.* (2nd ed.; ÄA 5; Wiesbaden: Harrassowitz,1971), 224–34; Rainer Stadelmann, "Die Abwehr der Seevölker unter Ramses III," *Saeculum* 19 (1968): 156–71.

57. Michael C. Astour, "New Evidence on the Last Days of Ugarit," *AJA* 69 (1965): 253–58; Gustav Adolf Lehmann, "Der Untergang des hethitischen Großreiches und die

The Philistines belong to the last great wave of this international storm during the reign of Ramses III (1184–1153). Having already repelled an invasion in the fifth year of his reign, Ramses III waged the decisive battle came both by water and by land in his eighth year. The final victory over the Sea Peoples was impressively and vividly immortalized in inscriptions and reliefs in his funerary temple of Medinet Habu. The report of the events of the pharaoh's eighth year recounts the threat by these groups, though the depiction is exaggerated in dramatic fashion by the expressive language of the courtly style:

> The foreign countries made a *conspiracy* in their islands. All at once the lands were removed and scattered in the fray. No land could stand before their arms, from Hatti, Kode, Carchemish, Arzawa, and Alashiya on, being cut off *at* [*one time*]. A camp [was set up] in one place in Amor. They desolated its people, and its land was like that which has never come into being. They were coming forward toward Egypt, while the flame was prepared before them. Their confederation was the Philistines, Tjeker, Shekelesh, Denye(n), and Weshesh, lands united. They laid their hands upon the lands as far as the circuit of the earth, their hearts confident and trusting: "Our plans will succeed!" Now the heart of this god, the Lord of the Gods, was prepared. (*ANET*, 262)

The analysis of the inscription is difficult and need not be treated here in further detail.[58] The name contained in the oldest mention of the Philistines in a nonbiblical source is Palastu (*p-l-s-t*).

The relief of Ramses III in Medinet Habu shows one battle of ships and another by foot soldiers. Whereas the sea battle clearly took place in the Nile Delta, the place of the land battle is debatable. It was probably not in remote Syria, but rather on the border of Egypt and thus in the area of the Delta (so Stadelmann). Like the rest of the Sea Peoples, the Philistines are distinguished

---

neuen Texte aus Ugarit," *UF* 2 (1970): 39–73; Heinrich Otten, "Zum Ende des Hethiterreiches aufgrund der Bogazköy-Texte," in *Jahresbericht des Instituts für Vorgeschichte der Universität Frankfurt am Main 1976* (Munich: Beck, 1977), 22–35; Kurt Bittel, "Das Ende des Hethiterreiches aufgrund archäologischer Zeugnisse," in *Jahresbericht des Instituts für Vorgeschichte*, 36–56.

58. See Günther Hölbl, "Die historischen Aussagen der ägyptischen Seevölkerinschriften," in *Griechenland, die Ägäis und die Levante während der "Dark Ages" vom 12. bis zum 9. Jh. v.Chr.: Acten des Symposions von Stift Zwettl (NÖ), 11–14 Oktober 1980* (ed. Sigrid Deger-Jalkotsky; Österreichische Akademie der Wissenschaften. Phil.-Hist. Klasse. Sitzungsberichte 418; Vienna: Österreichische Akademie der Wissenschaften, 1983), 121–38.

in the relief by their headgear, and the rest of the body is naked except for a loincloth. For a long time the particular Philistine helmet was mistakenly interpreted as a feathered crown or as a hairstyle, but it probably depicts a helmet. The additional armament consists of a round shield and sword. In addition to the Philistines' gear, women and children are represented on wagons pulled by zebu cattle.

Given the style of the available sources, there are no statements concerning the repercussions of the battle. After all, from what is gathered from the findings in Megiddo (stratum VII A) and Beth-Shan (stratum VI) indicate that Egyptian suzerainty over Canaan still existed during the reign of Ramses III and collapsed only under the later Ramessides. The Philistines' settlement in the southern coastal plains thus cannot have occurred without the knowledge and acceptance of the great Egyptian power. It is unknown whether the Philistines' settlement in the Pentapolis was a conscious measure on the part of the pharaoh, since this thesis depends on *Papyrus Harris I* (*ANET*, 260–62), which does not provide a clear statement.[59] In any case, the land acquisition by the Philistines—as well as the other Sea Peoples—had to have occurred during the reign of Ramses III just after 1177 and prior to the end of Egyptian dominance over Canaan during the second half of the twelfth century.

By naming the "islands" as the origin of the Philistines, the inscription of Ramses III gives only a vague indication that cannot be further verified or substantiated. The homeland is assumed to be the Aegean region, where, around 1200, massive political changes took place as the centers of Mycenaean culture were annihilated in the context of the so-called Doric Migration.[60] The possible connection between the events in the Aegean and the movement of the Sea Peoples certainly requires further clarification. The previous position of scholarship, that Cilicia in southeast Asia Minor was the original land of the Philistines, is in any case to be given up.

The biblical tradition gives an indication of the Philistine's homeland, as Amos 9:7 states, "Did I not bring Israel up from the land of Egypt, and the Philistines from Caphtor and the Arameans from Kir?" The saying puts into perspective the salvific significance of the exodus for Israel and probably does not stem from the prophets, but rather was first composed as part of a Deuter-

---

59. See Albrecht Alt, "Ägyptische Tempel in Palästina und die Landnahme der Philister," in idem, *Kleine Schriften zur Geschichte des Volkes Israel I* (2nd ed.; Munich: Beck, 1959), 216–30; Itamar Singer, "The Beginning of Philistine Settlement in Canaan and the Northern Boundary of Philistia," *Tel Aviv* 12 (1985): 109–22.

60. Per Ålin, *Das Ende der mykenischen Fundstätten auf dem griechischen Festland* (SMA 1; Lund: C. Bloms, 1962); V. R. d'A. Desborough, *The Last Mycenaeans and Their Successors: An Archaeological Survey, c. 1200–c. 1000 B.C.* (Oxford: Clarendon, 1964).

onomistic redaction.⁶¹ Regardless of authorship, the tradition records a saying about the origin of the Philistines (cf. Jer 47:4), but the derivation of the saying cannot be traced back further. Since in Hebrew Caphtor signifies either Crete or Cyprus, the biblical tradition likewise takes into account the arrival of these peoples by sea. Caphtor is probably not meant as the land of origin, but rather at most as a stopover point. The question concerning the Philistines' homeland cannot be answered on the basis of Amos 9:7. From the Egyptian sources, it can only be gathered that the Philistines belong to the land-seeking groups from the Aegean region whose campaign of conquest came to an end at the borders of Egypt. The Philistines then, as also the Tjeker, found a new homeland in the Egyptian-controlled Canaan, whereas the "Shardana, Teresh, and Shekelesh, after their brief Egyptian adventure (were) broken up into further migrations towards the west, where in the islands of Sicily, Sardinia, and the middle Italian mainland in Etruria they found a new homeland and made their mark through their names" (Stadelmann, *LÄ* 5:819).

II.7.2. Settlement History

Four of the five Philistine cities have been identified. The cities Ashdod (Tel er-Rās at Esdūd), Ashkelon (Tel er-Ḫaḍra), Gaza (Ġazze), and Ekron (Ḫirbet el-Muqannaʿ) lie on the coast. The location of Gath is still uncertain, but currently there is broad agreement that the place is located at Tel eṣ-Ṣāfī in the Shephelah, although the latest confirmation is still outstanding.⁶² Up to now the Philistine cities Ashdod, Ashkelon, and Ekron have been the subjects of archaeological research. Although the findings have only been partially published thus far, the excavations present their own picture of the Philistines' land occupation.

---

61. Hartmut Gese, "Das Problem von Amos 9,7," in *Textgemäss: Aufsätze und Beiträge zur Hermeneutik des Alten Testaments. Festschrift für Ernst Würthwein zum 70. Geburtstag* (ed. A. H. J. Gunneweg and Otto Kaiser; Göttingen: Vandenhoeck & Ruprecht, 1979), 33–38; Volkmar Fritz, "Amosbuch, Amos-Schule und historischer Amos," in *Prophet und Prophetenbuch: Festschrift für Otto Kaiser zum 65. Geburtstag* (ed. Volkmar Fritz et al.; BZAW 185; Berlin: de Gruyter, 1989), 29–43.

62. Anson F. Rainey, "The Identification of Philistine Gath," *Eretz Israel* 12 (1975): 63*–70*; but see now Aren M. Maeir and Carl S. Ehrlich, "Excavating Philistine Gath: Have We Found Goliath's Hometown?" *BAR* 27.6 (2001): 22–31; Carl S. Ehrlich, "Die Suche nach Gat und die neuen Ausgrabungen auf Tell es-Sāfī," in *Kein Land für sich allein: Studien zum Kulturkontakt in Kanaan, Israel/Palästina und Ebirnari für Manfred Weippert zum 65. Geburtstag* (ed. Ulrich Hübner and Ernst Axel Knauf; OBO 186; Fribourg: Universitätsverlag; Göttingen: Vandenhoeck & Ruprecht, 2002), 56–69.

Ashdod shows the settlement history in clear succession: from the last Canaanite city of stratum XIV there follows in stratum XIII a shift in the settlement according to which vessels in the tradition of Late Bronze Age pottery are represented alongside those of Mycanaean III C:1b. In stratum XII the two-color painted vessels first emerge, which had developed out of Mycanaean III C:1b vessels and having been identified as Philistine pottery. The same succession of settlement history has been attested in strata VIII–VI in Ekron.[63] The stratigraphic findings are clear, but the dating is debatable. At this point the so-called Philistine pottery is found in Ashdod—but also in Gezer—along with objects furnished with the cartouche of Ramses III. This means, however, that the two-colored Philistine pottery must have already come into use prior to the end of the reign of this pharaoh in 1153. The development of this new style is thus to be dated from circa 1160 or a bit earlier. This Philistine pottery must be from an earlier period and merely imitated the vessels of Mycanaean III C:1b. But the destruction of the last Canaanite city of Ashdod cannot have taken place prior to the appearance of the Sea Peoples at the beginning of the reign of Ramses III. Thus, the settlement history yields the following chronology:

	Ashdod	*Ekron*
Canaanite ends ca. 1180	Stratum XIV	Stratum XIII
Mycanaean IIIC:1b ends ca. 1160	Stratum XIII	Stratum VII
Philistine pottery	Stratum XII	Stratum VI

Ashdod stratum XIII and Ekron stratum VIII existed for only a short period, but the end of this settlement history marks the beginning of the Philistine settlement around 1160. The cultural imprint of both settlement histories thus indicates the continuation of Canaanite successors rather than a new beginning made solely by foreign conquerors. Therefore, it can be deduced that the Philistines by no means exterminated the local population. At most they assumed power as the ruling class; their land acquisition thus consists of taking over and conquering Canaanite city-states in the southern coastal plains. "The Philistines were integrated into the existing pattern of settlement, their integration being attested by the continuity of the socio-

---

63. Seymour Gitin and Trude Dothan, "The Rise and Fall of Ekron of the Philistines," *BA* 50 (1987): 197–222; see now Mark W. Meehl, Trude Dothan, and Seymour Gitin, eds., *Tel Miqne-Ekron Excavations, 1995–1996: Field INE East Slope, Iron Age I (Early Philistine Period)* (Jerusalem: W. F. Albright Institute of Archaeological Research and Institute of Archaeology, Hebrew University of Jerusalem, 2006).

political system of city-states as existed in Philistia during most of the Late Bronze Age" (Bunimovitz, "Problems," 211–12).

After securing their control in the Pentapolis and after the collapse of Egyptian supremacy, the Philistines first attempted to broaden their ascendance to include additional parts of the land. They could have established or conquered villages in the coastal plains as shown in the example of the established settlement of Tel Qasile in the middle of the twelfth century. In the remote mountain regions they could have exerted their control by means of military power and administrative measures, although this is unknown, given the lack of examples in the sources. This political expansion must have led to altercations with the Israelite tribes, especially those that had settled in the mountains. Because of their military superiority, the Philistines were initially victorious, and they successfully brought additional regions of Israelite settlement into political subjugation. The political oppression by the Philistines first came to an end as a result of the strong political power gained by the establishment of the monarchy in Israel.

II.7.3. Material Culture

Except for a seal that has proved controversial in both its wording and its interpretation (T. Dothan, *Philistines*, 45, pls. 6 and 7) no inscriptional evidence of the Philistines has been discovered. This is not remarkable, given that the use of writing before 1200 in the Aegean had not spread widely to other advanced cultures.[64] The Phoenician alphabet was first taken up by the Greeks in the eighth century. Additionally, the elements of Philistine culture can only be made out with difficulty, since the Philistines' land acquisition came about as an adaptation of the culture of the Canaanites. Given the political and social conditions in which the city-states were conquered and taken over by the Philistines, which therefore entails interaction from the outset, it is difficult to determine what would characterize typical Philistine culture. Nevertheless, the attempt must be made to determine independent Philistine elements.

II.7.3.1. Architecture

Thus far only a few buildings of the Philistine settlement history have been

---

64. On prealphabetic writing systems, see Alfred Heubeck, "Schrift," *Archaeologia Homerica III*, X (Göttingen: Vandenhoeck & Ruprecht, 1979), 1–73, with literature given on pp. 185–96.

excavated that do not stand in the tradition of Canaanite building. In Ashdod strata XIII and XII, a domed building was uncovered, but its total size cannot be determined (T. Dothan, *Philistines*, 39 fig. 2). This design element is foreign to Canaanite courtyard houses. It is assumed that Ekron stratum VII has a Megaron, a clear illustration of a type of Mycenaean construction, but the foundation is still not completely documented.[65] The stove house in Tel Qasile stratum XII represents another characteristic of the architecture of the Early Iron Age. It likewise has not been completely uncovered, but its characteristic feature is a free-standing hearth otherwise unknown in Canaan.[66] These few examples, apart from the cultic buildings, attest to a foreign influence on the architecture of the era, which can definitely go back to the Philistines. The Philistine construction tradition was, however, operative only in a very small area.

II.7.3.2. Cult

Independent cultic buildings are evident only in Tel Qasile strata XII–X, but there are various indications of cultic practices in dwellings and in palace architecture. In Ekron a structure was uncovered in stratum V for which the findings suggest a cultic function (Dothan, "The Rise and Fall of Ekron," 203). In this city a palace was dug out in stratum IV in which at least the furnishings and the findings indicate a room for performing cultic activities, although the possibility must always be admitted that these pieces were deposited in this room only temporarily. The building stands in the Egyptian tradition, meaning that the rooms are arranged in single rows.[67]

A small sanctuary could endure over the course of three settlement strata in the Early Iron Age at Tel Qasile.[68] In stratum XII there is a building 6.4 x 6.6 m that has only one room with a platform at the back wall. In the following stratum XI, the sanctuary was broadened to 8.5 x 7.9 m; at the same time, the entrance was shifted to the northern corner and separated within a smaller

---

65. Trude Dothan, "The Rise and Fall of Ekron of the Philistines," *BA* 50 (1987): 203.

66. Amihai Mazar, "Excavations at Tell Qasile, 1982–1984, Preliminary Report." *IEJ* 36 (1986): 3–6.

67. See Eliezer D. Oren, "Governors' Residences," in *Canaan under the New Kingdom: A Case Study of Egyptian Administration, Journal of the Society for the Study of Egyptian Antiquities* 14.2 (1985): 37–56; see now also Carolyn R. Higginbotham, *Egyptianization and Elite Emulation in Ramesside Palestine: Governance and Accommodation on the Imperial Periphery* (CHANE 2; Leiden: Brill, 2000).

68. Amihai Mazar, *Excavations at Tell Qasile I: The Philistine Sanctuary. Architecture and Cult Objects* (Qedem 12; Jerusalem: Institute of Archaeology, 1980) and *II: The Philistine Sanctuary. Various Finds, the Pottery, Conclusions, Appendixes* (Qedem 20; Jerusalem: Institute of Archaeology, 1985).

room. By the latest reconstruction, stratum X, the building was enlarged to approximately 14 x 8 m and partitioned into a vestibule, a main room, and a small adjoining room (fig. 17). The entrance to the vestibule was at a right angle to the longitudinal axis of the building. Like the previous buildings, the vestibule and main room have benches along the walls for storing sacrifices. In the main room two pillars are found, and the heightened platform was approachable by steps.

The cultic function is apparent from the arrangement of the building as well as from a large number of discoveries. The arrangement is that of a one-room temple, which was enlarged with a vestibule in the first of its two renovations. Parallels to such cultic rooms are common in the cultic sites of the Late Bronze Age as have been excavated in Hazor area C at Tel Mubarak and in the temple in front of the wall (the so-called Fosse Temple) in Lachish.[69] These do not follow any particular building tradition but instead represent a local development.

Rich cultic inventories were found in all three settlement sites, and, in addition to Philistine elements, Canaanite, Cypriot, and Egyptian influences are noticeable. Among the objects found are anthropomorphic vessels, cultic stands, hollow rings with applications (*kernoi*), and assorted vessels for libation.

Comparable cultic vessels from Ashdod and Gezer indicate that there are more cultic sites in these places that have not yet been discovered. Additionally, there are signs of the household cult. To these belong especially clay figures, which appear in the entire catchment area of the Philistines and follow the pattern of comparable pieces of Mycenaean culture (see T. Dothan, *Philistines*, 234–49). The chair figurine from Ashdod, in which the seated goddess would be fused to her throne, is unique and is called an "Ashdoda" (fig. 18). This clearly follows the model of the figurines of an enthroned goddess from the realm of Mycenaean culture. There are also the so-called lamentation figurines from the Aegean tribes. According to this type, a woman is posed with one or both hands raised over her head in a lamentation rite; the lamentation figurines were placed up at the edge of jars or deep bowls (*lekane*). The Philistines brought both forms of figurines with them from their homeland in the region of the Aegean, as these figurines were previously unknown in Canaanite culture. Since they do not appear among the extensive stock of cultic artifacts from the temple at Tel Qasile, they evince rites within the confines of household cultic practice.

---

69. See Amihai Mazar, *Excavations at Tell Qasile, Part 1: The Philistine Sanctuary: Architecture and Cult Objects* (Qedem 12; Jerusalem: Institute of Archaeology, Hebrew University of Jerusalem, 1980), 63 fig. 15.

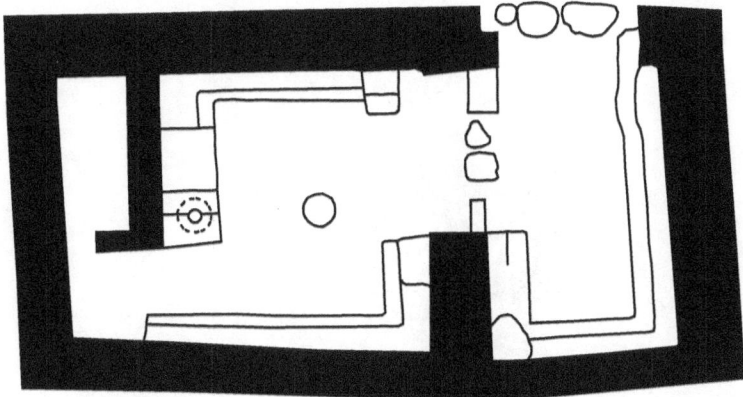

Figure 17. Isometric reconstruction of the temple at Tel Qasile stratum X.

II.7.3.3. Burial

There is still not much that can be said concerning death and burial among the Philistines, since none of the cities of the Pentapolis excavated thus far contains a cemetery. The two burial rites that have previously been brought into connection with the Philistines have nothing to do with this, since they can definitely be traced back to a provenance outside the Aegean. From numerous places derive anthropoid clay sarcophagi, which imitate the wooden coffins having a painted face in Egypt and owe to Egyptian burial rites. Burial in clay coffins having facemasks shows the cultural influence in Canaan during the New Kingdom; the custom was probably imported to Canaan primarily by Egyptian officials and soldiers in order to maintain a proper burial even far away from home. There is thus no particular connection to the Philistines, although it cannot be ruled out that Philistine soldiers in Egyptian service were buried in the same manner (see T. Dothan, *Philistines*, 252–88).

In the burial places in the vicinity of Tell el-Fārʻa (south), cemetery 900 goes back to an early group of Sea Peoples, and cemetery 500 is assigned to Philistines on the basis of pottery.[70] Both cemeteries are rock-cut tombs with benches, whose origin in Mycenaean culture is presumed. Rock-cut tombs

---

70. Jane C. Waldbaum, "Philistine Tombs at Tell Fara and Their Aegean Prototypes," *AJA* 70 (1966): 331–340; cf., in contrast, William H. Stiebing, "Another Look at the Origins of the Philistine Tombs at Tell el-Farʻah (S)," *AJA* 74 (1970): 139–93.

Figure 18. Philistine figurine from Ashdod.

already had a long tradition in Canaan, so the examples in the vicinity of Tell el-Fār'a (south) can be explained as a development from local tradition rather than as the adoption of an Aegean chamber. Typical Philistine burials have still not been proven, if there were special burial rites, so this must still be investigated.

II.7.3.4. Pottery

Around the middle of the twelfth century a new pottery appeared that differs in particular ways in form and decoration from the local vessels of the Early Iron Age. The dissemination of this so-called Philistine pottery is not limited to the coastal plains; fragments are scattered over the entire land (T. Dothan, *Philistines*, 25–93). Yet even in certain Philistine locations, these particular vessels never constitute more than 30 percent of the total material findings. In form and decoration, the Philistine pottery represents a development of Mycenaean III C:1b vessels as shown in particular by the appropriated motifs of white primer and the two-colored painting in red and black (T. Dothan,

Philistines, 94–218). Although the majority of forms in the repertoire are taken from Mycenaean vessels, some forms go back to Cypriot, Egyptian, and Canaanite prototypes. Geometric patterns predominate in the decorations, but there are also stylistic depictions of birds and fish, and the painting can be exceptionally variegated and extensive.

Based on the form and their provenance Trude Dothan has divided Philistine pottery into five groups with eighteen total types (see fig. 19):

1. Vessels derived from Mycenaean prototypes: bowl, krater, stirrup jar, pyxis and amphoriskos, three-handled jar, strainer-spout jug, jug with basket handle and spout, and juglet with pinched-in girth.
2. Vessels that go back to Cypriot types: cylindrical bottle, horn-shaped vessel, and gourd-shaped jar.
3. Jugs with a high neck under Egyptian influence.
4. Vessels developed from Canaanite types: small bowl with bar handle, jugs, juglets, and trefoil-mouth juglets.
5. Types first developed at the end of the era: jug with strainer spout and basket handle, deep krater with horizontal handle.

The vessels characteristic in shape and decorative painting developed from circa 1160 in the Philistine centers of the coastal plains; this followed a phase of local imitation of Mycenaean III C:1b vessels dating from 1180 to 1160. Although the emergence of local emulation of Mycenaean pottery can be connected directly to the arrival of the Philistines, the development of the so-called Philistine pottery cannot go back to an unmediated influence of Philistine culture, since the mixing of styles from different cultures shows up in the design shape and decoration. "This pottery was not the product of a people coming directly from their country of origin with a homogenous tradition but rather reflects the cultural influences in the long, slow, meandering immigration from their Aegean homeland" (T. Dothan, *Philistines*, 217).

The development of the so-called Philistine pottery represents a complex cultural-historical phenomenon that was indeed initiated by the arrival of the Sea Peoples but that was also carried out independently of the influence of Philistine culture. One cannot conclude, on the basis of the Philistine pottery, that the Philistines were the ultimate bearers of the culture. On the contrary, Philistine culture appears to have come about largely within Canaanite culture, with a particular development in pottery. The so-called Philistine pottery is therefore not a cultural or an ethnic indicator, but rather vessels of particular quality as opposed to conventional pottery. It is thus at most a social indicator.

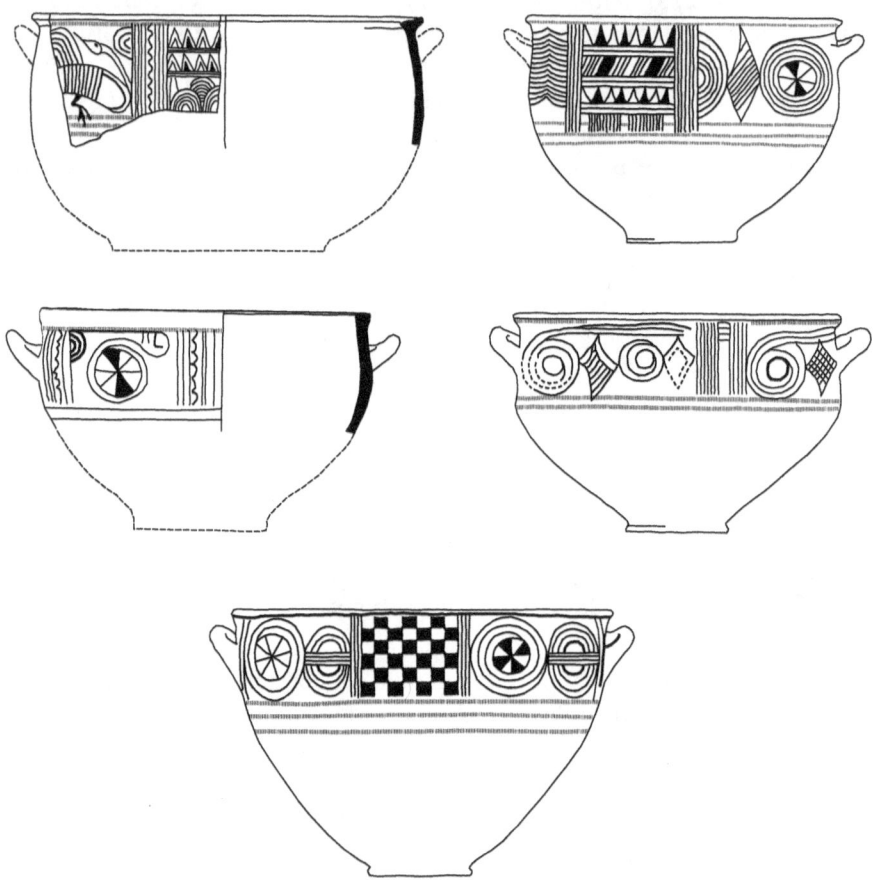

Figure 19. Philistine pottery with painting.

In the course of conducting trade as well as migratory movement, these vessels were disseminated over the entire land of Canaan. The appearance of Philistine pottery in numerous locations is not a fixed criterion by which "to delineate the expansion of the Philistine's political sphere of influence or other groups of Sea Peoples in Palestine" (Lehmann, "Die 'Seevölker,'" 80). In any case, after the collapse of Egyptian rule in Canaan, the Philistines filled the resulting power vacuum by rapidly assuming power throughout the entire land. With the collapse of the political hegemony of the Philistine coastal plains in connection with the military expeditions of David, Philistine pottery vanishes from the material culture of Palestine at the beginning of the tenth century.

II.7.3.5. Metallurgy

From circa 1200 on, the use of iron in addition to bronze appears increasingly for the production of weapons and equipment.[71] The particulars of the advancement in metallurgy are unknown, but the increased appropriation of iron owes to at least three definite factors: (1) the collapse of Mycenaean culture ended trade in copper and tin, which were necessary alloys for the production of bronze; (2) technical progress came to a satisfactory solution for tempering iron and for its forging process even if the melting point of 1530° C was still unreachable by the means available; and (3) iron ore was mined easily in the deposits after the local copper deposits were largely exhausted by a century of extraction.

The available technology was thus advancing for forging iron, but without completely replacing bronze. The Philistines had already mastered the forging process in their land of origin. As archaeological findings reveal, iron processing had fully developed at the end of the Mycenaean III B era (ca. 1200) in the Aegean. Daggers and other weapons as well as jewelry and other utensils made of iron have been found in all of the Philistine locations; for the most part the daggers are furnished with expensive grips made from ivory.[72] Nevertheless, the Philistines did not possess a monopoly on iron working, given that there are findings made out of iron in every Early Iron Age settlement excavated thus far; although these consist predominantly of agricultural tools. That such tools for practical use were produced in Early Iron Age villages and not imported is attested to by a smelting furnace for the production of iron in Tell Yin(am and by a blacksmith workshop at Hirbet el-Msas stratum II.[73] Thus, in Canaan the smelting and processing of iron developed independently of the Philistines, although the production of agricultural tools corresponding to the agrarian structure of the villages is conspicuous.

---

71. James D. Muhly, "How Iron Technology Changed the Ancient World—And Gave the Philistines a Military Edge," *Biblical Archaeology Review* 8 (1983): 40–54.

72. Mazar, *Excavations at Tell Qasile*, 6–8; Trude Dothan, "Iron Knives from Tel Miqne-Ekron," *Eretz Israel* 20 (1989): 154–63.

73. Harold Liebowitz and Robert L. Folk, "The Dawn of Iron Smelting in Palestine: The Late Bronze Age Smelter at Tell Yin'am. Preliminary Report," *Journal of Field Archaeology* 11 (1984): 265–80; Volkmar Fritz, "Eine Metallwerkstatt der frühen Eisenzeit (1200–1000 v.Chr.) auf der *Hirbet el-Msas* im Negeb," in *Archäometallurgie der Alten Welt: Beiträge zum Internationalen Symposium "Old World Archaeometallurgy," Heidelberg 1987 = Old World Archaeometallurgy: Proceedings of the International Symposium "Old World Archaeometallurgy," Heidelberg 1987* (ed. Andreas Hauptmann, Ernst Pernicka, and Günther A. Wagner; Der Anschnitt Beiheft 7; Bochum: Selbstverlag des Deutschen Bergbau-Museums, 1989), 223–26.

In the light of the archaeological findings, 1 Sam 13:19–21 must be read anew. The note establishes the Israelites' lack of iron weapons in the time of Saul, but the use of iron tools for agriculture is assumed. A Philistine prohibition against ironworking by the Israelites hardly stands behind these verses; on the contrary, at most the fact is that the Philistines alone had command of iron weapons. However, this discovery of the different use of iron reflects social conditions rather than political ones. The rural society in Early Iron Age villages had no need for weapons, since agricultural production determined their lives. By contrast, the Philistines comprised a military elite who saw their meaning of life in war and battle. The clear military advantage of the Philistines does not, then, establish the use of iron for the production of weapons—the metal alone determined no advantage at all. On the contrary, the Philistines were militarily superior because, as a warrior people, they were essentially more trained and adept in their use of weapons than the inhabitants of the Early Iron Age villages. The narrative of David's victory over the individual combatant Goliath in 1 Sam 17 clearly evinces the Philistines' manifestly greater fighting strength with respect to armament.[74] The later military success of David over the Philistines, therefore, does not in the end owe to the formation of a powerful and combat-experienced mercenary force.

Thus, according to 1 Sam 13:19–21 there were social and economic differences between the Philistines and Israelites that would necessarily have an impact on military conflicts; however, in view of the archaeological findings, the notion that there was some difference in metalworking clearly needs to be corrected. Both populations smelted and forged iron, but the group that produced agricultural equipment would have been inferior in military confrontations to the group equipped with weapons and trained in battle. The findings with respect to metallurgy thus support the hypothesis that the Philistines, after suffering defeat against Egypt, became established as the ruling class in the cities still existing in the coastal plains; then after the ultimate collapse of Egyptian dominance, the Philistines exerted and enforced their supremacy in Canaan based on their military superiority.

II.7.4. History and Significance

The Philistines come onto the scene in connection with the defense of Ramses III against the Sea Peoples, but the history, origin, and ethnic identification of

---

74. On this point, see Kurt Galling, "Goliath und seine Rüstung," in *Volume du Congrès: Genève 1965* (VTSup 15; Leiden: Brill, 1966), 150–69; see now also Israel Finkelstein, "The Philistines in the Bible: A Late-Monarchic Perspective," *JSOT* 27 (2002): 131–67.

the Philistines are unknown. After the failure of their invasion into Egypt, the Philistines settled in the five cities of the coastal plains (Ashkelon, Ashdod, Gaza, Ekron, and Gath), an act presumably tolerated by Egypt. There they appear to have comprised the upper class of the city population, which in the course of two or three generations brought the cities under their control. After the collapse of Egyptian domination under the later Ramessides, they exerted their power in the coastal plains. The later expansion of their ruling territory into the regions of the Judean and Ephraimite mountains led necessarily to conflict with the Israelite tribes residing there.

The hostility with the Philistines forms the background for the tradition of Samson in Judg 13–16—whenever its final form is to be fixed. The ark narrative of 1 Sam 4–6 and 2 Sam 6 reflects the inferiority of premonarchic Israel with respect to military altercations. Only after the Israelite tribes reached the political agreement to come under the rule of a king did Saul prove successful at breaking the dominance of the Philistines and establishing an independent state (1 Sam 13–14). When Saul's hostility toward David became clear, David consistently put himself in the service of Achish of Gath (1 Sam 21:11–16). In battle with the Philistines at the mountain of Gilboa, Saul eventually loses his crown and his life (1 Sam 31). Only his successor, David, could ultimately ward off the continuing danger by achieving victories in numerous battles (2 Sam 5:17–25; 8:1).

The ensuing history appears to be characterized by a peaceful coexistence; at least the sources remain silent concerning further altercations. The succession of five settlement strata in Ashdod (X–VI) during Iron Age II shows, however, that the era of the monarchy did not simply proceed peacefully, but the details are unknown. Not until the conquests by Tiglath-pileser III (745–726) would these particular cities reemerge in connection with the anti-Assyrian coalition (see *TUAT* 1:373, 375, 379, 290, 406), but they are not characterized specifically as Philistines. The concept of a Philistine people thus remains limited to the biblical tradition pertaining to the early monarchy; in the ensuing history the Philistines appear as independent city-states.

II.8. Neighboring Peoples

Little can be known of the peoples neighboring the Israelite tribes in Iron Age I, since there are concrete findings only as of 1000 B.C.E. The two kings Sihon and Og, named in the context of the march through the land east of the Jordan in Num 21:21–35 (cf. Deut 2:26–37; 3:1–11) cannot be verified. Given the late composition of these texts, a memory of a historical occurrence is improbable (see §I.2.3); Sihon and Og are fictional kings from traditions no longer extant.

In the book of Judges, then, Moabites, Midianites, and Ammonites appear along with Canaanites and Philistines as enemies of Israel in the period after the land acquisition (see Judg 3:12–30; 6–8; 10:17–12:6). These narratives actually deal with the traditions of the monarchy and project military self-assertion back to the time before the formation of the state. The biblical report is to be ruled out as a historical source for the history of the neighboring peoples in the time before the formation of the state. The extrabiblical literary traditions for the neighboring peoples and states are first attested in Iron Age II, leaving any statements Iron Age I dependent on the results of archaeological research and conclusions from later sources.

II.8.1. Phoenicians

The Phoenician cities were located either on an island off the coast or on the coast in the area of Lebanon, where the natural conditions made possible the construction of a harbor.[75] The most important cites were, from the south to the north, Tyre, Sidon, Beirut, Byblos, and Arvad. The history of the Phoenician cities reaches back to the early Bronze Age, a time characterized by intensive trade with Egypt; but the name Phoenician properly denotes only the population of the Iron Age. The name is used by the Greek authors Homer, Thucydides, and Herodotus, but its meaning is unclear, as is the origin of the designated people-group. The name probably has to do with the descendents of the inhabitants of the city-states in the Bronze Age. It probably has to do with the descendants of the inhabitants of the city-states in the Bronze Age. Extant inscriptions show clearly that the Phoenicians belonged to the Northwest Semitic language group. The Phoenician population took over the settlement form of the city and from there reached out to the hinterland that belonged to the sphere of influence of the city in order to secure the necessary supplies. It is difficult to establish the settlement history in all of the coastal cities, since they were built over heavily in later eras. Thus far only the history of Tyre has been investigated through the stratigraphic layers of the settlement.[76] According to the stratigraphy, the city was first founded toward the end of Middle

---

75. See Sabatino Moscati, *The World of the Phoenicians* (trans. Alastair Hamilton; London: Weidenfeld & Nicolson, 1968); Dimitri Baramki, *Phoenicia and the Phoenicians* (Beirut: Khayats, 1961); André Parrot, Maurice H. Chéhab, and Sabatino Moscati, *Les Phéniciens: l'expansion phénicienne, Carthage* (L'universe des forms 23; Paris: Gallimard, 1975); María Eugenia Aubet, *The Phoenicians and the West: Politics, Colonies, and Trade* (trans. Mary Turton; Cambridge: Cambridge University Press, 1993).

76. Patricia Maynor Bikai, *The Pottery of Tyre* (Warminster: Aris & Phillips, 1978).

Bronze IIB around 1600 B.C.E. (stratum XVIII), and it also existed later during the Late Bronze Age (strata XVII–XIV). Later still, circa 1150 B.C.E., the city decays and is characterized by Canaanite culture. A gap in settlement follows, because the resettlement first reappears in the middle of the eleventh century B.C.E. (stratum XIII). Thereafter the settlement continues in unbroken succession until around 700 B.C.E. (strata XII–I). The Phoenicians' habitation of this Iron Age city drove trade and established businesses throughout the entire Mediterranean region. Their extensive control of sea trade was fully established by the middle of the tenth century, because Solomon allocates the construction of the temple entirely to his trade partner Hiram of Tyre (1 Kgs 9:27; 10:11–12). He would not only supply the materials of wood and bronze but also see to the skilled labor. The Phoenicians probably arose as the dominant trade power in the Mediterranean already during the eleventh century. At that time the independent city-states on the Lebanese coast profited from the power vacuum created by the decline of Mycenean and Canaanite culture and built up far-reaching trade relations in the entire Mediterranean region. During the course of Iron Age II, the Phoenicians decidedly contributed to negotiations among the different cultures of the Mediterranean.

II.8.2. ARAMEANS

According to the annals of Tiglath-pileser I (1115–1077; see *ANET*, 275), the Arameans originally inhabited the Syrian plains. From there the Aramean tribes advanced to Mesopotamia in the eleventh century, initially merging with the settlements in the area of the bend of the Euphrates as well as the valleys of Balīḫ and Ḫābūr.[77] From the tenth century on they built a series of cities in the area of the Euphrates and Syria, which would become the provinces of the Assyrian Empire after the Assyrian conquest in the eighth century. The following cities of southern Syria neighbored Israel:

---

77. Albrecht Alt, "Die syrische Staatenwelt vor dem Einbruch der Assyrer," in idem, *Kleine Schriften zur Geschichte des Volkes Israel* (3 vols.; Munich: Beck, 1953), 3:214–32; Abraham Malamat, "The Aramaeans," in *Peoples of Old Testament Times* (ed. D. J. Wiseman; Oxford: Clarendon, 1973), 134–55; Martin Noth, "Die Nachbarn der israelitischen Stämme in Ostjordanlande," *ABLAK* 1 (1971): 434–75; Gotthard G. G. Reinhold, *Die Beziehungen Altisraels zu den aramäischen Staaten in der israelitisch-judäischen Königszeit* (Europäische Hochschulschriften, Reihe 23, Theologie 368; Frankfurt am Main: Lang, 1989). See now also Paul-Eugène Dion, *Les araméens à l'âge du fer: Histoire politique et structures socials* (Études bibliques NS 34; Paris: Lecoffre/Gabalda, 1997); Edward Lipiński, *The Arameans: Their Ancient History, Culture, Religion* (OLA 100; Leuven: Peeters, 2000).

Zobah	northeast of Antilebanon
Beth-rehob	on the eastern border of 'Aǧlūn
Maacath	south of Lebanon and Antilebanon
Geshur	in northeast Ġōlān
Damascus	east of Hermon

These cities were subjugated by David (see 2 Sam 8:3-5; 10:6-8, 15-19), but the wars against the Arameans would have a decided influence on the subsequent history of Israel up to the beginning of the eighth century.

Any contact between the Israelite tribes and the Arameans in premonarchic times is improbable, although the history of Aramean settlement patterns and city building in the region of Syria runs parallel to that of Israel's history. The extent to which these parallels develop during the monarchy remains an open question. The tradition would produce an explicit connection between Israel and the Arameans: the patriarchal narratives mention several times the relation of Abraham and Jacob to clans living in an Aramean settlement region. In the later formulation of the so-called little historical credo (Deut 26:5), the unnamed father becomes the "wandering Aramean." The consciousness of this close relationship can be no older than the monarchic period, when the numerous military contests and the associated contacts with the Arameans in language and culture first become clear. Aramaic belongs to the Northwest Semitic language family, and, over the course of the first millennium B.C.E., it replaced Hebrew as the spoken language in the southern Levant. Since the Israelite tribes do not belong to the groups that penetrated the cultivated land of the Syrian plains (see §II.4), Israel's land acquisition cannot be understood as part of the Aramean migration, although it did occur at approximately the same time as the founding of the state.

II.8.3. Ammonites

The Ammonites are a tribe or group of tribes of unknown origin, who in the early Iron Age assumed a firm place of residence at the eastern edge of Belqā in the region of the upper reaches of Jabbok (Nahr ez-Zerqā).[78] The borders

---

78. Ulrich Hübner, *Die Ammoniter: Untersuchungen zur Geschichte, Kultur und Religion eines transjordanischen Volkes im 1. Jahrtausend v.Chr.* (ADPV 16; Wiesbaden: Harrassowitz, 1992); Rudolph Henry Dornemann, *The Archaeology of Transjordan in the Bronze and Iron Ages* (Milwaukee Public Museum Publications in Anthropology and History 4; Milwaukee: Milwaukee Public Museum, 1983); Walter E. Aufrecht, *A Corpus of*

of their settlement region cannot presently be determined with certainty. Their later urban center was the city Rabbah, in present-day ʿAmmān. The early Iron Age settlement is outside of ʿAmmān, still in Abū Billāna and at the Ǧebel et-Tuwēm, as well as in Ḫirbet el-Ḥaǧǧar and Saḥab as proved by excavations. Nevertheless, the material culture of this era has not yet been determined in adequate detail. The point in time of the transition to city building is unknown. The wars of Saul (1 Sam 11) and David (2 Sam 10) against the Ammonites nevertheless presume the establishment of kingship and thus statehood for this people by the end of the eleventh century. This state borders on the vicinity of the territories given to the tribes east of the Jordan in the area of Belqā and ʿAǧlūn and so necessarily would have come into the military contestations of the early monarchy. After David's final victory, the Ammonites served the Israelites as corvée (2 Sam 12:26–31). King Shobi's providing supplies for David and his court during his flight to Mahanaim is probably to be understood in terms of a faithful vassal.[79] The sources are silent about any further development; the kingdom of Ammon was probably too small to represent a serious threat to the regions of Israel east of the Jordan. Nevertheless, it remains suspect that Ammon would simply be inactive when Israel was embattled in war with the Arameans during the entire ninth century (see 1 Kgs 20:1).

In Gen 19:38 the Ammonites are placed in relationship with Israel such that the fictional father of the tribe Ben-ammi, the future Ammonites, is made out to be Lot's son; at the same time, that the ancestor of the Ammonites was conceived by incest between Lot and his own daughter signifies a devaluation of the people. In Jephthah's battles with the Ammonites in Judg 11:23, 32, 33 (see §I.2.3.1), the military events of the monarchy are projected back into premonarchic times. Thus, in Judges, the Ammonites are the enemies of Israel along with the other neighboring peoples. This labeling is based on the outlook of the monarchic period and has no basis in the preceding era. From the parallel development of the land acquisition and state formation of Ammon and the immediate vicinity of the settlement territories of the Israelite tribes and the Ammonites, one can nevertheless expect that the relationship was not exactly peaceable in the time before Saul and David, since every expansion must have led to conflicts between the neighboring tribes and peoples. Apparently the tribes east of the Jordan could nevertheless hold their ground

---

Ammonite Inscriptions (Ancient Near Eastern Texts and Studies 4; Lewiston, N.Y.: Mellen, 1989); Burton MacDonald, *"'East of the Jordan': Territories and Sites of the Hebrew Scriptures* (ASOR Books 6; Boston: American Schools of Oriental Research, 2000).

79. Mahanaim has still not been located. For the location and lower reaches of Jabbok, see Robert A. Cooghanour, "A Search for Mahanaim," *BASOR* 273 (1989): 57–66.

well enough against the Ammonites, since the highlands in the western parts of the eastern Transjordan were able to be conquered; this area was far better suited for agriculture than the regions occupied by the Ammonites on the eastern edge of Belqā.

According to the few inscriptions discovered thus far, the Ammonite language shows a close connection to North Arabian, Moabite, and Hebrew; it thus belongs in the group of Northwest Semitic languages. From the eleventh century to the eighth century, Ammon was a small independent kingdom that became a tributary vassal to the Assyrians after the conquest. The material culture of Iron Age II shows an independent expression throughout, while the panorama of the powerful settlement mounds of the Citadel by ʿAmmān evinces a certain closeness to Aramean art of the first half of the first millennium.[80]

II.8.4. Moabites

As 1 Sam 22:3–4 indicates, there was already a king of Moab by the time of David, albeit one who goes unnamed.[81] (In this context the city named Mizpeh in Moab is not located and does not appear again in the sources.) The king named Eglon of Moab in Judg 3:12–30 has not been verified historically. The narrative concerning Eglon's death at the hands of the left-handed Ehud originated in the time of the monarchy, and the history of tradition hardly reaches back to the time before the state (see §I.2.3.1). In the Egyptian texts Moab is mentioned as a place name only once, on the base of a statue in front of the northern pylon of the temple of Ramses II in Luxor.[82] As in the case of the Ammonites, the sources are thus lacking with respect to the history of Moab in the twelfth and eleventh centuries.

The Moabites derive their name from the settlement regions they took during the course of the early Iron Age. Their origin is unknown but, like that of the Arameans and the Israelites, probably involves nomadic groups migrating and then becoming settled. The archaeological record indicates as much.[83]

---

80. See Ali Abou-Assaf, "Untersuchungen zur ammonitischen Rundbildkunst," *UF* 12 (1980): 7–102.

81. John R. Bartlett, "The Moabites and Edomites," in *Peoples of Old Testament Times* (ed. D. J. Wiseman; Oxford: Clarendon, 1973), 229–58; Piotr Bienkowski, ed., *Early Edom and Moab: The Beginning of the Iron Age in Southern Jordan* (Sheffield Archaeological Monographs 7; Sheffield: J. R. Collis, 1992).

82. Jan Jozef Simons, *Handbook for the Study of Egyptian Topographical Lists Relating to Western Asia* (Leiden: Brill, 1937), no. XXII:d10.

83. See the findings of the initial research by J. Maxwell Miller, *Archaeological Survey*

Since east of the Dead Sea there is only a narrow strip of cultivated land usable for agriculture, only a few late Bronze Age cities existed in this region. After the collapse of the Canaanite city-states, the number of settlements increased considerably, and these are indicative of a new population. The transition to city building probably took place during the eleventh century, although the exact date is unknown. Under David this neighboring state was a tributary vassal (see 2 Sam 8:2–12), but its subjugation by Saul is uncertain historically, since 1 Sam 14:47 represents only a brief summary statement.

The original settlement region of the Moabites was on the plateau east of the Dead Sea between the Arnon (Sēl el-Mōğib) and the Sered (Wādi el-Ḥesā), the two deep incisions in the plateau that constituted natural borders. Furthermore, Num 21:13 and 22:36 as well as Judg 11:18 establish the Arnon as the border with Moab. The city center lay in Kir Moab, present-day el-Kerak. According to the identification from the Mesha Stele (*TUAT* 1:646–50), in the ninth century the Moabites extended their territory northward from Arnon to the point where the Israelites had conquered the territory of the mountains at the north end of the Dead Sea. In the premonarchic period, the Arnon thus constituted the clear boundary for the expansion of the settlement territory by the tribes east of the Jordan (see §II.5.3).

The Mesha Stele and later inscriptions show Moabite as its own language in the Northwest Semitic family bearing a close relation to Hebrew. The awareness of a certain nearness between the Moabites and the Israelite tribes is expressed in the patriarchal narratives where the fictional father of the tribe of Moab is said in Gen 19:37 to be the son of Lot. At the same time, Lot's procreation by incest with his own daughter nevertheless entails a devaluing dissociation that is reflected in the wider course of history between Judah and Moab and in the necessary ethnic differentiation in the time after the Assyrian conquest.

II.8.5. Edomites

Bartlett, John R. *Edom and the Edomites* (JSOTSup 77; Sheffield: Sheffield Academic Press, 1989). **Bennett,** Crystal M. "Neo-Assyrian Influence in Transjordan," *SHAJ* 1 (1982): 181–187. **Bienkowski,** Piotr, ed. *Early Edom and Moab: The Beginning of*

---

of the Kerak Plateau: Conducted during 1978–1982 under the Direction of J. Maxwell Miller and Jack M. Pinkerton (ASOR Archaeological Reports 1; Atlanta: Scholars Press, 1991). The conclusions of Nelson Glueck (*Explorations in Eastern Palestine I* [AASOR XIV; Baltimore: J. H. Furst, 1933–34], 1–113) are dated. See also James A. Sauer, "Transjordan in the Bronze and Iron Ages: A Critique of Glueck's Synthesis," *BASOR* 263 (1986): 1–26.

the Iron Age in Southern Jordan (Sheffield Archaeological Monographs 7; Sheffield: J. R. Collis, 1992). **Bienkowski.** "Umm el-Biyara, Tawilan and Buseirah in Retrospect," *Levant* 22 (1990): 91–109. **Finkelstein**, Israel. "Edom in the Iron I," *Levant* 24 (1992): 159–69. **Knauf**, Ernst Axel. "Alter und Herkunft der edomitischen Königsliste Gen 36:31–19," *ZAW* 97 (1985): 245–53. **Maag**, Victor. "Jakob–Esau–Edom," in *Kultur, Kulturkontakt und Religion: gesammelte Studien zur allgemeinen und alttestamentlichen Religionsgeschichte; Victor Maag zum 70. Geburtstag* (ed. H. H. Schmid and O. H. Steck; Göttingen: Vandenhoeck & Ruprecht, 1980), 99–110. **Oakeshott**, M. F. "The Edomite Pottery," in *Midian, Moab and Edom: The History and Archaeology of Late Bronze and Iron Age Jordan and North-west Arabia* (ed. John F. A. Sawyer and David J. A. Clines; JSOTSup 24; Sheffield: JSOT Press, 1983), 53–63. **Weippert**, Manfred. "Remarks on the History of Settlement in Southern Jordan during the Early Iron Age," *SHAJ* 1 (1982): 153–62. See now also: **Levy**, Thomas E., et al. "Reassessing the Chronology of Biblical Edom: New Excavations and 14C Dates from Khirbat en-Nahas (Jordan)," *Antiquity* 78 (2004): 863–76. **Levy** et al. "High-Precision Radiocarbon Dating and Historical Biblical Archaeology in Southern Jordan," *Proceedings of the National Academy of Sciences* 105 (2008): 16460–65.

Edom "the Red" is originally the designation for the narrow strip of cultivated land at the drop-off at the east Jordan high plateau, but it would be transferred to the name of the landscape of the entire region east of Arabah. The name emerges for the first time during the reign of Ramses II in Papyrus Anastasi VI in the context of the border crossing of the Shasu nomads (*ANET*, 259); it occurs also in extrabiblical Ugaritic and Akkadian texts. In the Bible Edom is synonymous with Seir, meaning "hairy" (the original designation used for the middle tier of Mount Seir made of Nubian sandstone) and is also synonymous with Teman, meaning "south." The region reaches in the north to Wādi el-Ḥesā, constituting the boundary with Moab, and in the south to the gulf of el-'Aqaba. In the west, the escarpment of the plateau to the Arabah forms a barrier difficult to cross over, whereas crossing over the steppe into the wilderness is rather fluid in the east. The Edomites thus bear the name of their inhabited region, and these nomadic people are designated in the Egyptian sources of the New Kingdom as Shasu (šꜣśw) (see §II.4.2). In any case Edom does not belong to the catchment area of the Canaanite city-states during the Late Bronze Age. Nevertheless, modest settlement remains during Iron Age II indicate the transition to at least sporadic settlements. The assimilation of agriculture and the building of stone houses can signify a transitional establishment without them necessarily having given up the herding associated with their nomadic lifestyle. The urbanization associated with the formation of the state appeared in Edom in the eighth century at the earliest, as was proved by the excavations at Buṣērā, Ṭawīlān, and Umm el-Biyāra. The revival of mining and smelting of copper in the territory of

Fēnān since the eleventh century assumes far-reaching trade relationships for their marketing, but these have not been clearly demonstrated thus far. In any case, over the course of Iron Age II a pottery evolved that was independent in style and decoration and is clearly differentiated from the common goods in other regions. Following the Assyrian conquest of Edom in the last third of the eighth century, a strong influence of Neo-Assyrian culture is apparent. Edomite culture in Iron Age I is as yet unavailable.

In the Bible, the Edomites are counted as the offspring of Esau, which should indicate a strong kinship relationship to the Israelites. As such, the Edomites do not appear as enemies of Israel before or after the land acquisition. With Saul, the Edomites first show up as enemies in the summary of the routed neighboring peoples (1 Sam 14:47). The biblical tradition has preserved the names of the Edomite clans in the compiled list in Gen 36, which can hardly reach back to the early Iron Age. Historically there is no further validation of this list, and any other attestations from inscriptions or other sources are lacking. Furthermore, the list of the kings of Edom (Gen 36:31–39) does not yield additional historical knowledge. This compilation does draw on historical figures, but it is not possible to reconstruct a chronology, given the lack of any fixed point for determining a date. In the early monarchic period, David would conquer the Edomites and make them pay tribute, as was the case with all the other neighbors of Israel (2 Sam 8:13–15); however, having escaped to Egypt during David's reign, Hadad the Edomite would restore the autonomy of the region upon the accession of Solomon (1 Kgs 11:14–22).

II.8.6. Midianites

In the traditions about the judge Gideon in Judg 6–8, the Midianites, along with the Amalekites, are the enemies of Israel who are depicted as camel-riding plunderers from the east. They are also identified as nomadic tribes from the Arabian wilderness. The naming of the two kings Zebah and Zalmunna is unverifiable; since the traditions date from the time of the monarchy (see §I.2.3.1), they can hardly refer to historical figures of the twelfth or eleventh century. The Midianites also appear elsewhere as nomadic inhabitants of the southeastern wilderness (see Isa 66:6; Hab 3:7). The land of Midian lies south of Edom on the way to Egypt in the vicinity of Paran (1 Kgs 11:18). Like other nomads of the Arabian Peninsula, the Midianites were projected back as descending from a concubine of Abraham in Gen 25:4 and were thus depicted as having a kinship connection to Israel. According to the pre-Priestly pentateuchal narrative, Moses marries a daughter of Jethro, one of the priests in Midian (Exod 2:16–22; 3:1) and celebrates a sacrificial meal with his father-in-law at the mountain of God in the wilderness (Exod 18:1–12). In the postexilic additions to the pentateuchal narratives, the Midianites appear as enemies of Israel who must be fought and defeated. Like the other peoples east of the Jordan, at a later time the Midianites were counted among the adversaries of Israel who obstructed Israel's journey into the promised land. The five kings named in this context, Evi, Rekem, Zur, Hur, and Reba, come from an uncertain literary tradition. The "Day of Midian" in Isa 9:3 (Eng. 9:4), in the framework of a prophecy of salvation, is presumably an allusion to Gideon's victory over the Midianites and thus already presupposes Judg 6–8. Except for their classification as nomads, the history of the Midianites is as yet completely unknown; the biblical tradition offers no concrete references.

Midian was originally the name of a territory, and the inhabitants called themselves by their settlement region.[84] The name Midian appears as the city Madiama/Madyan according to ancient and Arabian geography.[85] This city is compared with the oasis el-Badʿ east of the Gulf of Aqaba. In this proximity, the remains of several settlements are located from the thirteenth and twelfth centuries as well as from the Nabatean-Roman period.[86] The land of Midian is thus not only "the surrounding region of this city" (Knauf) but also probably encompassed the coastal mountains and the plateau el-Ḥisma. The entire region has still not been explored to any great extent, but there is evidence of sporadic settlements in the area of a considerable number of oases starting from the second millennium. Thus, if the Midianites were nomads, their lifestyle precluded neither their building settlements to occupy the oases nor their practicing agriculture in suitable regions. It is unknown whether the Midianites went beyond their constitution as a tribe and established a state. In any case the borders of the land of Midian were not sharply delineated.

The so-called Midianite pottery is associated with the Midianites as their only type of monuments. These are vessels of fine yellowish clay having two-colored decorations, which can be made up of geometric patterns as well as figured images. Based on the details of their discovery, they can be assumed to date from the thirteenth to the eleventh centuries. From preliminary reports, this pottery is attested in many places in the region of Midian; its center of

---

84. For this point, see Ernst Axel Knauf, *Midian: Untersuchungen zur Geschichte Palästinas und Nordarabiens am Ende des 2. Jahrtausends v.Chr.* (ADPV 7; Wiesbaden: Harrassowitz, 1988).

85. Evidence by Alois Musil, *The Northern Ḥeğâz: A Topographical Itinerary* (American Geographical Society of New York, Oriental Explorations and Studies 1; New York: American Geographical Society, 1926), 278–82.

86. M. L. Ingraham et al., "Preliminary Report on a Reconnaissance Survey of the Northwestern Province," *Aṭlāl* 5 (1981): 59–84, esp. 74–75.

production appears to have been in Qurayyah in the southern portion of the plateau el-Ḥisma.[87] The scattering of these vessels reaches to the southern Levant; they are found not only in the mining regions of el-Meneʿīyeh and Fēnān at the edge of Arabah, but shards have been found also in the early Iron Age layers of Ḫirbet el-Mšāš, Tell el-Fārʿa (south) in the Negeb, and Ǧedur in the Shephelah. If these vessels are to be connected with the Midianites, it would indicate the wide dissemination of this people and yet another activity. The Midianites not only were familiar with camel breeding but also were masters of a special kind of axe in addition to smelting and finishing copper. In this respect, in the early Iron Age the Midianites were presumably the ones who mediated the technology of copper mining and the manufacture of weapons and tools out of bronze to the Egyptians in the mining regions of el-Meneʿīyeh, to the Edomites in Fēnān, and to the Judean tribal groups settled in the Negeb and the Shephelah.

II.8.7. Amalekites

Along with the Midianites, the Amalekites appear as the enemies of Israel in the narratives about Gideon (see Judg 6:3; 7:12). This is the traditional role for these people, as seen elsewhere in the biblical tradition. According to Gen 36:12, the Amalekites were counted among the Edomite tribes that were considered the offspring of Esau. The so-called banner speech of Exod 17:16 is attached to the pre-Priestly narrative about the attack by Amalek, which expresses the enemy connection between Israel and the Amalekites according to the terminology of holy war:

> A hand upon the banner of Yahweh,
> Yahweh will have war with Amalek
> from generation to generation.

Even if the speech were to be older than the preceding narrative, the account reflects the situation of the monarchic period. In Deut 25:17–19 the military

---

87. Peter J. Parr et al., "Preliminary Survey in North-West Arabia," *Bulletin of the Institute of Archaeology of the University of London* 8–9 (1970): 193–242; 10 (1972): 23–61; Beno Rothenberg and Jonathan Glass, "The Midianite Pottery," in *Midian, Moab and Edom: The History and Archaeology of Late Bronze and Iron Age Jordan and North-west Arabia* (ed. John F. A. Sawyer and David J. A. Clines; JSOTSup 24; Sheffield: JSOT Press, 1983), 65–124; Peter J. Parr, "Contacts between North West Arabia and Jordan in the Late Bronze and Iron Ages," *SHAJ* 1 (1982): 127–33.

conflict with the Amalekites worsens further to the point of their annihilation. The same is true of the third oracle of Balaam in Num 24:20. These negative attitudes toward the Amalekites were first established on the basis of historical experience over the course of the monarchy.

Since the premonarchic period, the Amalekites were a nomadic tribe whose catchment area was in the plains region south of the Negeb. Given that the southern plains zone can be used only for pasture, it was apparently never settled by these nomads. (As named in 1 Sam 15, King Agag is an anachronism, although there could have been an Agag who was a tribal leader.) The land seizure by the Israelite tribes and their claim to the conquered settlement territory necessarily led to military confrontations. Southern Judah and the Negeb were captured by different clans, the latter being absorbed into the tribe of Judah. Saul had already commanded a campaign of predatory attacks in order to defend the new Israelite territories in southern Judah and the Negeb from plundering (1 Sam 15); in doing so he pushed far forward into the center of the Amalekite territory called "the city of the Amalekites." (This unnamed city does not necessarily refer to a fixed settlement; it could also indicate an oasis or a tent camp.) Even though nomads could retreat to the distant plains, they could never be decisively defeated except by the loss of a part of their herds. As of the time of Saul, the Amalekites had conducted a raid against Ziklag (Tell es-Sebaʿ) and had abducted the women and children (1 Sam 30); Ziklag was the city given to David by Achish of Gath.[88] David, along with his men, set out in pursuit and not only brought back his original property but also collected a large amount of booty, which he distributed among the other villages in the region. Thereafter the Amalekites begin to disappear from the historical sources, although they were also an unsettling element during the monarchic period for farmsteads located in the Negeb and in the plains, despite the Judean kings having transportation routes in this region through a system of armed fortresses.

---

88. On the site of Ziklag, see Volkmar Fritz, "Der Beitrag der Archäologie zur historischen Topographie Palästinas am Beispiel von Ziklag," *ZDPV* 106 (1990): 78–85.

III. The Literature of the Era

Almost nothing has survived of the literature of the era, since stories and accounts were recited and transmitted orally and had probably already become lost during the course of the monarchy. The composition of individual forms as substantial works was first introduced during the monarchy. Thus, songs predating the formation of the state were preserved only by their integration in prose narratives. But apparently there was still a collection of premonarchic songs in the early monarchic period, because Josh 10:13 and 2 Sam 1:18 mention explicitly a "Book of the Upright" (ספר הישר; "Book of Jashar") as a source. This reference, however, does not prove the existence of such a collection, since the statement could be the work of the Deuteronomistic Historian. Similar reservations apply to the name "Book of the Wars of Yahweh" (ספר מלחמות יהוה) in Num 21:14.

From the context of the books of Joshua and Judges, the only portions expressed as songs are the fragment in Josh 10:12b–13a and the elements of the Song of Deborah in Judg 5:12–17, 18b, 19–22, 24–30. Yet the hymns of praise in Gen 4:23 and 1 Sam 18:7 = 21:11 probably originated prior to the formation of the state, and the two funeral or lamentation songs in 2 Sam 1:19–27 and 3:33–34 belong to the beginning of the monarchic period. All the remaining songs, which otherwise might be considered just as old, must be dated to the monarchic period based on their content and language; to those belong the Song of Miriam in Exod 15:21 and the Well Song in Num 21:17–18. Nevertheless, different forms of songs with distinguishable *Sitze im Leben* can be assumed for the time before the formation of the state of Israel.

Additional genres were admitted into the prose narratives of the book of Judges, and their development prior to the monarchic period is at least possible. Riddles stand in the middle of the narrative of Samson's marriage (Judg 14:14, 18); this simple form is connected with no particular era and can thus be assumed from an early time, even if Solomon's riddle sayings cannot be dated precisely. A fable is found in connection with the traditions about Abimelech in Judg 9:8–15, which evinces a critical *Tendenz* against the monarchy and thus originated in the monarchic period. Regardless of the unquestionably old age of the genre of funeral songs—since those first appear in the books of Samuel—only hymns of praise, riddles, and fables can be treated as biblically attested genres from the books of Joshua and Judges.

III.1. HYMNS OF PRAISE

Ackerman, James S. "Prophecy and War in Early Israel: A Study of the Deborah-Barak Story," *BASOR* 220 (1975): 5–13. **Bechmann**, Ulrike. *Das Deboralied zwischen Geschichte und Fiktion: Eine exegetische Untersuchung zu Richter 5* (St. Ottilien: EOS, 1989). **Blenkinsopp**, Joseph. "Ballad Style and Psalm Style in the Song of Deborah: A Discussion," *Biblica* 42 (1961): 61–76. **Coogan**, Michael D. "A Structural Analysis of the Song of Deborah," *CBQ* 40 (1978): 132–66. **Craigie**, Peter C. "The Song of Deborah and the Epic of Tukulti-Ninurta," *JBL* 88 (1969): 253–65. **Gerleman**, Gillis. "The Song of Deborah in the Light of Stylistics," *VT* 1 (1951): 168–80. **Gray**, John. "Israel in the Song of Deborah," in *Ascribe to the Lord: Biblical and Other Studies in Memory of Peter C. Craigie* (ed. Lylel M. Eslinger and Glen Taylor; JSOTSup 67; Sheffield: JSOT Press, 1988), 421–55. **Mayes**, A. D. H. "The Historical Context of the Battle against Sisera," *VT* 19 (1969): 353–60. **Müller**, Hans-Peter. "Der Aufbau des Deborahliedes," *VT* 16 (1966): 446–59. **Murray**, D. F. "Narrative Structure and Technique in the Deborah-Barak Story (Judges IV 4-22)," in *Studies in the Historical Books of the Old Testament* (VTSup 30; Leiden: Brill, 1979), 155–89. **Neef**, Heinz-Dieter. "Der Sieg Deboras und Baraks über Sisera," *ZAW* 101 (1989): 28–49. **Stager**, Lawrence E. *Archaeology, Ecology, and Social History: Background Themes in the Song of Deborah* (VTSup 40; Leiden: Brill, 1988), 221–34. **Weiser**, Artur. "Das Deboralied—eine gattungs- und traditionsgeschichtliche Studie," *ZAW* 71 (1959): 67–97. **Zobel**, Hans-Jürgen. *Stammesspruch und Geschichte: Die Angaben der Stammessprüche von Gen 39, Dtn 33, und Jdc 5 über die politischen und kultischen Zustände im damaligen "Israel"* (BZAW 95; Berlin: Töpelmann, 1965), 44–52. See now also: **Fritz**, Volkmar. "The Complex of Traditions in Judges 4 and 5 and the Religion of Pre-state Israel," in *"I Will Speak the Riddles of Ancient Times": Archaeological and Historical Studies in Honor of Amihai Mazar on the Occasion of His Sixtieth Birthday* (ed: Aren M. Maeir and Pierre de Miroschedji; 2 vols.; Winona Lake, Ind.: Eisenbrauns, 2006), 2:689–98. **Ackerman**, Susan. "Digging Up Deborah: Recent Hebrew Bible Scholarship on Gender and the Contribution of Archaeology," *NEA* 66 (2003): 172–84. **Vincent**, Mark A. "The Song of Deborah: A Structural and Literary Consideration," *JSOT* 91 (2000): 61–82.

Since the Song of Deborah in Judg 5 is older than the prose narrative in Judg 4, it can be treated independently. Indeed, the view predominates today that the song is not a literary unity, but opinions are deeply divided as to the formation of the composition. Against the view espousing the growth of multiple layers, it seems more probable to assume the expansion of a foundational element by adding pieces in praise of Yahweh and Israel (H.-P. Müller). Thus, the criteria for the two different layers can be abstracted simply from the text itself.

The two sentences in Judg 5:1 and 31b constitute the necessary transitions and thus are not original, constituent parts of the song. The point of departure for any further differentiation of layers is the observation of the double preludes that signal the singing in verses 2–3 and 12. The double usage of the same grammatical form of the imperative is functionally unwarranted and thus provides the decisive clue that the song at one time originally began with the invocation in verse 12. Verses 2–11, with invocation, depiction of the theophany, description of the conditions, and hymn of praise to Yahweh, thus represent a later addition, to which the conclusion in verse 31a also belongs. According to this framework, the original song did not express the participation of Yahweh (vv. 4, 5, 9–11) or add the necessary description of the situation (vv. 6–8).

The remaining core of the song consists of a succession of scenes, in which the curse of Meroz (v. 23) merely comprises foreign material. Moreover, there still appear to be short additions where the name of a tribe is repeated in another location, thereby breaking the principle of only naming each tribe a single time. This is the case once in verse 15 with the words יששכר כן ברק; Barak's participation in the battle should already be clear from verse 12. Furthermore, the tribe of Zebulun, which was already named as a participant in the battle in verse 14, is mentioned again in verse 18a, whereas the continuation in verse 18b connects to verse 17; so this is also to be counted as an addition. Further additions to the song are not apparent, so the foundational song comprised verses 12–17, 18b, 19–22, and 24–30.

After the prelude in Judg 5:12, the text gives four unconnected, successive scenes:

1. The Mustering of the Militia (vv. 13–17, 18b)
2. The Depiction of Battle (vv. 19–22)
3. Jael Killing Sisera (vv. 24–27)
4. Mocking the Enemies (vv. 28–30)

The text depicts the scenes in a tight succession of images, although some details remain incomprehensible. Below, modifications to the Masoretic Text and omissions generally follow the apparatus of *Biblia Hebraica Stuttgartensia* and are marked with an asterisk.

12   Awake, awake, Deborah!
     Awake, awake, utter a song!
     Arise, Barak,
     lead away your captives, O son of Abinoam.

1. The Mustering of the Militia (vv. 13–17, 18b)

13   Then down marched the remnant of the noble;
     the people of Yahweh marched down for him against the mighty.
14   From Ephraim they set out into the valley,
     following you, Benjamin, with your kin;
     from Machir marched down the commanders,
     and from Zebulun those who bear the marshal's staff;
15   the chiefs of Issachar came with Deborah*
     into the valley they rushed out at his heels.
     Among the clans of Reuben there were great searchings of heart.
16   Why did you tarry among the sheepfolds,
     to hear the piping for the flocks?*
17   Gilead stayed beyond the Jordan
     and Dan, why did he abide with the ships?
     Asher sat still at the coast of the sea,
     settling down by his landings,
18b Naphtali, too, on the heights of the field.

2. The Depiction of Battle (vv. 19–22)

19   The kings came, they fought;
     then fought the kings of Canaan
     at Taanach, by the waters of Megiddo;
     they got no spoils of silver.
20   The stars fought from heaven;
     from their courses they fought against Sisera.
21   The torrent Kishon swept them away,
     the onrushing torrent, the torrent Kishon.
22   Then loud beat the horses' hoofs
     with the galloping, galloping of his steeds.

3. Jael Killing Sisera (vv. 24–27)

24   Most blessed of women be Jael,*
     of tent-dwelling women most blessed.
25   He asked water and she gave him milk;
     she brought him curds in a lordly bowl.
26   She put her hand to the tent peg,

and her right hand to the workmen's mallet;
she struck Sisera a blow, she crushed his head,
she shattered and pierced his temple.
27 He sank, he fell, he lay still at her feet,
at her feet he sank, he fell.
Where he sank, there he fell dead.

4. Mocking the Enemies (vv. 28–30)

28 Out of the window she peered,
the mother of Sisera gazed through the lattice.
"Why is his chariot so long in coming?
Why tarry the hoofbeats of his chariots?"
29 Her wisest ladies make answer,
indeed, she answers the question herself:
30 "Are they not finding and dividing the spoil?
A girl or two for every man,
spoil of dyed stuffs for Sisera,*
a dyed garment, two garments
for my neck as spoil?"

Literarily this song is a unity, even if there is a change in location in each of the individual scenes. All four sections have as a theme the victory over the Canaanite foes. The prelude names Deborah as the singer, and thus the author of the song, as well as Barak as the commander of the army.

The army is mustered in the first scene (vv. 13–17, 18b), and all the tribes are listed that were obligated to service in the army. The tribes that presumably complied with the call were explicitly praised, and the absent members of the alliance were rebuked. The federation of ten tribes is based on the mutual obligation to participate in holy war (see §II.5.2). The naming and reproof of the missing tribes are necessary for the preservation of the covenant existing among the members of the confederation. The comments to the individual tribes are contingent on the situation and have nothing to do with the so-called blessings of the tribes in Gen 49 and Deut 33, according to which the individual tribes are characterized by different formulaic sayings (see §II.5.1). It is instead comparable to the list of participating and nonparticipating tribes in the so-called ships catalogue in the *Iliad* (lines 494–760), in which the commanders participating in the battle against Troy are presented individually with the name of their region and the number of their equipped ships. In the case at hand, the named participants constitute the "people of Yahweh" (עם יהוה).

The second section (vv. 19–22) does not cover details of the battle. The only aspect emphasized is a concern for the forces of nature in the victory;

these are assumed to be separate powers, and there is no mention of their dependence on Yahweh. The human success in fighting is not depicted further.

The third scene (vv. 24–27) presents Jael's heroic deed extensively. The killing of the fleeing and exhausted Sisera by a woman is described in detail. The demise of the enemy leader appears as the climax of the victory over the enemies.

The fourth part (vv. 28–30) transitions to the women of the enemies, so the hearer or reader can determine based on the preceding description that the scene is a derision of the enemies. Without knowing the course of the battle and the fate of Sisera, the women console themselves with the expectation of a victorious outcome and portray, as it were, the horrors of warfare directed against themselves. The song leaves the depiction of the women's reaction to the actual facts up to the listener. This scene concerning the situation of the enemy brings to mind the horrible fate that could befall one's family in war, namely, rape and pillage.

Despite the change from scene to scene, the song represents a literary unity. Regarding content, all the pieces serve to glorify the achieved victory, although quite different means can be used. The concise style is characteristic, and at times the message is reinforced by repetitions in the form of parallelism. Lacking any depiction of missing details, the statements are often in close succession, one after the other, so that the event is impressive. Each of the four scenes shows a structure complete in itself; with the exception of the list of tribes. The active person is introduced at the beginning, then the event is described, and finally the outcome is established. Nevertheless, all of the sections together present a whole, because only the totality of the depictions allows the magnitude and the effect of the events to become clear.

The genre is that of a song whose individual strophes glorify the victory achieved. This glorification entails the enumeration of the allies at the beginning as well as the ironic exposure of the enemies at the conclusion. Indeed, Jael's extraordinary deed, albeit standing in the middle of the song, is in praise of the victory rather than the magnificence of a hero. As such, the tribes' contribution to the victory remains oddly in the dark. Since it is not heroic poetry, the Song of Deborah can only be designated as a hymn of praise. There could also have been additional hymns of praise prior to the formation of the state that were not handed down; at the latest, this form of poetic literature became extinct and was replaced by the form of prose narratives at the beginning of the monarchic period. Despite the discernible beginnings as a hymn of praise, there is therefore no formation of epic poems in Israel. As the hymnic songs in the book of Psalms show, there were poetic means available for it, but they were not employed to describe human actions and accomplishments. The basis for this can only be assumed. Probably the conception predominated in Israel that praise and glory in song could only be performed with respect to Yahweh as the guide of all fortune. Only in a short song could humans be praised, as in the case of the women singing in the round dance, "Saul has killed his thousands, and David his ten thousands" (1 Sam 18:7 = 21:12, Eng. v. 11). An additional formulation of this song had exalted David over humans in a manner unbefitting to him. The narratives of the books of Samuel also portray David as a man full of contradictions whose actions were not only glorious but also imperfect. Since only the prose narrative permits a differentiated representation of its character, the hymn of praise with its panegyric purpose could have no continued existence. The hymnic song of praise remains reserved for Yahweh alone, and the Song of Deborah could therefore be passed on only by framing it with additional hymnic pieces (Judg 5:2–11, 31a) that would add in the praise of Yahweh.

The fragment of a longer hymn of praise is contained in Josh 10:12b–13a:

> Sun, stand still at Gibeon,
> and Moon, in the valley of Aijalon.
> And the sun stood still,
> and the moon stopped,
> until the nation took vengeance on their enemies.

This fragment has to do with the influence of the heavenly powers sun and moon on a specific place,[1] precisely elucidated as "Gibeon" and the "valley of Aijalon." Presumably it also has to do with a battle, but additional circumstances are unknown. In the continuation of Josh 10:13b–14, the statements are reinterpreted to the effect that a time delay occurred when the sun and the moon stood still so that Israel could achieve its victory to the fullest extent. The cosmic dimension of the original saying was reinterpreted in the sense of a real event. The influence of the sun and moon as cosmic powers was turned into a historical occurrence of the lengthening of a day in order to allow the battle to come to a close; that is, the army was proceeding toward victory, but at the onset of night all the fighting would have come to a natural end. The allpowerful celestial bodies become heavenly bodies that indicate day and night, and their course could absolutely be influenced by Yahweh, since all power belongs to the God of Israel alone.

---

1. See John S. Holladay, "The Day(s) the Moon Stood Still," *JBL* 87 (1968): 166–97.

III.2. Riddles

Gunkel, Hermann. "Simson," in idem, *Reden und Aufsätze* (Göttingen: Vandenhoeck & Ruprecht, 1913), 38–64. **Jäger**, Martin. "Assyrische Rätsel und Sprüchwörter," *Beiträge zur Assyriologie* 2 (1884): 274–305. **Jolles**, André. *Einfache Formen: Legende, Sage, Mythe, Rätsel, Spruch, Kasus, Memorabile, Märchen, Witz* (2nd ed.; Darmstadt: Wissenschaftliche Buchgesellschaft, 1958). **Klein-Franke**, Aviva. "Die Königin von Saba in der jüdischen Überlieferung," in *Die Königin von Saba: Kunst, Legende und Archäologie zwischen Morgenland und Abendland* (ed. Werner Daum; Stuttgart und Zürich: Belser, 1988), 105–10. **Müller**, Hans-Peter. "Der Begriff 'Rätsel' im Alten Testament," *VT* 20 (1970): 465–89. **Nel**, Philip J. "The Riddle of Samson (Judg 14,14.18)," *Biblica* 66 (1985): 534–45.

The riddle is a simple literary form that is essentially connected to oral tradition. The exceptional record of riddles, either in collections of sayings or in a narrative framework, covers a wide dissemination through all the ancient cultures of the Mediterranean and Near East. The essence of the riddle is always a question to which the answer must be given (Jolles, *Einfache Formen*, 129). The characteristic question clearly differentiates the riddle from the wisdom aphorism, proverb, and nursery rhyme. The form presupposes that a riddle will always be put forth from one person to another person or group in order to receive an answer. The situation for the riddle always has something to do with a competition or test. The one who solves the riddle therefore proves intellectual equality, knowledge, astuteness, and last of all the ability to cope with life. The riddle has the character of a playful confrontation, but it can also be a life-or-death challenge. In the Riddle of the Sphinx, which exists in many variations in Greek literature, the person who was unable to solve the riddle was killed. Homer would die from grief because he could not answer the riddle of the head lice/catch of fish.[2] Upon answering the riddle's question, the test was considered passed, and the one answering was considered equal to the one questioning. Thus a power struggle also always existed, and anyone involved could try to determine the outcome for himself or herself: the one

---

2. See Konrad Ohlert, *Rätsel und Rätselspiele der alten Griechen* (2nd ed.; Berlin: Mayer & Müller, 1912; repr., Hildesheim: Olms, 1979); Wolfgang Schultz, *Rätsel aus dem hellenischen Kulturkreise* (2 vols.; Mythologische Bibliothek 3.1, 5.1; Leipzig: Hinrichs, 1909, 1912). See now also Claudia V. Camp, "Riddlers, Tricksters and Strange Women in the Samson Story," in idem, *Wise, Strange and Holy: The Strange Woman and the Making of the Bible* (JSOTSup 320 = Gender, Culture, Theory 9; Sheffield: Sheffield Academic Press, 2000), 94–143.

asking the riddle by making the ciphering as difficult as possible and the one solving the riddle by finding the correct answer in order to achieve equality.

In the framework of the Samson tradition, two riddles (חידות) are conveyed that are of the same formal construction and associated closely with the narrative of Samson's marriage in Judg 14:10–19. Samson puts the first one to the wedding guests with a prize associated with the question: "Out of the eater came something to eat. Out of the strong came something sweet." Since the ones who were asked the question could not solve it, they turn to Samson's unnamed wife, who finally elicits the secret from her husband by means of her tears. The solution likewise had the form of a riddle: "What is sweeter than honey? What is stronger than a lion?"

This competition simultaneously alludes to the narrative in Judg 14:5–9, according to which Samson slew a lion with his bare hands and later got the honey produced by a swarm of bees in the lion's carcass. Since it was originally a self-contained piece, however, the riddle cannot have been formulated as an allusion to Samson's deed. On the contrary, both riddles precede the narratives tradition-historically and are thus independent of the context in which they are handed down. "The narrator of the tradition obtained both riddles and ingeniously employed the second one as the solution to the first" (Gunkel, "Simson," 54: "Beide Rätsel hat der Erzähler der Überlieferung entnommen und das zweite geistreich als Lösung des ersten verwandt"). The riddles are linked to each other not only by the narrative but also by the choice of words. As such, the question arises as to their original meaning.

The answer is made clear only by the second question's governing concepts of "honey" and "lion": *love* alone is sweeter and stronger. The solution is not apparent with respect to the first riddle but must be sought in the horizon of the event of love: the topic inquired about must then fulfill the contradiction that is expressed twice: the one eating (אכל) produces food, and sweetness is not usually attached to one who is strong. With the mystery so enciphered, only the act of love can be meant, which the named terms alone can fulfill so that the meaning is lewdly but clearly divulged. Such a riddle is suitable within the scope of the narrative about Samson's wedding, given that elsewhere the popular tradition also shows an acquaintance with lewdness and ambiguity in the form of a riddle within the scope of wedding festivities. In the context of the Samson narrative, the crass joke is obscured by being placed in connection with the preceding story.

With respect to genre, a popular riddle thus has to do with both pieces by which a concept or topic is obscured in images or other designations. At the same time, the images used for the concealment can definitely go in a completely different direction, so the riddle practically aims at ambiguity. The riddle about sleep by Mecklenburg serves as an example of this far-reaching form in the German language. The intentional lewdness clearly emerges from the text:

> Ole, Ole.
> he seet bi mi up'n Stohle,
> he wenk mi,
> ick wehr mi.
> He würn mi so sööt
> Vergüng mi Ogen und Fööt.

> Der Alte, der Alte,
> auf dem Stuhl ich mich halte
> er winkte mir zu,
> ich will meine Ruh,
> er wurde so süß
> vergingen mir Augen und Füß.

> Old one, old one,
> On the stool I keep my balance / I hold (onto) myself
> he winked at me
> I'll have my peace
> he was so sweet
> passing by me, eyes and feet.

As in the narrative of Judg 14:10–19, there are also in the German language riddles that allude to a situation known to the questioner alone and thus are not to be deciphered by outsiders. With recourse to an incident in one's own life, the questioner provides himself or herself with an advantage that cannot be compensated for so that a riddle can serve to save the life of a condemned person. By still greater cleverness, one can overcome a death sentence. The best known of such "neck-riddles" is the so-called Ilo-riddle, according to which the condemned woman manufactured a pair of shoes out of the fur of her dog, named Ilo. She alludes to that event in a riddle designed to pull her head out of the noose:

> Auf Ilo geh ich,
> auf Ilo steh ich,
> auf Ilo bin ich hübsch und fein,
> rat't meine Herren, was soll das sein?

> Into Ilo I go,
> In Ilo I stand,
> In Ilo I am pretty and fine,
> Riddle me gentlemen, what should that be?

Despite their reference to one incident, Samson's two riddles are not "neck-riddles" but were instead originally self-contained sayings. An answer independent of context can be determined for both riddles, so that they contain their meaning in themselves and need no further explanation to be carried out by narration. The *narratives* originated as literary framing for the *riddles*.

Even if the origin of the riddle is not assuredly dated to the premonarchic period, this form of question and answer can nevertheless by reckoned as very old. The assumption of a very old age of the riddle is supported by ancient Near Eastern parallels. As early as the third millennium, riddles in the Sumerian language were compiled into collections along with their solutions.[3] These riddle sayings already show the typically characteristic picturesque ciphering of meaning:

> I am small—(since) I am the child of a drill.
> I am grown-up—(since) I am the body of a god.
> I am old—(since) I am the physician of the land of Sumer.
> The answer therefore: it is linen.

But also in the Assyrian and Babylonian texts, along with aphorisms and proverbs, riddle-like questions are found to challenge one's knowledge:

> What becomes pregnant, without conceiving,
> what becomes heavy, without eating?

The answer is not actually imparted but comes forth from the text indirectly in that "heavy" and "pregnant" are Assyrian designations for the clouds. Thus, the riddle's meaning is contained in itself.

No further riddles are preserved in the biblical literature, but there are hints that they were well liked and popular. In the legendary narrative of 1 Kings concerning Sheba's visit with Solomon, riddle play is named explicitly as the explanation of the visit (1 Kgs 10:1), even if proof of wisdom knowledge is actually meant. (Josephus transferred the same form of discussion to Solomon and Hiram of Tyre; see *Ant.* 8.5.3 §§141–49.) Filling in missing riddle questions and solutions out of the biblical narrative is a popular theme in later Jewish and Arabic tradition. In addition to numerous hints in the biblical narratives, there are also riddles that relate to the general knowledge of nature as human living space:

---

3. Bendt Alster, "A Sumerian Riddle Collection," *JNES* 35 (1976): 203–67; Robert D. Biggs, "Pre-Sargonic Riddles from Lagash," *JNES* 32 (1973): 26–33; Miguel Civil, "Sumerian Riddles: A Corpus," *Aula Orientalis* 5 (1987): 17–37.

> What is this? As long as it is living, it moves, and if its head
> Is cut off, it moves also.
> It is a ship in the water.

Reminiscent of the riddle about linen is the description of flax and the products manufactured from it, for example, garments, headscarves, burial shrouds, rope (to hang those condemned to death), and nets:

> What is this? A storm wind goes ahead of everything, as it withstands a great obstacle it cries out bitterly, its head is like reed; it is an adornment for the free, a thing of beauty for the poor, an adornment for the dead, a disgrace for the living, a joy for the birds, a sorrow for the fish.
> It is flax.

A disguised riddle without a solution is perhaps preserved among a list of sayings in Prov 30:15a. In general, the list of sayings is understood simply as answers to riddles (cf. Prov 6:16–19; 30:15b–31; Sir 25:1–2). In other respects, occasional riddles are found interspersed with their solutions only in the collections of wisdom sayings from the Hellenistic period:

> What is stronger than frothy wine? — The maiden. (*Ahiqar* XI,1)

> What is heavier than lead? And what is its name except "Fool"? (Sir 22:14)

Bound to oral transmission and practiced in the framework of playful competition, the riddle in Israel found no further admittance into the literature. The two examples from the Samson narrative nevertheless indicate well enough the essence and function of this form.

III.3. Fables

Bartelmus, Rüdiger. "Die sogenannte Jothamfabel—eine politisch-religiöse Parabeldichtung," *TZ* 41 (1985): 97–120. **Crüsemann**, Frank. *Der Widerstand gegen das Königtum: d. antikönigl. Texte d. Alten Testamentes u. d. Kampf um d. frühen israelit. Staat* (WMANT 49; Neukirchen-Vluyn: Neukirchener, 1978), 19–42. **Diels**, Hermann. "Orientalische Fabeln im griechischen Gewande," *IWW* 4 (1910): 993–1002. **Ebeling**, Erich. *Die babylonische Fabel und ihre Bedeutung für die Literaturegeschichte* (MAOG 2/3; Leipzig: Eduard Pfeiffer, 1927; repr., Osnabrück: Zeller, 1972). **Lindars**, Barnabas. "Jotham's Fable—A New Form-Critical Analysis," *JTS* 24 (1973): 355–66. **Maly**, Eugene H. "The Jotham-Fable—Anti-monarchical?" *CBQ* 22 (1960): 299–302. **Meuli**, Karl. "Herkunft und Wesen der Fabel," *SAVK* 50 (1954): 65–88. **Perry**, Ben E. "Fable," *Studium generale* 12 (1959): 17–37. **Schnur**, Harry C. *Fabeln der Antike:*

Griechisch und lateinisch (Munich: Heimeran, 1978). See now also: **Ruprecht**, Eberhard, *Die Jothamfabel und außerisraelitische Parallelen* (Göttingen: Vandenhoeck & Ruprecht, 2003).

The fable in Judg 9:8–15 was originally a self-contained unit and was only inserted into the context of the Abimelech narrative by means of the Jotham episode in Judg 9:7–16a, 19b–21. The piece is a self-enclosed form that ends with a concrete result. Only the threat at the end in Judg 9:15b is worked in afterward, and because of its reference to the end of the story of Abimelech it is to be considered an outgrowth of the original form of the text. The point is achieved clearly in verse 15a:

> 8 The trees once went out
> to anoint a king over themselves.
> So they said to the olive tree,
> "Reign over us."
> 9 The olive tree answered them,
> "Shall I stop producing my rich oil
> by which gods and mortals are honored,
> and go to sway over the trees?"
> 10 Then the trees said to the fig tree,
> "You come and reign over us."
> 11 But the fig tree answered them,
> "Shall I stop producing my sweetness
> and my delicious fruit,
> and go to sway over the trees?"
> 12 Then the trees said to the vine,
> "You come and reign over us."
> 13 But the vine said to them,
> "Shall I stop producing my wine
> that cheers gods and mortals,
> and go to sway over the trees?"
> 14 So all the trees said to the thornbush,
> "You come and reign over us."
> 15a And the thornbush said to the trees,
> "If in good faith you are anointing me king over you,
> then come and take refuge in my shade!"

The intention is clear from the course of the dialogue. All the trees value their fruit over the offer to assume the office of a king. Only the fruitless thorn bush accepts the nomination, even though it is completely inadequate given that it cannot at all contribute the shade it offered. The fable thus has a clear critical *Tendenz* against the monarchy: only an inadequate person who has nothing to offer will become king. This rejection is not directed against any particular king but instead represents a fundamental critique of this office, not only by sarcastic harshness but also by scathing irony: "The monarchy is unproductive, bears no fruit, and cannot fulfill the protective function that it claims" (Crüsemann, *Der Widerstand*, 29: "Das Königtum ist unproduktiv, bringt keine Frucht und kann die Schutzfunktion, die es sich anmaßt, nicht ausfüllen"). That is, shade is not only, in addition to fruit, an additional pleasant aspect of every tree, but at the same time it is a symbol for the protection expected from and granted by a king; it is practically a "*topos* of ancient Near Eastern kingly ideology" (ibid., 21: "Topos altorientalischer Königsideologie"). The fable thus accepts an existing idea of kingship by its use of figurative language "and carries it ad absurdum: the king, to live in whose shade guarantees the highest degree of security, is compared to the thorn bush. To speak of the thorn bush's shade is pure scorn, and the king nevertheless offers even this" (ibid., 22: "und führt sie ad absurdum: Der König, in dessen Schatten zu leben höchste Sicherheit verbürgt, wird mit einem Dornstrauch verglichen, bei dem von Schatten zu sprechen, purer Hohn ist, und der dennoch eben diesen offeriert"). Thus, the punch line is increased to the maximum: someone will become king who cannot hold this office at all, given his lack of qualifications; at the same time, the king, who was chosen in misjudgment of the actual situation, offers to fulfill the expected function. Thus, the king not only makes a point of his own inability but also at the same time mocks everyone who helped establish him in this position.

The dating of the fable is decided by asking when this devastating opinion of the monarchy could have been expressed. According to its content, the fable is a document of opposition to the monarchy. At present Frank Crüsemann has shown that at the very earliest the rejection of this institution could have been voiced only around the time of the establishment of the institution. The wealthy landowners, who were the sponsors of the opposition in question, were subsequently integrated into the appointed social order of the monarchy under Solomon, so the protest disappeared. The fable thus originated at the earliest in the early monarchic period when the new form of government must have been asserted against contrary opinions and when recourse to this kingly ideology could also have been determined by a criticism against accepting non-Israelite ideas. The only alternative to this dating comes by accepting the consideration that Judg 9:8–15a is a "deliberate literary construct in the framework of an equally deliberate programmatic speech worked into the final individual narrative of the book of Judges" (Bartelmus, "Die Jothamfabel," 117: "absichtvolles literarisches Konstrukt im Rahmen einer ebenso absichtsvoll in die letzte Einzelerzählung des Retterbuches eingebauten programmatischen Rede"). However, the poetic form speaks against this view of the piece as a postexilic construction, given that in the surrounding Deuteronomistic theology there is no indication whatsoever of reservations toward the monarchy.

The possible context of the fable at the beginnings of monarchic power plays in the periods of Saul and David presupposes that the creative means were already in place. Although the fable in Judg 9:8–15a cannot be dated back to the premonarchic period, given its fashioning, it nevertheless probably stands in a literary tradition that does reach back before the monarchic period. Even if no examples are preserved, this genre would already have been cultivated in the premonarchic period, but a conclusive decision on this subject cannot be reached.

The fable is an invented story, by which a truth should be clarified. As such, it can deal with worldly wisdom or a special solution to a concrete situation. The genre was defined in this way already by Theon of Alexandria as, "an invented story that exemplifies a truth." Very commonly, the plot occurs in the world of animals or plants, so its fictive nature is apparent from the outset. The genre presupposes of its hearer or reader a knowledge of the traits of animals or plants, since otherwise the main point cannot be understood. It is practically part of the essence of the fable that the animals and plants that appear do not need to be described precisely; instead, the determination of their nature—unlike in a fairy tale perhaps—is always already determined according to people's prior understanding. Additional characteristics of the genre are its allegorical mode of expression and the way it conveys the intended knowledge over the course of the plot.

The fable is not represented in ancient Near Eastern literature. Nevertheless, debates and short stories do make use of the characteristics of trees and animals (see W. von Soden, *TUAT* 3:180–88); these are most likely to be seen as the precursors to the fable. General comparisons from the animal world are nevertheless widely disseminated in ancient Near Eastern and ancient Israelite wisdom sayings. The fable goes beyond the merely pictorial manner of speaking in treating animals or plants as "persons." Thus, a narrative event is constructed whose result is understandable only based on the respective characteristics of the persons involved. The meaning of the fable is the illustration of a truth in order to obtain the correct outlook. In Greek and Latin literature, this form was handled with great perfection and fixed in written collections. But also among the wisdom sayings of Ahiqar, a fable is found interspersed in VII,7–8, whose moral is given clearly from the comparison of the plants involved:

> The thornbush sent the following message to the pomegranate: "The thornbush to the pomegranate: Of what use is the load of your thorns? Whoever touches (you) (surely) gets caught by you." But the pomegranate answered

and said to the thornbush: "You are good for nothing to the one who touches you ... only thorns."

The popularity of the fable, which found expression in numerous collections from Aesop through the Middle Ages, goes back to the point that this simple form mediates universal truth. The existing circumstances are not reversible. In nature an order is set that holds true for humans in their societal and political integration. At the same time, the prevailing fact clarified by the fable is that humans are relegated to a fixed role in which they have to accept the analogy to the area of nature, because humans cannot alter nature. The fable thus becomes the repository of worldly wisdom, and it should mediate the necessary insight to accept a given situation. The fable in Judg 9:8–15a falls short of that understanding insofar as the plot is applied to a political situation. Yet it is not only the expression of a protest but also an example of coping with a new situation. Indeed, the characterization of the monarchy is less than flattering, but the situation entered into could not be helped. This act of God in the conditions also characterizes the second fable contained in the biblical literature in 2 Kgs 14:9, which belongs to the context of the middle of the monarchic period. It is introduced as the answer of Jehoash of Israel (802–787) to Amaziah of Judah (801–773):

> The thornbush that is in Lebanon sent to the cedar in Lebanon and told him: "Give your daughter to my son as a wife!" But the deer in Lebanon ran over the thornbush and crushed him.

This fable also uses strong contrasts from the plant world to express the superiority of Israel over Judah in addition to well-founded relationships in social distinction. This was probably also an originally independent piece that was taken up at this point by the narrator as an illustration. Rooted in universal worldly wisdom, the fable could be applied to different situations in both political and personal areas. Despite its high esteem, no further fables are handed down and there is no collection of such compositions in Israelite literature.

III.4. The Role of Oral Tradition

Culley, Robert C. "An Approach to the Problem of Oral Tradition," *VT* 13 (1963): 112–25. **Nielsen**, Eduard. *Oral Tradition: A Modern Problem in Old Testament Introduction* (SBT 11; Chicago: A. R. Allenson, 1954). **Warner**, Sean M. "Primitive Saga Men," *VT* 29 (1979): 325–35. **Wolf**, Alois. "H. Gunkels Auffassung von der Verschriftung der Genesis im Licht mittelalterlicher Literarisierungsprobleme," *UF* 12 (1980): 361–74.

The literature of premonarchic Israel is lost except for minor remnants. The few pieces that remain, however, show that the tribes of Israel were not a pre-literary society. On the contrary, there were two basic literary forms, both of which in different ways managed to survive without being recorded in writing. The two are differentiated according to their fundamental *Sitz im Leben*: the hymn of praise and the various simple forms (e.g., the riddle).

The hymn of praise was probably performed by singers who were employed as profession poets. To be sure, direct evidence for the existence of such singers is lacking in the premonarchic period, but they are attested in 2 Sam 19:3b for the court of David. David himself had played the lyre in the court of Saul, and at least the funeral song in 2 Sam 1:19–27 and 3:33–34 goes back to David's court. Singers are thus assumed in Israel in analogy to other cultures that wrote and performed songs of different kinds. The transmission of these songs was exclusively oral by means of memorization. The implication in the reference to the unpreserved Book of Jashar (Josh 10:13) that such songs were written down signifies already a break with this tradition. Also, since this written record is not preserved, the entire corpus of song materials from the premonarchic era is lost, except for the Song of Deborah. Furthermore, it appears that in early Israel no heroic poetry existed, so there was no development of epic poetry.

In the monarchic period, then, the prose narrative became the appropriate form of tradition, whereas songwriting was mostly restricted to the cult. This later development was probably a factor in the disappearance of the hymn of praise, and the practitioners disappeared along with the literary form. The later temple singers are not comparable to those of the early period, since they had a different task.[4]

The other bearer of literary references is the so-called vernacular; that is, the people made themselves a part of the tradition. The author is always anonymous, and the transmission passed from mouth to mouth over generations. To these forms, which are based solely on continuously repeated oral communication, belong today the most abbreviated genres: jokes, anecdotes, proverbs, riddles, and certain forms of lyric poetry such as oath formulas and nursery rhymes. The biblical literature contains an array of sayings of differ-

---

4. Historically these singers' guilds are first in evidence in the postexilic period; see Hartmut Gese, "Zur Geschichte der Kultsänger am zweiten Tempel, " in idem, *Vom Sinai zum Zion: Alttestamentliche Beiträge zur biblischen Theologie* (BevT 64; Munich: Kaiser, 1974), 147–58.

ent kinds and distinguishable circumstances; proverbs are attested by several examples, but it is not surprising that jokes are not in evidence because of their strong situational references.[5] Since the originator is unknown, these short forms likewise cannot be dated. The transmission over several generations and thus the recirculation in the premonarchic period can in no case be proven—but, at the same time, it also cannot be ruled out with certainty. In specific cases, however, an individual saying or proverb can go back prior to the monarchic period; this only occurs in exceptional cases that include criteria for the time of the formation of the saying, for example, the proverb "Is Saul also among the prophets?" (1 Sam 10:12). The tracing back of a saying to premonarchic times is in no case conclusive. At most, a great age can be claimed for the formulas that were uttered during the vicissitudes of life—for example, divorce: "She is not my wife, and I am not her husband" (Hos 2:4); or the death of a child: "Yahweh gave, and Yahweh has taken away; blessed be the name of Yahweh" (Job 1:21). One old formula may be attested in David's cry in pain, "My son Absalom! Would I had died instead of you" (2 Sam 19:1). Yet the saying "Do not be afraid, for you have born a son" (1 Sam 4:20; cf. Gen 35:17) could just as well have originated in a distant past, since the difficulty of birth and the joy over a living child belong to the basic sensitivities of human life.

In addition, the two riddles conveyed in the framework of the Samson narrative do not simply date back to the time narrated. Since the two riddle questions in Judg 14:14, 18 apply to universal human experiences, they are independent of the political situation and could have originated prior to the formation of the state. As the collections in Sumerian and Babylonian-Assyrian languages show, riddles belong to the foundational mode of human debate. With riddles, the self-assertion on the part of the questioner and the challenge on the part of the solver could lead to an intellectual duel; victory in the competition led to triumph over the losing opponent. The Samson narrative in Judg 14:10–19 is also fashioned as a confrontation in which Samson retaliates for his defeat by a massacre of his guests. Thus of all the simple forms, the riddle is still the most likely one assumed for the premonarchic period, yet it can also be reckoned that further sayings and other short forms circulated in the setting of daily life, ones that were necessarily omitted at all points in the writing process of the literature that was produced. By its close connection to its *Sitz im Leben*, this simple form of literature vanished almost completely,

---

5. See the compilation of all the nonwisdom proverbs and sayings by Otto Eissfeldt, *The Old Testament: An Introduction* (trans. Peter R. Ackroyd; New York: Harper & Row, 1965), 64–86; for jokes, see the unsuccessful demonstration of Frank Crüsemann, "Zwei alttestamentliche Witze," *ZAW* 92 (1980): 215–27.

inasmuch as it was connected primarily to oral tradition. Literature in narrative prose was not preserved prior to the formation of the state. Whether any accounts even existed is very questionable. The phase of the composition literature first began with the monarchy. Everything in the combined narratives of the books of Joshua and Judges originated in the monarchic period at the earliest, and its final arrangement in the framework of the Deuteronomistic History followed in the exilic or postexilic period at the earliest. Thus, none of the narratives concerning the taking of the land and the era of the judges originated in the time about which they report. Between the narrated time and the time of composition lies a span of several centuries. Only in the early monarchic period in the books of Samuel were narrative complexes available that actually originated and were written down in immediate temporal proximity to the narrated events.

This enormous gap between the event and the report of the event is generally bridged by the notion of a more or less long-lasting oral tradition. This assumption underlies the conjecture that, in analogy to epics, different genres of narrative such as fables, sagas, or legends were definitely transmitted by oral recitation over a long span of time before they were put into writing. According to this assumption of an oral tradition, the prevailing narrative was connected with the narrated event in such a way that, despite later formulation and linguistic shaping, that which was narrated was ultimately deeply rooted in an experiential or transpiring reality. The assertion of oral tradition practically becomes a trick to bring the written record into correlation or even harmony with the reports, even if the two are separated from one another by several centuries. The unproven and unprovable assertion of a long tradition-history of the narratives therefore belongs to the methodological fundamentals of exegesis and has become a foundational presupposition for the assessment of ancient Israelite historical writing.

In view of the body of source material, this methodological principle of a long tradition-history must undergo a critical examination. On the assumption of continuity between the time before and the time of the formation of the state of Israel, one must inquire about the possibilities and limits of orally communicated narrative genres over several generations. In so doing, one must proceed so that possible development from unwritten to written narrative can be obtained from the biblical texts themselves. Thus, the transition does not take place according to the concept of the legend, as Hermann Gunkel introduced it to Old Testament study,[6] since this genre classification

---

6. Hermann Gunkel, *Genesis* (1901; trans. M. E. Biddle; Mercer Library of Biblical Studies; Macon, Ga.: Mercer University Press, 1997), vii–lxxxvi.

was obtained from texts of other cultures and was subsequently transferred to the biblical narratives. This approach disregards from the outset the fact that the shaping of literature took place differently in every culture and thus is always represented differently. Furthermore, even the epic poems, for which a long oral tradition is always assumed, may not be adduced as a comparison since they follow their own rules, which can in no way be transferred to prose genres. Like the song, the epic was performed again and again; eventually it remained firmly fixed in form and content.

Further, certain convention are to be assumed also for prose narratives. To them belong the naming of space and time, the introduction of the acting persons, the attainment of a climax or a goal of the action, and a conclusion, which can be formulaic. Within this formal structure, however, the narrator had great design possibilities regarding language, the course of the action, and the stylistic means used. Within oral transmission, a narrative was continually changing because only its content was fixed, whereas there was a great deal of leeway with regard to the form. This means, however, that with narratives, every proposed delineation from the present version to an older version remains always in the realm of hypothesis. The narrative materials as they exist in the books of Joshua and Judges can therefore be reckoned with a long oral tradition only if the ones responsible for this act of repetition and circulation identified themselves. Such circles of preservation of oral tradition over many generations can neither be proven nor postulated; this is because the development of a chain of tradition can be assumed at most with a certain probability for the simple forms, not for the narratives. Unless the narratives stem from the monarchic period and do not represent later literary formation, the accounts in the books of Joshua and Judges do not reach back to the premonarchic period in which their plot is set. Therefore, no development of tradition can be derived from the biblical narratives that reaches back to the time depicted in the accounts. On the contrary, even in places where older traditions were assumed on account of the literary form, these narratives are not to be credited with a long process of tradition. The fashioned narrative is thus in no way the result of lengthy oral tradition; it assumed its extant form—as opposed to the finished literary product—only over the course of its retelling. The literary product became fashioned and written down by an author who possessed the appropriate abilities to adopt names and materials and to adhere to conventions of narration.

The development of this to the form of the narrative contained when committed to writing can be reconstructed within the biblical literature of the monarchic period. Prior to the developed form of the historical narrative stand the note and the short story as preliminary stages.

Note

By "note" I mean a short message through which a particular deed or a particular event is recorded and passed down. From the early monarchic period two types of notes in connection with the lists of David's heroes have been preserved in 2 Sam 23:8–38 and 21:15–22.[7] The heroes are men named as outstanding and well-armed individual fighters who not only put themselves in single combat but also distinguished themselves in military expeditions through courage, bravery, and boldness. Their outstanding accomplishments, attaching the deeds directly to the name of the hero (גבור), are listed in 2 Sam 23:8–15. On the other hand, in 2 Sam 21:15–22 such notes are compiled concerning the heroic deeds accomplished by the men from David's entourage (עבד) against the so-called giants. Despite certain differences in details, these notes evince the same formal characteristics. These should be clear from the example of 2 Sam 23:11–12:

> Next to him [Eleazar] was Shammah son of Agee, the Hararite. The Philistines gathered together at Lehi, where there was a plot of ground full of lentils; and the army fled from the Philistines. But he took his stand in the middle of the plot, defended it, and killed the Philistines; and God brought about a great victory.

The note is connected to the names of *the three* named heroes and names the event in which each one proved himself. Only the place of the event is named, while every form of temporal classification is lacking. After stating the situation in order to indicate the immediate circumstances, the actual heroic deeds are communicated with extreme brevity, and an interpretive remark then follows. The note forgoes all details and simply reports the brute facts. The process is reduced to the succession of actions, and only the event is conveyed without any embellishment. A narrative thus does not exist—at most a short report. This presupposes an oral tradition, since the author is hardly an eyewitness to the event.

The tradition of Shammah's heroic deed is connected to the person, and its characteristic is the summarized brevity and lack of narrative embellishment. The rest of the notes evince the same features, and they represent a particular form of communication that goes back to the oral report. Their concern is the transmission of an outstanding action in order to preserve the

---

7. For a treatment of their content as factual, see Karl Elliger, "Die dreißig Helden Davids," in idem, *Kleine Schriften zum Alten Testament* (TB 32; Munich: Kaiser, 1966), 72–118.

memory; there is neither narrative design nor comparative assessment. Event and tradition are bound together temporally and practically, so an oral phase precedes their being committed to writing.

Short Story

The short story marks the first step in the course of literary shaping, which distinguishes it formally from the notes. By "short story" I mean narratives that depict a particular action in a few sentences. Whereas a location is necessarily constitutive to the piece, the date remains vague. For the most part an otherwise well-known person stands in the center, and the minor characters enter only as is absolutely necessary for the course of the action. Joshua 5:13–15 and Judg 7:23–25; 8:1–3; 16:1–3 can count as examples, but additional pieces are found also in 1–2 Samuel. The formal characteristics should become clear in the piece from the Samson complex of Judg 16:1–3, which represents a literarily self-contained unit:

> Once Samson went to Gaza, where he saw a prostitute and went in to her. The Gazites were told, "Samson has come here." So they circled around and lay in wait for him all night at the city gate. They kept quiet all night, thinking, "Let us wait until the light of the morning; then we will kill him." But Samson lay only until midnight. Then at midnight he rose up, took hold of the doors of the city gate and the two posts, pulled them up, bar and all, put them on his shoulders, and carried them to the top of the hill that is in front of Hebron.

With regard to content, the narrative is as unusual as it is improbable. Indeed Gaza presumably stood as a fortified city in the time of the action, and Samson is probably a historical person. The depicted deed, however, can make no claim to historical reality. According to human judgment, dismantling the city gates and managing the load are just as impossible as the traveled distance of about thirty-seven miles. Thus, this is not the tradition of a historical occurrence; on the contrary, the narrative owes its formation to a particular intent—to demonstrate the superhuman strength of Samson in an individual case and, in the process, to include characteristics that are familiar from other stories in the Samson complex, namely, his enmity with the Philistine men and his loose behavior with Philistine women. These traits thus stem from the general portrait of his character as a berserker and a creature of instinct. As such, the motif of wish fulfillment serves only as the foundation for the whereabouts of the hero. The prostitute is not given a name and does not make a further appearance. In the center, standing alone, is the graphic presentation of Samson's extraordinary strength, which exceeds all human measure. In the description, the untamable feat of Samson is played off against the unsuccessful cunning of the city residents in order to mock them as helpless and foolish. The narrator achieves this particular effect by making a scene change within the narrative. Further details are not conveyed over the course of the action; the short story runs straightaway to its climax, carrying the city gates away from Gaza.

The short story hardly goes back to an event that took place at one time in this or in a similar form; thus the short story is not based on oral tradition. On the contrary, the narrator credited the hero with a further achievement to match the situation biographically and geographically. There is in the background, then, not a tradition concerning the loss of the city gates in Gaza but rather the desire to report an additional triumph by Samson over his enemies. The person may be historical, but the entire plot is based solely in the concern to narrate further heroic deeds. The literary shaping cannot be traced back to a concrete situation; rather, the short story derives solely from the creativity of the composer. Despite its brevity, it does show an artful construction with regard to the scene change, which can only be achieved by a deliberate intention.

The short story thus indicates a narrative tradition, and it can have been constructed only by a gifted writer or professional narrator. It is not just a piece handed down orally among the people but is rather the result of an artistic creation that was committed to writing without a lengthy tradition history. Thus, the short story is distinguished from the note by its lack of a connection to the narrated event and predominantly fictional character, so the possibility of a historical evaluation does not apply. The question as to the historical event cannot be put to the short story, since it serves only to illustrate a trait and at most assumes general ideas and particular features of a character or a person's position. The short story places the acting person in a particular light by means of its representation. The specific character of the short story suggests that this form of narrative first came about in the monarchic period. Literarily it constructs the stage for the historical narrative.

Historical Narrative

The historical narrative is distinguished from the short story by its greater detail. This is shown by the detailed description of particulars and the use of additional creative means, given that the need arises for verbal discourse. The strict orientation toward an end remains unchanged, though, as does the limited number of active characters; only occasionally do additional minor characters appear. Even if the historical narrative stands in a larger context, it nonetheless always represents a self-contained literary unity. All the narrative pieces of the books of Joshua and Judges belong to this form of historical narrative, and Josh 7 can serve as an example.

The narrative about the sin and punishment of Achan in Josh 7 is essentially unified, and apart from some short additions, only verses 8–9 represent a later expansion. After the heading in verse 1, a number of scenes follow that yield a consistent plot sequence: dispatch of the spies (vv. 2–3), defeat at Ai (vv. 4–5), Joshua's lamentation and inquiry of Yahweh (vv. 6–7), Yahweh's answer and instruction (vv. 10–15), finding out the guilty (vv. 16–23), the punishment of Achan (vv. 24–25), and a concluding comment (v. 26). The narrative is part of a unified whole and runs straightaway from the exposition of the investigation to the execution. The action of the plot is narrated consistently without digression; in the middle stands Joshua as the undisputed leading figure, but his antagonist will also be named. The multiple speeches by the main characters have the function of establishing and authenticating the course of the plot. At the same time, Yahweh's long speech in verses 10–15 occupies a prominent position, since it not only explains the cumulative events thus far but also establishes the subsequent action. At the end stands an etiological formula that is linked to the narrative by means of the verb עכר, from which the homonymous toponym Achor (עכור) is derived.

The narrative evinces a clear and consistent construction without discrepancies or details that would indicate a lengthy tradition. The content concerns the stringent implementation of the commandments about things devoted to destruction; since the narrative does not amount to an explanation of the place name, it also cannot originally have been limited to that purpose. Nothing points to an older version that would have been handed down and rearranged through oral tradition. On the contrary, the contentual and linguistic shaping renders possible the late composition on the assumption of the idea of devoting things to destruction (חרם). Since the historical point of origin is not recognizable, the narrative of Achan's sin regarding the things consecrated for destruction can only be regarded as a model case that was transferred back to the time of the land acquisition. The historical narrative in Josh 7 indeed presupposes the practice of experienced acts of war that was established in the framework of the war commandments in Deut 20:10–18. This section explicitly commands carrying out the destruction of things taken in the conquest of the land, even though a portion of the booty is excluded from the practice. Joshua 7 tells of the punishment for the unauthorized appropriation of booty pieces that, as lifeless objects, are not consecrated for destruction. The narrative thus intensifies the demand of Deuteronomic war commandments, according to which all living things are forfeited to destruction. The construction, style, and its didactic character indicate that the narrative of the sin and punishment of Achan in Josh 7 was probably first written by the Deuteronomistic Historian.

In the example of Achan's fate, the consequences of sin were exemplified. Thus, at the beginning of the narrative there is not a particular event but rather a definite intent. The historical narrative, by means of a fictive plot, elucidates the consequences of sin in connection with the consecrated destruction of certain goods and thus the consequences of transgressing a divine commandment. Having been created as an illustration of the absolute value of divine instruction, this story does not retain a tradition but rather proclaims a *Tendenz*. Since an orally transmitted early stage of Josh 7 is not to be discovered, neither the material nor a tradition-historical kernel reaches back to the premonarchic period. On the contrary, the prose narrative was created in connection with the Deuteronomistic History on the assumption of a highly advanced narrative tradition.

The historical narrative thus constructs its own reality in the frame of fiction and does not primarily serve to preserve a tradition. In particular, the artistic literary formulation shows a considerable distance from the reported reality, a distance that cannot be closed by postulating a lengthy oral tradition from the narrative to a historical event. Nevertheless, the adoption of traditions pertaining to historical events is not ruled out on principle, but the question as to historical reality must always be put anew and cannot simply be postulated on the presupposition of lengthy oral tradition.

The free interaction of the narrator with the existing tradition is made clear in the example of the conquest of Jericho in Josh 2 and 6. In the original version, the city fell because of treason on the part of Rahab, and this is still discernible in the detail of the red scarf in the window through which the spies escaped. The received tradition establishes Rahab's survival by her salvific act (Josh 2). With the acceptance of this tradition in the land-taking narrative, the conclusion was nevertheless replaced by a new narrative of the fall of the city (Josh 6), which was created by the author of the Deuteronomistic History. According to this version, the walls of the city collapsed by a miraculous event in connection with a mere war cry. Both versions thus aim at the conquest and destruction of Jericho in connection with the land-taking narrative, but they differ fundamentally with respect to implementation. The new version actually changed the event on the basis of a different theological view: The conquest of the city was effected not by humans who outwitted their opponents, but rather by God's miraculous intervention. The historical narrative in Josh 6 is thus constituted essentially by a theology that traces historical actions back to God alone; the older narrative that was connected to Rahab was replaced and outdone. This reorganization is a pure literary occurrence and is completely uninfluenced by oral tradition.

The historical narrative is first and foremost literature designed to sketch the portrait of a hero or a certain era. The extent to which the hero can be identified with a historical person can no longer be determined in most cases, but for the most part the identification of the name with a figure who actually lived is to be presupposed. The geographic frame is frequently coherent because the topographic data underwent little or no change. Also, a definite oral tradition is assumed for individual persons, as shown by the biographical notes of the early monarchic period. Nevertheless, as a general rule the form of the short story is already a literary fiction lacking the background of historical events. The historical narrative is completely the product of artistic shaping and is not the result of lengthy oral tradition. Its historical value can be verified only if a written source can serve as a control. If no such criterion exists, then nothing beyond a historical kernel can be assumed for the historical narrative. The place name alone is inadequate to determine that an event transpired, given that in the majority of cases the place name is not the center point of the tradition but is instead merely the starting point for the shaping of a narrative. In many cases the place name is in fact only coupled with the etiological point, as verified by the example of Josh 7:24. As a general rule, the historical narrative thus includes no oral tradition, but instead shapes a tradition according to a certain view and thereby forms and establishes a picture of the past.

Only in exceptional cases is there recourse to a written tradition. All the same, according to the proof of the hymn of praise in Judg 5, it is conceivable that there existed a collection of such songs originally performed orally. As an analogy to the prose writing of the song in Judg 4, it is conceivable that occasionally historical narratives go back to older songs. As such, it must be understood from the outset that a a song does not have the truthful description of an occurrence in mind but rather the glorification of a communal or personal deed.

The connection of a narrative to its poetic *Vorlage* can be illustrated in the only extant example available by comparing the prose record in Judg 4 to the hymn of praise in Judg 5:12–17, 18b, 19–22, 24–30. Except for the Deuteronomistic frame in Judg 4:1–3 and 23–24, the narrative shows few additions that can be attributed to later alignment with the theology of the Deuteronomistic History. Essentially the insertion turns the well-known King Jabin of Hazor in Josh 11:1–2 into the actual opponent of Israel, so that Sisera as the chief of the enemies was made to be Jabin's general (Judg 4:7). Furthermore, several comments were added concerning Heber the Kenite (Judg 4:11, 17b). With the exception of these expansions, the narrative is consistent and subdivides into three passages of approximately equal length, which correspond to three of the four "strophes" of the song (see §III.1):

Preparation	Judg 4:4–6, 8–10	par. Judg 5:12–17, 18b
Combat	Judg 4:12–16	par. Judg 5:19–22
Jael's deed	Judg 4:17a, 18–22	par. Judg 5:24–27

In comparing the prose report to the song, it is apparent that the first two parts, "Preparation" and "Combat," differ greatly from each other, whereas the third part, "Jael's deed," shows only minor difference.

In the first part, Deborah and Barak are introduced similarly, but the prose version omits the enumeration of the ten tribes, so Kedesh in Naphtali is inserted as the place of action. The biggest difference from the song, however, is the naming of Naphtali and Zebulun as the ones actually conducting the combat; in the song, Ephraim, Benjamin, Machir, Zebulun, and Issachar are named as the participants in the battle, and Naphtali is listed behind Reuben, Gilead, Dan, and Asher as one of the tribes who refused the notice to levy the army. (On the naming of Zebulun in Judg 5:18a, see the literary criticism in §III.1) This discrepancy cannot be reconciled, according to Artur Weiser ("Das Deboralied"), by assuming that Judg 5:13–17 quotes only the participants in the victory celebration that follows the combat. On the contrary, there exists a fundamentally incompatible naming of participants that cannot be clarified by additional hypotheses. Since the prose report clearly follows the song in its construction, the song must be considered the older text. Therefore, it must be asked why the author of the prose version in Judg 4 deviates from the clear statement of the song. The reason cannot lie in the number of tribes but must rather be connected to a fundamental understanding of the reported events.

In the narratives of the book of Judges, local conflicts of individual tribes are described throughout, such that affiliation with additional tribes is not precluded. The Song of Deborah, however, praised the battle with the Canaanites as an event in which not all the tribes really participated in a confederation with one another, even though all of them were called. Thus, the "people of Yahweh" (Judg 5:13) comprise only the ten named tribes. The author of Judg 4 could not employ this historical reality anchored in the song. On the one hand, the view contradicts what is presupposed in the Deuteronomistic History, namely, a unified Israel consisting of twelve tribes. On the other hand, the conception of individual actions on the part of tribes during the time of the judges does not agree with the adoption of the five names of widely scattered tribes.

The answer to the question as to why in Judg 4:6 Naphtali and Zebulun are fighting the battle emerges from the context and from the intention of the prose narrator: For these tribes, the battleground was in the immediate vicinity of their settlement territories. Indeed, even in the prose report the place of the battle is not specified adequately, but it is outlined closely enough by the designations Mount Tabor, Harosheth-ha-goiim, and Kishon. Although Harosheth-ha-goiim has not been identified, the rest of the place names point to the region of the plain of Jezreel and Tabor. The territories of the tribes Naphtali and Zebulun border on this prominent mountain (see Josh 19:10–16, 32–39). In any case, the author reduced the participants to the inhabitants of the region and thus altered the data of the *Vorlage*. Since the grounds for the ensuing change are determined, this cannot be connected to an alternate tradition.

In the second part the events of the battle are put in concrete terms. The hymn of praise in Judg 5:19–22 was exceptionally vague; it named the opposition and set the place as the location at Tanaach but did not supply details. The process remains obscure, and the reference to the intervention of cosmic powers elevated the event in the sense of a mythical worldview without describing it precisely. By contrast, the prose report named concrete data, although formulaic language predominates in the description of the events. The formulation of the battle scene is shaped by universal ideas and phrases, and the narrative is predominately fantasy and does not go back to the view of a participant or an eyewitness. The character of the piece indicates that the formulation is that of the author. An oral type of source beyond the song was not utilized, and the prose version follows with the embellishment of narrative necessities by way of seemingly concrete details.

The third part shows the greatest agreement. The killing of the enemy by a woman was depicted already in the song in extensive detail. By reorganizing the song into a prose narrative, the details were painted in further, while a divergence does ensue insofar as now Sisera is slain in battle. The heroic deed of the woman so dramatically highlighted in the song comes closer to cunning and to assassination. This reorganization presumably owes to the preconceived depiction of women, according to which a woman could indeed be considered brave but not strong, and thus she could not act heroically. So the deed was still described as such, albeit according to a certain modification owing to the self-image of the narrator. The comparison shows that the narrator referred solely to the existing song and did not have additional sources in oral or written form. All deviations stem from the author of the prose version and are therefore conditioned insofar as in the reshaping of the song version, the conventions of narrative representation, and the conditions of the literary environment were operative in the form of the narratives of the book of Judges. In his portrayal of the event, the narrator stands no closer than this; instead, he merely attempted by narrative means to lead the target audience closer to the event. With the exception of Jael's deed, the event in the course of the prose version remains every bit as approximate as in the song. Both forms of linguistic mediation of an event simply follow their own conventions. Concerning the historical reality, there is little to be extracted from the song and even less from the prose report, given its conscious alterations.

In view of the fact that no written tradition existed prior to the formation of the state, no such tradition can even be postulated. The written songs, if there ever were such a collection, are irretrievably lost. The oral tradition is limited to names of persons and places. Even if it cannot be ruled out that these certain incidents are or were connected, the literature concerning the premonarchic period does not preserve oral tradition, which for the early period is demonstrable only in the form of songs and not for prose narrative. The historical narrative did not grow from popular narrative traditions but rather goes back to a creative individual during the middle of the monarchy. What had been narrated and passed on in the time before the formation of the state had, by the time of the monarchy, already been lost or replaced by new narratives. The developed form of the hymn of praise was presumably bound to a certain circle of professional singers and probably was suppressed or became extinct in the monarchic period. An oral tradition regarding historical events and deeds existed in early Israel at most in the very sparse form of short communications or notes. The narratives about occurrences in the premonarchic period first developed in the monarchic period, and a literature based on oral tradition apparently existed prior to the monarchy only in the form of hymns of praise.

III.5. On the Concept of the Legend

Gunkel, Hermann. *Die israelitische Literatur* (Leipzig, 1925; repr., Darmstadt, 1963).
Petzoldt, Leander. *Märchen, Mythos, Sage: Beiträge zur Literatur und Volksdichtung* (Marburg: Elwert, 1989). **Petzoldt**, ed. *Vergleichende Sagenforschung* (Wege der Forschung 152; Darmstadt: Wissenschaftliche Buchgesellschaft, 1969).

The legend is a literary form that originated at a set location and was orally transmitted for a certain time. In addition to the attachment to one place, the point of departure for this tradition is also a connection to one person. Additional criteria are the straightforwardness of the plot, which moves directly to its goal, the limited number of acting persons, and the recourse to ideas from the past. This reference back to the history thus feigns a historical truth, one that does not stand up to critical examination. The point of origin for the legend is not an event of the past, but rather only a place or a figure that can be connected with events in the story. The event depicted in the legend is always rooted in an idea or a particular image from the story. The legend thus does not reflect events that took place, but rather only an idea of experiences or incidents, ones that did not happen in the way communicated. Like the historical narrative, the legend thus turns out to be a literary form made up of fictional characters and not an early mode of historiography. The legend establishes an idea as reality and connects a fictional event to the real facts of a place or person. The kernel of a legend, regardless of when it was conjured up, exists only in that the respective name is verifiable. All the descriptions connected to a name owe to narrative shaping. As such, as a general rule, the age of the legend is greatly overestimated. Hermann Gunkel (*Genesis*, xlviii) considered the legends age-old and bridged over the temporal gap by assuming a long oral tradition between the narrated time and the time of the narrator.

Modern research on legends, however, has determined that legends were preserved no longer than one hundred to two hundred years in oral transmission; after a few generations without being written down, they disappeared from the tradition. Since the requirements are the same for popular traditions even among different cultures, and the popular traditions cannot change or can change hardly at all over the course of the eras, similar circumstances can be assigned to ancient Israel. This means that the legends written during the monarchic period reach back only a few generations. The formation of a legend in an early period can be reckoned only if it can be shown to have been written in the early monarchic period. Yet, since none of the great historical works can be dated with certainty to the period of David and Solomon, the creation of legends must not be moved back to the premonarchic period. The legends included in the books of Joshua and Judges cannot have existed in the time of their story lines, since they were composed as part of the Deuteronomistic History no earlier than the end of the seventh century. All the legends included in the narratives concerning the taking of the land and the judges thus in no way go back further than to the middle of the monarchic period in the ninth and eighth centuries. As a literary form, the legend therefore belongs to the literature of the monarchic period.

Of the historical narratives of the books of Joshua and Judges, only a few reveal the reception of older traditions. Based on their local attachment, the following pieces from the book of Joshua could stem from oral tradition:

— The spies in Jericho (Josh 2:1–3, 4b, 5–7, 15–17a, 18, 19, 21–23)
— The conquest of Ai (Josh 8:10–12, 14, 15, 19, 21, 23, 29)
— The demise of the kings in the cave at Makkedah (Josh 10:16–23a, 24–27)

From the Judges narratives, the following traditions are traceable to the monarchic period:

— Ehud's murder on the toilet (Judg 3:12–30)
— Gideon's fight against the Midianites (Judg 6:2–6, 33–35; 7:1–25; 8:4–21)
— The Gaal episode in Shechem (Judg 9:26–41)
— Jephthah and his daughter (Judg 11:29–40)
— Samson's marriage and revenge (Judg 14:1–15:8)

For these narratives, a version in oral tradition can at least be supposed, albeit with considerable reshaping either in transmission or by the narrator. Just as the narrative of the victory over the Canaanites in Judg 4 refers back to the Song of Deborah in the written version of Judg 5:12–17, 18b, 19–22, 24–30, so could these narratives also have been shaped by including circulated materials. As the typical characteristic of the legend, either local attachment or connection to a hero shows through every time in the historical narrative. A certain legendary formation is thus to be accounted to the monarchic period, which had to preserve a portrait of the past. In no case, though, does this legendary tradition go back to the narrated event. Instead, the legend mediates a fictional reality based on general experience and historical ideas. As such, ideals and experiences from the time of the formation of the legend were transferred back to the time of the plot.

The legends are thus literary fiction and do not qualify for use as historical sources. Formally, the legend corresponds in many elements to the historical narrative; yet since the elements from oral tradition are not very pronounced, though, the legend remains fully back behind the historical narrative. Presumably the historical narrative lost the simpler form of the legend when there came about a complete transfer to written tradition at the end of the monarchic period, such that oral tradition vanished along with the form of the legend.

As a literary form, the legend can only have developed in the monarchic period. The genre was transmitted orally, but written versions or collections cannot be ruled out. However, the biblical literature did not preserve such old compilations. In the composition of the great historical works, the legend came to be replaced by the historical narrative and was taken up into it, such that only occasionally do legendary elements still shine through.

IV. The Theological Significance of the Era

Because of the paucity of sources, the theological significance of the era can no longer be ascertained. Like the actual course of the history, religious practice and conviction remain unknown. At most it can be assumed that certain circumstances, as would be laid out in the books of Samuel, already existed in premonarchic times (see §II.6). Presumably one would offer a sacrifice and inquire about God's will by means of an oracle. Any further details of cultic practice and theological substance would develop only during the monarchic period. Thus, there is no attestation of the era in question prior to the institution of the monarchy. Given the absence of any form of theological reflection, premonarchic Israel can be called an archaic age only in terms of theological significance.

There are two songs that speak about this period with any degree of certainty, and both reveal that the time before the formation of the state was dominated by a faith in the heavenly bodies. The fragment in Josh 10:12b–13a is probably part of a longer hymn of praise, the one remaining portion of which reads:

> Sun, stand still at Gibeon,
> and Moon, in the valley of Aijalon.
> And the sun stood still,
> and the moon stopped,
> until the nation took vengeance on their enemies.

The sun and the moon are heavenly powers that remain over the place of battle so that through their influence Israel could secure victory. In this fragment, the sun and moon are understood as cosmic powers that can exert influence over actual events by their very presence. In the wider context, the original meaning of the saying was reinterpreted as a prolonging of the day, and the victory would be attributed to Yahweh alone (see Josh 10:13b–14).

The two heavenly bodies are consequently not to be understood as having the substance of gods, but merely as bearing special power.

Analogously, the Song of Deborah in Judg 5:20–21a gives praise to heavenly and earthly powers that helped Israel achieve victory:

> The stars fought from heaven,
> from their courses they fought against Sisera.
> The torrent Kishon swept them away,
> the onrushing torrent, the torrent Kishon.

With the help of the stars of heaven and the torrent of Kishon, the tribes achieved victory over their enemies. These are not purely natural phenomena or natural powers that entered in on Israel's side in the battle against the Canaanite kings in order to bring victory to the "people of Yahweh." Yahweh does not appear, and the verses do not reflect on the relationship of God to the stars and nature. This archaic level of Israelite religion is not discernible in any further detail; in the monarchic period the notions of Yahweh as creator of heaven and earth and as lord over the heavenly bodies would prevail. Nevertheless, in Job 38:7 the stars again appear as independent beings that join together with the sons of God in praise of Yahweh.

In the Song of Deborah, Judg 5:13 is the only biblical reference to Yahweh from premonarchic times. Whether or not Yahweh is the single God of the tribes does not emerge from the text. The phrase עם יהוה, "the people of Yahweh," can be understood in such a way that the common God Yahweh had become a constitutive element for the entire collective of the tribes. Nevertheless, if Yahweh has not (yet) become the one and only God, Yahweh has played a special role from the beginning of the written tradition and in its ensuing history. The actual means of worshiping Yahweh are almost entirely unrecoverable. Furthermore, archaeological discoveries are of no help, given that no official cults from premonarchic times have been proven with certainty. Although the name of God had not been settled on once and for all, that Yahweh was worshiped as the God of the tribes in premonarchic times has in fact been shown.

Since it is entirely improbable that adoption of Yahwism coincided with settlement, the practice of Yahwism must have been adopted prior to the acquisition of the land. It has already been pointed out that there is extrabiblical attestation of *yhw₃* as the name of a geographic region most likely found in northwest Arabia (see §II.6). If Yahweh was the name of a region, then Yahweh must have originally been the God of the inhabitants of that region. The confinement to one region presupposes that Yahweh must appear continually anew from this region in order to be amid his current group of people. The arrival of Yahweh from the remote wilderness of the southeast would be emphasized in the theophany narratives of Judg 5:4; Deut 33:2; and Hab 3:3. Not until the course of the monarchy and in connection with temple theology did the development of the idea of a residence develop; additionally, the theophany from the south, under the influence of Canaanite religion, was superimposed with the mythical story of a mountain of God in the north.

The theological significance of the era thus consists in that Yahweh, who was originally the God from the nomadic past, became the God of all the tribes. While space does not permit a wider examination of this particular point, during this period Yahweh was well on the way to becoming the God of the tribes of Israel and eventually the God of all peoples (see Deut 4:35, 39; Isa 44:6; 45:5, 6, 18). We have no evidence, however, and the beginning of the Yahweh cult lies in darkness. Moreover, if Yahweh was perhaps not the one and only God in premonarchic times, Yahweh was from the beginning the God whose worship established and preserved the commonality of the tribes. Since no other statements are available, the essence of Yahweh cannot be addressed. However, from the very beginning of any sense of interrelatedness, Israel portrayed itself in terms of the one God Yahweh, and a summary statement of Yahwism would accompany every mighty act in history. Consequently, the origin and development of the religion of Israel will be embedded in the history prior to the taking of the land. The broad historical-theological brushstrokes of these eras stand out as the point of departure for everything from the monarchic, pre-Priestly narratives of Genesis–Numbers to the postexilic, Priestly Document. The entire body of history places the decisive event for the gradual knowledge of God in a time past, a time from which there can be no verifiable historical tradition. In fact, the narrative design of historical progress prior to the land acquisition is a literary fiction grounded in historical-theological conceptions that are characterized differently according to the historical standpoint of each author.

In the pre-Priestly historical writings Yahweh is known from the beginning of creation, and his worship begins even before the flood (Gen 4:2–4a). Noah, the sole survivor, built Yahweh an altar after the flood (Gen 8:20), thereby marking the beginning of cultic practice. By the epiphanies to the three patriarchs, Yahweh proves to be the God of the people from the beginning of history and thereafter. Becoming a people and worshiping Yahweh are thus interdependent. Abraham, Isaac, and Jacob establish cultic sites for Yahweh in the places of the epiphanies (Gen 12:6a, 7, 8; 13:18; 26:25; 28:16–19a). Yahweh will become the God of the people at the theophany at Sinai (Exod 19), having already revealed his identity to Moses (Exod 3). The theophanies manifest only that which was already stated in the history: Yahweh is Israel's God because he acted on behalf of his people in the exodus of Israel out of Egypt. Historical experience constitutes relationship to God in the following way: Yahweh is the God who brought Israel out of Egypt. Thus, history will become the mode for experiencing God. Israel's relationship to its God will not be set in myth but will be based in a narrative of history.

The name of God is initially concealed in the historical work of the Priestly Document. Moses is the first to learn the identity of Yahweh as the creator God and the God who appeared to the patriarchs as El Shaddai (Exod 6). What is revealed to the people at Sinai is not the deity but rather the tabernacle as the sole legitimate site for cultic practice (Exod 25–32). God is to be reached only in and through the cult. From then on, for the Priestly Document, the experience of God in history recedes. However, the point is not given up entirely, as shown by the overall historical sketch from creation to the exodus (Gen 1–Exod 14). With the foundation of the cult at Sinai, however, the Priestly Document has broken with the older historical sketch in favor of another emphasis. The shrine in the midst of the people manifests the unalterable bestowal of God to Israel. The notion of continuous expiation has superseded historical actions. God is no longer to be experienced in history, only in the cult. Thus, the older historical work and the Priestly Document have both grounded Yahwism in history, albeit in very different ways. Their different schemata can be said to have a guiding principle of historical reality only insofar as they reflect the different historical situations of their respective authors.

Historical reality and the biblical representation of history fall apart and cannot be reassembled when it comes to the origins of Yahwism. The historical writings, with Yahweh established as the God of Israel in history, is based on a conception of history fundamentally different from any modern understanding of history. In Israel, history is the domain of human and divine action: God determines the process of history, and humans are able to act only under the restricted possibilities imposed by God. Given these assumptions, what Israel conceptualized as a view of history is therefore contradictory to that which modern research can ascertain regarding historical processes and conditions. This applies especially to the formation of Israel in the twelfth and eleventh centuries.

The fictive representation of the era in the books of Joshua and Judges would come to be characterized by the theological framework found in the Deuteronomistic History. This picture of history emphasizes the era of land acquisition and premonarchic time according to a particular theological reflection—one that would precondition Israel's historical experiences. Through various theological statements this historical writing would not only provide insights into but would also determine the very dimensions of salvation.

The narrative of the land acquisition in Joshua shows a clear theological program. With God's assistance, Israel has come into possession of the land. At God's command the inhabitants were annihilated. In an order regulated according to the will of God, Joshua had at last apportioned the land to the tribes so that every tribe had obtained its God-given portion. In the land's capture and distribution, Yahweh had unequivocally and irrevocably secured the land for Israel. The land came to Israel not through human choice or historical chance but through God himself. Israel and its land will forever be inextricably linked because the gift of God cannot be sold or rescinded. The book of Joshua is thus a theological outline for the justification of Israel's possession of the land.

The theological conception of the land acquisition in Joshua would be fleshed out in Deuteronomy as a theology of possessing the land. According to Deuteronomy's legal code, the land is deemed the gift of Yahweh to his people; as "an inherited possession" (נחלה; RSV: "inheritance"; NRSV: "possession"), it is given to Israel (Deut 12:9–10; 19:10, 14; 20:16; 21:23; 24:4; 25:19). The land and the people are inextricably linked, and only in the land can Israel remain what it is. The existence of Israel without the land that was promised to the ancestors is simply unthinkable according to Deuteronomistic theology. With the conquest and allocation of the land as depicted in Joshua, the promise to the patriarchs comes to fulfillment—a promise already embedded in the pre-Priestly narratives of Genesis.

This outline is further put in concrete terms in the book of Judges with respect to the threat of enemies. The oldest portion is set out in Judg 3–16, which alone describes any action taken against enemies; the prologue of Judg 1–2 and the appendix of Judg 17–21 describe "internal" contestation. The individual narratives are integrated into a framework that, with its chronological statements, offers not only the necessary temporal transitions and establishes the literary connection of the individual narratives but also conveys a theological assessment. The historical-theological schema is based on the connection between deed and consequence, according to which the people will be judged by their obedience to God. Behavior acceptable to God results in periods of calm for the people, and improper conduct is punished by oppression by their enemies. Improper conduct is never clearly defined but can be determined on the basis of the preceding speech in Josh 24, which treats faithless conduct and turning away from God as part of the programmatic institution of the covenant with Yahweh. The recent appointment of salvation determined the people's history, at least insofar as they were committed to Yahweh. To be sure, the land was their possession and could not be lost. Nevertheless, the people could incur heavy losses to their newly possessed salvific reality because of constant threat and periodic oppression from their enemies.

The history of the judges is already embedded in a historical-theological concept in such a way that God also effects salvation. The individual hero is gifted with the spirit of God and hence is equipped with special power and ability to carry out his assignment. Already before their admittance to the Deuteronomistic History, different individual histories were composed as a type of biography, as in the cases of Gideon (Judg 6–8), Jephthah (Judg 10–12), and Samson (Judg 13–16). The basis of the tradition is nevertheless the individual narrative accompanied by a surprising and successful conclusion. The major units of collected traditions depict the three figures quite differently. Gideon is an experienced contender for the pure Yahweh cult who nevertheless fails in the end with regard to cultic practice owing to his own presumptuousness. Jephthah is a superior general who falls only under the shadow of a hasty vow. Samson is the only brave fighter whose courage and power are truly admirable, but whose addiction to Philistine women would in the end bring him to catastrophe. In their present context, the narrative complexes thus have a definite didactic character. In addition, the strong men have their weaknesses, namely, when their whole person does not stand in the service of Yahweh. In the editing of the materials, the three savior figures have received a reduced sentence. The premonarchic period was an era of struggles. Yahweh truly cares about these means of deliverance, but the people constantly put their entrusted salvation at risk. Through Deuteronomistic theology, the people's own transgression brought about the ability to blame themselves for calamity, and the time of the judges will be the precursor to the era of the monarchy. Yahweh is not to blame when disaster strikes; on the contrary, by their misconduct the people force God into constant oppressions by their enemies. Humans must themselves bear the consequences of their actions, and the standard for assessing their actions is fidelity to Yahweh as the God of Israel.

The tradition of the "major" judges would be placed within the frame of theological historiography, which attests to the saving action of Yahweh in addition to human failures. Thus, the book of Judges does not preserve historical traditions, but instead lays out a theological program. As a historical work, it deals only with the "present" insofar as the Deuteronomistic Historian, writing from the horizon of his own experience, describes the time of the exile. The recorded heroic narratives have no claim to authenticity, since they first stem from the monarchic period, when acts of heroism from David's wars were possible and communicable.

The books of Joshua and Judges turn out to be characterized by Deuteronomistic theology and deliver nothing for the theological significance to the era. Even with these limitations, the books nevertheless played a decisive role, even if their details are no longer recoverable. For now, with the strong conviction from the premonarchic period that Yahweh is the God of the people, Israel could take up contestation with other gods in the monarchic period and in the postexilic period could assert the recognition of Yahweh as the one and only existing God.

Index of Place Names

Abel-shittim 3, 15
Abū Billāna 197
Acco 56, 71, 75, 150, 152
Achshaph 75, 76, 126
Ai 5, 9, 27, 28, 60, 62, 87, 89, 90, 95, 101, 117, 118, 134, 227, 234
Aijalon 44, 56, 60, 211, 237
'Ammān 21, 197, 198
Aphek 71, 74, 75, 76, 97, 170
Arad 19, 98, 100, 101, 157, 178
Arpad 130
Arvad 194
Ashdod 179, 182, 183, 184, 186, 188, 193
Ashkelon 79, 80, 179, 182, 193
Bamoth 20
Beersheba 98, 153, 164, 165, 175, 176
Beirut 194
Bethel 28, 52, 55, 57, 71, 84, 89, 118, 148, 165, 175, 176
Beth Horon 148
Bethlehem 44
Beth-shean 55, 71, 72, 74, 75, 76, 112, 126
Beth-shemesh 56, 71, 170
Bochim 35, 56
Buṣērā 200
Byblos 194
Dan 50, 51, 56, 175, 176
Dor 55
Ebal 5, 92, 96, 177
Ebenezer 170
Ekron 179, 182, 183, 185, 190, 193
el-Mene'īyeh 203
En-Harod 40

Eshtaol 51, 151
Ezion-geber 15
Fēnān 112, 200, 203
Gath 54, 179, 182, 193, 204
Gaza 48, 179, 182, 193, 225, 226
Ǧedur 203
Ǧenīn 177
Gezer 55, 71, 75, 76, 80, 103, 126, 133, 183, 186
Gibeah 52
Gibeon 5, 28, 29, 30, 60, 211, 237
Gilgal 4, 26, 57, 175, 176
Gīlō 96
Guzana 130
Hazor 5, 30, 38, 71, 72, 74, 75, 76, 87, 126, 176, 186, 230
Hebron 5, 31, 54, 68, 226
Heshbon 2, 13, 20, 21
Ḥirbet Bēt Lēy 157
Ḥirbet ed-Dawwara 91, 96, 100
Ḥirbet el-Ḥaǧǧar 197
Ḥirbet el-Mšāš 82, 94, 99, 100, 101, 102, 103, 105, 115, 203
Ḥirbet el-Qōm 29, 157
Ḥirbet Ǧel'ad 151
Ḥirbet Raddāne 90, 95, 101
Ḥirbet Sēlūn 88, 170, 176
Hormah 2, 19, 54
Ibleam 55
Iye-abarim 20
'Izbet Ṣarṭah 93, 97, 101, 105, 113, 114
Jabesh-gilead 52
Jahaz 21
Jericho 1, 2, 4, 9, 10, 26, 27, 37, 60, 62, 71, 117, 118, 148, 228, 229, 234

Jerusalem	5, 11, 20, 23, 30, 48, 54, 55, 75, 77, 79, 81, 82, 96, 113, 116, 117, 125, 126, 144, 148, 149, 160, 161, 163, 170, 171, 175, 176, 177, 179, 185, 186	Sela-rimmon	52
		Ṣerabit el-Ḫādem	114
		Shamir	44
		Shechem	7, 33, 34, 41, 42, 43, 63, 71, 74, 75, 76, 84, 125, 147, 149, 166, 175, 234
Kadesh-barnea	24, 159, 161	Shiloh	8, 88, 89, 105, 108, 117, 134, 170, 171, 176
Kadesh (Naphtali)	1, 12, 19, 23		
Kamon	44		
Kiriath-jearim	148, 170	Sidon	56, 194
Kir Moab	199	Succoth	40, 41
Lachish	5, 74, 75, 76, 126, 157, 186	Taanach	55, 112, 137, 143, 208
Lehi	49, 224	Tappuah	147, 148
Madiama	202	Ṭawīlān	200
Mahanaim	138, 197	Tēl ʿIsdār	98, 101
Makkedah	5, 29, 60, 117, 234	Tell Deir ʿAllā	17
Mamre	175	Tell el-Farʿa	187
Megiddo	7, 55, 71, 72, 74, 75, 76, 87, 88, 112, 126, 132, 133, 134, 137, 143, 181, 208	Tell el-Fārʿa	203
		Tell el-Mazar	178
		Tell es-Saʿīdīye	112
Meribath-kadesh. *See* Kadesh barnea		Tell es-Sebaʿ	87, 94, 97, 98, 101, 102, 204
Michmethath	33	Tell Qirī	88
Mizpah (Benjamin)	52, 175	Tel Mubarak	186
Mizpah (Gilead)	47, 175	Tel Qasile	184, 185, 186, 187
Mizpeh (Moab)	198	Til Barsip	130
Nob	176	Timnah	109
Oboth	20	Tyre	179, 194, 195, 215
Ophrah	40, 41	Umm el-Biyāra	200
Penuel	40, 41	Yanoam	80
Pirathon	44	Ziklag	204
Qurayyah	202	Zoan	68
Ramses	15	Zorah	51, 151
Saḥab	197		
Samʾal	130		

Index of Modern Authors

Abba, Raymond 156
Abou-Assaf, Ali 198
Ackerman, James S. 206
Aharoni, Miriam 178
Aharoni, Yohanan 30, 31, 77, 115, 149, 178
Ahlström, Gösta W. 79, 115
Albertz, Rainer 167
Albright, William Foxwell 114, 115, 160
Ålin, Per 181
Alster, Bendt 215
Alt, Albrecht 31, 76, 106, 115, 119, 120, 123, 167, 168, 181, 195
Amiran, Ruth 111
Amit, Yairah 38, 50
Astour, Michael C. 75, 156, 180
Aubet, María Eugenia 194
Auld, A. Graeme 8, 24, 39, 40, 53
Axelsson, Lars Eric 82
Bächli, Otto 30, 136
Baramki, Dimitri 194
Bartelmus, Rüdiger 34, 42, 216
Bartlett, John R. 18, 198, 199
Bechmann, Ulrike 206
Becker, Uwe 34, 46, 51
Bennett, C.-M. 199
Ben-Tor, A. 88
Beyerlin, Walter 39, 57
Bienkowski, Piotr 198, 200
Biggs, Robert D. 215
Bikai, Patricia Maynor 195
Bittel, Kurt 180
Blenkinsopp, Joseph 48, 206
Boling, Robert G. 40
Boogaart, Thomas Arthur 42
Borowski, Oded 102
Bottéro, Jean 124
Braemer, François 108
Braulik, Georg 155
Brenner, Athalya 38
Brentjes, Burchard 128
Brownlee, William Hugh 156
Brug, John F. 178
Buber, Martin 158
Buccellati, Giorgio 70
Budde, Karl 170
Bulliet, Richard W. 128
Bull, R. J. 42
Bunimovitz, Shlomo 178, 183
Callaway, Joseph A. 95, 116
Campbell, Edward F., Jr., 42
Chaney, Marvin L. 116
Chéhab, Maurice H. 194
Civil, Miguel 215
Coats, George W. 15
Cohen, Rudolph 97
Coogan, Michael D. 206
Cooghanour, Robert A. 197
Cooley, Robert E. 95
Coote, Robert B. 82, 116
Craigie, Peter C. 206
Crenshaw, James L. 48
Cross, Frank Moore 8, 11, 31, 113, 156, 165
Crüsemann, Frank 42, 106, 216, 217, 221
Culley, Robert C. 220
Davies, G. I. 15
Delekat, Lienhard 156
Demsky, Aaron 113
Desborough, V. R. d'A. 181

Dever, William G.	70	Glueck, Nelson	82, 84, 199
Dexinger, F.	37	Gonen, Rivka	72
Dibelius, Martin	170, 171	Görg, Manfred	78, 127, 156
Diels, Hermann	216	Gottwald, Norman K.	116, 121, 122
Dietrich, Walter	9, 156	Gray, John	206
Dommershausen, Werner	173	Greenberg, Moshe	124, 171
Donner, Herbert	16, 18	Gressmann, Hugo	170
Dornemann, Rudolph Henry	197	Gross, Walter	16
Dorsey, David A.	29	Gunkel, Hermann	48, 211, 213, 223, 232, 233
Dothan, Moshe	178	Gunneweg, A. H. J.	58
Dothan, Trude	178, 183, 184, 185, 186, 188, 189, 190	Haag, Herbert	39
Draffkorn, A. E.	171, 172	Hackett, Jo Ann	17
Dumbrell, William J.	14	Halbe, J.	28
Dus, J.	26	Halpern, Baruch	28, 34, 116
Ebeling, Erich	216	Haran, Menahem	28, 170
Eissfeldt, Otto	14, 52, 160, 171, 221	Hartmann, Richard	170, 171
Elliger, Karl	224	Hauptmann, Andreas	112
Emerton, J. A.	39	Hauser, Alan J.	43, 116
Engel, Helmut	79	Helck, Wolfgang	70, 127, 179
Esse, Douglas L.	111	Heltzer, Michael	125
Exum, J. Cheryl	48	Henninger, Joseph	127, 130
Faegre, Torvald	129	Herrmann, Siegfried	115, 116, 136, 156
Fecht, Gerhard	79	Hertzberg, Hans-Wilhelm	44
Feilberg, Carl Gunnar	129	Herzog, Ze'ev	97
Finkelstein, Israel	82, 83, 84, 86, 88, 96, 97, 116, 200	Heubeck, Alfred	115, 184
Fohrer, Georg	136, 141	Hoffner, Harry A.	171
Folk, Robert L.	191	Hoftijzer, J.	17
Freedman, David Noel	127, 156, 157	Hölbl, Günther	180
Frenzel, Elisabeth	52	Holladay, John S.	211
Friedman, Richard Elliott	9	Hopkins, David C.	102
Friedrich, Ingolf	173	Hornung, Erik	69, 79
Fritz, Volkmar	12, 24, 25, 32, 33, 42, 47, 72, 77, 82, 99, 100, 108, 112, 116, 123, 144, 177, 182, 191	Hübner, U.	37
		Hübner, Ulrich	196
		Ibrahim, M. M.	111
Galling, Kurt	192	Ingraham, M. L.	202
Gal, Zvi	82	Ishida, Tomoo	44
Gerleman, Gillis	206	Isserlin, Benedikt, S.J.	116
Gerstenblith, Patty	70	Jäger, M.	211
Gese, Hartmut	182, 221	Jeremias, Jörg	161, 171
Geus, C. H. J. de	116, 121, 136	Jirku, Anton	171
Gitin, Seymour	183	Jolles, André	211, 212
Giveon, Raphael	127	Jüngling, Hans-Winfried	52
Glass, Jonathan	203	Kaiser, Otto	4
		Kallai-Kleinmann, Z.	31

INDEX OF MODERN AUTHORS

Kallai, Zecharia	15, 18, 30, 144	Margalith, Othniel	48, 78
Kearney, Peter J.	28	Maxwell-Hyslop, K. R.	112
Keel, Othmar	156	Mayes, A. D. H.	28, 38, 136, 206
Kelm, George L.	109	Mazar, Amihai	70, 96, 109, 116, 177, 178, 185, 186, 190
Kempinski, Aharon	72, 99		
Klein-Franke, Aviva	212	Mazar, Benjamin	71, 75, 116, 149, 178
Klengel, Horst	128	McCarter, P. Kyle	17
Klopfenstein, Martin A.	156	McCarthy, Dennis J.	32
Knauf, Ernst Axel	14, 112, 157, 161, 200, 202	McKenzie, John L.	23
		Mendenhall, George E.	116, 120, 121
Knudtzon, J. A.	123	Meuli, Karl	216
Kochavi, Moshe	98	Miller, J. Maxwell	15, 116, 199
Koch, Klaus	127, 169	Mittmann, Siegfried	23, 54, 82, 84, 85
Köckert, Matthias	167, 168	Mölle, Herbert	32
Kohata, F.	18	Moore, Michael S.	16
Kooij, G. van der	17	Morgenstern, Julian	170
Kraeling, Emil Gottlieb Heinrich	37	Moscati, Sabatino	194
Kuschke, Arnulf	28, 118	Mowinckel, Sigmund	16, 157
Kutsch, Ernst	39	Muhly, James D.	112, 190
Labuschagne, C. J.	171	Mullen, E. Theodore, Jr.	44, 53, 56
Lang, Bernhard	156	Müller, Hans-Peter	17, 158, 206, 212
Langlamet, F.	26	Murray, D. F.	206
Lapp, Paul W.	116	Musil, Alois	202
Lasine, Stuart	52	Na'aman, Nadav	19, 31, 77, 124, 135
Lehmann, Gustav Adolf	178, 180, 190	Namiki, K.	136
Lemaire, André	149	Naveh, Joseph	113
Lemche, Niels Peter	44, 75, 76, 116, 121, 122, 127	Neef, Heinz-Dieter	206
		Negbi, Ora	112
Liebowitz, Harold	191	Nel, P.	48, 212
Lindars, Barnabas	42, 144, 216	Nelson, Richard D.	9, 11
Lindblom, Johannes	158	Nielsen, Eduard	154, 220
Lipiński, Eduard	173, 174	Niemann, Hermann Michael	50
Liver, Jacob	28	Noort, Edward	179
Lohfink, Norbert	23	North, Robert	78
Loretz, Oswald	124	Noth, Martin	9, 12, 13, 14, 15, 16, 18, 20, 28, 29, 30, 31, 44, 50, 51, 116, 118, 136, 141, 144, 149, 171, 195
Maag, Victor	200		
MacLaurin, E. C. B.	157		
Macuch, Rudolf	155	Oakeshott, M. F.	200
Maddin, R.	112	O'Doherty, Eamonn	53
Maiberger, Paul	161	Ohlert, Konrad	212
Maier, Johann	26, 170, 173	Oren, Eliezer D.	185
Malamat, Abraham	50, 116, 195	Otten, Heinrich	180
Malul, Meir	169	Otto, Eckart	26, 79, 115, 163, 171
Maly, Eugene H.	42, 216	Parrot, André	194
Marcus, David	47	Parr, Peter J.	203

Peckham, Brian	9, 26	Schnutenhaus, Frank	161
Perlitt, Lothar	19, 23, 24, 32, 33	Schoors, Antoon	116
Perry, Ben E.	216	Schroer, Silvia	172
Petzoldt, Leander	232	Schultz, Wolfgang	212
Polzin, Robert	9	Schunck, Klaus-Dietrich	44, 52, 144, 148
Porter, J. R.	26, 48		
Portugali, Y.	88	Schwienhorst-Schönberger, Ludger	27
Preuss, Richard	173	Seebass, Horst	136
Pritchard, James B.	28	Sellin, Ernst	173
Propp, William H. C.	19	Selms, A. van	48
Rad, Gerhard von	142	Shiloh, Yigal	108, 117
Rainey, Anson F.	31, 123, 182	Simons, Jan Jozef	152, 198
Redford, Donald B.	79	Singer, Itamar	79, 181
Reinhold, Gotthard G. G.	195	Smend, Rudolf	9, 11, 24, 53, 136, 142, 143
Revell, E. J.	52		
Reviv, H.	42	Soden, Wolfram von	157
Richter, Wolfgang	34, 44, 45, 62	Soggin, J. Alberto	26, 34, 37, 42, 44, 52, 163
Ricke, Herbert	100		
Robertson, Edward	173	Sperling, S. David	32
Rösel, Hartmut N.	37, 39, 42, 44, 45, 57, 77	Stadelmann, Rainer	179, 182
		Stager, Lawrence E.	79, 117, 206
Rose, Martin	157	Staubli, Thomas	128, 131
Ross, J. F.	42	Stech-Wheeler, Tamara	112
Rothenberg, Beno	203	Stiebing, William H.	187
Rouillad, H.	171	Stolz, Fritz	142, 163
Rowton, Michael B.	116	Stuart, Aaron	12
Rudolph, Wilhelm	12	Sypherd, Wilbur Owen	47
Sachsse, E.	79	Talmon, Shemaryahu	52
Saebø, Magne	158	Thiel, Winfried	102, 108, 117
Safren, Jonathan D.	16	Tropper, J.	171
Sass, Benjamin	113	Tubb, Jonathan N.	71
Sasson, Victor	17	Van Seters, John	18, 24, 32, 75
Sauer, G.	36	Vaux, Roland de	117
Sauer, James A.	199	Veijola, Timo	9, 11, 23, 154, 155
Saydon, Paul P.	26	Vieweger, Dieter	117
Schäfer-Lichtenberger, Chr.	28	Vogt, Ernst	26
Schleif, A.	157	Vollborn, W.	36
Schmid, H.	157, 160	Vorländer, Hermann	167
Schmid, H. H.	42	Vriezen, Th. C.	158
Schmidt, Ludwig	16, 39	Waldbaum, Jane C.	112, 187
Schmidt, W. H.	158	Walsh, Jerome T.	15
Schmitt, Götz	32	Walz, Reinhard	128
Schmitt, H.-Ch.	18, 21	Warner, Sean M.	36, 220
Schmitt, Rainer	170	Weimar, P.	38
Schnur, Harry C.	216	Weinfeld, Moshe	53, 117

Weinstein, James M.	71	Wissowa, Georg	173
Weippert, Helga	9, 17, 71, 115, 118, 136	Wolf, A.	220
Weippert, Manfred	17, 18, 76, 115, 117, 118, 124, 128, 142, 157, 160, 200	Wolff, Hans Walter	9
		Wright, G. Ernest	31, 77
Weiser, Artur	206, 230	Wüst, Manfried	18, 22, 45
Weisgerber, G.	112	Yadin, Yigael	87, 117, 176
Weisman, Zeev	44	Yassine, Khair N.	178
Wenning, Robert	177	Yeivin, Shmuel	117
Wertime, Theodore A.	112	Zenger, Erich	177
Whitelam, Keith W.	82	Zertal, Adam	96, 177
Whitley, Charles Francis	39	Zevit, Ziony	28
Williams, R. J.	42	Zobel, Hans-Jürgen	16, 58, 206
Willoughby, B. E.	127	Zwickel, Wolfgang	15

Index of Biblical References

Genesis
3:18	104	26:24	169
4:2–4	239	26:25	164, 239
4:23	205	27:28	104
4:26	154, 164, 169	27:37	104
8:20	239	28:10–22	55
9:26	168	28:11	165
10:15–18	77	28:12	165
10:16	79	28:13	168, 169
12–36	168	28:16–19	239
12:6	33, 239	28:17	165
12:7	33, 239	28:18	165, 175
12:7–8	175	28:20	165
12:8	164, 239	28:21	165
13:3	175	28:22	165
13:4	164, 175	29:31–30:12	139, 140
13:7	79	31	172
13:18	175, 239	31:5	168
15:19–21	77	31:13	55, 165
16:1	163	31:19	172
16:2	163	31:29	168
16:4–7	163	31:30	172
16:8	163	31:34–35	172
16:11–14	163	31:42	168, 169
16:14	163	31:53	168, 169
19:1–11	52	32:10	168
19:37	199	32:29	81
19:38	197	33:18–20	33, 175
21:22–34	164	33:20	166
21:32	164	34	33
21:33	164, 175	34:30	79
24:27	169	35:1–5	165
25:4	201	35:3	165
25:24	168	35:7	55, 165, 175
26:23–25	175	35:14	175
		35:16–20	139, 140

Genesis (cont.)		Exodus	
35:17	222	1–14	1, 64
35:22–26	139	1:1–4	36
36	201	1:2–4	139
36:2	78	1:15	127
36:12	203	1:19	127
36:31–39	201	2:7	127
38:6–10	107	2:13	127
39:14	127	2:16–22	201
39:17	127	3	6, 162, 239
40:15	127	3:1	201
41:12	127	3:6	168, 169
43:2	78	3:8	1, 77
43:18	146	3:9–14	158
43:19	146	3:13	169
43:23	168	3:14	157, 158
43:32	127	3:15	168
46:1–4	175	3:15–16	168, 169
46:3	166, 168	3:16	168
46:8–25	13, 139	3:17	77
47:29	169	3:18	127
48:1–20	146	4:5	168, 169
49	58, 138, 209	5:3	127
49:1–27	139	6	240
49:3–4	59	7:16	127
49:8	59	9:1	127
49:9	59	9:13	127
49:10	59	10:3	127
49:10–12	59	12:37	15
49:13	59, 150	13:5	77
49:14	59, 150	14	26
49:15	59	15–18	1
49:16	59	15–Num 20	15, 21, 22, 59
49:17	59, 151	15:2	168
49:19	59	15:21	205
49:20	152	15:22	19
49:21	59, 152	15:22–18:27	1
49:22	59	17:8–16	6
49:23–24	59, 168	17:15	175
49:25–26	59	17:16	203
49:27	59, 147	18:1–12	201
50:8	146	18:4	168
50:17	168	19	161, 162, 239
		19–40	3
		19:1–Num 10:10	1

INDEX OF BIBLICAL REFERENCES

19:18	160	13:4–56	16		
21:26	172	13:16	6		
23:23	77	13:22	68, 69		
23:28	77	13:29	77		
24:12–14	6	14	31, 54		
25–32	240	14:6–38	6		
25:7	173	14:10–35	1		
28:4–30	173	14:39–45	1		
28:30	174	14:45	19		
28:31–35	173	15:1–16	14		
32	41	20	18		
32:17	6	20:1–3	14		
33:2	77	20:1–13	18		
33:11	6	20:14–21	18, 20		
34:11	77	20:22	1, 19		
35:9	173	20:22–29	19		
35:27	173	21	13, 16, 18, 24, 60		
39:1–21	173	21–36	2, 3, 9, 12, 22		
39:22–29	173	21:1–3	2, 18, 19, 54		
		21:4	19, 20		
Leviticus		21:4–9	2, 18, 19		
1–7	14	21:10–20	2, 18, 20		
1–27	3	21:13	78, 199		
8:8	174	21:14	205		
23	14	21:17–18	20, 205		
		21:21–25	21		
Numbers		21:21–31	18, 20, 22		
1	139	21:21–35	2, 194		
1–9	3	21:25	21		
1–10	2	21:25–26	21		
1:5–15	16, 139	21:27–30	20		
1:20–47	13, 14, 139	21:31	21		
2:3–31	139	21:32	18, 21		
7:12–83	139	21:33–35	18, 21		
10–20	1	22–24	2, 13, 16, 18		
10–32	23, 24	22:1	21		
10:11–20:29	1	22:1–24:25	16		
10:12	160	22:2–4	16		
10:14–28	139	22:4–6	17		
10:36	81	22:7–20	17		
11:28	6	22:21	17		
12:16	160	22:22–35	17		
13	31, 54	22:35	2		
13–14	5, 24	22:36	199		
13:4–15	139	22:36–41	17		

Numbers (cont.)			
22:41	20	32:41	44
23:1–25	17	33	13
23:14–15	20	33–36	13
23:26–24:44	17	33:1–49	3, 15
23:28	20	33:5–34:29	15
24:20	204	33:44	20
24:25	17	33:48	21
25	13	33:49	21
25–31	13	33:50	21
25:1–5	2, 13	33:50–34:29	3, 13
25:1–15	15, 18	33:50–56	15
25:6–18	2	34:1–12	16, 25
25:16–18	14	34:13–15	16
26	2, 13	34:17–18	16
26:3	21	35	13
26:5–51	139	35:1	21
26:23	44	36	13, 14
26:26	45	36:13	21
26:28–37	138	24:1–24	17
26:30–32	149	**Deuteronomy**	
26:33	14	1–3	3, 4, 10, 21, 23, 24
26:63	21	1–34	3
26:65	6	1:2	161
27:1–11	2, 13, 14	1:19	161
27:12–23	2, 13, 14	1:44	19
27:21	174	1:46	161
28–30	2	2:7	68
28:1–30:1	13, 14	2:13	20
30:2–17	13, 14	2:14	161
31	2, 13, 14	2:26–37	194
31:8	18	3:1–3	21
31:12	21	3:1–11	194
31:16	18	3:13–14	149
32	3, 13, 16, 18, 24, 30, 60, 150	3:13–15	138
32:1	21, 22	3:23–29	14
32:1–38	22	3:29	13
32:3	21	4:10	161
32:16	22	4:15	161
32:17	22	4:26	58
32:20	22	4:35	155, 239
32:24	22	4:38	155
32:34–38	22, 151	4:39	239
32:35	21	4:46	13
32:39–42	21, 138, 147, 149	6:4	154, 155

7:1	77	34	3
7:1–6	29, 117	34:1	14, 19, 21, 25
7:2	54	34:1–9	4
8:2	68	34:6	13
8:8	104	34:7–9	14, 19, 25
8:19–20	58	34:8	21
9:23	161		
11:17	58	**Joshua**	
12:9–10	241	1	24
19	25	1–12	1, 2, 3, 6, 22, 24, 33
19:10	241	1–24	4, 9, 22, 24, 25
19:14	241	1:1	14
20:10–18	29, 228	1:1–6	6, 25
20:16	241	1:2	14
20:16–18	54	1:7–9	25
20:17	77	1:10	25
21:23	241	1:11	25
23:5–6	17	1:12–18	25
24:4	241	2	4, 25, 26, 60, 117, 228, 229
25:17–19	203	2:1–3	26, 234
25:19	241	2:4	26, 234
26:5	196	2:5–7	26, 234
27:5–7	28	2:8–14	25
28:22	104	2:9	26
29:4	68	2:10	78
30:18	58	2:12–14	26
31:1–8	14	2:15–17	26, 234
32:10	20	2:18	26, 234
32:48–52	14	2–19	60
33	3, 58, 138, 141, 209	2:19	26, 234
33:2	159, 160, 161, 239	2:21	26
33:6	59	2:21–23	26, 234
33:7	59	3	26
33:8	174	3:1	26
33:8–10	59	3:4	4, 175
33:11	59	3:10	77
33:12	59	3:14	26
33:13–16	59	3:15	26
33:17	59	3:16	26
33:18–19	59	4	26
33:20–21	59	4:1–9	26
33:22	59, 151	4:11	26
33:23	59	4:18	26
33:24	152	4:19	57
33:24–25	59	4:20	57

Joshua (cont.)		8:21	27, 234
5:1	27	8:23	28, 234
5:1–9	4	8:29	28, 234
5:2	27	8:30	166, 175
5:3	27	8:30–35	5, 28
5:4–7	27	9	5
5:6	68	9:1	29, 77
5:8	27	9:1–4	9
5:9	27, 57	9:2	29
5:10	27, 57	9:3–7	29
5:10–12	27	9:3–15	28
5:11	27	9:6	57
5:12	27	9:7	78
5:13	27	9:8	29
5:13–15	4, 6, 27, 225	9:9	29
5:14	27	9:10	29, 78
6	5, 9, 10, 26, 27, 118, 143, 228, 229	9:11–15	29
6:1	27	9:15	29
6:2	27	9:16	29
6:3	27	9:17	29
6:4	27	9:18–21	29
6:5	27	9:22–26	29
6:7	27	10	5, 9, 30
6:14	27	10:1	9
6:15	27	10:1–14	5
6:20	27	10:1–15	29, 30
6:21–24	27	10:1–27	117
7	5, 27, 227, 228	10:2	9
7:1	227	10:6	57
7:2–3	227	10:7	57
7:4–5	227	10:9	57
7:6–7	227	10:12	29, 60, 61, 63
7:10–15	227	10:12–13	205, 211, 237
7:13–14	173	10:13	29, 60, 61, 63, 205, 220
7:14–18	106	10:13–14	211, 237
7:16–23	227	10:15	57
7:24	229	10:15–27	5
7:24–25	227	10:16	29
7:26	227	10:16–23	234
8	9, 27, 52, 60, 117, 118	10:16–27	29, 60
8:10–12	27, 234	10:24–27	234
8:14	234	10:28–43	5, 29
8:14–15	27	10:33	55
8:15	234	10:43	57
8:19	27, 234	11	9

INDEX OF BIBLICAL REFERENCES

11:1	38	15:13–19	31, 60, 63
11:1–2	230	15:17	37
11:1–3	9	15:20–63	31, 32, 60
11:1–9	30	15:30	19
11:1–15	29	15:46–47	55
11:1–23	5	15:63	79
11:3	77, 78	16	31
11:10–15	30	16–17	5
11:16–20	25, 30	16:2	148
11:19	78	16:3	148
11:21–23	30	16:5–9	147
12	9, 25, 30, 33, 61	16:9	31
12:1–24	5, 6, 25	17	31
12:1	30	17:1	149
12:1–6	30	17:2	149
12:7–24	30	17:7	33
12:8	77	17:7–13	147
12:10–24	60	17:9	31
12:12	55	17:11–13	55
12:14	19	17:14	32
13	5, 25, 30	17:14–18	31
13–19	16, 25, 30, 33, 34, 54	17:15	32, 79
13–24	6	17:16	32
13:1	25, 30	17:17	32, 146
13:7	25, 30	17:18	32
13:15–20	30	18	32, 61
13:15–23	151	18–19	5
13:23	30	18:1–10	32
13:24–26	30	18:5	146
13:24–31	151	18:11–20	60, 148
13:25	21	18:11–28	32
13:27	30	18:16	54, 79
13:28	30	18:21–28	31, 60, 148
13:29–31	147	18:28	79
13:30–32	149	19	32, 56, 61
13:32	21	19:10–16	150, 231
14	5, 31	19:10–39	61
14:6	57	19:15	56
15	5, 31, 32, 61	19:18–20	150
15–19	30, 145, 146	19:24–31	152
15:1–12	31, 60	19:28	56
15:5–9	148	19:30	56
15:8	79	19:32–39	152, 231
15:9	54	19:38	56
15:13–14	54	19:41–46	51, 61, 151

Joshua (cont.)		**Judges**	
19:42	56	1	7, 34, 35, 53, 54
19:49	6, 25, 32	1–2	241
19:50	32	1–21	6, 9, 34
19:51	32	1:1	54
20	25	1:1–2:5	57
20–21	16, 25	1:1–3:6	35
20–24	26	1:1–21	53
20:7	33	1:2–10	54
21	5, 25, 141	1:4	79
21:21	33	1:5	79
21:39	21	1:8	55
22	5, 16, 25	1:9	55
22:22	166	1:11	54
23	25, 33, 57	1:13	37
23:1–24:28	5	1:16	54
24	25, 32, 241	1:17	19, 54
24:1	33	1:18	54
24:1–28	6, 25, 33, 34	1:19	55
24:2	33	1:20	55
24:2–13	33	1:21	55, 79
24:2–24	32	1:22	146
24:3	33	1:22–26	55
24:4	33	1:22–36	53
24:5	33	1:23	146
24:6	33	1:27	55
24:7	33	1:29	55, 56
24:8	33, 78	1:30	56
24:9	33	1:30–36	56
24:9–10	17	1:31	56
24:10	33	1:33	56
24:11	33, 77	1:34–35	56
24:12	33	1:35	146
24:13	33	1:36	56
24:16–18	33	2	35, 53
24:19–24	33	2:1–5	7, 35, 56, 57
24:25	33	2:6–10	7, 35, 57
24:25–28	33	2:10	57
24:26	33, 175	2:11	35, 36
24:27	33	2:11–16	57
24:28	33	2:11–23	7, 35, 57
24:29–31	6, 25, 34, 35, 41, 57	2:12	35
24:29–33	5	2:13	35
		2:14	35
		2:14–16	35

INDEX OF BIBLICAL REFERENCES

2:17	35, 57	5:2–3	207
2:18	35, 57	5:2–11	39, 207, 211
2:19	35, 57	5:3	39, 81
2:20–23	35, 57	5:3–5	39
3–9	62	5:4	159, 160, 162, 207, 239
3–16	35, 36, 60, 241	5:5	81, 207
3:1	35, 36	5:6–8	207
3:1–6	7, 36	5:7	81, 137
3:3	36, 78	5:8	81, 137
3:5	36, 77	5:9	81
3:7	36	5:9–11	207
3:7–11	35, 36	5:11	81, 137
3:7–31	7	5:12	108, 207
3:8	36, 46, 67	5:12–17	61, 63, 136, 142, 205, 207, 230, 234
3:9	36		
3:11	36, 46, 67	5:12–31	39
3:12	36	5:13	108, 143, 157, 231, 238
3:12–30	35, 37, 61, 194, 198, 234	5:13–17	207, 208, 209, 230
3:14	36, 46, 67	5:13–18	58
3:15	36	5:14	38, 137, 147, 148, 207
3:15–30	147	5:14–17	138, 140, 154
3:30	36, 46, 67	5:14–18	108
3:31	35, 37, 38	5:15	38, 137, 207
4	7, 35, 38, 229, 231, 234	5:15–17	137
4–5	153	5:17	149, 151, 152, 207
4:1	36	5:18	61, 63, 136, 137, 138, 140, 142, 149, 154, 205, 207, 208, 209, 230, 234
4:1–3	38, 230		
4:2	36	5:19	137
4:3	36, 46, 67	5:19–22	39, 61, 63, 136, 142, 205, 207, 208, 209, 230, 231, 234
4:4–6	38, 230		
4:4–22	38	5:20–21	143, 238
4:6	38, 149, 231	5:23	207
4:7	38, 230	5:24	54
4:8–10	38, 230	5:24–27	38, 207, 208, 209, 230
4:11	38, 54, 230	5:24–30	61, 63, 136, 142, 205, 207, 230, 234
4:12–16	230		
4:12–17	38	5:28–30	207, 209, 210
4:17	38, 54, 230	5:31	36, 39, 46, 67, 207, 211
4:18–22	38, 230	6–8	7, 8, 15, 35, 39, 40, 108, 194, 201, 202, 242
4:23	36, 38		
4:23–24	230	6:1	36, 40, 46, 67
4:24	38	6:2–6	40, 41, 61, 234
5	7, 8, 35, 38, 39, 58, 138, 140, 206, 229	6:3	203
5:1	207	6:6	36
5:2	81, 137	6:7	36

Judges (cont.)

6:7–10	40	9:22	42
6:11–24	41	9:23	42
6:24	175	9:24	42, 43
6:25–32	39, 41	9:25	42
6:32	39	9:26–41	42, 46, 61, 63, 234
6:33–35	41, 61, 234	9:28	39
6:33–40	40	9:42–45	42
6:36–40	41	9:49–59	42
7	41	9:50–54	42
7:1	39	9:55	42
7:1–25	40, 41, 61, 234	9:56	42
7:12	203	9:57	39, 42, 43
7:23–25	225	10–12	242
7:24	146	10–13	108
8	41	10–16	46
8:1–3	41, 48, 225	10:1	46
8:4–21	40, 41, 61, 234	10:1–5	7, 35, 41, 43, 45, 61, 108, 141
8:10	40	10:2	36, 67
8:22	41	10:3	36, 46, 67
8:23	41	10:6	36
8:24–27	41	10:6–16	7, 35, 44, 46, 57
8:28	36, 40, 46, 67	10:7	36
8:29	39	10:8	78
8:29–31	41	10:10	36
8:29–35	41	10:12	36
8:30	41	10:17	47
8:31	40, 41	10:17–12:6	35, 44, 45, 194
8:35	39	10:17–12:7	7, 8, 47
9	33, 35, 39, 41, 43	10:18	47
9:1	39	11:1–11	47
9:1–5	42	11:11	175
9:5	39, 42	11:12–28	47
9:6	42	11:18	199
9:7–15	42	11:19	47
9:7–16	216	11:20	78
9:8–9	104	11:23	197
9:8–15	61, 206, 216, 218, 219	11:29–40	47, 61, 234
9:13	104	11:32	47, 197
9:15	216	11:33	36, 47, 197
9:16	39, 42	12:1–6	48, 52
9:16–19	42, 43	12:7	36, 44, 46, 47, 67
9:18	39	12:8	46
9:19	39	12:8–15	7, 35, 41, 43, 45, 48, 61, 108, 141
9:19–21	42, 216	12:9	36, 67

12:11	36, 46, 67	21:13	52
12:13	46	21:15–25	88
12:14	67	21:25	8, 53
13	7, 39, 49		
13–16	8, 35, 48, 193, 242	**1 Samuel**	
13:1	36, 46, 48, 50	1	49, 105
13:2–25	50	1–4	88
13:25	50, 151	1:9	176
14–16	7	2:18	173
14:1–15:8	49, 50, 61, 234	2:28	81, 173
14:5–9	213	3:3	176
14:10–19	212, 214, 222	3:20	51, 81
14:14	205, 222	4–6	170
14:18	205, 222	4:6	127
15:9–17	49, 50	4:9	127
15:18	49, 50	4:18	68
15:19	49, 50	4:20	221
15:20	36, 48, 50, 67	7:17	175
16	48	8–11	47
16:1–3	48, 225	10:12	221
16:1–31	50	10:19–21	106
16:4–22	48	10:20	81
16:23–31	48	11	197
16:31	36, 48	11:4	52
17	35, 51	12:11	39
17–18	8, 50, 151, 174, 175	13–14	193
17–21	35, 50, 241	13–2 Sam 24	63
17:5	172	13:1	45, 68
17:6	8, 53	13:3	127
17:8	146	13:19	127
18	35, 51	13:19–21	192
18:1	8	14:3	173
18:2	146	14:11	127
18:14	172	14:18	173
18:17–18	172	14:21	127
18:20	172	14:35	175
18:30	51	14:41	174
19–21	8, 35, 52, 53, 147, 175	14:47	199, 201
19:1	8, 146	15	204
19:16	146	15:6	54
19:16–26	52	15:23	172
19:18	146	17	192
19:29	52	17:52	81
20:45	52	18:7	205, 211
20:47	52	18:16	81

1 Samuel (cont.)		11:3–24			78
19	172	11:11			171
19:13	172	11:21			39, 43
19:16	172	12:26–31			197
21:2–10	176	14:7			107
21:10	173	16:5–14			147
21:11	205, 211	19:1			221
21:11–16	193	19:3			220
22:3–4	198	19:21			146
22:6–23	176	20			147
22:18	173	20:1			138
23:2	174	21			104
23:9–12	173	21:1–14			28
23:12	174	21:15–22			37, 224
25	106	23:1			168
25:2	105	23:8–15			224
25:42	106	23:8–22			37
26:6	78	23:8–38			224
28:6	174	23:11–12			224
29:3	127	24			175
30	204	24:5			21
30:7–9	173				
30:30	19	**1 Kings**			
		2:10–12			45
2 Samuel		2:11			68
1:18	205	4:7–19			76, 138, 146
1:19–27	205, 220	4:8			147
2:1–4	140	4:9			56
2:8–9	138	4:11			55
2:9	153, 154	4:12			55
3:10	51	4:15			152
3:33–34	205, 220	4:16			151
5:6–10	54	4:18			148
5:17–25	193	4:19			151
5:19	174	6:1			68
6	170	8:1–11			170
6:14	173	9:15			55
8:1	179, 193	9:16			56
8:2–12	199	9:20			77
8:3–5	196	9:21			55
8:13–15	201	9:27			195
10	197	10:11–12			195
10:6–8	196	10:29			78
10:15–19	196	11:1			78
11	43	11:14–22			201

INDEX OF BIBLICAL REFERENCES

11:18	201	34:3	168
11:28	146		
11:41–43	45	**Ezra**	
12:16	138	2:63	174
12:26–32	176	9	13
12:28–29	55	9:1	77
12:28–30	50		
12:28–32	51	**Nehemiah**	
15:20	51	7:65	174
17:1	104	9:8	77
18:36	168	11:31–35	148
20:1	197	13:2	17
2 Kings		**Job**	
2:14	168	1:21	221
7:6	78	6:5	150
8:1	104	11:12	150
9:27	55	38:7	238
10:5	168	39:5–8	150
14:9	219		
15:29	51	**Psalms**	
18:4	20	6:4	81
23:24	172	18:7–15	161
		20:1	168
1 Chronicles		46:7	168
1:1–28	36	47:9	168
2:1	139	48:2	160
2:2	139	50:1	166
6	141	50:3	161
6:66	21	75:9	168
8:7	77	76:6	168
11:4	79	78:60	176
12	141	81:1	168
26:31	21	81:4	168
27:16–22	139	84:8	168
28:9	168	89:36	158
29:10	168	90:13	81
		94:7	168
2 Chronicles		97:2–5	161
17:4	168	99:5	170
20	143	104:15	104
21:12	168	104:32	161
28:2	170	114:7	168
30:6	168	126:4	81
32:17	168	132:7	170

Proverbs
6:16–19	216
30:15	216
30:15–31	216

Isaiah
2:3	168
9:4	202
14:13	160
16:8	21
38:5	168
44:6	155, 239
45:5	155, 239
45:6	155, 239
45:18	155, 239
46:9	155
66:6	201

Jeremiah
7:12	176
7:14	176
26:6	176
26:9	176
47:4	182
49:7	161
49:20	161

Ezekiel
21:26	172
25:13	161
47:15–20	16

Daniel
3:28	168
6:26	168
11:37	169

Hosea
2:4	221
3:4	172
4:15	176
9:10	13
10:5	176
12:4–5	81
12:12	176

Joel
1:2	104

Amos
1:3	104
1:12	161
3:14	55
4:4	176
4:4–5	55
4:9	104
5:5	176
5:6	146
7:1	104
7:2	104
8:14	176
9:7	181, 182

Obadiah
1:9	161
18	146

Micah
4:2	168
4:13	104

Habakkuk
3:3	160, 161, 239
3:7	201

Haggai
2:17	104

Zechariah
10:2	172
10:6	146

www.ingramcontent.com/pod-product-compliance
Lightning Source LLC
Chambersburg PA
CBHW030338240426
43661CB00052B/1668